# The Last of the Mohicans

*A Thrilling Tale of Wilderness Warfare, Honor*
*& Survival in Colonial America*

## A Modern Translation
Adapted for the Contemporary Reader

James Fenimore Cooper

Translated by Tim Zengerink

# Table of Contents

Preface Message to the Reader.................................................. 1

Introduction ................................................................. 2

Chapter I.................................................................... 8

Chapter II. ................................................................. 19

Chapter III. ................................................................ 30

Chapter IV. ................................................................ 41

Chapter V. ................................................................. 51

Chapter VI. ................................................................ 62

Chapter VII. ............................................................... 76

Chapter VIII. .............................................................. 89

Chapter IX. ............................................................... 101

Chapter X. ................................................................ 111

Chapter XI. ............................................................... 125

Chapter XII. .............................................................. 139

Chapter XIII. ............................................................. 156

Chapter XIV. ............................................................. 168

Chapter XV. .............................................................. 185

Chapter XVI. ............................................................. 198

Chapter XVII. ............................................................ 212

Chapter XVIII. ........................................................... 229

Chapter XIX. ............................................................. 243

Chapter XX. ...................................................................... 258

Chapter XXI. ..................................................................... 272

Chapter XXII. .................................................................... 285

Chapter XXIII. ................................................................... 299

Chapter XXIV. ................................................................... 314

Chapter XXV. .................................................................... 328

Chapter XXVI. ................................................................... 343

Chapter XXVII. .................................................................. 356

Chapter XXVIII. ................................................................. 368

Chapter XXIX. ................................................................... 380

Chapter XXX. .................................................................... 395

Chapter XXXI. ................................................................... 409

Chapter XXXII. .................................................................. 419

Chapter XXXIII. ................................................................. 437

Thank You For Reading ....................................................... 452

# Preface
# Message to the Reader

### Rebuilding the Greatest Library in Human History

Thousands of years ago, the Library of Alexandria was the heart of global knowledge — a sanctuary where the wisdom of every known civilization was gathered and shared freely.

And then, it was lost.

Now, we're rebuilding it — and you are invited to join us.

At the Library of Alexandria, we've set out to make every book available to every person on Earth — not just in print, but in every language, every format, and for every reader.

Here's how we do it:

- **Deluxe Print Editions at True Printing Cost** - Order any book as a high-quality paperback, elegant hardcover, or stunning boxset — and only pay what it costs to print. No markups. No middlemen.
- **Unlimited Access to the Greatest Works** - Enjoy thousands of timeless classics — from Plato to Shakespeare to Tolstoy — in beautiful, modern eBook and audiobook editions. Read and listen without limits — for every reader, everywhere.
- **Modern Translations for Every Language & Dialect** - We're reimagining the classics in clear, accessible language — and translating them into every dialect imaginable. Everyone deserves to understand humanity's greatest ideas.

When you visit **LibraryofAlexandria.com**, you're not just accessing books — you're joining a global movement to restore, preserve, and share the wisdom of civilization.

Join us today at LibraryofAlexandria.com

Together, we'll ensure the light of human wisdom never fades again.

With gratitude,

### The Modern Library of Alexandria Team

**Visit:**
**www.libraryofalexandria.com**
**Or scan the code below:**

# Introduction

## The Frontier as Stage: Honor, Identity, and Conflict in the American Wilderness

James Fenimore Cooper's *The Last of the Mohicans*, first published in 1826, remains one of the most widely read and influential novels in American literature. Set during the French and Indian War in 1757, this tale of brutal combat, shifting alliances, tragic love, and vanishing cultures has captivated generations of readers with its gripping plot and richly drawn landscapes. More than just a romantic adventure, however, the novel stands at a crossroads in American identity: dramatizing the complex relationships among British colonists, French forces, Native American tribes, and the wilderness itself.

As the second installment in Cooper's five-part *Leatherstocking Tales* series—featuring the noble frontiersman Natty Bumppo (also known as Hawkeye)—*The Last of the Mohicans* serves as both a historical novel and a mythic origin story for American character and values. With Hawkeye at its center, the novel offers readers a new kind of hero: one who is European by blood but Native American by culture, morally upright but brutally effective in battle, ruggedly individualistic yet committed to justice and loyalty. Hawkeye's deep bond with the Mohican father-and-son duo, Chingachgook and Uncas, serves as the emotional and ethical heart of the story, even as tragedy looms over the fate of indigenous peoples in a colonized world.

The novel unfolds during a pivotal moment in the struggle for control over North America. Against a backdrop of wilderness forts, mountain passes, and war-torn forests, Cooper weaves a story involving two British sisters—Cora and Alice Munro—their protector Duncan Heyward, the treacherous Huron Magua, and the trio of Hawkeye, Uncas, and Chingachgook. Their journey through contested territory, evading capture and enduring battle after battle, is as much a physical test as it is a philosophical journey into questions of race, loyalty, cultural collision, and what it means to be American.

Though often critiqued for its romanticized and occasionally stereotypical portrayal of Native Americans, *The Last of the Mohicans* was revolutionary in its time for giving indigenous characters complex moral and emotional lives. Uncas and Chingachgook are not merely sidekicks—they are figures of nobility, courage, and tragic depth. Magua, the novel's primary antagonist, is not a one-dimensional villain, but a man shaped by personal betrayal and historical injustice. In these portrayals, Cooper reveals a culture in flux, a world where heroism and savagery are not bound by skin color or nationality, but by choice and circumstance.

Above all, *The Last of the Mohicans* is a story of vanishing worlds—of lost love, lost tribes, and lost innocence. It captures a moment just before the frontier would be irrevocably changed by European dominance. Its title refers not just to Uncas, the literal "last" of the Mohicans, but to an entire way of life that is passing away. It is both a celebration of wilderness freedom and an elegy for what is lost when empires carve borders into wild lands.

## Heroism, Race, and the Making of American Myth

The success and legacy of *The Last of the Mohicans* owe much to the complex figure of Hawkeye, one of the earliest American fictional heroes to embody a new national identity distinct from European models. Unlike British officers such as Duncan Heyward or the aristocratic Colonel Munro, Hawkeye is a man of the land. He shuns titles, mocks bureaucracy, and mistrusts civilization's pretensions. Though white by birth, he lives as an adopted member of the Mohican tribe, guided more by the forest's natural law than by any formal allegiance to crown or country.

Hawkeye's unique position allows him to serve as an intermediary between cultures. He translates languages, brokers alliances, and makes moral judgments independent of imperial politics. This places him in the tradition of the "noble frontiersman"—a literary archetype that would influence later American heroes from Davy Crockett to the cowboys of the Western genre. Yet Hawkeye's nobility is always tinged with melancholy. He knows he cannot fully belong to the world of the Mohicans, and he remains painfully aware of the brutal fate awaiting Native peoples as colonization advances.

Uncas, the young and courageous Mohican, is the novel's tragic figure. As the last heir to his tribe, he represents a dying nobility—a people who have maintained honor, strength, and tradition in the face of relentless displacement. His bond with Cora Munro, the darker-skinned of the two British sisters, carries implicit commentary on race and romance. Their unfulfilled relationship offers both a critique of racial prejudice and a lament for the barriers that even love cannot overcome. Cora's character—strong, independent, and ultimately heroic—stands in contrast to the more delicate and conventional Alice, further complicating the novel's gender and racial dynamics.

Magua, the Huron antagonist, is one of Cooper's most compelling characters. Though portrayed as ruthless and cunning, Magua's motives are deeply personal: betrayal, loss of status, and a desire for revenge against the colonial powers that wronged him. His villainy is tragic rather than arbitrary, reflecting the violence that colonialism inflicts on individuals and cultures. In Magua, Cooper shows how the tools of war and manipulation—learned from the British and French alike—can be turned back against them. Magua is not an alien force; he is a product of the very world the colonists created.

Cooper's attempt to grapple with these racial and cultural complexities was ambitious for its time, even if flawed by the assumptions of his era. His depiction of Native Americans blends noble-savage tropes with genuine admiration. He often contrasts their honor, courage, and spiritual connection to the land with the petty scheming of European politics. At the same time, he cannot fully escape the romanticization and essentialism common in 19th-century portrayals of Indigenous people. Still, within these limitations, *The Last of the Mohicans* offers one of the earliest literary efforts to portray Native Americans as multifaceted individuals navigating an unjust world.

In this sense, the novel is more than just historical fiction—it is national mythmaking. It seeks to define what it means to be American through figures who live between cultures, between nature and civilization, between past and future. Hawkeye's wilderness ethic, Uncas's tragic purity, and Magua's haunted rage are all facets of a nation still forming its self-image. That this image includes both heroic idealism and violent contradiction makes the novel all the more powerful—and all the more relevant.

## Wilderness, War, and the Narrative of Loss

Cooper's portrayal of the American wilderness is one of the novel's greatest achievements. The forests, rivers, mountains, and fortresses of colonial America are more than mere settings—they are active forces in the drama, shaping every decision, every conflict, and every transformation. The natural world in *The Last of the Mohicans* is both sublime and deadly: a place of breathtaking beauty and unsparing danger. It is a realm where human strength, cunning, and morality are tested to their limits.

The wilderness also functions as a battleground—not only for armies, but for ideologies. British discipline and French strategy are constantly undermined by the fluid, unpredictable terrain. Native tribes, more attuned to the land, use it to ambush, escape, and survive. The forest undermines civilization's assumptions. It offers freedom but demands humility. It strips away artifice, exposing the true character of those who travel through it.

Cooper's descriptions are often lavish, filled with romantic awe. But they are never merely decorative. The wilderness is a moral and symbolic space—a testing ground for courage, loyalty, and identity. It reflects the novel's deeper theme of transition: from old worlds to new, from natural innocence to industrial domination, from tribal tradition to national formation.

The novel's warfare—brutal and constant—is depicted with visceral intensity. Sieges, massacres, ambushes, and duels drive the plot forward and reflect the chaos of a world in flux. The French and Indian War, while historically a conflict between imperial powers, is here reimagined as a more intimate and morally complex struggle. No side is wholly righteous; no victory is free from consequence. Cooper challenges readers to see war not as a noble enterprise but as a destructive force that leaves ruin in its wake—especially for those caught in the middle.

What gives *The Last of the Mohicans* its enduring power, however, is its elegiac tone. The novel is filled with scenes of loss—loss of life, love, culture, and innocence. The death of Uncas, the heartbreak of Cora, the extinction of the Mohican line—all speak to a broader historical tragedy: the erasure of Native cultures in the face of colonization. Cooper, writing from the vantage point of a newly expanding United States, understood that the frontier was not just a place of adventure but of disappearance. His tale preserves what is vanishing even as it narrates its demise.

As you step into the pages of *The Last of the Mohicans*, prepare for more than a tale of muskets and moccasins. This is a story of elemental forces: love and hate, honor and treachery, survival and extinction. It is a novel that celebrates heroism while mourning its futility, that admires strength while acknowledging its cost. In Hawkeye's stoic resolve, in Chingachgook's final lament, in the silence of the forest after battle—we hear the echoes of a deeper, more lasting truth: that the shaping of a nation is not only a triumph, but a tragedy.

James Fenimore Cooper, through this sweeping epic, gives voice to that truth. He invites us to see the wilderness not just as a setting, but as a mirror of our collective soul—wild, beautiful, conflicted, and haunted by what has been lost. The novel's richness lies in its refusal to simplify, in its refusal to resolve all tensions. It asks us to witness, to remember, and to reckon with the foundations of the American experience. That reckoning begins here.

# Chapter I.

"My ear is open, and my heart is ready:
The worst is worldly loss you can reveal:—
Tell me, is my kingdom lost?"—Shakespeare

The colonial wars of North America had a unique characteristic: armies had to face the hardships and perils of the wilderness before they could even confront each other. A vast and seemingly impenetrable barrier of forests separated the territories belonging to the warring French and English provinces. The tough colonists and the professional European soldiers fighting alongside them often spent months battling against rushing river rapids or navigating treacherous mountain passes, all in search of a chance to demonstrate their bravery in actual combat. However, by copying the patience and discipline of experienced native warriors, they mastered every obstacle. Eventually, it appeared that no corner of the forest was too remote or hidden, and no secret sanctuary too beautiful, to escape the attacks of those who had sworn their lives to satisfy their desire for revenge or to serve the calculating and selfish interests of Europe's distant rulers.

Perhaps no region across the vast expanse of the borderlands can provide a more vivid depiction of the brutality and savagery of the fierce conflicts during those times than the territory situated between the headwaters of the Hudson River and the neighboring lakes.

The natural advantages that this region offered for military movements were too clear to ignore. Lake Champlain extended from the Canadian border deep into New York territory, creating a natural corridor across half the distance the French needed to travel to reach their enemies. Near its southern end, it connected with another lake whose waters were so clear that Jesuit missionaries chose it exclusively for performing baptisms, earning it the name Lake "du Saint Sacrément." The less devout English believed they honored these pristine waters sufficiently by naming the lake after their ruling monarch, the second king from the House of Hanover. Both groups stripped the original inhabitants of their ancestral right to preserve the lake's native name of "Horican."

As each Indian nation had its own language or dialect, they typically gave different names to the same places, although nearly all of their names described the object itself. Therefore, a literal translation of the name for this beautiful body of water, as used by the tribe that lived on its shores, would be "The Tail of the Lake." Lake George, as it is commonly called today and now legally recognized, forms a kind of tail to Lake Champlain when you look at it on a map. This explains the origin of the name.

Winding through countless islands and nestled among mountains, the "holy lake" stretched another dozen leagues toward the south. Where the high plateau blocked the water's further passage, a portage of several miles began, leading travelers to the Hudson River's banks at a location where, despite the typical obstacles of rapids or rifts as they were called in the local language of that time, the river became navigable all the way to the tide.

While pursuing their bold plans of harassment, the restless ambition of the French even reached the distant and challenging mountain passes of the Alleghany, so it's easy to imagine that their legendary shrewdness wouldn't miss the natural strategic benefits of the area we've just described. This region became, without question, the bloody battlefield where most of the fights for control of the colonies took place. Military posts were built at various locations that controlled access to the route, and these were captured and recaptured, destroyed and reconstructed, as victory shifted between the opposing forces. While farmers retreated from the dangerous mountain passes to the safer borders of the older settlements, armies larger than those that had often decided the fate of empires were seen disappearing into these forests, from which they seldom emerged except as remnants of units, worn down by hardship or broken by defeat. Although the peaceful arts were foreign to this deadly region, its forests teemed with soldiers; its shadows and valleys echoed with the sounds of military music, and the mountain echoes carried back the laughter, or repeated the carefree shouts, of many a brave and reckless young man, as he passed through them, in the height of his enthusiasm, to rest in a long night of oblivion.

It was during this violent and bloody conflict that the events we will try to tell took place, in the third year of the war that England and France most recently fought over control of a territory that neither nation would ultimately keep.

The incompetence of her military commanders overseas and the devastating lack of determination in her government at home had brought down Great Britain's reputation from the lofty heights where it had been positioned by the abilities and boldness of her previous soldiers and political leaders. No longer feared by her adversaries, her officials were rapidly losing their sense of confidence and self-worth. In this humiliating decline, the colonists, though blameless for her incompetence and too modest to be responsible for her mistakes, naturally shared in this degradation. They had recently witnessed a select army from that nation, which they revered as a mother country and had naively believed to be unbeatable—an army commanded by a leader who had been chosen from among many experienced warriors for his exceptional military skills, shamefully defeated by a small group of French and Indians, and only rescued from complete destruction by the composure and courage of a young Virginian, whose later renown has since spread, with the enduring power of moral truth, to the farthest reaches of the Christian world. A vast frontier had been left exposed by this unforeseen catastrophe, and more concrete threats were accompanied by countless imagined and fictitious dangers. The frightened colonists believed that the screams of the savages mixed with every irregular burst of wind that came from the endless forests of the west. The terrifying nature of their ruthless enemies vastly amplified the inherent horrors of war. Countless recent slaughters remained fresh in their memories; nor was there any person in the provinces so unaware as not to have eagerly absorbed the account of some dreadful story of nighttime killing, in which the inhabitants of the forests were the main and savage perpetrators. As the gullible and agitated traveler recounted the dangerous uncertainties of the wilderness, the blood of the fearful froze with dread, and mothers looked worriedly even at those children who slept safely within the protection of the largest cities. In essence, the amplifying power of fear began to override logical thinking and to make those who should have maintained their courage become prisoners of the most degrading emotions. Even the most assured and the bravest individuals began to believe the outcome of the conflict was becoming uncertain; and that cowardly group was constantly growing in size, who believed they could foresee all the territories of the English crown in America conquered by their Christian enemies, or devastated by the attacks of their merciless allies.

Washington, who had warned the European general about the danger he was carelessly rushing into—though his warnings went unheeded—ended up saving what remained of the British army through his decisive action and bravery. The reputation Washington gained from this battle became the main reason he was later chosen to lead the American forces. It's worth noting that while all of America celebrated his well-deserved fame, his name doesn't appear in any European reports of the battle—at least the author couldn't find it despite thorough searching. This shows how the mother country manages to claim even the glory under such a system of governance.

When intelligence was received at the fort that protected the southern end of the portage between the Hudson River and the lakes that Montcalm had been spotted moving up Lake Champlain with an army "numerous as the leaves on the trees," this news was accepted with the cowardly reluctance of fear rather than the fierce joy a warrior should experience when finding an enemy within striking distance. The report had arrived toward the end of a midsummer day, delivered by an Indian messenger who also carried an urgent request from Munro, the commander of a fortification on the shore of the "holy lake," asking for swift and substantial reinforcement. It has already been noted that the distance between these two military posts was less than five leagues. The rough trail that originally served as their communication route had been expanded to allow wagon passage, so the distance that the forest dweller had covered in two hours could easily be traveled by a military detachment with their essential supplies between sunrise and sunset of a summer day. The faithful servants of the British crown had named one of these wilderness strongholds William Henry, and the other Fort Edward, naming each after a beloved prince of the ruling family. The experienced Scottish officer just mentioned commanded the first fort with a regiment of regular soldiers and a few provincial troops—a force truly far too small to stand against the formidable power that Montcalm was bringing to the base of his earthen fortifications. At the second fort, however, was stationed General Webb, who commanded the king's armies in the northern provinces, with a force of more than five thousand men. By combining the various detachments under his command, this officer could have assembled nearly twice that number of fighters against the bold Frenchman who had ventured so far from his own reinforcements with an army only slightly larger in size.

Under the pressure of their declining circumstances, both the officers and soldiers seemed more inclined to wait for their powerful enemies to arrive at their fortifications than to stop their advance by following the successful strategy the French had used at Fort du Quesne and attacking them while they marched.

After the initial shock of the news had somewhat subsided, a rumor spread throughout the fortified camp, which extended along the banks of the Hudson River, forming a series of defensive positions connected to the main fort. The rumor claimed that a specially selected force of fifteen hundred men would leave at dawn for William Henry, the outpost located at the northern end of the portage. What began as mere rumor quickly became fact, as orders were issued from the commanding general's headquarters to the various units he had chosen for this mission, instructing them to prepare for immediate departure. All uncertainty about Webb's intentions now disappeared, and the next hour or two brought hurried footsteps and worried expressions. The inexperienced soldier rushed from place to place, actually slowing down his own preparations through excessive and somewhat frantic enthusiasm; meanwhile, the seasoned veteran organized his gear with careful deliberation that showed no sign of urgency, though his serious expression and worried eyes clearly revealed that he had little professional enthusiasm for this unfamiliar and feared type of wilderness combat. Eventually the sun set in magnificent splendor behind the distant western mountains, and as darkness spread its cover over the isolated location, the sounds of preparation faded; the final light vanished from the log quarters of some officer; the trees cast deeper shadows across the earthworks and the flowing stream, and soon a silence settled over the camp as profound as that which filled the vast forest surrounding it.

Following the orders given the night before, the army's deep sleep was interrupted by the rolling beat of warning drums, whose echoing sounds could be heard drifting through the damp morning air from every opening in the woods, just as daylight began to outline the rough shapes of some tall nearby pines against the growing brightness of a gentle and clear eastern sky. Immediately the entire camp sprang into action; even the lowest-ranking soldier rose from his sleeping place to watch his fellow soldiers depart and to take part in the excitement and events of the moment. The basic formation of the selected group was quickly arranged. While the professional and trained soldiers serving the king marched proudly to the right side of the line, the more modest colonists took their less prominent position on the left, with an obedience that long experience had made natural. The scouts set out; strong guards went before and after the heavy wagons that carried the supplies; and before the gray morning light was softened by the sun's rays, the main force of fighters formed into a column and departed the camp with a display of impressive military discipline that helped to calm the hidden fears of many a beginner who was about to experience his first battle. While still visible to their admiring comrades, they maintained the same dignified appearance and orderly formation, until the sound of their fifes grew weaker with distance, and the forest finally seemed to absorb the living mass that had slowly moved into its depths.

The deepest sounds of the retreating and hidden column had stopped carrying on the wind to those listening, and the last straggler had already vanished in pursuit; but there were still signs of another departure in front of a log cabin of unusual size and comfort, before which sentinels walked their rounds, known to guard the English general. At this location were gathered about half a dozen horses, equipped in a way that showed at least two were meant to carry women of high social standing, unusual to encounter so deep in the country's wilderness. A third horse bore the gear and weapons of a staff officer; while the others, judging by their plain coverings and the travel bags they carried, were clearly prepared for several servants, who appeared to be already waiting for their masters' orders. At a respectful distance from this uncommon display, various groups of curious onlookers had gathered; some admiring the breeding and build of the spirited military horse, and others staring at the preparations with the dull amazement of common curiosity. There was one man, however, who by his appearance and behavior stood out markedly from those in the latter group of observers, being neither idle nor apparently very ignorant.

This person's physical appearance was extremely awkward, though he wasn't actually deformed in any specific way. He possessed all the same bones and joints as other people, but none of their proper proportions. When standing upright, he towered above his companions; however, when sitting down, he seemed to shrink to normal human size. This same contradiction appeared throughout his entire body. His head was oversized; his shoulders were narrow; his arms hung long and loose at his sides; while his hands were surprisingly small, even delicate. His legs and thighs were thin to the point of being skeletal, yet extraordinarily long; and his knees would have seemed enormous, if they hadn't been overshadowed by the even broader base upon which this bizarre mixture of human features was so strangely assembled. The man's mismatched and poorly chosen clothing only made his clumsiness more obvious. A sky-blue coat with short, wide tails and a low collar exposed his long, skinny neck and even longer, skinnier legs to harsh criticism from anyone inclined to judge. His lower garment consisted of yellow nankeen fabric, tightly fitted to his shape and tied at his knobbly knees with large bows of white ribbon that had become quite dirty from wear. Mottled cotton stockings and shoes—one of which bore a metal spur—completed the outfit covering the lower half of this figure, whose every curve and angle was not only visible but seemed deliberately displayed, whether through the vanity or innocence of the wearer.

From beneath the flap of a huge pocket in a dirty embossed silk vest, heavily decorated with tarnished silver lace, stuck out an instrument that, given the military setting, could have easily been mistaken for some dangerous and unfamiliar weapon of war. Though small, this unusual device had sparked the curiosity of most of the Europeans in the camp, while several of the local colonists were observed handling it not only without fear, but with complete ease. A large, formal three-cornered hat, similar to those worn by clergymen in the past thirty years, topped off the entire appearance, lending dignity to a kind-hearted and somewhat blank expression that clearly needed such artificial help to maintain the seriousness required for some important and exceptional responsibility.

While the ordinary soldiers kept their distance out of respect for Webb's quarters, the figure we have described walked boldly into the center of the servants, openly voicing his criticisms or praise about the quality of the horses, depending on whether they disappointed or pleased his expert eye.

"This animal, I believe, friend, isn't raised locally, but comes from foreign countries, or perhaps from that small island across the blue water?" he said, speaking in a voice as notable for its gentle and sweet tones as his body was for its exceptional build. "I can speak about these matters without boasting, since I've been to both ports—the one located at the mouth of the Thames that's named after the capital of Old England, and the one called 'Haven' with 'New' added to it. I've watched the flat-bottomed boats and two-masted ships gathering their herds, like animals coming to the ark, heading out to Jamaica to trade in livestock. But I've never before seen an animal that so perfectly matched the true biblical war-horse described in scripture: 'He paws in the valley and rejoices in his strength; he goes out to meet armed men. He says among the trumpets, Ha, ha; and he smells the battle from far away, the thunder of the captains, and the shouting.' It seems like the bloodline of Israel's horses has survived to our present day, doesn't it, friend?"

Receiving no response to this remarkable outburst, which truly deserved some kind of acknowledgment given how forcefully and resonantly it had been delivered, the man who had proclaimed these sacred words turned toward the silent figure he had unknowingly been addressing, and discovered an even more striking subject for wonder in what met his eyes. His gaze landed on the motionless, erect, and stiff form of the "Indian runner," who had brought the disturbing news to the camp the previous evening. Though completely at rest and seemingly ignoring the commotion and activity surrounding him with characteristic stoicism, there was a brooding ferocity mixed with the savage's calm that would likely capture the attention of far more seasoned observers than the one now studying him in open astonishment. The native carried both the tomahawk and knife of his people; yet his overall appearance was not entirely that of a warrior. Instead, there was a disheveled quality about him, as if he had recently undergone great physical strain that he hadn't yet had time to address. The pigments of his war paint had smeared together in dark disorder across his fierce face, making his dark features appear even more savage and frightening than if such an effect had been deliberately created rather than happening by accident. Only his eye, which gleamed like a blazing star among threatening clouds, could be seen in its natural, untamed state. For just a moment his probing yet cautious stare met the amazed look of the other man, and then shifting its focus, partly from cunning and partly from contempt, it remained fixed as if piercing through the distant air.

It's impossible to know what unexpected comment this brief and wordless exchange between two such unusual men might have prompted from the white man, if his restless curiosity hadn't been drawn to other matters. A stirring among the servants and the soft murmur of quiet voices signaled the arrival of those whose presence was the only thing needed for the group to begin their journey. The humble admirer of the war-horse immediately stepped back to a thin, bony, scraggly-tailed mare that was absentmindedly nibbling the withered grass near the camp; there, resting one elbow on the blanket that covered what passed for a saddle, he watched the departure unfold, while a young foal quietly enjoyed its morning meal on the other side of the same horse.

A young man dressed as an officer led two women to their horses, and it was clear from their clothing that they were ready to face the hardships of traveling through the forest. One of them, who looked younger though both were young, allowed glimpses of her radiant skin, beautiful golden hair, and bright blue eyes to be seen as she carelessly let the morning breeze lift the green veil that hung low from her hat.

The glow that still remained above the pine trees in the western sky was no brighter or more delicate than the color in her cheek; nor was the beginning of day more uplifting than the lively smile she gave the young man as he helped her into the saddle. The other woman, who seemed to receive equal attention from the young officer, hid her beauty from the soldiers' stares with a caution that appeared better suited to someone with four or five more years of experience. It was clear, however, that her figure, though shaped with the same perfect proportions that were not diminished by the traveling clothes she wore, was somewhat fuller and more developed than that of her companion.

As soon as the women had taken their seats, their escort quickly mounted his war-horse, and all three bowed to Webb, who politely waited at his cabin doorway to see them off. They turned their horses and began moving at a leisurely pace, followed by their group, toward the northern entrance of the camp. During this short journey, none of them spoke, but the younger woman let out a small gasp when an Indian runner suddenly appeared beside her and took the lead along the military road ahead of them. While this unexpected and startling appearance of the Indian drew no sound from the other woman, her surprise caused her veil to fall open, revealing an expression that mixed pity, admiration, and horror as her dark eyes tracked the graceful movements of the native warrior. This lady's hair was glossy and black, like a raven's feathers. Her skin wasn't dark, but seemed filled with rich blood that appeared ready to overflow. Yet her face showed neither roughness nor lack of delicate features—it was perfectly proportioned, noble, and extraordinarily beautiful. She smiled, as though pitying her own brief lapse of composure, revealing teeth that would put the finest ivory to shame. Then, pulling her veil back into place, she lowered her head and continued riding in silence, like someone whose mind was focused elsewhere.

---

# Chapter II.

"Sola, sola, wo ha, ho, sola!"
—Shakespeare

While one of the beautiful women we have so briefly introduced to the reader was lost in thought, the other quickly recovered from the fear that had caused her outcry, and, laughing at her own vulnerability, she asked the young man who rode beside her:

"Do these ghostly figures appear often in the woods, Heyward, or is this display a special show arranged just for us? If it's the latter, we should be grateful and say nothing; but if it's the former, both Cora and I will need to rely heavily on that inherited bravery we're so proud of, even before we have to face the formidable Montcalm."

"That Indian is a 'scout' for the army, and according to the customs of his people, he can be considered a hero," the officer replied. "He has offered to lead us to the lake using a route that few people know about, which will get us there faster than if we followed the slow progress of the main force, and therefore more pleasantly."

"I don't like him," said the lady, shuddering, partly from pretended fear, but mostly from genuine terror. "You know him, Duncan, or you wouldn't trust yourself so freely to his care?"

"Let me put it differently, Alice—I simply wouldn't trust you with this. I do know him, or he wouldn't have my confidence, especially not at a time like this. People say he's Canadian, yet he fought alongside our allies the Mohawks, who are part of the six allied nations, as you're aware. From what I've been told, he came to be among us through some unusual circumstances that involved your father, where the native was treated quite harshly. But I'm forgetting the details of that old story—what matters is that he's our friend now."

"If he was my father's enemy, then I dislike him even more!" cried the girl, now genuinely worried. "Won't you speak to him, Major Heyward, so I can hear how he sounds? It might seem silly, but you've often heard me say that I trust what I can learn from a person's voice!"

"It would be pointless, and would most likely be met with an outburst. Although he might understand what we're saying, he pretends, like most of his people, not to know English. He certainly won't lower himself to speak it, especially now that the war requires him to maintain his full dignity. But he's stopping— the hidden trail we need to take is probably nearby."

Major Heyward's guess was correct. When they arrived at the place where the Indian was standing and pointing into the dense brush that bordered the military road, they could see a narrow, hidden trail that would allow only one person to pass through at a time, though with some difficulty.

"This is our path," the young man said quietly. "Don't show any suspicion, or you might bring about the very danger you seem to fear."

"Cora, what do you think?" asked the hesitant young woman. "If we travel with the soldiers, even though we might find their company annoying, won't we feel more confident about our safety?"

"Since you're not very familiar with how the natives fight, Alice, you're misunderstanding where the real danger lies," Heyward said. "If enemies have actually made it to the portage—which isn't very likely since our scouts are out there—they'll definitely be found moving along the edges of the main column, where there are plenty of scalps to be taken. The detachment's route is well-known, but ours was only decided within the last hour, so it must still be a secret."

"Should we distrust the man because his manners are not our manners, and because his skin is dark?" Cora asked coldly.

Alice didn't hesitate any longer; giving her Narragansett a sharp crack of the whip, she was the first to push aside the thin branches of the bushes and follow the runner along the dark and twisted path. The young man looked at the last speaker with obvious admiration, and even allowed her fairer, though certainly not more beautiful companion, to proceed without assistance, while he carefully cleared the way himself for the passage of the one who has been called Cora. It appeared that the servants had been given instructions beforehand; for, instead of pushing through the thicket, they followed the route of the column; a decision which Heyward explained had been suggested by the wisdom of their guide, in order to reduce the signs of their trail, if, by chance, the Canadian savages should be hiding so far ahead of their army. For many minutes the complexity of the route allowed for no further conversation; after which they emerged from the wide border of undergrowth that grew along the line of the highway, and entered under the high but dark arches of the forest. Here their progress was less hindered; and the moment the guide saw that the women could control their horses, he moved on, at a pace between a trot and a walk, and at a speed which kept the sure-footed and distinctive animals they rode at a fast yet comfortable gait. The youth had turned to speak to the dark-eyed Cora, when the distant sound of horses' hooves, clattering over the roots of the broken path behind him, caused him to stop his horse; and, as his companions pulled their reins at the same moment, the whole party came to a halt, in order to get an explanation of the unexpected interruption.[1]

[1] In Rhode Island, there's a bay called Narragansett, named after a powerful Native American tribe that once lived along its shores. By chance, or through one of those mysterious quirks that nature occasionally produces in the animal kingdom, a breed of horses developed that became well-known throughout America, distinguished by their natural pacing gait. Horses from this breed were, and still are, highly valued as riding horses because of their toughness and smooth movement. Since they were also sure-footed, Narragansett horses were especially popular with women who had to travel across the rough terrain of tree roots and holes found in the frontier regions.

In just a few moments, a young horse appeared, moving like a deer through the straight pine tree trunks. An instant later, the awkward man described in the previous Chapter came into sight, riding as fast as he could push his thin horse without causing it to completely break down. Up until this point, this character had avoided being noticed by the travelers. If he had the ability to catch someone's attention when showing off his impressive height while walking, his horseback riding skills were even more certain to draw people's eyes.

Despite constantly pressing his one good heel into the mare's sides, the fastest pace he could manage was an uneven canter with the back legs, while the front legs helped out only occasionally, usually preferring to maintain a steady loping trot. The rapid shifts between these different gaits might have created a visual trick that made the horse appear more capable than it actually was; what's certain is that Heyward, who had a keen eye for judging horses, couldn't figure out despite his best efforts exactly how his persistent pursuer managed to follow his winding trail with such determined endurance.

The rider's activity and movements were just as remarkable as those of his horse. With each change in the horse's maneuvers, the rider lifted his tall frame up in the stirrups, causing his legs to stretch unnaturally and creating such sudden increases and decreases in his height that it was impossible to guess his actual size. Add to this the fact that because he applied the spur only to one side, one flank of the mare seemed to move faster than the other, and the irritated side was clearly shown by the constant swishing of her thick tail, and we complete the picture of both horse and rider.

The frown that had formed on Heyward's handsome, open, and masculine forehead slowly eased, and his lips curved into a faint smile as he looked at the stranger. Alice didn't try very hard to contain her amusement, and even Cora's dark, contemplative eyes brightened with humor that appeared to be held back more by habit than by her natural disposition.

"Are you looking for anyone here?" Heyward asked when the other person had come close enough to slow down. "I hope you're not bringing bad news?"

"Even so," the stranger replied, working his triangular hat vigorously to stir the stagnant air in the dense woods, leaving his listeners uncertain which of the young man's questions he was answering; after he had cooled his face and caught his breath, he went on, "I understand you're traveling to William Henry; since I'm heading in that direction myself, I thought good company would suit both our interests."

"You seem to have the deciding vote," Heyward replied; "there are three of us, while you haven't consulted anyone but yourself."

"Even so. The first thing you need to achieve is understanding your own mind. Once you're certain of that—and when it comes to women, that's not easy—the next step is to follow through on your decision. I have tried to do both, and here I am."

"If you're heading to the lake, you've taken the wrong path," Heyward said arrogantly. "The main road there is at least half a mile back the way you came."

"Even so," replied the stranger, completely undeterred by this chilly welcome; "I've been staying at the 'Edward' for a week, and I'd have to be mute not to have asked about the route I needed to take; and if I were mute, that would put an end to my profession." After smiling slightly, like someone whose modesty prevented a more obvious display of his appreciation for a joke that made no sense whatsoever to his listeners, he went on, "It's not wise for anyone in my line of work to get too close to those I'm supposed to teach; that's why I don't travel with the army; besides, I believe that a gentleman of your standing has the best sense when it comes to travel matters; I've therefore decided to join your group, so that the journey might be pleasant and we can enjoy each other's company."

"What an arbitrary, if not reckless decision!" Heyward exclaimed, unsure whether to unleash his rising anger or burst out laughing at the man. "But you mention instruction and a profession; are you attached to the provincial forces as an instructor in the noble art of warfare and tactics; or perhaps you're someone who sketches diagrams and geometric figures while claiming to teach mathematics?"

The stranger looked at the person questioning him for a moment in amazement; and then, losing all signs of self-satisfaction and taking on an expression of serious humility, he replied:

"I hope I haven't offended anyone on either side. As for defending myself, I won't do that—by God's good mercy, I haven't committed any obvious sin since I last asked for his forgiveness. I don't understand what you're referring to with lines and angles, and I'll leave explaining such things to those who have been called and appointed to that sacred duty. I don't claim to have any greater gift than a small understanding of the glorious art of making requests and giving thanks, as it's practiced in singing psalms."

"The man is clearly a follower of Apollo," exclaimed Alice with amusement, "and I'm taking him under my special protection. Come now, put away that scowl, Heyward, and for the sake of my eager ears, let him travel with our group. Besides," she added quietly and quickly, glancing toward Cora in the distance, who was slowly following behind their quiet but moody guide, "he might prove to be an ally who could strengthen us when we need it most."

"Do you think, Alice, that I would bring those I love along this secret path if I thought such danger could arise?"

"No, no, I'm not thinking about that now; but this strange man amuses me, and if he 'has music in his soul', let's not rudely reject his company." She pointed persuasively along the path with her riding whip, while their eyes met in a look that the young man lingered a moment to extend; then, giving in to her gentle influence, he dug his spurs into his horse, and in a few leaps was once again at Cora's side.

"I'm happy to meet you, friend," the young woman continued, gesturing for the stranger to keep going as she encouraged her Narragansett horse to resume its gentle pace. "Biased family members have nearly convinced me that I'm not completely terrible at singing duets myself; and we could make our journey more enjoyable by engaging in our favorite activity. It would be extremely beneficial for someone as inexperienced as I am to hear the thoughts and expertise of someone skilled in this art."

"It's refreshing for both the spirit and the body to sing psalms at the right times," replied the music teacher, readily agreeing to her suggestion that he follow along. "Nothing would ease the mind more than such comforting fellowship through song. However, four vocal parts are absolutely essential for perfect harmony. You possess all the qualities of a gentle and rich soprano voice; with special effort, I can carry a full tenor part to the highest notes; but we're missing alto and bass voices! That officer of the king, who was reluctant to welcome me into his group, could handle the bass part, if one can tell from how his voice sounds in regular conversation."

"Don't judge too quickly based on hasty and misleading appearances," said the lady, smiling; "though Major Heyward can produce such deep notes when the situation calls for it, believe me, his natural voice is better suited for a smooth tenor than the bass you just heard."

"Is he, then, well-versed in the art of singing psalms?" asked her innocent companion.

Alice felt like laughing, though she managed to hold back her amusement before she replied:

"I suspect that he's quite fond of vulgar songs. A soldier's way of life offers little opportunity to develop more serious interests."

"A person's voice is given to them, just like their other talents, to be used properly and not misused. No one can say they have ever seen me neglect my gifts! I am grateful that, although my childhood could be described as having been dedicated, like the youth of the royal David, to the purposes of music, no word of crude poetry has ever defiled my lips."

"So you've focused your efforts only on sacred music?"

"Even so. Just as David's psalms surpass all other forms of language, the musical settings created for them by the religious scholars and wise men of our land exceed all meaningless poetry. I'm pleased to say that I speak only the thoughts and desires of the King of Israel himself; for while the times may require some minor adjustments, this version we use in the New England colonies far surpasses all other versions. Through its richness, its precision, and its spiritual simplicity, it comes as close as possible to the great work of the inspired author. I never stay anywhere, whether sleeping or awake, without a copy of this remarkable work. It is the twenty-sixth edition, published in Boston in the year 1744, and is titled, 'The Psalms, Hymns, and Spiritual Songs of the Old and New Testaments; faithfully translated into English Metre, for the Use, Edification, and Comfort of the Saints, in Public and Private, especially in New England'."

During this praise of the exceptional work of his homeland's poets, the stranger had pulled the book from his pocket, and after placing a pair of iron-rimmed spectacles on his nose, he opened the volume with the care and reverence appropriate for its sacred purpose. Then, without beating around the bush or offering any apology, he first spoke the word "Standish," and positioning the mysterious instrument, already described, to his mouth, from which he produced a high, piercing sound, followed by a note an octave lower from his own voice, he began singing the following words in rich, sweet, and melodious tones that overcame the music, the poetry, and even the restless movement of his poorly trained horse:

"How good it is to see,
And how pleasing it is,
For brothers to live together
In perfect unity.

It is like precious oil
That flows from the head to the beard;
Down Aaron's head it runs,
All the way to the edges of his robes."

The delivery of these skillful rhymes was accompanied by the stranger's regular rising and falling of his right hand, which ended on the downward motion by letting his fingers rest for a moment on the pages of the small book, and on the upward motion by such a flourish of his hand that only those with proper training could ever hope to copy. It appeared that long practice had made this hand movement necessary, as it continued until the preposition that the poet had chosen to end his verse had been properly delivered like a two-syllable word.

This kind of disruption to the quiet solitude of the forest was bound to catch the attention of those traveling just a short distance ahead. The Indian mumbled a few words in broken English to Heyward, who then spoke to the stranger, immediately interrupting and temporarily ending his musical performance.

"Even though we're not in immediate danger, basic common sense tells us we should travel through this wilderness as quietly as we can. So please forgive me, Alice, if I have to spoil your fun by asking this gentleman to hold off on his singing until we're somewhere safer."

"You'll definitely make them smaller," the mischievous girl replied; "I've never heard such a terrible combination of performance and words as what I just listened to; and I was deep into a scholarly investigation of what causes such a mismatch between sound and meaning, when you interrupted my thoughts with that deep voice of yours, Duncan!"

"I don't know what you mean by my bass," said Heyward, irritated by her comment, "but I know that your safety, and Cora's safety, means far more to me than any of Handel's orchestral music ever could." He stopped speaking and quickly turned his head toward a cluster of bushes, then looked suspiciously at their guide, who kept walking at his steady pace with undisturbed seriousness. The young man smiled to himself, believing he had mistaken some bright berry in the forest for the gleaming eyes of a lurking savage, and he continued riding forward, resuming the conversation that had been interrupted by the fleeting thought.

Major Heyward's only mistake was letting his youthful and noble pride override his careful vigilance. The group of riders hadn't traveled far when the branches of the bushes forming the thicket were carefully pushed apart, and a human face—made fiercely wild by savage artistry and uncontrolled passions—peered out at the departing footsteps of the travelers. A flash of triumph crossed the darkly painted features of this forest dweller as he tracked the route of his intended victims, who rode onward without suspicion, the light and graceful forms of the women moving among the trees along the curves of their path, followed at each turn by Heyward's masculine figure, until finally the awkward form of the singing master disappeared behind the countless tree trunks that rose in dark rows throughout the space between them.

———————————

# Chapter III.

"Before these fields were cut and cultivated,
Our rivers flowed completely full;
The music of waters filled
The fresh and endless forest;
And torrents crashed, and streams danced,
And springs bubbled up in the shadows."—Bryant

Leaving the unsuspecting Heyward and his trusting companions to venture even deeper into a forest that harbored such dangerous inhabitants, we must exercise an author's privilege and move the scene several miles west of where we last observed them.

On that day, two men were waiting by the banks of a small but fast-moving stream, less than an hour's travel from Webb's camp, like people waiting for someone to arrive or for some anticipated event to occur. The enormous canopy of forest stretched all the way to the river's edge, hanging over the water and casting shadows that made the dark current even darker. The sun's rays were starting to become less intense, and the day's scorching heat was beginning to fade as the cooler mist from springs and streams rose above their leafy surroundings and hung in the air. Still, that quiet stillness that characterizes the sleepy heat of an American landscape in July filled the isolated location, broken only by the men's quiet voices, the occasional lazy tapping of a woodpecker, the harsh call of some brightly colored jay, or a sound that grew louder in their ears from the muted roar of a distant waterfall. These weak and scattered sounds were, however, too familiar to the woodsmen to distract their attention from the more compelling subject of their conversation. While one of these men waiting around displayed the red skin and wild gear of a native of the forest, the other showed, beneath the disguise of his crude and almost savage equipment, the lighter, though sun-darkened and elongated complexion of someone who could claim European ancestry. The first man was sitting on the end of a moss-covered log, in a position that allowed him to enhance the impact of his serious words with the calm but meaningful gestures of an Indian participating in discussion. His body, which was almost completely bare, displayed a frightening symbol of death, painted in mixed colors of white and black. His closely-shaved head, on which no hair remained except the famous and warrior-like scalp lock was kept, had no decoration of any sort, except for a single eagle feather that crossed his head and hung down over his left shoulder. A tomahawk and scalping knife, made in England, were tucked in his belt; while a short military rifle, the type that white people's policies provided to their savage allies, rested casually across his bare and muscular knee. The broad chest, well-developed limbs, and serious expression of this warrior would indicate that he had reached his prime years, though no signs of decline seemed to have yet diminished his strength. [1]

> [1] The North American warrior had all the hair removed from his entire body, except for a small tuft that remained on the top of his head so that his enemy could grab it when tearing off the scalp if he was defeated. The scalp served as the only acceptable trophy of victory. Therefore, taking the scalp was considered more significant than actually killing the person. Certain tribes placed great importance on the honor of striking a dead body. These customs have almost completely vanished among the Indian tribes of the Atlantic states.

The white man's body, based on the parts visible beneath his clothing, showed the signs of someone who had endured hardship and physical labor since childhood. Though muscular, his frame appeared lean rather than robust, yet every sinew and muscle seemed toughened and hardened by constant exposure to the elements and demanding work. He dressed in a forest-green hunting shirt trimmed with faded yellow fringe, and wore a summer cap made from fur-stripped animal skins. A knife hung from a wampum belt similar to those that secured the simple clothing of Native Americans, though he carried no tomahawk. His moccasins displayed the colorful decorative style favored by the indigenous people, while the only visible portion of his undergarments beneath the hunting coat consisted of buckskin leggings that tied along the sides and were secured above the knees with deer sinew. A pouch and powder horn rounded out his personal equipment, while a very long rifle—which the more sophisticated whites had determined to be the most lethal of all firearms—rested against a nearby young tree. The hunter's eyes, or scout's if that's what he was, appeared small, alert, sharp, and constantly moving, scanning in all directions as he spoke, as though searching for prey or watching for the unexpected arrival of some hidden foe. Despite these signs of ingrained wariness, his face showed no trace of deception, and at this moment of introduction, it conveyed an expression of solid integrity.[2]

> [2]The hunting shirt is a picturesque work shirt that's shorter and decorated with fringes and tassels. The colors are designed to mimic the shades of the forest for camouflage purposes. Many units of American riflemen have worn this outfit, and it's one of the most distinctive uniforms of modern times. The hunting shirt is often white.

The military rifle is short; the hunter's rifle is always long.

"Even your traditions support my argument, Chingachgook," he said, speaking in the language that was familiar to all the native peoples who once lived in the territory between the Hudson and Potomac rivers, and which we will translate freely for the reader's understanding while attempting to maintain some of the distinctive characteristics of both the speaker and the language itself. "Your ancestors came from the west, crossed the great river, battled the inhabitants of this land, and claimed it as their own; while mine came from the eastern dawn, across the ocean, and carried out their mission in much the same manner that your people had shown them; so let God be the judge between us, and let friends hold their tongues!"[3]

> [3] The Mississippi. The scout refers to a tradition that is very popular among the tribes of the Atlantic states. Evidence of their Asian origin is drawn from these circumstances, though great uncertainty surrounds the entire history of the Indians.

"My ancestors battled against the bare-skinned red man!" the Indian replied harshly, speaking in the same tongue. "Tell me, Hawkeye, isn't there a distinction between a warrior's stone-tipped arrow and the lead bullet you use to kill?"

"An Indian can think logically, even though nature gave him red skin!" the white man said, shaking his head like someone who wasn't unmoved by such an appeal to his sense of fairness. For a moment he seemed aware that he was losing the argument, but then he recovered and responded to his opponent's objection as best as his limited knowledge would allow:

"I'm not a scholar, and I don't care who knows it; but based on what I've observed during deer hunts and squirrel hunting trips with the young men of today, I believe a rifle in the hands of their grandfathers wasn't as deadly as a hickory bow with a sharp flint arrowhead could be when drawn with Native American skill and aimed by a Native American eye."

"You have the story told by your fathers," the other replied, dismissing him with a cold wave of his hand. "What do your elders say? Do they tell the young warriors that the white men encountered the red men, painted for war and armed with stone hatchets and wooden guns?"

"I'm not a prejudiced man, and I don't boast about my natural advantages, though even my worst enemy on earth—and he happens to be an Iroquois—wouldn't dare deny that I'm genuinely white," the scout responded, examining with hidden satisfaction the weathered color of his lean and muscular hand. "And I'm willing to admit that my people have many customs that, as an honest man, I cannot approve of. One of their habits is to write down in books what they have accomplished and witnessed, rather than sharing these stories in their villages, where a lie can be called out directly to a cowardly braggart's face, and where a brave soldier can ask his fellow warriors to confirm the truth of his account. Because of this poor practice, a man who is too principled to waste his time among the women learning to read those black marks on paper may never learn about his ancestors' achievements, nor feel the pride that comes from trying to surpass them. As for myself, I believe the Bumppos were skilled marksmen, since I have a natural ability with a rifle that must have been passed down through the generations, just as our sacred teachings tell us that all good and evil talents are given to us; though I would hesitate to vouch for others in such matters. But every tale has two perspectives; so I ask you, Chingachgook, what happened, according to the traditions of the red men, when our ancestors first encountered each other?"

A minute of silence followed, during which the Native American remained quiet; then, filled with the dignity of his position, he began his short story with a seriousness that made it seem more truthful.

"Listen, Hawkeye, and you'll hear nothing but the truth. This is what my ancestors have said, and what the Mohicans have done." He paused for just a moment, casting a careful look at his companion before continuing in a way that seemed both questioning and stating a fact. "Doesn't this stream at our feet flow toward the south until its waters become salty and the current runs upstream?"

"There's no denying that your traditions are accurate about both of these things," the white man said. "I've been there myself and witnessed them firsthand, though I've never been able to explain why water that tastes so sweet in the shade turns bitter when exposed to the sun."

"And the current!" the Indian demanded, expecting his reply with the kind of interest a man feels when seeking confirmation of testimony that amazes him even as he respects it; "the fathers of Chingachgook have not lied!"

"The holy Bible is no more true, and that represents the truest thing in nature. People call this upstream current the tide, which can be easily explained and is clear enough to understand. For six hours the waters flow in, and for six hours they flow out, and here's why: when the water level in the sea is higher than in the river, the water flows in until the river reaches its highest point, and then it flows back out again."

"The water in the forests and on the large lakes flows downhill until it becomes level like my hand," the Indian said, extending his arm straight out in front of him, "and then it stops flowing."

"No honest person would deny it," said the scout, somewhat irritated by the suggestion that his explanation of how tides work might be wrong; "and I'll admit that's true on a small scale, where the land is flat. But everything depends on the perspective you take when looking at things. Now, on a small scale, the earth appears flat; but when you look at the big picture, it's round. This way, pools and ponds, and even the large freshwater lakes, can remain still, as both you and I know they do, since we've seen them ourselves; but when you spread water across a vast area, like the ocean, where the earth is round, how could anyone reasonably expect the water to stay calm? You might as well expect the river to remain motionless at the edge of those dark rocks a mile upstream from us, even though your own ears can hear it rushing over them right now."

If the Indian found his companion's philosophy unsatisfying, he was far too dignified to reveal his doubt. He listened as though he were convinced and continued his story with the same solemn manner as before.

"We came from the land where the sun hides at night, across vast plains where buffalo roam, until we reached the great river. There we battled the Alligewi until the earth was stained red with their blood. From the shores of the great river to the edges of the salt lake, no one stood against us. The Maquas followed from far behind. We declared that the land should belong to us from the place where the water no longer flows upstream, to a river twenty days' journey toward summer. We forced the Maquas into the forests with the bears. They could only taste salt at the natural licks; they caught no fish from the great lake; we threw them nothing but bones."

"I've heard all of this and I believe it," said the white man, noticing that the Indian had stopped speaking; "but this happened long before the English arrived in the country."

"A pine tree grew where this chestnut tree now stands. The first white people who came to live among us didn't speak English. They arrived in a large canoe during the time when my ancestors had made peace with the Native American tribes around them. Then, Hawkeye," he went on, showing his deep feelings only by letting his voice drop to those low, throaty tones that make his language sound so beautiful when he speaks like that; "then, Hawkeye, we were united as one people, and we lived in happiness. The ocean provided us with fish, the forest gave us deer, and the sky offered us birds. We married women who gave birth to our children; we honored the Great Spirit; and we kept the Maquas far away from hearing our victory songs."

"Do you know anything about your own family from that time?" the white man asked. "But you are quite a man, for an Indian; and since I assume you possess their natural abilities, your ancestors must have been brave warriors and wise men at the council fire."

"My tribe is the ancestor of nations, but I am a man of pure blood. The blood of chiefs flows through my veins, where it will remain forever. The Dutch arrived and brought my people alcohol; they drank until the sky and earth appeared to touch, and they mistakenly believed they had discovered the Great Spirit. Then they gave away their land. Step by step, they were forced back from the coastline, until I, who am both a chief and a Sagamore, have never seen the sun shine except through the forest canopy, and have never been able to visit my ancestors' burial grounds."

"Graves bring solemn feelings to the mind," the scout replied, deeply moved by his companion's quiet suffering; "and they often help a man with his good intentions; though, for myself, I expect to leave my own bones unburied, to bleach in the woods, or to be torn apart by the wolves. But where can we find those of your people who came to their relatives in the Delaware territory, so many summers ago?"

"Where are the flowers of those summers!—fallen, one by one; so all of my family left, each in their turn, to the land of spirits. I am on the hilltop and must go down into the valley; and when Uncas follows in my footsteps there will no longer be any of the blood of the Sagamores, for my boy is the last of the Mohicans."

"Uncas is here," said another voice in the same soft, throaty tones, close to his elbow; "who speaks to Uncas?"

The white man loosened his knife in its leather sheath and instinctively moved his hand toward his rifle at this sudden interruption, but the Indian remained calm and didn't turn his head at the unexpected sounds.

In the next moment, a young warrior moved silently between them and sat down on the bank of the rushing stream. The father showed no sign of surprise, and no questions were asked or answers given for several minutes. Each seemed to be waiting for the right moment to speak without showing feminine curiosity or childish impatience. The white man appeared to follow their customs and, releasing his grip on the rifle, he too remained quiet and composed. Finally, Chingachgook slowly turned his eyes toward his son and asked:

"Do the Mohawks dare to leave the mark of their moccasins in these woods?"

"I've been tracking them," the young Indian replied, "and I know there are ten of them, but they're hiding like cowards."

"The thieves are waiting out there for scalps and loot," said the white man, whom we'll call Hawkeye, following the custom of his companions. "That scheming Frenchman, Montcalm, will send his spies right into our camp, but he'll find out which route we're taking!"

"That's enough," the father replied, glancing toward the setting sun. "They'll be driven out like deer from their hiding places. Hawkeye, let's eat tonight and show the Maquas tomorrow that we are men."

"I'm just as ready to do one thing as the other; but to fight the Iroquois we need to find those hiding enemies, and to eat we need to catch some game—speak of the devil and he appears; there's a pair of the largest antlers I've seen all season, moving through the bushes down the hill! Now, Uncas," he went on in a hushed voice, chuckling with a quiet internal sound like someone who had learned to stay alert, "I'll wager my powder horn filled three times over against a foot of wampum that I can hit him right between the eyes, and closer to the right side than the left."

"That's impossible!" the young Indian exclaimed, jumping to his feet with youthful excitement. "Everything except the tips of his horns is hidden!"

"He's just a boy!" the white man said, shaking his head as he spoke and turning to address the father. "Does he really think that when a hunter spots part of an animal, he can't figure out where the rest of it must be!"

Adjusting his rifle, he was about to demonstrate the skill he took such pride in, when the warrior knocked the weapon aside with his hand, saying:

"Hawkeye! Will you fight the Mohawks?"

"These Indians understand the forest as if it's second nature to them!" the scout replied, lowering his rifle and turning away like someone who had realized his mistake. "I'll have to let you take the shot at that buck, Uncas, or we might end up providing dinner for those thieves, the Iroquois."

As soon as the father confirmed this signal with a meaningful gesture of his hand, Uncas dropped to the ground and moved toward the animal with careful, cautious steps. When he came within a few yards of the hiding place, he carefully fitted an arrow to his bow, while the antlers shifted as if their owner sensed danger in the contaminated air. In the next instant, the sharp sound of the bowstring rang out, a white flash was seen streaking into the bushes, and the wounded deer leaped from its cover, landing right at the feet of its concealed enemy. Dodging the horns of the enraged animal, Uncas sprang to its side and drew his knife across its throat, and as it bounded toward the river's edge, it collapsed, staining the waters red with its blood.

"It was done with Indian skill," said the scout, laughing quietly to himself but with great satisfaction. "And it was a beautiful sight to see! Though an arrow makes a close shot, it still needs a knife to complete the job."

"Hugh!" his companion exclaimed, spinning around quickly like a hunting dog that had caught the scent of prey.

"Good Lord, there's a whole group of them!" shouted the

scout, whose eyes started to shine with the excitement of his familiar work; "if they get close enough for a shot, I'll take one down, even if all the Six Nations are hiding within earshot! What do you hear, Chingachgook? because to me the forest is completely silent."

"There's only one deer, and it's dead," said the Indian, leaning down until his ear almost touched the ground. "I can hear footsteps!"

"Maybe the wolves have forced the deer to take cover and are tracking him down."

"No. The white men's horses are approaching!" the other replied, rising with dignity and settling back onto the log with his previous calm composure. "Hawkeye, these are your people; you should speak with them."

"I will, and I'll speak in English that the king wouldn't be ashamed to hear," the hunter replied, using the language he took pride in. "But I don't see anything, and I don't hear any sounds from people or animals. It's odd that an Indian would pick up on white men's sounds better than someone who—even his enemies would admit—has no mixed blood, though he's lived among the red men long enough to raise suspicions! Wait! There's something that sounds like a dry branch snapping—now I can hear the bushes rustling—yes, yes, there's a trampling sound that I mistook for the waterfall—and—but here they come! God protect them from the Iroquois!"

---

# Chapter IV.

"Well go thy way: thou shalt not from this grove
 Till I torment thee for this injury."—A Midsummer
Night's Dream.

The scout was still speaking when the leader of the group, whose approaching footsteps the Indian's sharp ears had detected, appeared in plain sight. A well-worn trail, like those created by deer traveling the same route season after season, curved through a small valley nearby and met the river exactly where the white man and his Native American companions had positioned themselves. Following this path, the travelers who had caused such an unexpected encounter in the deep woods moved slowly toward the hunter, who stood ahead of his companions, prepared to meet them.

"Who's there?" the scout called out, casually shifting his rifle across his left arm while keeping his right index finger on the trigger, though he was careful not to appear threatening. "Who comes here, into this wilderness full of wild animals and dangers?"

"We're religious believers and loyal supporters of the law and the king," replied the rider in front. "We're men who have been traveling since sunrise through the shadows of this forest without food, and we're exhausted from our journey."

"So you're lost," the hunter interrupted, "and you've discovered how helpless it is when you don't know whether to go right or left?"

"Even so; nursing infants are no more dependent on those who guide them than we who are fully grown, and who may now be said to have the physical stature without the wisdom of men. Do you know the distance to a crown outpost called William Henry?"

"Ha!" the scout called out, not holding back his open laughter, though he quickly controlled the risky sounds and enjoyed his amusement with less chance of being heard by any hidden enemies. "You're as far off track as a hunting dog would be with Fort William Henry standing between it and its prey! William Henry, my friend! If you're loyal to the king and have business with the army, you should follow the river downstream to Fort Edward and present your case to Webb, who's stationed there, rather than pushing into these narrow passes and forcing this bold Frenchman back across Lake Champlain into his stronghold again."

Before the stranger could respond to this surprising proposal, another rider burst through the bushes and spurred his horse onto the path, positioning himself in front of his companion.

"So how far are we from Fort Edward?" asked someone else. "You're telling us to go to the place we left this morning, and we're trying to get to the head of the lake."

"Then you must have lost your eyesight before losing your way, because the road across the portage is cut to a good two rods wide, and is as grand a path, I figure, as any that runs into London, or even before the palace of the king himself."

"We won't argue about how excellent this route is," Heyward replied with a smile, for as the reader has already guessed, it was indeed him. "What matters right now is that we put our trust in an Indian guide to lead us along a shorter but more obscure trail, and we were wrong about his expertise. To put it simply, we have no idea where we are."

"An Indian lost in the woods!" said the scout, shaking his head with doubt. "When the sun is burning the treetops, and the waterways are flowing full; when the moss on every beech tree he sees will tell him which direction the north star will shine at night. The woods are filled with deer trails that lead to streams and salt licks, places well known to everyone; and the geese haven't finished their migration to the Canadian waters yet! It's strange that an Indian would be lost between Horican and the river bend! Is he a Mohawk?"

"Not by birth, though he was adopted into that tribe; I believe his birthplace was farther north, and he is one of those you call a Huron."

"Hugh!" shouted the two companions of the scout, who had remained seated and motionless throughout this part of the conversation, appearing completely indifferent to what was happening, but who now jumped to their feet with such sudden energy and interest that it clearly caught them off guard and broke through their usual restraint.

"A Huron!" the tough scout said again, shaking his head with obvious suspicion. "They're a dishonest people, and I don't care who takes them in—you can never turn them into anything but sneaks and wanderers. Since you put yourself under the protection of someone from that tribe, I'm only surprised you haven't run into more of them."

"There's little danger of that, since William Henry is so many miles ahead of us. You're forgetting that I told you our guide is now a Mohawk, and that he's serving with our forces as an ally."

"And I'm telling you that someone born a Mingo will die a Mingo," the other replied with certainty. "A Mohawk! No, give me a Delaware or a Mohican for honesty; and when they're willing to fight, which they don't all do, having allowed their cunning enemies, the Maquas, to make them weak—but when they do decide to fight, look to a Delaware, or a Mohican, for a true warrior!"

"That's enough," Heyward said impatiently. "I don't want to discuss the character of a man I already know, especially with someone who must be a stranger to him. You still haven't answered my question: how far are we from the main army at Edward?"

"It seems that may depend on who is your guide. One would think such a horse as that might get over a good deal of ground between sunrise and sunset."

"I don't want to argue over meaningless words with you, friend," said Heyward, controlling his frustrated attitude and speaking in a gentler tone; "if you tell me how far it is to Fort Edward and guide me there, I'll make sure you're paid for your trouble."

"And by doing this, how do I know that I'm not leading an enemy and a spy of Montcalm to the army's fortifications? Not every man who can speak English is a loyal subject."

"If you serve with the military forces, and I believe you to be a scout, you should be aware of one of the king's regiments known as the Sixtieth."

"The Sixtieth! You can't tell me much about the Royal Americans that I don't already know, even though I wear a hunting shirt instead of a scarlet jacket."

"Well, then, among other things, you might know the name of its mayor?"

"He's a major!" the hunter interrupted, straightening his body like someone who took pride in being trusted with such information. "If there's anyone in this country who knows Major Effingham, you're looking at him."

"It's a military unit that has many majors; the gentleman you're referring to is the senior one, but I'm talking about the most junior of them all; the one who commands the companies stationed at the garrison in William Henry."

"Yes, yes, I've heard that a young man of great wealth from one of the southern provinces has gotten the position. He's too young to hold such a high rank and to be placed above men whose hair is starting to turn gray; yet they say he's knowledgeable as a soldier and a brave gentleman!"

"No matter who he is or what qualifications he has for his position, he's speaking to you now and obviously can't be an enemy you need to fear."

The scout looked at Heyward with surprise, and then removing his cap, he replied in a voice that was less certain than before—though still showing doubt.

"I heard that a group was supposed to leave the camp this morning to head to the lake shore?"

"You have heard the truth; but I chose a shorter path, relying on the knowledge of the Indian I mentioned."

"And he deceived you, and then abandoned you?"

"I don't think either one is true; definitely not the second option, since you'll find him at the back."

"I'd like to get a look at this person; if he's a real Iroquois, I can tell by his cunning expression and his war paint," the scout said, stepping past Heyward's horse and moving onto the path behind the singing master's mare, whose young foal had used this break to nurse from its mother. After pushing through the bushes and walking a short distance, he came upon the women, who were waiting anxiously for the outcome of their discussion, feeling more than a little uneasy. Behind them, the messenger was leaning against a tree, where he endured the scout's careful examination with complete composure, though his expression was so dark and fierce that it could frighten anyone just by itself. Content with what he had observed, the hunter quickly moved away from him. As he walked back past the women, he stopped briefly to admire their beauty, responding to Alice's smile and nod with a look of genuine delight. From there he approached the maternal horse, and after spending a moment trying unsuccessfully to figure out what kind of person her rider was, he shook his head and walked back to Heyward.

"A Mingo is a Mingo, and God having made him so, neither the Mohawks nor any other tribe can change him," he said, once he had returned to his earlier position. "If we were by ourselves, and you would abandon that magnificent horse to the wolves tonight, I could guide you to Edward myself within an hour, since it's only about an hour's travel from here; but with such ladies accompanying you, it's impossible!"

"And why? They are tired, but they can easily handle riding a few more miles."

"It's absolutely impossible!" the scout said again. "I wouldn't walk a single mile through these woods once darkness falls with that messenger for company, not even for the finest rifle in all the colonies. These forests are crawling with scattered Iroquois war parties, and your half-breed Mohawk knows exactly where to locate them—far too well for me to trust him as a traveling companion."

"Do you really think so?" Heyward asked, leaning forward in his saddle and lowering his voice to almost a whisper. "I'll admit I've had my own doubts, though I've tried to hide them and pretended to have confidence I didn't always feel, for the sake of my companions. It was precisely because I suspected him that I refused to follow any longer, forcing him to follow me instead, as you can see."

"I could tell he was a fraud the moment I saw him!" the scout replied, putting a finger to his nose as a warning gesture.

"The thief is leaning against the base of the young sugar maple tree that you can see beyond those bushes. His right leg is aligned with the tree's bark, and," he said, patting his rifle, "I can hit him from right here, somewhere between his ankle and knee, with just one shot. That would put an end to his wandering through the forest for at least a month. If I were to go back toward him, the crafty scoundrel would become suspicious and start weaving through the trees like a startled deer."

"This won't work. He might be innocent, and I don't like doing this. However, if I were certain he had betrayed us—"

"It's safe to assume an Iroquois will be treacherous," said the scout, instinctively bringing his rifle forward.

"Wait!" Heyward interrupted, "that won't work—we need to come up with a different plan—and yet, I have good reason to believe the scoundrel has deceived me."

The hunter, who had already given up his plan to wound the runner, thought for a moment, then made a gesture that immediately brought his two Native American companions to his side. They spoke together seriously in the Delaware language, though quietly; and from the white man's gestures, which were often directed toward the top of the young tree, it was clear he was pointing out where their hidden enemy was located. His companions quickly understood what he wanted, and setting aside their guns, they separated, taking opposite sides of the trail, and concealed themselves in the dense brush with such careful movements that their footsteps made no sound.

"Now, go back," said the hunter, speaking once more to Heyward, "and keep the devil busy talking; these Mohicans here will capture him without disturbing his war paint."

"No," said Heyward, proudly, "I will seize him myself."

"Listen! What could you possibly accomplish on horseback against an Indian hiding in the bushes!"

"I will get down."

"Do you really think that when he noticed one of your feet slipping from the stirrup, he would wait for the other one to come free? Anyone who enters the wilderness to negotiate with the natives must adopt their customs if they want to succeed in their endeavors. Go ahead then; speak frankly to that villain, and act as though you believe he's the most loyal friend you have on earth."

Heyward got ready to follow through, even though he felt strong revulsion at what he was being forced to do. With each passing moment, he became more aware of the dangerous situation he had allowed his precious responsibility to fall into because of his own overconfidence. The sun had already set, and the forest, suddenly stripped of its light, was taking on a dark appearance that sharply reminded him that the time when savages typically carried out their most brutal and merciless acts of revenge or attack was quickly approaching. Driven by fear, he left the scout, who immediately began talking loudly with the stranger who had so boldly joined their group of travelers that morning. As he passed his more delicate companions, Heyward spoke a few encouraging words and was relieved to discover that, although they were tired from the day's journey, they seemed to have no idea that their current predicament was anything more than an accident. Making them think he was simply discussing their future path, he urged his horse forward and pulled back on the reins when the animal had brought him to within a few yards of where the grim runner still stood, leaning against the tree.[1]

[1] The setting of this story was at the 42nd degree of latitude, where twilight never lasts very long.

"You can see, Magua," he said, trying to appear relaxed and confident, "that night is falling around us, and yet we're no closer to William Henry than we were when we left Webb's camp at sunrise."

"You've lost your way, and I haven't had any better luck. But fortunately, we've come across a hunter—the one you hear speaking with the singer—who knows the deer trails and hidden paths through these woods, and he's promised to guide us to a place where we can rest safely until morning."

The Indian fixed his burning eyes on Heyward as he asked in his broken English, "Is he alone?"

"Alone!" Heyward replied hesitantly, since he wasn't used to lying and felt uncomfortable doing it. "Oh! surely not alone, Magua, because you know we're here with him."

"Then Le Renard Subtil will leave," the runner replied, calmly picking up his small pouch from where it had been resting at his feet; "and the white men will see only others of their own race."

"Go! Who are you calling Le Renard?"

"That's the name his Canadian fathers have given to Magua," the runner replied, with an expression that showed his pride in the distinction. "Night is the same as day to Le Subtil, when Munro waits for him."

"And what explanation will Le Renard offer the commander of William Henry about his daughters? Will he have the courage to tell the fiery Scotsman that his children have been abandoned without a guide, even though Magua had promised to serve as one?"

"Even though the gray-haired man has a powerful voice and a long reach, Le Renard will not listen to him or be affected by him in the forest."

"But what will the Mohawks say? They will make him wear women's clothing and tell him to stay in the lodge with the women, because he can no longer be trusted with men's responsibilities."

"Le Subtil knows the path to the great lakes, and he can find the bones of his fathers," was the response of the unshaken runner.

"That's enough, Magua," Heyward said. "Aren't we friends? Why should we exchange harsh words? Munro has promised to reward you for your services once they're completed, and I'll owe you a debt as well. Rest your tired body, then, and take out your food to eat. We have some time available; let's not waste it arguing like quarreling women. Once the ladies have rested, we'll continue on."

"The pale faces make themselves dogs to their women," the Indian muttered in his native language, "and when they want to eat, their warriors must put down the tomahawk to feed their laziness."

"What do you say, Renard?"

"Le Subtil says it is good."

The Indian then fixed his gaze intently on Heyward's open face, but when their eyes met, he quickly looked away and deliberately sat down on the ground, pulling out the remains of an earlier meal and beginning to eat, though not before slowly and carefully scanning his surroundings.

"That's good," Heyward went on; "and Le Renard will have the strength and eyesight to find the trail in the morning"; he stopped, because sounds like the breaking of a dry branch and the whisper of leaves came from the nearby bushes, but quickly collecting his thoughts, he continued, "we need to get moving before sunrise, or Montcalm might block our route and prevent us from reaching the fort."

Magua's hand fell from his mouth to his side, and while his eyes remained fixed on the ground, he turned his head to one side, his nostrils flared, and his ears appeared to stand even more upright than normal, making him look like a statue carved to show complete focus and alertness.

Heyward, who observed his actions with a watchful gaze, casually freed one of his feet from the stirrup while moving his hand toward the bear-skin cover of his holsters.

Every attempt to figure out what the runner was looking at was completely thwarted by the restless movements of his eyes, which seemed unable to focus on any single object for even a moment, yet at the same time could barely be said to move at all. While he wondered what to do next, Le Subtil carefully stood up, moving so slowly and cautiously that the change made absolutely no sound. Heyward realized he now had to take action. Swinging his leg over the saddle, he got off his horse, determined to move forward and capture his deceitful companion, leaving the outcome to his own courage. However, to avoid causing unnecessary panic, he maintained an appearance of calm and friendliness.

"Le Renard Subtil does not eat," he said, using the name he had discovered was most appealing to the Indian's pride. "His corn isn't properly roasted, and it looks dry. Let me take a look; maybe I can find something among my own supplies that will improve his appetite."

Magua extended the wallet toward the other man's offer. He even allowed their hands to touch without showing the slightest emotion or changing his fixed posture of alertness. However, when he felt Heyward's fingers moving softly along his bare arm, he knocked away the young man's limb and let out a sharp cry as he ducked beneath it and leaped in a single bound into the thicket on the opposite side. The next moment, Chingachgook's figure emerged from the bushes, appearing ghostlike with his war paint, and glided swiftly across the path in pursuit. This was followed by Uncas's shout, as the woods suddenly lit up with a bright flash accompanied by the sharp crack of the hunter's rifle.

---

# Chapter V.

"In such a night
Did Thisbe fearfully step over the dew;
And saw the lion's shadow before seeing the lion itself."—
The Merchant of Venice

The sudden departure of his guide and the wild shouts of those giving chase left Heyward frozen in place for several moments, stunned into inaction. Then, remembering how crucial it was to capture the runaway, he pushed through the nearby bushes and rushed forward eagerly to help with the pursuit. However, before he had traveled even a hundred yards, he encountered the three woodsmen already coming back from their failed chase.

"Why are you giving up so quickly!" he shouted; "that villain must be hiding behind one of these trees, and we might still be able to catch him. We won't be safe as long as he's running free."

"Would you set a cloud to chase the wind?" replied the disappointed scout. "I heard that devil moving through the dry leaves like a black snake, and catching a glimpse of him just over there beyond that big pine tree, I fired what should have been a perfect shot. But it didn't work! Still, for a well-aimed shot, if anyone other than myself had pulled the trigger, I would call it excellent marksmanship. I have considerable experience in these matters and should know what I'm talking about. Look at this sumac—its leaves are red, even though everyone knows the fruit comes from yellow blossoms in July!"

"It's the blood of Le Subtil! He's wounded and might still fall!"

"No, no," the scout replied, firmly rejecting this view, "I may have scraped some bark off a branch, but the animal jumped even farther because of it. When a rifle bullet grazes a running animal, it affects them much like spurs affect a horse—it speeds up their movement and energizes their body rather than slowing them down. However, when the bullet tears through and creates a jagged wound, after a jump or two, the leaping typically comes to a complete stop, whether it's an Indian or a deer!"

"We have four healthy men for every one who's injured!"

"Is life troubling you?" the scout interrupted. "That red devil over there would lure you within striking distance of his companions' tomahawks before you even got warmed up in the pursuit. It was a thoughtless action for a man who has so often slept while war cries echoed through the air, to fire his weapon within hearing range of an ambush! But then it was a natural temptation! It was very natural! Come, friends, let us change our position, and do it in such a way that will put a Mingo's cunning on the wrong trail, or our scalps will be drying in the wind in front of Montcalm's tent by this time tomorrow."

This terrifying statement, which the scout delivered with the calm confidence of someone who completely understood the danger while showing no fear of confronting it, reminded Heyward of how crucial the mission he had been entrusted with really was. He looked around, trying unsuccessfully to see through the darkness that was growing thicker under the leafy canopy of the forest, and felt as though, isolated from any human help, his defenseless companions would soon be completely at the mercy of those savage enemies who, like wild predators, were simply waiting for the approaching darkness to make their attacks more deadly and accurate. His heightened imagination, fooled by the misleading light, transformed every swaying bush or piece of fallen tree into human shapes, and countless times he thought he could make out the horrible faces of his hidden enemies, watching from their concealed positions, constantly monitoring every move his group made. When he looked up, he saw that the thin, wispy clouds that evening had painted across the blue sky were already losing their faintest hints of pink, while the embedded stream that flowed past where he stood could only be traced by the dark outline of its tree-lined banks.

"What should I do!" he said, feeling completely helpless and uncertain in such an urgent crisis; "don't abandon me, for God's sake! stay to protect those I'm escorting, and feel free to name whatever reward you want!"

His companions, who spoke privately in their tribal language, paid no attention to this sudden and urgent request. Although they kept their conversation quiet and careful, barely louder than a whisper, Heyward, who was now getting closer, could easily tell the difference between the passionate voice of the younger warrior and the more measured words of the older men. It was clear that they were arguing about whether to take some action that would significantly affect the travelers' safety. Driven by his intense interest in what they were discussing, and frustrated by a delay that seemed to bring even more danger, Heyward moved even closer to the shadowy group, planning to make his offer of payment more specific, when the white man gestured with his hand, as if he was giving in on the disputed matter, turned away, and said in a kind of soliloquy, speaking in English:

"Uncas is right! It wouldn't be the action of real men to abandon such innocent people to whatever happens to them, even if it means destroying our safe hiding place forever. If you want to rescue these delicate souls from the clutches of the most evil predators, gentlemen, you don't have any time to waste or courage to squander!"

"How could anyone question such a desire! Haven't I already offered—"

"Pray to the One who can grant us the wisdom to outwit the clever devils that inhabit these forests," the scout said calmly, cutting him off, "but keep your money to yourself—you might not live to pay it, and I might not survive to collect it. These Mohicans and I will do everything humanly possible to protect such delicate flowers, who, despite their beauty, were never meant for the harsh wilderness, and we'll do it without expecting any reward except what God always provides to those who act with honor. But first, you must promise me two things, both for yourself and your companions, or we'll end up hurting ourselves instead of helping you!"

"Name them."

"One condition is that you must remain as silent as these sleeping woods, no matter what happens, and the other is that you must keep the location where we will take you a secret from all people forever."

"I will do everything in my power to make sure both of these requirements are met."

"Then follow me, because we're wasting moments that are as precious as the heart's blood to a wounded deer!"

Heyward could make out the scout's impatient gestures through the deepening shadows of evening, and he quickly followed in his footsteps toward the spot where he had left the rest of their group. When they reunited with the waiting and worried women, he briefly informed them about their new guide's situation and explained why they needed to suppress all fears and focus on immediate, serious action. Though his alarming news filled the listeners with hidden terror, his sincere and compelling manner, perhaps helped by the very real nature of the danger, managed to strengthen their resolve to face whatever unexpected and extraordinary ordeal lay ahead. Without speaking and without wasting a single moment, they allowed him to help them down from their horses, and they quickly made their way to the water's edge, where the scout had gathered the rest of their party, communicating more through meaningful gestures than through spoken words.

"What should I do with these foolish creatures!" grumbled the white man, who seemed to have complete responsibility for deciding their next actions. "It would be a waste of time to kill them and throw their bodies into the river, but leaving them here would signal to the Mingoes that they don't need to look far to find their owners!"

"Then give them their bridles, and let them roam the woods," Heyward ventured to suggest.

"No; it would be better to trick the devils and make them think they need to match a horse's speed to catch their prey. Yes, yes, that will fool their blazing eyes! Chingach—Listen! what's moving in the bushes?"

"The colt."

"That young horse has to die, at least," the scout muttered under his breath, reaching for the mane of the quick animal, which easily slipped away from his grasp; "Uncas, your arrows!"

"Stop!" shouted the owner of the doomed animal loudly, ignoring the hushed voices of the others around him. "Save Miriam's foal! It's the beautiful child of a loyal mother, and it wouldn't hurt anything on purpose."

"When people fight for the one life God has given them," the scout said harshly, "even their own people seem no different from wild animals. If you speak again, I'll abandon you to the mercy of the Maquas! Pull your arrow back to full draw, Uncas; we don't have time for a second shot."

The low, threatening murmur of his voice could still be heard when the wounded foal first reared up on its hind legs, then plunged forward onto its knees. Chingachgook met the animal, his knife slicing across its throat faster than thought itself, and then, following through with the movements of the struggling creature, he pushed it into the river, where it drifted downstream, gasping audibly for breath as its life ebbed away. This act of apparent cruelty, though born of real necessity, struck the travelers' spirits like a terrible warning of the danger they faced, made even more intense by the calm yet unwavering determination of those who carried out the deed. The sisters trembled and pressed closer together, while Heyward instinctively placed his hand on one of the pistols he had just pulled from their holsters, positioning himself between those under his protection and the thick shadows that seemed to draw an impenetrable curtain across the heart of the forest.

The Indians, however, didn't hesitate for even a moment, but grabbed the bridles and led the frightened and unwilling horses into the riverbed.

A short distance from the shore, they turned and were quickly hidden by the jutting bank, moving beneath its edge in a direction opposite to the water's flow. Meanwhile, the scout pulled a bark canoe from where it was hidden under some low bushes, whose branches swayed with the swirling current, and he quietly gestured for the women to get in. They did so without hesitation, though they cast many fearful and worried looks back toward the deepening darkness, which now stretched like a dark wall along the edge of the stream.

As soon as Cora and Alice were seated, the scout, without worrying about the water, told Heyward to support one side of the fragile vessel, and positioning himself at the other side, they carried it upstream against the current, followed by the disheartened owner of the dead foal. They continued this way for many yards, in a silence that was only broken by the gentle splashing of the water as its currents swirled around them, or the quiet sound made by their own careful footsteps. Heyward left the steering of the canoe completely to the scout, who moved closer to or farther from the shore to avoid rock fragments or deeper sections of the river, with an ease that demonstrated his familiarity with the path they were taking. From time to time he would pause; and in the middle of a hushed stillness that the distant but growing rumble of the waterfall only made more striking, he would listen with intense concentration to catch any sounds that might come from the sleeping forest. When convinced that everything was quiet, and unable to detect, even with the help of his experienced senses, any sign of their approaching enemies, he would carefully resume his slow and cautious advance. Eventually they reached a spot in the river where Heyward's wandering gaze became fixed on a group of dark objects gathered at a place where the high bank cast a deeper shadow than usual on the black waters. Uncertain about moving forward, he pointed out the location to draw his companion's attention.

"Yes," replied the calm scout, "the Indians have hidden the animals with the wisdom of natives! Water doesn't leave any tracks, and even an owl's sharp eyes would be useless in the darkness of a place like that."

The entire group quickly came back together, and the scout held another discussion with his new companions. During this meeting, those whose lives depended on the trustworthiness and skill of these unfamiliar woodsmen had some time to examine their circumstances more carefully.

The river flowed between towering, jagged rocks, with one massive stone hanging over the place where the canoe had come to rest. These rocky walls were crowned with tall trees that seemed to lean precariously over the edge of the cliff, making the stream look as though it was flowing through a deep, narrow valley. Everything beneath the twisted branches and rough treetops, which appeared faintly outlined against the star-filled sky, was hidden in dark shadows. Behind them, the curved riverbanks quickly blocked their view with the same dark, tree-covered silhouette; but ahead, seemingly not far away, the water appeared to rise up toward the sky, then cascade down into hidden caves from which came the deep, rumbling sounds that had filled the evening air. It truly seemed like a place meant for solitude, and the sisters felt a comforting sense of safety as they looked upon its wild yet somewhat frightening beauty. A sudden stirring among their guides, however, quickly pulled them away from admiring the untamed splendor that the night had helped give to this place, bringing back the harsh reality of their dangerous situation.

The horses had been tied to scattered bushes growing in the cracks of the rocks, where they stood in the water and were left for the night. The scout told Heyward and his dejected companions to sit in the front of the canoe, while he took his position at the back, standing as upright and steady as if he were in a boat made of much stronger material. The Indians carefully made their way back toward where they had come from, while the scout pressed his pole against a rock and with a forceful push sent his fragile vessel straight into the rushing water. For several minutes, the battle between the lightweight craft they rode in and the fast-moving current was intense and uncertain. Told not to move even a finger, and almost too scared to breathe for fear they might expose their delicate boat to the river's violence, the passengers stared at the flashing waters with anxious dread. Twenty times they believed the spinning whirlpools were carrying them toward certain death, when their pilot's skilled hand would turn the front of the canoe to face the rapids head-on. A long, powerful, and what seemed to the women a hopeless struggle finally ended. Just as Alice covered her eyes in terror, thinking they were about to be pulled into the whirlpool at the base of the waterfall, the canoe came to rest motionless beside a flat rock that sat level with the water's surface.

"Where are we, and what should we do next!" Heyward demanded, noticing that the scout had stopped his efforts.

"You're at the base of Glenn's," the other replied, speaking loudly without worrying about being overheard above the thundering waterfall. "Now we need to make a careful landing, or the canoe will tip over and you'll go back down the difficult route we just traveled much faster than you came up. It's a tough current to fight against when the river is running high, and five people is too many to keep dry in a rush, with just a small birch bark canoe and some gum to seal it. Go ahead, all of you get on the rock, and I'll bring the Mohicans up with the deer meat. A man would be better off sleeping without his scalp than starving when there's plenty of food around."

The passengers willingly followed these instructions. As soon as the last person stepped onto the rock, the canoe spun away from its position, and for a brief moment, they could see the scout's tall figure moving across the water before he vanished into the complete darkness that covered the riverbed. Abandoned by their guide, the travelers stood for several minutes in complete confusion, too frightened to even move across the jagged rocks, worried that one wrong step might send them plunging into one of the numerous deep, thundering caverns where the water appeared to cascade all around them. Their anxiety was quickly eased, however, because with the natives' expertise, the canoe darted back into the swirling current and returned to float beside the low rock before they even believed the scout had enough time to reunite with his companions.

"We're now fortified, garrisoned, and well-supplied," Heyward called out cheerfully, "and we can stand up to Montcalm and his allies without fear. Tell me, my watchful guard, can you spot any of those Iroquois you mentioned on the mainland?"

"I call them Iroquois, because to me every native who speaks a foreign language is considered an enemy, even though he may claim to serve the king! If Webb wants loyalty and honesty from an Indian, let him bring out the Delaware tribes, and send these greedy and deceitful Mohawks and Oneidas, with their six nations of scoundrels, where they naturally belong, among the French!"

"We would be trading a warrior for a worthless ally! I've heard that the Delawares have put down their weapons and are willing to accept being called women!"

"Yes, shame on the Dutch and Iroquois, who tricked them through their cunning schemes into such an agreement! But I have known them for twenty years, and I call anyone a liar who says cowardly blood flows in the veins of a Delaware. You have forced their tribes away from the coast, and now you want to believe what their enemies tell you, so you can sleep peacefully at night with a clear conscience. No, no; to me, every Indian who speaks a foreign language is an Iroquois, whether his tribe's stronghold is in Canada or in New York."[1]

[1] The main villages of the Native Americans are still referred to as "castles" by the white residents of New York. "Oneida castle" is nothing more than a dispersed hamlet, but this terminology remains commonly used.

Heyward realized that the scout's unwavering loyalty to his friends the Delawares, or Mohicans, since they were branches of the same large tribe, would likely drag out a pointless argument, so he changed the topic.

"Whether there's a treaty or not, I know perfectly well that your two companions are brave and careful warriors! Have they heard or seen anything of our enemies?"

"A Native American can be sensed before he's spotted," the scout replied, climbing up the rock and casually tossing down the deer. "I rely on other signs besides what the eye can see when I'm tracking the Mingoes on their trail."

"Do your ears tell you that they have tracked our retreat?"

"I would hate to think they were here, although this is a place where brave fighters could hold their ground in a fierce battle. I won't deny, however, that the horses shrank back when I walked past them, as if they could smell wolves nearby; and a wolf is an animal that tends to lurk around an Indian ambush, hoping for the scraps from the deer that the warriors have killed."

"You're forgetting about the deer right at your feet! Or maybe their visit has something to do with the dead young horse? Wait! What's that sound?"

"Poor Miriam!" whispered the stranger; "your young one was destined from the beginning to fall victim to hungry wild animals!" Then, suddenly raising his voice above the endless roar of the rushing waters, he sang out loud:

"He struck down the firstborn of Egypt,
both people and animals alike:
O Egypt! He sent wonders among you,
against Pharaoh and all his servants!"

"The death of the colt weighs heavily on its owner's heart," the scout said, "but it's encouraging to see someone who cares about his animals. He has the right spiritual understanding, believing that what's meant to happen will happen; and with that kind of comfort, it won't be long before he accepts the logic of killing a four-legged animal to save human lives. It may be as you say," he continued, returning to the main point of Heyward's previous comment; "and all the more reason why we should cut our meat and let the body float downstream, or we'll have the wolf pack howling along the cliffs, resenting every bite we take. Besides, though the Delaware language is like a closed book to the Iroquois, those crafty scoundrels are quick enough to understand what a wolf's howl means."

The scout gathered the tools he needed while he spoke; when he finished talking, he quietly moved past the group of travelers, joined by the Mohicans, who appeared to understand his plans with natural intuition, and then all three of them disappeared one after another, seeming to fade away against the dark surface of a steep rock wall that stood several yards high, just a few feet from the water's edge.

---

# Chapter VI.

"Those melodies that once flowed sweetly in Zion;
He chooses a portion with thoughtful care;
And 'Let us worship God', he says, with solemn
reverence."—Burns

Heyward and the women watched this strange behavior with hidden anxiety; although the white man's conduct had been beyond criticism so far, his crude gear, harsh manner, and intense prejudices, combined with the nature of his quiet companions, all gave reasons for suspicion in minds that had been so recently disturbed by Native American betrayal.

The stranger paid no attention to what was happening around him. He sat down on a rocky ledge, showing no awareness of his surroundings except through the turmoil of his emotions, which revealed itself in repeated deep sighs. Muffled voices could then be heard, as if people were calling to one another from deep underground, when a sudden burst of light illuminated those outside and revealed the highly valued secret of this location.

At the far end of a narrow, deep cave in the rock, whose length seemed much longer due to the perspective and the type of light illuminating it, sat the scout, holding a burning piece of pine. The bright glow of the fire shone directly on his sturdy, weathered face and wilderness clothing, giving a romantically wild appearance to someone who, if seen in ordinary daylight, would have shown the distinctive qualities of a man notable for his unusual dress, the steel-like rigidity of his build, and the remarkable combination of sharp, alert intelligence and refined simplicity that alternately took control of his strong features. A short distance ahead stood Uncas, his entire figure prominently displayed. The travelers nervously observed the upright, flexible form of the young Mohican, elegant and natural in his postures and movements. Although his body was more covered than usual by a green fringed hunting shirt like the white man's, there was no hiding his dark, flashing, fearless eyes, both frightening and peaceful; the bold outline of his high, proud features, pure in their natural red color; or the dignified height of his sloping forehead, along with all the finest qualities of a noble head, exposed except for the generous scalp lock. This was the first chance Duncan and his companions had to examine the distinct facial features of either of their Indian guides, and each member of the group felt freed from uncertainty, as the proud and resolute, though untamed expression on the young warrior's face caught their attention. They sensed this might be someone partially lost in ignorance, but it could not be one who would willingly use his abundant natural talents for deliberate betrayal. The innocent Alice stared at his free manner and proud bearing, as she might have gazed upon some valuable remnant of Greek sculpture brought to life through divine intervention; while Heyward, though used to seeing the physical perfection common among unspoiled natives, openly showed his admiration for such a flawless example of man's finest proportions.

"I could sleep peacefully," Alice whispered in response, "with such a brave and noble-looking young man standing guard over me. Certainly, Duncan, those brutal killings and horrific scenes of torture that we read and hear so much about could never happen in the presence of someone like him!"

"This is certainly a remarkable and outstanding example of those natural traits that these distinctive people are known to possess," he replied. "I share your opinion, Alice, that such a face and gaze were designed more to command respect than to mislead; however, we shouldn't fool ourselves by expecting any display of what we consider virtue beyond what fits the savage's way of life. Just as shining examples of noble character are far too rare among Christians, they are equally uncommon and isolated among the Indians; yet, to the credit of our shared humanity, both groups are capable of producing such individuals. Let us therefore hope that this Mohican will not let us down, but will prove to be what his appearance suggests—a courageous and loyal friend."

"Now Major Heyward speaks as Major Heyward should," said Cora; "who that looks at this natural man remembers the color of his skin?"

A brief and seemingly uncomfortable silence followed this comment, which was broken when the scout called out loudly for them to come in.

"This fire is starting to burn too brightly," he continued as they followed his instructions, "and it might guide the Mingoes straight to us and lead to our destruction. Uncas, lower the blanket and show those scoundrels its dark side. This isn't the kind of meal that a major of the Royal Americans should expect, but I've seen tough detachments from the corps happy to eat their venison raw, and without any seasoning too. Here, you can see, we have plenty of salt and can cook this quickly over the fire. There are fresh sassafras branches for the ladies to sit on, which might not be as fancy as their mahogany chairs, but they give off a sweeter scent than the hide of any pig could, whether it's from Guinea or anywhere else. Come now, friend, don't feel sad about the young horse; it was an innocent creature that hadn't experienced much suffering. Its death will spare the animal many painful backs and tired feet!"[1]

> [1] In everyday speech, Americans call the seasonings of a meal "a relish," using the thing itself to describe its effect. These regional terms are often placed in the mouths of speakers based on their different social positions in life. Most of these expressions are used locally, while others are quite specific to the particular group of people that the character represents. In this case, the scout uses the word with direct reference to the "salt" that his own group was lucky enough to have with them.

Uncas followed the other man's instructions, and when Hawkeye stopped speaking, the thundering of the waterfall sounded like distant thunder rolling across the sky.

"Are we completely safe in this cave?" Heyward asked. "Is there no risk of being caught off guard? One armed man at the entrance could have us completely at his mercy."

A ghostly figure emerged from the darkness behind the scout, grabbing a burning torch and holding it toward the far end of their hiding place. Alice let out a weak cry, and even Cora stood up as this frightening figure stepped into the light; but a single word from Heyward reassured them that it was only their companion,

Chingachgook, who lifted another blanket and revealed that the cave had two exits. Then, carrying the torch, he crossed a deep, narrow gap in the rocks that ran perpendicular to the passage they were in, but which, unlike theirs, was open to the sky, and entered another cave that matched the description of the first one in every important detail.

"Experienced old foxes like Chingachgook and myself don't often get trapped in a burrow with only one exit," Hawkeye said with a laugh. "You can easily see how cleverly this place is designed—the rock is black limestone, which everyone knows is soft. It makes a comfortable enough pillow when brush and pine wood are hard to find. Well, the waterfall was once located just a few yards below where we're standing, and I'd venture to say it was, in its day, as steady and beautiful a sheet of water as any you'd find along the Hudson. But old age does terrible things to beauty, as these lovely young ladies have yet to learn! This place has changed dramatically! These rocks are riddled with cracks, and in some spots they're softer than in others. The water has carved out deep hollows for itself, causing it to retreat—yes, several hundred feet back—breaking away here and wearing down there, until the falls have lost both their shape and their substance."

"Where exactly are we positioned within their territory?" Heyward asked.

"Well, we're close to the place where God first put them, but it appears they were too defiant to remain there. The rock turned out to be softer on both sides of us, so they left the middle of the river exposed and dry, after first carving out these two small caves for us to take shelter in."

"We are then on an island!"

"Yes! There are waterfalls on both sides of us, and the river flows above and below. If you had daylight, it would be worth the effort to climb up to the top of this rock and observe how unpredictable the water behaves. It follows no pattern whatsoever;

sometimes it leaps, sometimes it tumbles; there it skips; here it shoots; in one place it's white as snow, and in another it's green as grass; around here, it plunges into deep hollows that rumble and pound the earth; and over there, it ripples and sings like a brook, creating whirlpools and channels in the ancient stone, as if it were no harder than packed clay. The entire course of the river seems chaotic. First it flows smoothly, as if intending to descend the slope as nature intended; then it turns at angles and faces the shores; there are also places where it appears to flow backward, as if reluctant to leave the wilderness and mix with the salt water. Yes, lady, the fine lace-like fabric you wear at your throat is rough, like a fishing net, compared to the tiny spots I can show you, where the river creates all kinds of patterns, as if having broken free from order, it wants to try its hand at everything. And yet what does it all mean! After the water has been allowed to have its way for a while, like a stubborn person, it is brought together by the hand that created it, and just a few yards downstream you can see it all flowing steadily toward the sea, just as it was destined from the very beginning of the earth!"

While his listeners found comfort in this simple description from Glenn, which assured them their hiding place was secure, they were much more inclined to disagree with Hawkeye about the area's natural beauty. However, they weren't in a position to let their minds focus on the appeal of the landscape around them; and since the scout hadn't stopped his cooking duties while talking, except to gesture with a bent fork toward some particularly troublesome spot in the unruly stream, they now allowed their attention to turn to the practical, though less refined matter of their evening meal.[2]

> [2] Glenn's Falls are located on the Hudson River, approximately forty to fifty miles upstream from the head of tide, which is the point where the river becomes navigable for sloops. The scout's description of this

picturesque and remarkable small waterfall is accurate enough, although the use of the water for civilized purposes has significantly damaged its natural beauty. The rocky island and the two caves are familiar to every traveler, since the island now supports the pier of a bridge that spans the river directly above the falls. To understand Hawkeye's perspective, we should remember that people always value most highly what they experience least often. Therefore, in a new country, the forests and other natural features that would be preserved at great expense in an established country are simply removed in the name of what is called "improvement."

The meal, which was greatly enhanced by several delicacies that Heyward had wisely brought along when they left their horses, was extremely refreshing to the exhausted group. Uncas served as an attendant to the women, carrying out all the small tasks within his ability with a combination of dignity and eager grace that entertained Heyward, who understood well that this was a complete departure from Indian customs, which prohibited their warriors from engaging in any servant-like work, especially for their women. Since the rules of hospitality were considered sacred among them, however, this small deviation from masculine dignity provoked no spoken criticism. If someone there had been sufficiently free to observe closely, he might have imagined that the young chief's services were not entirely impartial. While he offered Alice the gourd of sweet water and the venison on a wooden plate, skillfully carved from the pepperidge tree knot, with adequate courtesy, when performing the same duties for her sister, his dark eyes lingered on her expressive, captivating face. Once or twice he was forced to speak to gain the attention of those he was serving. On such occasions he used English, broken and imperfect, but clear enough, which he made so gentle and melodious with his deep, throaty voice that it never failed to make both ladies look up in wonder and amazement. During these courteous exchanges, a few sentences were spoken that helped establish the appearance of friendly relations between the groups.

During this time, Chingachgook's serious demeanor remained unchanged. He had positioned himself closer to the circle of light, allowing his guests' frequent, restless glances to better distinguish his natural facial features from the frightening effects of his war paint. They noticed a strong similarity between father and son, with the differences one would expect from age and life's hardships. The fierce expression on his face now appeared dormant, replaced by the calm, emotionless composure that characterizes an Indian warrior when his abilities aren't needed for the more significant aspects of his life. However, it was easy to observe from the occasional flashes that crossed his dark face that it would only take stirring his emotions to fully activate the terrifying appearance he had created to frighten his enemies. In contrast, the scout's quick, wandering eyes rarely stayed still. He ate and drank with an enthusiasm that no sense of danger could disturb, yet his alertness never seemed to leave him. Twenty times he paused with the gourd or venison halfway to his mouth, turning his head to the side as if listening to some distant and suspicious sounds—a gesture that always brought his guests back from contemplating the unusual aspects of their circumstances to remembering the troubling reasons that had forced them to seek this refuge. Since these frequent interruptions were never accompanied by any comment, the brief anxiety they caused quickly faded away and was temporarily forgotten.

"Come on, friend," said Hawkeye, pulling out a keg from under a pile of leaves as the meal was ending, speaking to the stranger sitting beside him who was thoroughly enjoying his cooking, "try some spruce beer; it'll wash away any thoughts of the young horse, and give you new energy. I'm drinking to our improved friendship, hoping that a bit of horse meat won't cause any bad feelings between us. What's your name?"

"Gamut—David Gamut," replied the singing master, getting ready to drown his sorrows in a strong drink of the woodsman's richly flavored and well-spiked mixture.

"That's a very good name, and I'd say it was passed down from honest ancestors. I'm someone who appreciates names, though Christian naming customs fall far short of savage traditions in this regard. The biggest coward I ever knew was called Lyon; and his wife, Patience, would yell at you until you couldn't hear anything in less time than it would take a hunted deer to run a few yards. With an Indian it's a matter of principle; what he calls himself, he generally is—not that Chingachgook, which means Big Serpent, is actually a snake, big or small; but that he understands the twists and turns of human nature, and is quiet, and strikes his enemies when they least expect him. What might your profession be?"

"I am an unworthy teacher in the art of psalm singing."

"Anan!"

"I teach singing to the young men of the Connecticut militia."

"You could probably find better work to do. The young hunters are already making too much noise, laughing and singing as they move through the woods, when they should be staying as quiet as a fox hiding in its den. Can you shoot with a smoothbore musket, or do you know how to handle a rifle?"

"Thank God, I've never had any reason to get involved with deadly weapons!"

"Maybe you understand how to use a compass and can map out the rivers and mountains of the wilderness on paper, so that those who come after you can find these places by their proper names?"

"I don't engage in that kind of work."

"You have a pair of legs that could make a long journey feel short! I imagine you sometimes travel with news for the general."

"Never; I follow no other calling than my own noble vocation, which is teaching sacred music!"

"It's a strange profession!" muttered Hawkeye, with an inward laugh, "to go through life, like a catbird, mimicking all the highs and lows that may happen to come out of other men's voices. Well, friend, I suppose it is your talent, and shouldn't be denied any more than if it was shooting, or some other better skill. Let us hear what you can do in that way; it will be a friendly manner of saying good-night, for it is time that these ladies should be gathering strength for a hard and long journey, in the early morning, before the Maquas are awake."

"I gladly agree," said David, adjusting his wire-rimmed glasses and pulling out his cherished small book, which he immediately handed to Alice. "What could be more appropriate and comforting than to offer evening prayers after a day of such extreme danger!"

Alice smiled, but when she looked at Heyward, she blushed and hesitated.

"Treat yourself well," he whispered; "shouldn't the advice of the worthy person who shares the name of the Psalmist carry some influence at a time like this?"

Encouraged by his opinion, Alice did what her religious feelings and her strong love for beautiful music had already urged her to do. The book was open to a hymn that suited their situation well, and in it the poet, no longer driven by his ambition to surpass the inspired King of Israel, had shown some refined and admirable abilities. Cora showed she was ready to support her sister, and the sacred song began, after the necessary preparations with the pitch pipe, and the melody had been properly arranged by the systematic David.

The atmosphere was reverent and unhurried. Sometimes the music swelled to embrace the full range of the women's rich voices as they leaned over their small prayer book with sacred fervor, and then it would drop so quietly that the rushing water seemed to weave through their melody like a deep, echoing harmony. David's natural musical instinct and keen ear shaped and adjusted the sounds to fit the enclosed cave, filling every crack and crevice with the stirring notes of their supple voices. The Indians fixed their gaze on the stone walls and listened with such intense focus that they appeared to have turned to stone themselves. But the scout, who had rested his chin in his hand with an expression of cool detachment, slowly allowed his stern features to soften, until, as one verse followed another, he felt his hardened nature give way, while his memory drifted back to his childhood, when he had grown used to hearing similar songs of worship in the colonial settlements. His wandering eyes began to grow moist, and before the hymn concluded, burning tears spilled from wells that had long appeared dried up, streaming down cheeks that had more often felt heaven's storms than any signs of vulnerability. The singers were lingering on one of those soft, fading notes that the ear consumes with such eager delight, as though aware it is about to lose them, when a scream that seemed neither human nor of this world rose from the air outside, piercing not only the depths of the cave but reaching the very core of everyone who heard it. What followed was a silence apparently as profound as if the waters had been halted in their violent flow by such a terrible and strange disruption.

"What is it?" whispered Alice, after several moments of awful suspense.

"What is it?" Hewyard repeated out loud.

Neither Hawkeye nor the Indians responded. They listened carefully, as though waiting for the sound to come again, their expressions showing clear surprise. Eventually they spoke to each other seriously in the Delaware language, and then Uncas, moving through the inner and most hidden opening, carefully left the cave. After he had departed, the scout was the first to speak in English.

"What it is, or what it isn't, no one here can say, even though two of us have roamed these woods for more than thirty years. I thought there wasn't a sound that any Indian or animal could make that I hadn't heard before; but this has shown me that I was just a foolish and arrogant man."

"Wasn't that the war cry warriors use to frighten their enemies?" asked Cora, who stood wrapping her veil around herself with a composure that her distressed sister couldn't match.

"No, no; this was terrible and shocking, with an almost inhuman quality to it; but once you hear a war cry, you'll never confuse it with anything else. Well, Uncas!" he said, speaking in Delaware to the young chief as he came back in, "what do you see? Are our lights visible through the blankets?"

The response was brief and seemed final, delivered in the same language.

"There's nothing to see outside," Hawkeye continued, shaking his head with dissatisfaction; "and our hiding place remains shrouded in darkness. Go into the other cave, those of you who need rest, and try to sleep; we must be moving long before sunrise and make the best use of our time to reach Edward while the Mingoes are still taking their morning rest."

Cora demonstrated how to comply, showing a steadiness that taught the more fearful Alice that they needed to obey. Before leaving the area, though, she quietly asked Duncan to come with them. Uncas lifted the blanket so they could pass through, and when the sisters turned to thank him for this thoughtful gesture, they noticed the scout sitting once more in front of the fading embers, his face buried in his hands in a way that revealed how deeply he was thinking about the mysterious interruption that had cut short their evening prayers.

Heyward brought along a burning piece of wood, which cast a faint glow throughout the narrow space of their new shelter. After positioning it where it would provide the best light, he joined the

73

women, who now realized they were alone with him for the first time since leaving the protective walls of Fort Edward.

"Don't leave us, Duncan," Alice said. "We can't sleep in a place like this, with that terrible cry still echoing in our ears."

"First, let's look into how secure your fortress is," he replied, "and then we can talk about rest."

He walked toward the far end of the cave, approaching an exit that was hidden by blankets like the other openings; after pulling away the heavy covering, he breathed in the fresh, invigorating air flowing from the waterfall. One branch of the river ran through a deep, narrow gorge that its flow had carved into the soft rock directly below where he stood, creating what he believed was an effective barrier against any threat from that direction; the water, just a short distance upstream from their position, cascaded down while reflecting light and rushing along in its most turbulent and chaotic fashion.

"Nature has created an impassable barrier on this side," he went on, gesturing toward the steep drop into the dark water below before he let the blanket fall; "and since you know that good and trustworthy men are standing watch up front, I don't see any reason why we should ignore our honest host's advice. I'm sure Cora will agree with me that you both need sleep."

"Cora might agree with your reasoning, even though she can't act on it," replied the older sister, who had seated herself next to Alice on a sassafras couch. "There would be other reasons keeping us awake, even if we hadn't been startled by that strange sound. Think about it, Heyward—can daughters ignore the worry a father must feel when his children are staying somewhere unknown to him in such a dangerous wilderness, surrounded by so many threats?"

"He is a soldier, and knows how to assess the risks of the forest."

"He is a father, and cannot deny his nature."

"How kind he has always been with all my foolish mistakes, how gentle and understanding of all my desires!" Alice cried. "We have been selfish, sister, in pushing for our visit despite such danger."

"I might have been too hasty in pushing for his agreement when he was feeling so overwhelmed, but I wanted to show him that even if other people abandoned him during his difficult time, his children would remain loyal to him."

"When he learned that you had reached Edward," Heyward said with compassion, "there was an intense battle in his heart between fear and love; however, love, made stronger by such a lengthy separation, soon won out. 'It is the courage of my noble-hearted Cora that guides them, Duncan,' he said, 'and I will not stand in its way. If only the man who protects the honor of our royal master would display even half of her determination!'"

"And didn't he mention me, Heyward?" Alice asked, her voice filled with anxious love; "surely, he didn't completely forget his little Elsie?"

"That would be impossible," the young man replied; "he spoke of you using countless loving terms that I wouldn't dare repeat, but I can wholeheartedly confirm how fitting they were. On one occasion, he actually said—"

Duncan stopped talking; while his eyes were fixed on Alice's, who had turned toward him with the eagerness of a daughter's love to hear his words, the same powerful, terrible cry from before filled the air and left him speechless. A long, breathless silence followed, during which everyone looked at each other in fearful anticipation of hearing the sound again. Finally, the blanket was slowly lifted, and the scout appeared in the opening with an expression whose steadiness clearly began to weaken before a mystery that seemed to threaten some danger, one against which all his skill and experience might prove useless.

# Chapter VII.

"They do not sleep,
On yonder cliffs, a grizzly band,
I see them sit."—Gray

"It would be neglecting a warning that's given for our benefit to stay hidden any longer," said Hawkeye, "when such sounds are heard in the forest. These gentle ones may stay close, but the Mohicans and I will keep watch on the rock, where I assume a major of the Sixtieth would want to join us."

"Is our danger really that urgent?" asked Cora.

"The one who makes these strange sounds and sends them out to warn mankind is the only one who truly understands our danger. I would consider myself wicked, rebelling against His will, if I were to hide underground when such warnings fill the air! Even the weakest soul who spends his days singing is moved by this cry, and as he says, is 'ready to go forth to battle.' If it were only a battle, it would be something we could all understand and easily handle; but I have heard that when such screams echo between heaven and earth, it signals a different kind of warfare!"

"If all the things we have to fear, my friend, are limited to those that come from supernatural causes, then we don't have much reason to be worried," continued the calm Cora. "Are you sure that our enemies haven't come up with some new and clever way to frighten us, so that defeating us will be easier?"

"Lady," the scout replied seriously, "I have been listening to every sound in the woods for thirty years, the way a man listens when his life and death depend on how sharp his hearing is.

There's no cry from a panther, no call from a catbird, and no trick from those devilish Mingoes that can fool me! I have heard the forest groan like people do when they're suffering; many times I have listened to the wind making its music through the branches of stripped trees; and I have heard lightning crackling through the air like the snapping of burning brush as it shot out sparks and jagged flames; but I have never thought I was hearing anything more than the enjoyment of the one who played with the creations of his hands. But neither the Mohicans nor I, who am a white man without mixed blood, can explain the cry we just heard. We therefore believe it is a sign given for our benefit."

"This is incredible!" Heyward exclaimed, grabbing his pistols from where he had placed them when he entered. "Whether it's a sign of peace or a signal of war, we need to investigate. Lead the way, my friend; I'm right behind you."

When they emerged from their hiding place, the entire group immediately felt their spirits lift as they traded the stale air of their concealment for the fresh, revitalizing atmosphere that swirled around the whirlpools and cascades of the waterfall. A strong evening wind swept across the river's surface and seemed to push the thunderous roar of the falls back into the depths of their own cavern, from where it emerged deep and steady, like thunder rolling beyond far-off mountains. The moon had come up, and its light was already dancing here and there on the waters above them, though the edge of the rock where they stood remained cloaked in darkness. Apart from the sounds created by the rushing water and the occasional whisper of air as it drifted past them in irregular gusts, the scene was as quiet as night and isolation could make it. Each person strained their eyes along the far shores, searching for any signs of life that might explain what had caused the disturbance they had heard, but their worried and intense gazes were fooled by the misleading light or fell only upon bare rocks and rigid, motionless trees.

"There's nothing to see here except the darkness and stillness of a beautiful evening," Duncan whispered; "how much we should treasure such a scene, and all this peaceful solitude, at any other time, Cora! Imagine yourselves safe, and what now, perhaps, adds to your fear, could become a source of pleasure—"

"Listen!" interrupted Alice.

The warning wasn't needed. Once again the same sound rose up, as if coming from the riverbed, and after breaking free from the narrow confines of the cliffs, could be heard rolling through the forest in distant and fading echoes.

"Can anyone here identify what made such a cry?" Hawkeye asked, after the final echo faded away in the forest; "if someone can, let them speak up; as for me, I don't think it belongs to this earth!"

"Here's someone who can clear up your confusion," Duncan said. "I recognize that sound perfectly well, since I've heard it many times on the battlefield and in situations that come up often in a soldier's life. It's the terrible scream that a horse makes when it's suffering—usually caused by pain, though sometimes by fear. My horse is either being attacked by wild animals, or it can see danger coming but can't escape it. That sound might have fooled me inside the cave, but out here in the open air, I know it too well to be mistaken."

The scout and his companions listened to this straightforward explanation with the keen attention of men who absorb fresh concepts while simultaneously discarding old beliefs that had become unwelcome burdens. The two Indians voiced their characteristic meaningful exclamation of "hugh!" as understanding first dawned upon them, while the scout, after a brief, thoughtful pause, took it upon himself to respond.

"I can't argue with what you're saying," he said, "because I don't know much about horses, even though I was born in a place where there are plenty of them. The wolves must be lurking right above them on the riverbank, and those frightened animals are asking humans for help in the only way they know how. Uncas"—he switched to speaking in Delaware—"Uncas, get down into the canoe and wave a burning stick at that pack of wolves; otherwise fear might accomplish what the wolves themselves can't manage to do, and we'll be left without any horses come morning, when we'll desperately need them to travel quickly!"

The young Native American had already gone down to the water to follow the order, when a long howl echoed from the riverbank and quickly carried off into the deep forest, as if the wild animals were voluntarily abandoning their prey in sudden fear. Uncas, with natural quick reflexes, stepped back, and the three woodsmen held another one of their quiet, serious discussions.

"We've been like hunters who have lost their sense of direction, with the sun hidden from us for days," said Hawkeye, turning away from his companions. "Now we're starting to understand the signs of our path again, and the routes are clear of obstacles! Sit down in the shade that the moon casts from that beech tree over there—it's thicker than the shade from the pine trees—and let's wait for whatever the Lord decides to send us next. Keep all your talking to whispers; though it would be better, and perhaps wiser in the long run, if each of us spent some time thinking our own thoughts in silence."

The scout's demeanor was genuinely impressive, no longer showing any traces of unmanly fear. It was clear that his brief moment of weakness had disappeared along with the explanation of a mystery that his own experience hadn't been able to solve; and although he now understood the full reality of their current situation, he was ready to face it with the strength of his resilient character. This attitude seemed to be shared by the natives as well, who positioned themselves where they could see both shores completely, while keeping their own bodies effectively hidden from view. Under these circumstances, basic common sense required that Heyward and his companions follow the same careful approach that came from such a knowledgeable source. The young man gathered a pile of sassafras from the cave and placed it in the gap that divided the two caverns, where it was used by the sisters, who were thus shielded by the rocks from any projectiles, while their worry was eased by the knowledge that no threat could come near without advance notice. Heyward positioned himself close by, near enough that he could speak with his companions without having to raise his voice to a risky level; while David, copying the woodsmen's example, arranged himself among the cracks in the rocks in such a way that his awkward limbs were no longer unpleasant to look at.

Hours continued to pass without any further disturbance. The moon climbed to its highest point and cast its gentle light straight down on the beautiful scene of the sisters sleeping peacefully in each other's embrace. Duncan pulled Cora's wide shawl over the sight he loved so much to watch, and then let his own head find a resting place on the rock. David started making sounds that would have horrified his refined sensibilities during more alert moments; in essence, everyone except Hawkeye and the Mohicans lost all awareness, overcome by irresistible sleepiness. However, the alertness of these careful guardians never grew weary nor dozed. Motionless as the rock they each seemed to be part of, they remained positioned with their eyes constantly scanning the dark edge of trees that lined the nearby banks of the narrow waterway. No sound went unnoticed by them; the most careful observer couldn't have detected their breathing. It was clear that this extreme caution came from experience that taught them no cunning from their enemies could fool them. This vigilance continued without any obvious results until the moon had disappeared and a faint light above the treetops at the river's curve just downstream signaled that dawn was approaching.

Then, for the first time, Hawkeye was seen to move. He

crawled along the rock and shook Duncan from his deep sleep.

"Now is the time to travel," he whispered; "wake the peaceful ones, and be ready to get into the canoe when I bring it to the landing place."

"Did you have a peaceful night?" Heyward asked. "As for me, I think sleep overcame my watchfulness."

"Everything remains as quiet as midnight. Stay silent, but move quickly."

By this time Duncan was completely awake, and he quickly lifted the shawl from the sleeping women. The movement caused Cora to raise her hand as if to push him away, while Alice whispered in her soft, gentle voice, "No, no, dear father, we weren't abandoned; Duncan was with us!"

"Yes, sweet innocence," whispered the young man; "Duncan is here, and as long as life continues or danger remains, he will never leave you. Cora! Alice! wake up! The time has come to move!"

A loud scream from the younger sister and the sight of the other standing straight up in front of him, frozen in confused terror, was the unexpected response he got.

As Heyward was still speaking, such an explosion of screams and shouts erupted that it seemed to force the rushing blood in his veins to flow backward toward his heart. For nearly a minute, it felt as though devils from hell had taken control of the air around them, releasing their wild fury through savage sounds. The cries didn't come from any specific direction, though it was clear they filled the entire forest and, as the terrified listeners could easily picture, echoed through the caverns behind the waterfall, bounced off the rocks, rose from the riverbed, and filled the sky above. In the middle of this hellish noise, David stood up tall, pressing his hands against both ears as he cried out:

"Where does this conflict come from! Has hell broken free, that people should make sounds like these!"

The bright flashes and sharp cracks of a dozen rifles from the opposite banks of the stream followed this reckless exposure of his body, leaving the unfortunate singing master unconscious on the rock where he had been resting for so long. The Mohicans boldly returned the threatening war cry of their enemies, who raised a shout of savage victory at Gamut's fall. The rifle fire was then rapid and intense between them, but both sides were too experienced to leave even a limb exposed to enemy aim. Duncan listened with desperate anxiety for the sound of paddle strokes, believing that escape was now their only option. The river flowed past at its normal speed, but the canoe was nowhere to be seen on its dark waters. He had just imagined they were cruelly abandoned by their scout, when a stream of flame burst from the rock beneath them, and a fierce war cry, mixed with a scream of pain, announced that the messenger of death sent from Hawkeye's deadly weapon had found a target. At this minor setback the attackers immediately retreated, and gradually the area became as quiet as it had been before the sudden chaos.

Duncan took advantage of the opportunity to leap toward Gamut's body, carrying him to the safety of the narrow ravine where the sisters had taken shelter. Within moments, the entire group had gathered in this relatively secure location.

"The poor fellow has saved his scalp," said Hawkeye, calmly running his hand over David's head; "but he proves that a man can be born with too long a tongue! It was complete madness to expose six feet of flesh and blood on a bare rock to those furious savages. I'm only surprised he escaped with his life."

"Isn't he dead?" Cora asked, her voice rough and strained, revealing how her natural horror was fighting against the composure she was trying to maintain. "Is there anything we can do to help the poor man?"

"No, no! He's still alive, and after he sleeps for a while he'll wake up and be wiser for the experience, until his actual time comes," Hawkeye replied, glancing sideways at the unconscious body while he loaded his rifle with remarkable precision. "Carry him inside, Uncas, and put him on the sassafras. The longer he stays unconscious the better it will be for him, since I doubt he can find proper shelter for someone his size on these rocks; and singing won't help him with the Iroquois."

"Do you think they'll attack again?" Heyward asked.

"Do I expect a hungry wolf to be satisfied with just one bite! They've lost a man, and it's their way, when they suffer a loss and their surprise attack fails, to retreat; but they'll come at us again, with new plans to outsmart us and take our scalps. Our main hope," he continued, lifting his weathered face, across which a shadow of worry passed like a dark cloud, "will be to hold the rock until Munro can send a group to help us! God grant it may be soon and under a leader who understands Indian ways!"

"You've heard what we're likely facing, Cora," Duncan said, "and you know we can count on your father's concern and expertise to help us through this. Come with Alice into this cave, where you'll at least be protected from our enemies' deadly gunfire, and where you can provide the kind of tender care that comes naturally to you both for our wounded friend."

The sisters followed him into the outer cave, where David was starting to show signs of regaining consciousness through his sighs, and after entrusting the wounded man to their care, he immediately got ready to leave them.

"Duncan!" Cora called out in a shaking voice as he reached the cave entrance. He turned around and saw her standing there, her face drained of all color and her lips trembling as she watched him go, with such a look of concern that it immediately drew him back to her side. "Remember, Duncan, how essential your safety is to our survival—how you carry the sacred responsibility of a father's trust—how much relies on your careful judgment and caution—in short," she continued, as revealing blood rushed to her face, turning even her temples crimson, "how truly and deeply precious you are to everyone who bears the Munro name."

"If anything could strengthen my deep love of life," said Heyward, letting his unaware eyes drift toward the young figure of the quiet Alice, "it would be such a kind promise. As major of the Sixtieth, our trustworthy host will tell you I must do my part in the battle; but our job will be simple; we just need to hold these ruthless enemies back for a few hours."

Without waiting for a response, he pulled himself away from the sisters and rejoined the scout and his companions, who were still positioned within the safety of the small ravine between the two caves.

"I'm telling you, Uncas," said the first man as Heyward approached them, "you're wasting your gunpowder, and the rifle's recoil is throwing off your aim! A small amount of powder, a light bullet, and a long barrel rarely fail to bring the death cry from a Mingo warrior! At least, that's been my experience with those creatures. Come on, friends: let's get to our hiding places, because no one can predict when or where a Maqua will attack."[1]

[1] Mingo was the Delaware term for the Five Nations. Maquas was the name the Dutch gave them. The French, from their first contact with them, called them Iroquois.

The Indians quietly moved to their assigned positions, which were cracks in the rocks that allowed them to control the pathways leading to the base of the waterfall. In the middle of the small island, a few short and twisted pine trees had taken root, creating a dense cluster of vegetation that Hawkeye rushed into with the speed of a deer, with the agile Duncan close behind. Here they positioned themselves as securely as the situation allowed, hiding among the bushes and scattered pieces of stone throughout the area. Above them rose a smooth, rounded boulder, with water flowing playfully on both sides before cascading into the deep pools below in the way previously described. Since daylight had now broken, the far shores no longer appeared as an unclear silhouette, but they could now see into the forest and make out details beneath the dark canopy of pine trees.

A long and anxious period of watching followed, but there were no further signs of another attack. Duncan began to hope that their gunfire had been more deadly than they had thought, and that their enemies had been effectively driven back. When he dared to share this thought with his companions, Hawkeye responded with a disbelieving shake of his head.

"You don't understand what a Maqua is like if you think he can be driven off so easily without taking a scalp!" he replied. "If there was one of those devils screaming this morning, there were forty! And they know our numbers and our capabilities too well to abandon the chase this quickly. Listen! Look at the water upstream, right where it flows over the rocks. I swear I'm not human if those dangerous devils haven't swum down to this exact spot, and as our bad luck would have it, they've reached the head of the island. Listen! Stay down! Or your scalp will be taken faster than you can blink!"

Heyward raised his head from his hiding place and saw what he rightly thought was an incredible display of both recklessness and expertise. The river had eroded the edge of the soft rock in such a way that it made the initial drop less steep and vertical than what you typically see at waterfalls. Using nothing more than the ripples of the stream where it met the tip of the island as their guide, a group of their relentless enemies had dared to enter the current and had swum down to this spot, knowing that if they succeeded, it would give them easy access to their intended prey.

As Hawkeye finished speaking, four human heads appeared above some pieces of driftwood that had become stuck on these bare rocks, which had likely given them the idea that this dangerous plan might actually work. The next moment, a fifth figure could be seen floating over the green edge of the waterfall, slightly away from the island's edge. The warrior fought desperately to reach the safe spot, and helped by the rushing water, he was already extending his arm to grab hold of his companions when the swirling current swept him away again. He seemed to rise into the air with his arms raised and his eyes bulging, then suddenly plunged into the deep, gaping chasm over which he had been suspended. A single wild cry of despair echoed from the cavern, and then everything became as silent as a tomb.

Duncan's first generous impulse was to rush to the rescue of the unfortunate man, but he found himself held firmly in place by the iron grip of the motionless scout.

"Are you trying to get us all killed by letting the Mingoes know where we're hiding?" Hawkeye demanded harshly. "That's a waste of gunpowder, and right now ammunition is as valuable as air to a hunted deer! Check the priming on your pistols—the spray from the waterfall tends to dampen the gunpowder—and get ready for hand-to-hand combat while I shoot at them as they charge."

He put a finger to his mouth and let out a long, piercing whistle that echoed back from the rocks where the Mohicans stood guard. Duncan caught brief glimpses of heads appearing above the scattered driftwood when this signal rang through the air, but they vanished as quickly as they had appeared before his eyes. A soft rustling sound behind him drew his attention next, and when he turned his head, he saw Uncas just a few feet away, crawling toward his side. Hawkeye spoke to him in Delaware, and the young chief took his position with remarkable caution and calm composure. For Heyward, this was a moment of anxious and restless suspense, though the scout thought it was the perfect time to give a lesson to his younger companions about the proper use of firearms with good judgment.

"Of all weapons," he began, "the long-barreled, true-grooved, soft-metal rifle is the most dangerous in skilled hands, though it requires a strong arm, a quick eye, and great judgment in loading to bring out all its finest qualities. The gunsmiths can have but little understanding of their craft when they make their fowling pieces and short horsemen's—"

He was interrupted by Uncas's low but meaningful grunt.

"I can see them, boy, I can see them!" Hawkeye continued. "They're getting ready to charge, or else they'd keep their dark backs hidden behind the logs. Well, let them come," he added, checking his flint. "The man in front is definitely heading to his death, even if it turns out to be Montcalm himself!"

At that moment the woods erupted with another wave of shouts, and at this signal four warriors leaped from their hiding place behind the driftwood. Heyward felt an overwhelming urge to charge forward and confront them, so intense was his frenzied anxiety in that moment; but he held back, following the measured example set by the scout and Uncas.

When their enemies, who had jumped over the black rocks separating them with long leaps while screaming wild battle cries, came within just a few yards, Hawkeye's rifle slowly emerged from the bushes and discharged its deadly shot. The leading Indian leaped like a wounded deer and tumbled headfirst into the rocky crevices of the island.

"Now, Uncas!" shouted the scout, pulling out his long knife while his sharp eyes started to burn with fierce determination, "take down the last of those screaming devils; we've already taken care of the other two!"

He was obeyed, and only two enemies remained to be defeated. Heyward had given one of his pistols to Hawkeye, and together they charged down a small slope toward their opponents; they fired their weapons at the same moment, and both shots missed their targets.

"I knew it! And I said it!" muttered the scout, hurling the worthless little weapon over the falls with bitter contempt. "Come on, you bloodthirsty devils! You're facing a man without a cross!"

The words had barely been spoken when he came face to face with a massive savage with an extremely fierce appearance. At the same time, Duncan found himself locked in a similar hand-to-hand struggle with another warrior. With practiced skill, Hawkeye and his opponent each seized the other's raised arm that gripped the deadly knife. For nearly a minute they stood staring into each other's eyes, gradually applying all their muscular strength to gain the upper hand.

Eventually, the hardened muscles of the white man overcame the less experienced limbs of the native warrior. The native's arm slowly weakened against the scout's growing strength, and the scout suddenly broke free from his opponent's grip, driving his sharp blade through the man's bare chest straight to his heart. Meanwhile, Heyward found himself locked in an even more dangerous fight. His lightweight sword broke during their first clash. With no other weapon to defend himself, his survival now depended completely on his physical strength and determination. Although he possessed both qualities in good measure, he faced an opponent who matched him in every way. Fortunately, he managed to disarm his enemy, whose knife clattered onto the rock beneath their feet. From that point forward, it became a fierce battle to see who could throw the other over the dizzying cliff into a nearby cavern by the waterfall. Each struggle brought them closer to the edge, where Duncan realized the final, decisive effort would have to be made. Both fighters poured all their energy into that crucial moment, and the outcome was that they both swayed dangerously on the edge of the cliff. Heyward felt his opponent's grip around his throat and saw the grim smile on the savage's face, driven by vengeful hope that he was dragging his enemy to the same doom awaiting him. As Duncan felt his body slowly giving way to an unstoppable force, the young man experienced all the terror of such a moment in its full horror. At that instant of extreme peril, a dark hand and flashing knife appeared before him. The Indian let go as blood poured freely from the severed tendons in his wrist. While Duncan was pulled backward to safety by Uncas's rescuing hand, his mesmerized eyes remained fixed on the fierce and frustrated face of his enemy, who fell grimly and defeated down the unforgiving precipice.

"Take cover! Take cover!" shouted Hawkeye, who had just finished off the enemy; "take cover, for your lives! the job is only half done!"

The young Mohican let out a triumphant shout, and with Duncan following behind him, he moved swiftly up the slope they had come down to fight, looking for the protective cover of the rocks and bushes.

---

# Chapter VIII.

"They linger yet,
Avengers of their native land."—Gray

The scout's warning cry had good reason behind it. Throughout the deadly fight that had just taken place, the thundering of the waterfall remained uninterrupted by any human voice. It appeared that fascination with the outcome had held the natives on the far shores in silent, breathless anticipation, while the rapid movements and quick shifts in the fighters' positions effectively prevented any gunfire that might have endangered both allies and enemies alike. However, the instant the battle reached its conclusion, a shriek erupted as wild and brutal as untamed and vengeful emotions could hurl into the atmosphere. This was immediately followed by the rapid flashes of muskets, which hurled their lead projectiles across the rocky terrain in coordinated bursts, as if the attackers sought to unleash their helpless rage upon the unfeeling location of the deadly struggle.

A steady but deliberate shot came from Chingachgook's rifle, as he had held his position throughout the entire battle with unwavering determination. When Uncas's triumphant shout reached his ears, the proud father lifted his voice in a single answering cry, after which only his active weapon showed that he continued to guard his position with tireless vigilance. In this way many minutes passed by with the speed of thought; the rifles of the attackers firing sometimes in rapid bursts, and other times in sporadic, scattered shots. Though the rock, the trees, and the bushes were cut and damaged in countless places around those under siege, their shelter was so tight, and so strictly maintained, that so far, David had been the only one hurt in their small group.

"Let them waste their gunpowder," said the calm scout, while bullet after bullet whistled past the spot where he lay safely hidden; "there will be plenty of lead scattered around when this is finished, and I expect those devils will grow tired of this game before these ancient stones start begging for mercy! Uncas, boy, you're wasting your ammunition by using too much powder; and a rifle that kicks hard never shoots a straight bullet. I told you to aim at that running scoundrel below the white marking; now, if your bullet missed by even the smallest amount, it went two inches too high. A Mingo's vital organs sit low in his body, and basic decency tells us to put an end to these snakes quickly."

A quiet smile lit up the proud features of the young Mohican, revealing that he understood both the English language and the meaning behind the other man's words; however, he let the moment pass without defending himself or offering any response.

"I can't allow you to accuse Uncas of lacking judgment or skill," Duncan said. "He saved my life in the most composed and quick-thinking way possible, and he's gained a friend who will never need to be reminded of the debt he owes."

Uncas partially lifted himself up and extended his hand for Heyward to shake. During this gesture of friendship, the two young men shared meaningful glances that made Duncan momentarily forget about the background and circumstances of his untamed companion. Meanwhile, Hawkeye, who watched this display of youthful emotion with a detached yet benevolent expression, responded as follows:

"Life is a debt that friends frequently owe one another in the wilderness. I believe I may have done Uncas a similar favor myself in the past; and I clearly recall that he has saved my life on five separate occasions; three times from the Mingoes, once while crossing Horican, and—"

"That bullet was aimed much better than usual!" Duncan exclaimed, instinctively pulling back from a shot that hit the rock beside him and bounced off sharply.

Hawkeye placed his hand on the misshapen metal and shook his head as he studied it, saying, "Lead that falls naturally never gets flattened like this—if it had come from the clouds, this might have occurred."

Uncas deliberately raised his rifle toward the sky, drawing his companions' attention to a spot where the mystery became clear at once. A weathered oak tree grew on the river's right bank, almost directly across from where they stood. The tree had leaned so far forward in its search for open space that its upper branches hung over the part of the stream that flowed closest to its own shore. Hidden among the highest leaves, which barely covered the twisted and stunted branches, a warrior had positioned himself. He was partially hidden by the tree trunk and partially visible, as if he were looking down at them to see the results of his sneaky shot.

"These devils will climb all the way to heaven just to outmaneuver us and destroy us," said Hawkeye; "keep him engaged, boy, until I can get 'killdeer' into position, then we'll test what he's made of by attacking him from both sides of the tree at the same time."

Uncas held his fire until the scout gave the command.

The rifles fired, sending leaves and bark from the oak tree flying through the air before the wind scattered them, but the Indian responded to their attack with a mocking laugh, firing another bullet down at them that knocked Hawkeye's cap right off his head. The wild war cries erupted from the forest once again, and bullets whistled overhead like deadly rain, as if trying to pin down the defenders in a spot where they would become sitting ducks for the warrior who had climbed up into the tree.

"We need to handle this," said the scout, looking around with a worried expression. "Uncas, get your father; we're going to need all our weapons to force that crafty pest out of his hiding place."

The signal was given immediately, and before Hawkeye could reload his rifle, Chingachgook had joined them. When his son showed the experienced warrior where their dangerous enemy was positioned, the familiar exclamation "hugh" escaped from his lips; after that, he didn't allow any other expression of surprise or alarm to slip out. Hawkeye and the Mohicans spoke seriously together in Delaware for a few moments, then each quietly moved to his position to carry out the plan they had quickly developed.

The warrior positioned in the oak tree had kept up a rapid but ineffective barrage of gunfire from the instant he was spotted. However, his accuracy suffered due to the watchfulness of his adversaries, whose rifles immediately targeted any portion of his body that became visible. Nevertheless, his shots continued to land among the huddled group below. Heyward's clothing, which made him especially noticeable, was torn multiple times by bullets, and on one occasion he sustained a minor wound to his arm that drew blood.

Eventually, growing bold from watching his enemies for so long without being discovered, the Huron warrior tried to take a better and more deadly shot. The sharp eyes of the Mohican fighters spotted the dark outline of his legs carelessly visible through the sparse leaves, just a few inches away from the tree trunk. Both of their rifles fired at the same time, and as he collapsed onto his injured leg, part of the warrior's body became visible. Quick as lightning, Hawkeye took advantage of the moment and fired his deadly rifle toward the top of the oak tree. The leaves shook violently; the threatening rifle dropped from its high position, and after a few moments of futile struggle, the warrior's body could be seen hanging in the wind, his hands still desperately clutching a broken and bare tree branch.

"Please, have mercy and give him the bullets from another rifle," Duncan shouted, turning his eyes away in horror from the sight of a fellow human being in such terrible danger.

"Not a single grain!" declared the stubborn Hawkeye; "his death is inevitable, and we cannot afford to waste any gunpowder, since battles with Indians can go on for days; it's either their scalps or ours! And God, who created us, has placed within our very nature the desire to keep the skin on our heads."

Against this harsh and inflexible moral code, backed as it was by such clear strategic reasoning, there could be no argument. From that instant the screams in the woods fell silent once more, the fire was allowed to die down, and every gaze, from allies and enemies alike, became focused on the desperate plight of the unfortunate man who hung suspended between heaven and earth. His body swayed with the air currents, and although no sound or moan came from the victim, there were moments when he grimly stared at his enemies, and the agony of cold hopelessness could be seen, across the distance that separated them, written on his dark features. Three separate times the scout lifted his rifle in compassion, and just as often, caution overcoming his purpose, he quietly lowered it again. Finally one of the Huron's hands lost its grip and fell weakly to his side. A frantic and futile attempt to regain hold of the branch followed, and then the warrior was glimpsed for a brief moment, clutching desperately at nothing but air. Lightning moves no faster than the flash from Hawkeye's rifle; the victim's limbs shuddered and tightened, his head dropped to his chest, and his body cut through the churning waters like a stone, as the rushing current closed over it, and every trace of the unfortunate Huron vanished forever.

No triumphant shout followed this significant victory, but even the Mohicans looked at each other in silent terror. A single cry erupted from the forest, and then everything fell quiet again. Hawkeye, who seemed to be the only one thinking clearly in the moment, shook his head at his own brief moment of weakness, even voicing his self-criticism out loud.

"That was the last charge in my horn and the last bullet in my pouch, and it was the act of a boy!" he said; "what did it matter whether he struck the rock living or dead! feeling would soon be over. Uncas, lad, go down to the canoe, and bring up the big horn; it is all the powder we have left, and we shall need it to the last grain, or I am ignorant of the Mingo nature."

The young Mohican did as he was asked, leaving the scout to examine the worthless items in his pouch and shake his empty powder horn with growing frustration. This disappointing search was quickly interrupted by a loud, sharp cry from Uncas that even Duncan's inexperienced ears recognized as a warning of some fresh and unexpected disaster. His mind immediately filled with worry for the precious treasure he had hidden in the cave, and the young man jumped to his feet, completely ignoring the danger of exposing himself this way. As if driven by the same instinct, his companions copied his movement, and together they all rushed down the narrow path toward the protective crevice, moving so quickly that their enemies' scattered gunfire posed no threat at all. The unusual shout had drawn the sisters and the injured David from their hiding place, and with just one look, the entire group understood the nature of the catastrophe that had shaken even the calm composure of their young Indian guardian.

At a short distance from the rock, their small boat could be seen floating across the swirling water, moving toward the fast-flowing current of the river in a way that showed its path was being controlled by some unseen force. The moment this unwelcome sight caught the scout's eye, he instinctively raised his rifle and aimed, but the barrel produced no response to the bright sparks from the flint.

"It's too late, it's too late!" Hawkeye exclaimed, dropping the useless weapon in bitter disappointment; "the villain has reached the rapids; and even if we had gunpowder, it could hardly send the bullet faster than he's moving now!"

The bold Huron lifted his head above the protection of the canoe, and as it moved quickly down the river, he raised his hand and let out the cry that was the recognized signal of victory. His shout was met with a howl and laughter from the forest, as mockingly triumphant as if fifty devils were voicing their curses at the downfall of some Christian spirit.

"Go ahead and laugh, you devil's spawn!" the scout said, settling himself on a rocky ledge and letting his rifle drop carelessly to his feet. "The three fastest and most accurate shooters in these entire woods are now about as useful as dried weeds or last season's deer antlers!"

"What should we do?" Duncan asked, his initial disappointment giving way to a more determined need for action. "What's going to happen to us?"

Hawkeye responded only by running his finger around the top of his head in such a meaningful way that anyone who saw the gesture couldn't misunderstand what he meant.

"Surely, surely, our situation isn't that hopeless!" the young man cried out; "the Hurons aren't here; we can secure the caves, we can fight against their landing."

"With what?" the scout asked coolly. "The arrows of Uncas, or the kind of tears that women cry! No, no; you're young, wealthy, and you have friends, and I know that at your age it's difficult to face death! But," he said, looking toward the Mohicans, "let's remember that we are men without a cross, and let's show these forest natives that white blood can flow just as freely as red blood when our destined time arrives."

Duncan quickly turned to look where the other man's eyes were pointing, and what he saw in the Indians' behavior confirmed his worst fears. Chingachgook positioned himself with dignity on another piece of rock, having already set down his knife and tomahawk, and was now removing the eagle feather from his head while smoothing his single tuft of hair in preparation for its final and horrifying purpose. His face remained calm but serious, while his dark, shining eyes were slowly losing their battle intensity and taking on an expression more fitting for the transformation he expected to happen at any moment.

"Our situation isn't hopeless, and it can't be!" Duncan declared. "Help might arrive at any moment, even right now. I don't see any enemies around! They've grown tired of a fight where they're risking so much for so little chance of reward!"

"It might be a minute, or it could be an hour, before those cunning snakes creep up on us, and it's perfectly natural for them to be lying within earshot right at this very moment," said Hawkeye; "but they will come, and in such a way that will leave us with nothing to hope for! Chingachgook"—he spoke in Delaware—"my brother, we have fought our final battle together, and the Maquas will celebrate the death of the wise man of the Mohicans, and of the white man, whose eyes can turn night into day, and bring the clouds down to the mists of the springs!"

"Let the Mingo women weep for their dead!" the Indian replied with characteristic pride and unwavering resolve. "The Great Snake of the Mohicans has entered their homes and turned their victory bitter with the cries of children whose fathers will never return! Eleven warriors have vanished from their tribal burial grounds since the snow melted, and no one will know where to find them once Chingachgook's voice falls silent! Let them sharpen their keenest blade and swing their fastest tomahawk, for their most hated enemy is now in their grasp. Uncas, highest branch of a noble family tree, tell these cowards to hurry, or their courage will weaken and they will become like women!"

"They search among the fish for their dead!" replied the quiet, gentle voice of the young chief; "the Hurons drift alongside the slippery eels! They fall from the oak trees like ripe fruit ready to be picked! and the Delawares laugh!"

"Yes, yes," muttered the scout, who had listened to this unusual outburst from the natives with intense focus; "they have stirred up their Indian emotions, and they'll soon anger the Mohawks enough to bring about their quick death. As for me, who am of pure white blood, it is proper that I should die in a way that befits my race, with no mocking words on my lips, and without hatred in my heart!"

"Why should anyone have to die!" Cora exclaimed, stepping forward from the spot where natural terror had kept her frozen against the rock until that very moment. "The path is clear in every direction; escape to the forest and pray to God for help. Go, courageous men, we already owe you far too much; we must not continue to drag you into our cursed fate!"

"You don't understand much about how clever the Iroquois are, lady, if you think they've left the trail to the forest unguarded!" Hawkeye replied, though he immediately added with his straightforward honesty, "the downstream current would certainly carry us quickly beyond the range of their rifles or where they could hear our voices."

"Then try the river. Why wait around just to become another victim of our ruthless enemies?"

"Why," the scout repeated, looking around with pride; "because it's better for a man to die with a clear conscience than to live tormented by guilt! What answer could we give Munro when he asks us where and how we left his children?"

"Go to him and tell him that you left them with a message to hurry to their aid," Cora replied, moving closer to the scout with generous passion. "Tell him that the Hurons are taking them into the northern wilderness, but that with watchfulness and speed they might still be saved. And if, after everything, it should please heaven that his help arrives too late, carry to him," she continued, her voice gradually growing quieter until it seemed almost strangled, "the love, the blessings, and the final prayers of his daughters, and tell him not to grieve over their early death, but to look ahead with humble faith to the Christian's destination where he will meet his children again." The rough, weathered features of the scout began to shift, and when she had finished speaking, he lowered his chin to his hand, like a man thinking deeply about the nature of her suggestion.

"Her words make sense!" finally burst from his tight and shaking lips; "yes, and they carry the spirit of Christianity; what might be right and proper for a Native American, may be sinful for a man who doesn't even have mixed blood to excuse his ignorance. Chingachgook! Uncas! do you hear what the dark-eyed woman is saying?"

He now spoke in Delaware to his companions, and his words, though calm and measured, seemed very determined. The older Mohican listened with serious attention, and appeared to think carefully about what he had said, as if he understood how important it was. After a brief moment of uncertainty, he raised his hand in agreement, and spoke the English word "Good!" with the distinctive emphasis of his people. Then, putting his knife and tomahawk back in his belt, the warrior moved quietly to the edge of the rock that was best hidden from the riverbanks. Here he stopped for a moment, pointed meaningfully toward the woods below, and spoke a few words in his own language, as if showing the path he planned to take, then he dropped into the water and disappeared from the sight of those watching him.

The scout postponed leaving to talk with the kind-hearted young woman, whose breathing grew easier when she witnessed how effective her protest had been.

"Wisdom is sometimes given to the young, as well as to the old," he said; "and what you have spoken is wise, not to call it by a better word. If you are led into the woods, those of you who may be spared for a while should break the twigs on the bushes as you pass, and make the marks of your trail as clear as you can, because if human eyes can see them, you can count on having a friend who will follow to the ends of the earth before he abandons you."

He gave Cora a warm handshake, picked up his rifle, and after looking at it for a moment with sad concern, set it carefully aside and climbed down to the spot where Chingachgook had just vanished. For a moment he hung from the rock, and looking around with an expression of deep worry, he said bitterly, "If we hadn't run out of gunpowder, this humiliation never would have happened!" Then, letting go of his grip, the water closed over his head, and he too disappeared from sight.

All eyes turned to Uncas, who stood leaning against the jagged rock with unwavering composure. After waiting briefly, Cora pointed down the river and said:

"Your friends haven't been spotted, and they're most likely safe now. Isn't it time for you to follow them?"

"Uncas will stay," the young Mohican calmly replied in English.

"To make our capture even more terrifying, and to reduce any possibility of our freedom! Go, noble young man," Cora continued, lowering her eyes beneath the Mohican's gaze, and perhaps with an instinctive awareness of her influence; "go to my father, as I have told you, and be the most trusted of my messengers. Tell him to entrust you with whatever is needed to purchase his daughters' freedom. Go! It is my wish, it is my prayer, that you will go!"

The peaceful, composed expression on the young chief's face shifted to one of darkness, but he no longer wavered. Moving silently across the rock, he plunged into the churning waters below. Those watching from behind barely dared to breathe until they spotted his head breaking the surface for air far downstream, before he disappeared beneath the water once more and vanished from sight.

These quick and seemingly successful attempts had all happened within just a few minutes of time that had now become so valuable. After taking one final look at Uncas, Cora turned around and with a trembling lip, spoke to Heyward:

"I've heard about your famous swimming abilities, Duncan," she said; "so follow the wise example these simple and loyal creatures have shown you."

"Is this the kind of faith that Cora Munro would demand from her protector?" said the young man, smiling sadly, but with bitterness.

"This isn't the time for pointless arguments and mistaken beliefs," she replied; "but a moment when we must weigh every responsibility equally. You can't help us any more here, but your valuable life might be preserved for other friends who are closer to you."

He didn't respond, though his gaze lingered longingly on Alice's beautiful figure as she clung to his arm with the helplessness of a child.

"Think about it," Cora continued after a pause, during which she appeared to wrestle with a pain even sharper than any her fears had stirred up, "the worst thing that can happen to us is death—a price that everyone must pay when God decides the time is right."

"There are things worse than death," Duncan said, his voice

rough and strained, as though her persistent pleading irritated him, "but having someone willing to die for you might prevent those terrible fates."

Cora stopped pleading and, covering her face with her shawl, pulled the barely conscious Alice deeper into the farthest corner of the inner cave.

---

# Chapter IX.

"Be joyful without fear; dispel, my beautiful one, with smiles, the fearful clouds that hang upon your clear brow."—Death of Agrippina

The sudden and almost magical transformation from the intense action of battle to the silence that now surrounded him affected Heyward's excited imagination like a vivid dream. Though all the scenes and events he had witnessed remained vividly etched in his memory, he struggled to convince himself they had actually happened. Still unaware of what had become of those who had relied on the swift current's help, he initially strained to hear any signal or sounds of danger that might reveal whether their risky mission had succeeded or failed. His careful listening proved futile, however, because once Uncas vanished, every trace of the adventurers had disappeared, leaving him completely uncertain about their fate.

In a moment of such agonizing uncertainty, Duncan didn't hesitate to scan his surroundings, abandoning the protection of the rocks that had been so crucial to his survival just moments before. Every attempt to find even the slightest sign of their concealed enemies approaching proved as futile as searching for his missing companions. The tree-lined riverbanks appeared once again abandoned by all living creatures. The chaos that had recently thundered through the forest depths had vanished, leaving only the sound of rushing water to rise and fall with the air currents, carrying nature's pure and untainted melody. A fish-hawk, which had watched the battle from safety atop the highest branches of a dead pine tree, now dove down from its lofty and jagged perch, gliding in broad circles above its prey; meanwhile, a jay, whose raucous calls had been silenced by the harsher shouts of the savages, dared to open its harsh throat once more, as if reclaiming its undisturbed rule over these wilderness territories. Duncan drew from these natural elements of the isolated landscape a spark of hope; and he started to gather his mental strength for fresh efforts, with something resembling a renewed belief in success.

"The Hurons are nowhere to be found," he said, speaking to David, who had not yet recovered from the effects of the devastating blow he had received; "let us hide ourselves in the cave, and leave the rest to Providence."

"I remember joining with two beautiful young women in raising our voices in praise and thanksgiving," replied the confused singing teacher. "Since that time, I have been punished severely for my sins. I have been tormented with what seemed like sleep, while harsh and jarring sounds have torn at my ears—sounds that might signal the end of days, as if nature itself had lost all sense of harmony."

"Poor man! Your own time was, in truth, nearly finished! But wake up, and come with me; I will take you to a place where all other sounds except those of your own psalm singing will be shut out."

"There's music in the waterfall's cascade, and the sound of rushing waters delights the senses!" David said, pressing his hand frantically against his forehead. "Isn't the air still filled with screams and cries, as if the departed souls of the damned—"

"Not now, not now," the impatient Heyward interrupted, "they have stopped, and those who made them, I trust in God, are gone too! Everything except the water is quiet and peaceful; go in, then, where you can make those sounds you love so much to hear."

David smiled with sadness, though not without a brief flash of pleasure, at this reference to his cherished calling. He no longer hesitated to be guided to a place that promised such pure satisfaction to his exhausted senses; and resting on his companion's arm, he stepped into the narrow entrance of the cave. Duncan grabbed a pile of sassafras branches, which he pulled across the opening, carefully hiding every sign of an entrance. Behind this delicate barrier he arranged the blankets left behind by the woodsmen, darkening the inner depths of the cavern, while its entrance received a softened light from the narrow gorge, through which one branch of the river flowed rapidly to meet its companion stream just a few yards downstream.

"I don't like the philosophy of the natives, which teaches them to give up without fighting when situations seem hopeless," he said while working at this task. "Our own saying, which goes 'while life remains there is hope,' is more comforting and better suited to a soldier's nature. To you, Cora, I won't offer empty words of encouragement; your own courage and calm reasoning will show you everything that's appropriate for your gender; but can't we stop the tears of that shaking woman crying against your chest?"

"I'm feeling calmer now, Duncan," Alice said, lifting herself up from her sister's embrace and trying to appear composed despite her tears. "Much calmer. Surely we're safe here in this hidden place—we're concealed and protected from harm. We should put our hope in those brave men who have already risked so much for us."

"Now our gentle Alice speaks like a true daughter of Munro!" Heyward said, pausing to squeeze her hand as he moved toward the cave's outer entrance. "With two such examples of courage in front of him, a man would be ashamed to be anything less than a hero." He then sat down in the center of the cave, gripping his remaining pistol with a hand clenched tight, while his narrowed and scowling eyes revealed the grim determination of his intent. "The Hurons, if they come, may not take our position as easily as they think," he muttered quietly; and leaning his head back against the rock, he seemed to wait patiently for whatever would happen, though his eyes never stopped watching the open path to their hiding place.

As his voice faded away, a profound, extended, and nearly breathless quiet followed. The cool morning air had reached into their hiding place, and its effect was slowly being felt on the mood of those sheltered there. As one minute after another went by, leaving them in uninterrupted safety, the subtle feeling of hope was slowly taking hold of every heart, though each person felt hesitant to voice expectations that the next moment might so terrifyingly shatter.

David was the only one who didn't share these shifting emotions. A ray of light from the opening fell across his pale face and illuminated the pages of the small book he was leafing through once more, as though he were looking for a song better suited to their situation than any they had found so far. He was most likely acting during this entire time under a hazy memory of Duncan's promised comfort. Eventually, it seemed his persistent effort paid off; without any explanation or apology, he spoke the words "Isle of Wight" out loud, drew a long, beautiful note from his pitch-pipe, and then performed the opening musical phrases of the tune he had just named, using the melodious tones of his own singing voice.

"Could this turn out to be dangerous?" Cora asked, casting her dark eyes toward Major Heyward.

"Poor guy! His voice is too weak to be heard over the roar of the waterfall," came the reply; "besides, the cave will work in his favor. Let him give in to his emotions since he can do so without any danger."

"Isle of Wight!" David repeated, looking around with the same dignity he had long used to quiet the whispered echoes in his school. "It's a fine tune, set to serious words! Let it be sung with proper respect!"

After allowing a moment of silence to strengthen his resolve, the singer's voice could be heard in quiet, murmuring tones, slowly reaching their ears until it filled the small cave with sounds made even more moving by the weak and shaking delivery caused by his frailty. The melody, which no weakness could diminish, slowly worked its gentle magic on the senses of those who listened. It even overcame the poor imitation of David's song that the singer had chosen from a collection of similar religious pieces, making the listeners forget the words as they became absorbed in the captivating harmony of the music. Alice unconsciously wiped away her tears and fixed her tender gaze on Gamut's pale face, with an expression of refined joy that she neither pretended nor wanted to hide. Cora gave an approving smile to the devout efforts of the man who shared a name with the Jewish prince, and Heyward soon shifted his steady, serious gaze from the cave's entrance to focus it, with a gentler expression, on David's face, or to catch the wandering glances that occasionally drifted from Alice's moist eyes. The open sympathy of the listeners inspired the devoted musician, whose voice recovered its depth and power while keeping that moving gentleness that was its hidden appeal. Using his restored abilities to their fullest, he was still filling the cave's arches with long and rich notes when a scream erupted from outside, immediately silencing his sacred song and cutting off his voice suddenly, as if his heart had literally jumped into his throat.

"We're lost!" Alice cried out, throwing herself into Cora's arms.

"Not yet, not yet," replied the agitated but fearless Heyward: "the sound came from the center of the island, and it was caused by the sight of their dead companions. We haven't been discovered yet, and there is still hope."

Although the chance of escape seemed almost hopeless, Duncan's words weren't wasted, as they stirred the sisters' determination in such a way that they waited quietly for what would happen next. A second scream quickly followed the first, and then a flood of voices could be heard sweeping across the island from one end to the other, until they reached the bare rock above the caves, where, after a wild cry of savage victory, the air remained filled with terrible shouts and screams that only humans can make, and only when they're in a state of the most brutal savagery.

The sounds rapidly spread around them in all directions. Some called out to their companions from the water's edge, and received responses from the heights above. Shouts were heard in the alarming proximity of the gap between the two caves, which mixed with rougher howls that rose from the depths of the deep gorge. In essence, the wild sounds had spread so quickly across the barren rock that the worried listeners could easily imagine they were being heard from below, just as they truly were from above on every side of them.

In the middle of this chaos, a victorious shout erupted just a few yards from the cave's concealed entrance. Heyward gave up all hope, convinced this was the signal that they had been found. The feeling faded again when he heard voices gathering near the spot where the white man had so reluctantly left his rifle behind. Among the jumble of Indian languages he could now clearly hear, it was easy to pick out not just individual words, but complete sentences spoken in the French-Canadian dialect. A chorus of voices had cried out together, "La Longue Carabine!" making the woods across from them echo with a name that Heyward clearly remembered had been given by enemies to a famous hunter and scout from the English camp, and who, he now discovered for the first time, had been traveling with him.

"La Longue Carabine! La Longue Carabine!" spread from person to person, until the entire group seemed to gather around a prize that appeared to signal the death of its fearsome owner. Following a loud discussion that was occasionally drowned out by outbursts of wild celebration, they scattered once more, filling the air with the name of an enemy whose body, Heywood could understand from their expressions, they expected to discover hidden in some crack or crevice of the island.

"Now," he whispered to the trembling sisters, "this is the moment of uncertainty! If our hiding place escapes this search, we are still safe! In any case, we are assured by what we have heard from our enemies that our friends have escaped, and in two short hours we can expect help from Webb."

A few minutes of terrifying silence followed, and Heyward understood that the savages were now searching with increased alertness and systematic precision. He could hear their footsteps multiple times as they moved through the sassafras bushes, making the withered leaves crackle and causing branches to break. Eventually, the pile of debris shifted slightly, one corner of a blanket slipped down, and a weak beam of light penetrated into the cave's interior. Cora clutched Alice against her chest in anguish, while Duncan jumped to his feet. At that very moment, a shout echoed from what seemed like the heart of the rock itself, signaling that the adjacent cavern had finally been discovered. Within a minute, the volume and number of voices revealed that the entire group had gathered in and around that hidden location.

Since the inner passages to the two caves were so close together, Duncan realized that escape was no longer possible. He moved past David and the sisters to position himself between them and the initial attack of the terrifying encounter that was about to unfold. Driven to desperation by his circumstances, he approached the thin barrier that separated him by only a few feet from his ruthless pursuers. Pressing his face to the random opening in the barrier, he looked out at their movements with a kind of reckless indifference born of despair.

Within arm's reach stood the muscular shoulder of a massive Indian warrior, whose deep and commanding voice seemed to direct what his companions were doing. Past him, Duncan could see into the cave across from them, which was packed with natives who were overturning and ransacking the scout's simple belongings. David's wound had stained the sassafras leaves with a color that the warriors recognized as coming before its natural time. Seeing this evidence of their success, they let out a howl like a pack of hunting dogs that had picked up a lost scent. After this cry of victory, they ripped up the fragrant floor covering of the cave and carried the branches into the ravine, scattering the boughs as though they suspected the vegetation might be hiding the man they had hunted and feared for so long. One fierce and wild-looking warrior came up to the chief, carrying an armload of brush and pointing triumphantly to the dark red stains that spotted it, expressing his excitement in Indian war cries whose meaning Heyward could only understand because of how often they repeated the name "La Longue Carabine!" When his celebration ended, he threw the brush onto the small pile Duncan had built in front of the second cave's entrance, blocking the view inside. The other warriors followed his lead, and as they pulled branches from the scout's cave, they tossed them onto the same pile, unknowingly adding to the protection of the very people they were hunting. The weakness of this barrier was actually its greatest strength, because no one thought to disturb a heap of brush that they all assumed, in that moment of rush and chaos, had been accidentally created by members of their own group.

As the blankets gave way under the outward pressure, and the branches settled into the crack in the rock under their own weight, creating a solid mass, Duncan was able to breathe easily once again. Moving with a light step and an even lighter heart, he made his way back to the center of the cave and returned to the spot he had vacated, where he could keep watch over the opening that faced the river. While he was making this movement, the Indians, as though they had all suddenly changed their minds at the same moment, abandoned the chasm as a group and could be heard rushing back up the island toward the place where they had first come down. There, another mournful cry revealed that they had once again gathered around the bodies of their fallen companions.

Duncan finally dared to look at his traveling companions. Throughout the most dangerous moments they had just faced, he had been worried that the fear showing on his face might cause even more panic among those who were already struggling to cope with the situation.

"They're gone, Cora!" he whispered. "Alice, they've returned to where they came from, and we're saved! All praise goes to Heaven, which alone has delivered us from the grip of such a merciless enemy!"

"Then I'll give my thanks to Heaven!" cried the younger sister, pulling away from Cora's protective embrace and throwing herself down on the bare rock with passionate gratitude; "to that Heaven which has spared a gray-haired father from tears and has saved the lives of those I love so dearly."

Both Heyward and the more composed Cora watched this spontaneous display of emotion with deep sympathy, with Heyward privately thinking that devotion had never appeared as beautiful as it did now in Alice's young form. Her eyes shone with the warmth of grateful emotions; the rosy glow had returned to her cheeks, and her entire spirit seemed eager and ready to express its gratitude through her expressive face. But when her lips began to move, the words that should have come seemed frozen by some fresh and unexpected terror. Her healthy color drained away to a deathly pallor; her gentle and tender eyes became hard and appeared to shrink with fear; while her hands, which she had lifted and clasped together toward the sky, fell to hang straight in front of her, her fingers pointing forward in spasmodic movements. Heyward immediately turned in the direction that caught her attention, and looking just over the rocky edge that formed the entrance to the cave's opening, he saw the evil, fierce and brutal face of Le Renard Subtil.

In that moment of shock, Heyward managed to keep his composure. He noticed from the blank look on the Indian's face that his eyes, used to bright daylight, hadn't yet adjusted to the dim light that filled the deep cave. He had even considered backing away around a bend in the rock wall that might still hide him and his companions, but when a sudden flash of understanding crossed the warrior's face, he realized it was too late and that they had been discovered.

The expression of triumph and savage victory that revealed this horrifying truth was unbearably infuriating. Forgetting everything except the urges of his heated blood, Duncan raised his pistol and fired. The sound of the gun made the cave roar like a volcanic eruption; and when the smoke it released had been swept away by the air current flowing from the gorge, the spot recently occupied by his deceitful guide's face was empty. Racing to the opening, Heyward glimpsed his dark form slipping around a low and narrow rock shelf, which quickly concealed him completely from view.

Among the native warriors, an eerie silence followed the explosion that had just erupted from deep within the rock. However, when Le Renard lifted his voice in a long and clear war cry, it was met by an immediate shout from every Indian who could hear the sound.

The loud, chaotic sounds swept across the island once more, and before Duncan could recover from the shock, his weak barrier of brush was blown apart by the wind. The cave was invaded from both ends, and he and his companions were pulled from their hiding place and brought out into the daylight, where they found themselves surrounded by the entire group of victorious Hurons.

---

# Chapter X.

"I'm afraid we'll sleep through the morning that's coming, just as much as we've stayed awake too long tonight!"
—A Midsummer Night's Dream

As soon as the shock of this sudden disaster had subsided, Duncan started to observe the appearance and behavior of their captors. Unlike the typical customs of the natives when celebrating their victories, they had shown respect not only for the trembling sisters but for him as well. The elaborate decorations of his military uniform had been repeatedly examined by various members of the tribes, their eyes revealing a fierce desire to claim these treasures for themselves; however, before the usual violence could take place, a command spoken in the commanding voice of the large warrior previously described stopped their raised hands, and made Heyward realize that they were being saved for some purpose of special importance.

While the younger and more conceited members of the group displayed these signs of weakness, the seasoned warriors kept searching through both caves with an energy that showed they were far from satisfied with the spoils of victory they had already uncovered. When they couldn't find any new victims, these determined seekers of revenge soon turned to their male captives, repeating the name "La Longue Carabine" with an unmistakable ferocity. Duncan pretended not to understand what their repeated and aggressive questioning meant, while his companion was spared from having to make a similar pretense because he didn't know French. Eventually growing tired of their persistent demands and worried about angering his captors with continued stubborn silence, Duncan began looking around for Magua, who could translate his responses to questions that were becoming more urgent and menacing by the moment.

The behavior of this fierce warrior stood out completely from that of his companions. While the others were busy trying to satisfy their childlike desire for decorative items by stealing even the scout's meager belongings, or had been searching with murderous revenge written across their faces for the missing owner, Le Renard had positioned himself at some distance from the captives, displaying such a calm and content manner that it revealed he had already accomplished the main goal of his betrayal. When Heyward's eyes first locked with those of his former guide, he quickly looked away in revulsion at the menacing yet composed expression he saw there. Overcoming his repulsion, though, he managed to speak to his victorious enemy while keeping his face turned aside.

"Le Renard Subtil is too much of a warrior," said the hesitant Heyward, "to refuse telling an unarmed man what his conquerors say."

"They're looking for the hunter who knows the way through the forest," Magua replied in his broken English, placing his hand with a savage smile on the bundle of leaves that bandaged a wound on his shoulder. "La Longue Carabine'! His rifle shoots well, and he never misses; but like the pistol of the white leader, it's useless against the life of Le Subtil."

"Le Renard is too brave to dwell on the wounds suffered in battle, or to remember the hands that inflicted them."

"Was it war when the exhausted Indian stopped at the maple tree to eat his corn? Who filled the bushes with sneaking enemies? Who drew the knife, whose words spoke of peace while his heart was stained with blood? Did Magua say that the hatchet was dug up from the ground, and that his own hand had unearthed it?"

Since Duncan didn't dare fight back against his accuser by pointing out the man's own planned betrayal, and he refused to calm his anger with any apologetic words, he stayed quiet. Magua also seemed satisfied to leave both the argument and any further conversation at that point, as he returned to his relaxed position leaning against the rock from which he had briefly risen in a moment of intensity. However, the shout of "La Longue Carabine" started up again the moment the restless warriors realized that the brief exchange had come to an end.

"You hear," said Magua, with stubborn indifference: "the red Hurons are demanding the life of 'The Long Rifle', or they will spill the blood of whoever is hiding him!"

"He is gone—escaped; he is far beyond their reach."

Renard smiled with cold contempt as he replied:

"When the white man dies, he believes he has found peace; but the red men understand how to torment even the spirits of their enemies. Where is his body? Let the Hurons see his scalp."

"He is not dead, but escaped."

Magua shook his head in disbelief.

"Is he a bird that can spread his wings and fly, or is he a fish that can swim without needing air! The white chief has read his books, and now he thinks the Hurons are fools!"

"Even though he's not a fish, 'The Long Rifle' knows how to swim. He drifted downstream after all the gunpowder had been used up, while the Hurons couldn't see what was happening."

"And why did the white chief stay?" demanded the still disbelieving Indian. "Is he a stone that sinks to the bottom, or does the scalp burn his head?"

"If I weren't made of stone, your dead companion who fell into the waterfall might tell you the answer, if he were still alive," said the angry young man, using the kind of boastful speech that would most likely impress an Indian when he was furious. "White men believe that only cowards abandon their women."

Magua mumbled a few words under his breath that couldn't be heard, before he spoke out loud:

"Can the Delawares swim as well as they can crawl through the bushes? Where is 'Le Gros Serpent'?"

Duncan, who realized from hearing these Canadian names that his recent companions were far more familiar to his enemies than they were to him, replied reluctantly: "He also went down with the water."

"Le Cerf Agile' is not here?"

"I don't know who you're referring to when you say 'The Nimble Deer'," Duncan said, gladly taking advantage of any opportunity to buy more time.

"Uncas," Magua replied, struggling even more with the Delaware name than he did with his English words. "Bounding Elk' is what the white man calls the young Mohican."

"There seems to be some confusion about names between us, Le Renard," Duncan said, hoping to start a discussion. "Daim is the French word for deer, and cerf means stag; elan is the correct term when someone wants to refer to an elk."

"Yes," the Indian muttered in his native language, "the pale faces are chattering women! They use two words for everything, while a red man lets the sound of his voice speak for itself." Then, switching to English, he continued, using the incomplete vocabulary his local teachers had given him. "The deer runs fast but lacks strength; the elk runs fast and has strength; and the son of 'Le Serpent' is 'Le Cerf Agile.' Has he crossed the river to reach the woods?"

"If you're talking about the younger Delaware, he has also drowned in the water."

Since there was nothing unlikely about the escape method from an Indian's perspective, Magua accepted what he had heard as true, showing a willingness that provided further proof of how little value he placed on such worthless prisoners. However, his companions clearly felt differently about the situation.

The Hurons had waited for the outcome of this brief conversation with their typical patience, maintaining a silence that deepened until a complete stillness settled over the group. When Heyward stopped speaking, they turned their eyes as one toward Magua, demanding through this meaningful gesture an explanation of what had been discussed. Their interpreter gestured toward the river and informed them of the outcome, communicating as much through his actions as through the few words he spoke. When the situation became clear to everyone, the warriors let out a terrifying yell that revealed the depth of their frustration. Some rushed wildly to the water's edge, striking the air with frenzied movements, while others spat into the water to express their anger at what they saw as its betrayal of their rightful claims as victors. A few members of the group, among the most powerful and intimidating of the band, cast dark looks filled with fierce anger that was only restrained by their natural self-control at the prisoners who remained under their control, while one or two even expressed their hostile feelings through threatening gestures that offered no protection based on the captives' gender or the sisters' beauty. The young soldier made a desperate but unsuccessful attempt to rush to Alice's side when he witnessed a warrior's dark hand twisted in the abundant locks flowing over her shoulders, while a knife was held around the head from which her hair fell, as if to indicate the horrible way it was about to be stripped of its lovely adornment. However, his hands were tied, and at his first movement, he felt the grip of the powerful leader of the group pressing against his shoulder like a clamp. Immediately understanding how useless any resistance against such overwhelming strength would be, he accepted his situation, comforting his gentle companions with quiet and caring words of reassurance that the natives rarely carried out more than a fraction of their threats.

While Duncan offered these comforting words to calm the sisters' fears, he wasn't foolish enough to deceive himself. He understood perfectly that an Indian chief's authority was hardly based on formal rules, and was more often upheld through physical dominance than through any moral authority he might hold. The danger was therefore increased in direct proportion to the number of hostile warriors surrounding them. Even the most direct order from the man who appeared to be their recognized leader could be ignored at any moment by some impulsive warrior who decided to kill a captive as an offering to the spirit of a deceased friend or family member. So while Duncan maintained an outward show of composure and courage, his heart jumped into his throat whenever any of their fierce captors came closer than usual to the defenseless sisters, or fixed one of their dark, roaming stares on those delicate figures who were so poorly equipped to withstand even the smallest attack.

His fears were greatly eased when he saw that the leader had called his warriors together for a meeting. Their discussion was brief, and judging by how quiet most of the group remained, the decision appeared to be unanimous. From how often the few speakers gestured toward Webb's camp, it was clear they feared danger approaching from that direction. This concern likely sped up their decision-making and made their following actions more urgent.

During his brief meeting, Heyward found a break from his most serious worries and had time to appreciate the careful way the Hurons had advanced, even after the fighting had stopped.

It had already been mentioned that the upper half of the island was bare rock, lacking any defenses except for a few scattered pieces of driftwood. They had chosen this spot to make their way down, having carried the canoe through the forest around the waterfall for this very purpose. After placing their weapons in the small boat, a dozen men gripping its sides had entrusted themselves to the canoe's guidance, which was steered by two of the most experienced warriors positioned so they could see the treacherous passage ahead. Thanks to this strategy, they reached the head of the island at the same location that had proven deadly to their earlier companions, but now they had the benefits of greater numbers and firearms. The way they had made their descent became completely clear to Duncan, as they now carried the lightweight canoe from the upper end of the rock and set it in the water near the entrance to the outer cave. Once this move was completed, the leader gestured for the prisoners to come down and get in.

Since resistance was futile and protests would accomplish nothing, Heyward demonstrated compliance by stepping into the canoe first, where he quickly found himself seated alongside the sisters and the still bewildered David. Although the Hurons lacked knowledge of the narrow passages between the whirlpools and rushing waters of the river, they understood the basic principles of such navigation well enough to avoid any serious mistakes. Once the pilot selected to steer the canoe had assumed his position, the entire group waded back into the river, the boat drifted downstream with the current, and within minutes the prisoners discovered they were on the southern shore of the waterway, almost directly across from where they had reached it the night before.

Here was held another brief but serious discussion, during which the horses, whose panic their owners blamed for their greatest misfortune, were led from the shelter of the woods and brought to the protected location. The group now split up. The great chief, so frequently mentioned, mounting Heyward's horse, led the way directly across the river, followed by most of his people, and vanished into the woods, leaving the prisoners under the guard of six warriors, led by Le Renard Subtil. Duncan watched all their movements with fresh anxiety.

He had liked to believe, based on the unusual restraint shown by the natives, that he was being kept as a prisoner to be handed over to Montcalm. Since the minds of those who suffer rarely rest, and creativity is never sharper than when driven by hope, no matter how weak and distant, he had even convinced himself that Munro's fatherly emotions would be used as a tool to tempt him away from his loyalty to the king. While the French commander had a strong reputation for bravery and bold action, he was also considered skilled in those political tactics that don't always honor the finer points of moral duty, and which so commonly tainted European diplomacy during that era.

All those complex and clever theories were now completely destroyed by how his captors behaved. The part of the group that had followed the massive warrior headed toward the base of Lake George, leaving him and his companions with no other prospect than being held as prisoners without hope by their brutal captors. Eager to understand the full extent of their situation, and ready, in such a crisis, to test the power of money, he pushed past his hesitation to speak with Magua. Speaking to his former guide, who had now taken on the authority and demeanor of someone who would control the group's future actions, he said in the most friendly and trusting voice he could manage:

"I want to speak with Magua about something that only such a great chief should hear."

The Indian looked at the young soldier with contempt as he replied:

"Speak; trees have no ears."

"But the red Hurons are not deaf; and counsel that is fit for the great men of a nation would make the young warriors drunk. If Magua will not listen, the officer of the king knows how to be silent."

The warrior spoke casually to his companions, who were working in their clumsy way to prepare the horses for the sisters, and stepped slightly aside, where he used a careful gesture to encourage Heyward to follow him.

"Now, speak," he said; "if the words are what Magua should hear."

"Le Renard Subtil has shown himself deserving of the respected name his Canadian fathers gave him," Heyward began; "I recognize his wisdom and everything he has accomplished for us, and I will remember it when the time comes to reward him. Yes! Renard has demonstrated that he is not only a great chief in council, but also one who knows how to outwit his enemies!"

"What has Renard done?" the Indian asked coldly.

"What! Hasn't he seen that the woods were full of enemy scouting parties, and that the serpent couldn't slip through them without being spotted? Then, didn't he lose his trail on purpose to fool the Hurons? Didn't he pretend to return to his tribe, who had mistreated him and driven him from their lodges like a dog? And when we saw what he intended to do, didn't we help him by putting on a false front, so the Hurons would think the white man believed his friend was actually his enemy? Isn't all of this true? And when Le Subtil had blinded and deafened his nation through his cleverness, didn't they forget they had once wronged him and forced him to flee to the Mohawks? And didn't they leave him on the south side of the river with their prisoners, while they foolishly went north? Doesn't Renard plan to double back like a fox on his own trail and bring the wealthy, gray-haired Scotsman his daughters? Yes, Magua, I see it all clearly, and I've already been considering how such wisdom and loyalty should be rewarded. First, the commander of William Henry will pay as a great chief should for such service. Magua's medal will no longer be made of tin, but of hammered gold; his powder horn will overflow; silver dollars will be as common in his pouch as stones on the shore of Horican; and deer will come to lick his hand, knowing it's useless to run from the rifle he'll carry! As for myself, I don't know how to match the Scotsman's gratitude, but I—yes, I will—"[1]

> [1] It has long been a practice among white people to win over important Indian leaders by giving them medals, which they wear instead of their own simple ornaments. The medals given by the English typically feature an image of the current king, while those given by Americans show the president.

"What will the young chief, who comes from the direction of the sun, offer?" the Huron demanded, noticing that Heyward was hesitating in his attempt to conclude his list of benefits with something that might represent the ultimate fulfillment of an Indian's desires.

"He will make the liquor from the islands in the salt lake flow in front of Magua's dwelling, until the Indian's heart becomes lighter than hummingbird feathers, and his breath becomes sweeter than wild honeysuckle."

Le Renard had listened seriously as Heyward slowly delivered this clever speech. When the young man mentioned the deception he believed the Indian had used against his own people, the listener's face took on an expression of careful seriousness. At the reference to the wrong that Duncan pretended to think had forced the Huron away from his birth tribe, such a flash of uncontrollable rage shot from the other man's eyes that it made the bold speaker believe he had hit the right note. And by the time he reached the part where he so skillfully mixed the hunger for revenge with the desire for profit, he had at least gained complete control of the savage's deepest attention. The question Le Renard had asked was calm and carried all the dignity of an Indian; but it was quite clear from the thoughtful look on the listener's face that the answer had been very cleverly crafted. The Huron thought for a few moments, and then placing his hand on the rough bandages covering his wounded shoulder, he spoke with some force:

"Do friends make such marks?"

"Would 'La Longue Carbine' inflict such a minor wound on an enemy?"

"Do the Delawares sneak up on those they love like snakes, coiling themselves to attack?"

"Would 'Le Gros Serpent' have reached the ears of someone he wanted to remain deaf?"

"Does the white chief fire his weapons at his own brothers?"

"Does he ever miss his target when he's truly determined to kill?" Duncan replied, smiling with convincing sincerity.

Another long and deliberate pause followed these meaningful questions and quick replies. Duncan could see that the Indian was hesitating. To secure his victory completely, he was about to start listing the rewards again, when Magua made a significant gesture and spoke:

"Enough; Le Renard is a wise chief, and what he does will be seen. Go, and keep your mouth shut. When Magua speaks, it will be the time to answer."

Heyward noticed that his companion was carefully watching the rest of the group, so he quickly stepped back to avoid looking like he was conspiring with their leader. Magua walked over to the horses and pretended to be satisfied with his companions' hard work and cleverness. He then gestured for Heyward to help the sisters mount their horses, since he rarely bothered to speak

English unless something particularly important motivated him to do so.

There was no longer any believable excuse for delay, and Duncan was forced, though reluctantly, to go along with it. As he carried out this task, he whispered his renewed hopes to the frightened women, who rarely lifted their eyes from the ground out of fear of seeing the fierce faces of their captors. David's mare had been taken by the followers of the main chief, which meant that both its owner and Duncan had to travel on foot. Duncan didn't mind this situation too much, though, since it might allow him to slow down the group's pace. He kept looking back longingly toward Fort Edward, hoping in vain to hear some sound from that part of the forest that might signal help was coming. When everyone was ready, Magua gave the signal to move forward, taking the lead himself at the front of the group. David followed next, gradually becoming more aware of his situation as the effects of his injury became less noticeable. The sisters rode behind him, with Heyward walking alongside them, while the Indians spread out on the sides of the group and brought up the rear, maintaining a watchfulness that never seemed to fade.

They continued moving forward in unbroken silence, broken only when Heyward spoke a few comforting words to the women, or when David released his inner anguish through sorrowful cries that were meant to show humble acceptance of their fate. They were heading south, traveling in almost the opposite direction from the road to William Henry. Despite Magua's apparent commitment to his captors' original plan, Heyward couldn't believe that his appealing offer had been forgotten so quickly; he understood Indian travel routes too well to think that the obvious path led straight to the final destination when deception might be needed. Mile after mile passed through the endless forest in this agonizing way, with no sign that their journey would end anytime soon. Heyward watched the sun as it cast its midday light through the tree branches, longing for the moment when Magua's strategy would shift their route to something more promising for his plans. At times he imagined that the cautious savage, losing hope of safely passing Montcalm's army, was heading toward a famous border settlement where a prominent crown officer and trusted ally of the Six Nations maintained both his extensive lands and his regular home. Being handed over to Sir William Johnson would be much better than being taken into the Canadian wilderness; but even to achieve that outcome, they would need to travel through the forest for many exhausting leagues, with each step taking him farther from the battlefield and therefore from his position of both honor and responsibility.

Cora was the only one who remembered the scout's parting instructions, and whenever she got the chance, she reached out to bend back the branches that touched her hands. However, the Indians' constant watchfulness made this precautionary act both difficult and dangerous. She was frequently thwarted in her efforts when she caught sight of their alert eyes, forcing her to pretend to be startled when she wasn't and use her arm for some gesture of feminine fear instead. Only once was she completely successful; she managed to break down the branch of a large sumac, and in a moment of quick thinking, dropped her glove at the same time. This marker, meant for anyone who might be following them, was noticed by one of her captors, who picked up the glove and broke the remaining branches of the bush in such a way that it looked like some animal had been struggling through it, then placed his hand on his tomahawk with such a meaningful look that it effectively ended her attempts to leave these secret traces of their route.

Since there were horses in both groups of Indians that would leave footprints, this interruption eliminated any realistic chance of getting help by following their trail.

Heyward might have tried to protest if there had been anything hopeful in Magua's dark silence. However, throughout this entire journey, the Native American rarely turned to look back at those following him and never spoke a word. Using only the sun as his compass, or relying on subtle landmarks that only someone with his native expertise could recognize, he navigated through the barren pine forests, occasional small fertile valleys, across streams and creeks, and over rolling hills with the precision of natural instinct and almost the direct path of a flying bird. He never appeared to hesitate. Whether the trail was barely visible, whether it vanished completely, or whether it stretched clear and well-worn ahead of him made no noticeable difference in his pace or confidence. It appeared as though exhaustion could never touch him. Whenever the tired travelers lifted their eyes from the fallen leaves beneath their feet, they could see his dark figure moving swiftly between the tree trunks ahead, his head fixed steadily forward, with the bright feather on his head dancing in the breeze created entirely by his rapid movement.

But all this careful effort and quick pace had a purpose. After crossing a shallow valley where a rushing stream wound its way through, he suddenly climbed a hill so steep and challenging that the sisters had to get down and walk in order to keep up. When they reached the top, they discovered they were on a flat area sparsely dotted with trees, and under one of these trees Magua had positioned his dark figure, as if he was prepared and eager to find the rest that the entire group desperately needed.

--------

# Chapter XI.

"Cursed be my tribe If I forgive him."
—Shylock

The Native American had chosen for this strategic purpose one of those steep, pyramid-shaped hills that strongly resemble man-made mounds and appear frequently throughout American valleys. The hill he selected was tall and steep, with a flattened top as was typical, though one side was more jagged than usual. It offered no other obvious benefits as a resting spot beyond its height and shape, which would make defending it easier and being caught off guard nearly impossible. Since Heyward no longer held hope for the rescue that time and distance had made so unlikely, he looked at these minor features without interest, focusing entirely on providing comfort and consolation to his weaker companions. The Narragansett horses were allowed to graze on the branches of trees and bushes that grew sparsely across the hilltop, while what remained of their food supplies was laid out beneath the shade of a beech tree whose horizontal branches spread like a canopy overhead.

Despite how quickly they were moving, one of the Indians had managed to find a chance to shoot a wandering fawn with an arrow, and had carried the best pieces of the animal patiently on his shoulders to their resting spot. Without any help from cooking skills, he immediately joined his companions in devouring this nourishing food. Only Magua sat by himself, not taking part in the disgusting meal, and seemed lost in deep thought.

This remarkable self-restraint from an Indian, especially when he had the means to satisfy his hunger, eventually caught Heyward's attention. The young man readily assumed that the Huron was carefully considering the best way to escape the watchful eyes of his companions. Hoping to help his plans with any ideas of his own and to make the temptation stronger, he left the beech tree and wandered, as if aimlessly, to the place where Le Renard was sitting.

"Hasn't Magua traveled toward the sun long enough to get away from all the danger the Canadians pose?" he asked, as if he no longer questioned the good understanding they had reached. "And wouldn't the commander of William Henry be happier to see his daughters before another night passes and hardens his heart to losing them, making him less generous with his reward?"

"Do white people love their children less in the morning than at night?" asked the Indian, coldly.

"Absolutely not," Heyward replied, eager to correct his mistake if he had made one. "A white man might forget where his ancestors are buried, and often does. Sometimes he stops remembering those he should love and has promised to care for. But a parent's love for their child is never allowed to fade away."

"And is the heart of the gray-haired leader tender, and will he think of the children that his wives have given him? He is harsh with his warriors and his eyes are made of stone!"

"He is harsh with those who are lazy and evil, but to those who are responsible and worthy he serves as a leader who is both fair and compassionate. I have known many loving and caring parents, but I have never encountered a man whose heart was more tender toward his child. You have witnessed the gray-haired man leading his warriors, Magua; but I have seen his eyes filled with tears when he spoke of those children who are now under your control!"

Heyward stopped speaking, unsure how to interpret the striking expression that flashed across the dark features of the focused Indian. Initially, it appeared as though the memory of the promised reward became clear in his mind as he heard about the parental emotions that would guarantee he received it; however, as Duncan continued talking, the look of satisfaction turned so intensely malicious that it was impossible not to suspect it came from some darker motivation than simple greed.

"Go," said the Huron, instantly suppressing the alarming display with a deathly calm expression; "go to the dark-haired daughter, and tell her, 'Magua waits to speak.' The father will remember what the child promises."

Duncan, who understood this speech as expressing a desire for some additional assurance that the promised gifts would not be withheld, slowly and reluctantly made his way to the place where the sisters were now resting from their exhaustion, to share its meaning with Cora.

"You understand what an Indian desires," he concluded, as he guided her toward the place where she was expected, "and you must be generous with your offers of gunpowder and blankets. Strong liquor is, however, what such men value most; and it wouldn't hurt to add some gift from your own hand, with that charm you know so well how to use. Remember, Cora, that your quick thinking and cleverness may determine not only your own life, but Alice's as well."

"Heyward, and yours!"

"My life doesn't matter much; I've already pledged it to my king, and it's there for the taking by any enemy strong enough to claim it. I have no father waiting for me to return, and only a handful of friends who would mourn a destiny I've pursued with the relentless desire of youth seeking glory. But quiet now! We're getting close to the Indian. Magua, the woman you want to speak with is here."

The Indian slowly rose from his seat and stood silent and motionless for nearly a minute. He then gestured with his hand for Heyward to leave, saying coldly:

"When the Huron speaks to the women, his tribe closes their ears."

Duncan remained where he was, seemingly reluctant to follow the request, when Cora spoke with a serene smile:

"You hear what's being said, Heyward, and common decency should prompt you to step away. Go to Alice and reassure her with the news that our situation is improving."

She waited until he had left, and then turned to the native with the dignity of her gender evident in both her voice and bearing, adding: "What would Le Renard say to the daughter of Munro?"

"Listen," said the Indian, placing his hand firmly on her arm, as if he wanted to capture her complete attention for his words; a gesture that Cora just as firmly but quietly rejected by pulling her arm free from his grip: "Magua was born a chief and a warrior among the red Hurons of the lakes; he watched the suns of twenty summers melt the snows of twenty winters into flowing streams before he ever laid eyes on a pale face; and he was content! Then his Canadian fathers entered the woods and taught him to drink the firewater, and he became a scoundrel. The Hurons banished him from his ancestors' burial grounds, just as they would drive away a hunted buffalo. He fled along the lakeshores and followed the waterway to the 'city of cannon.' There he hunted and fished until the people drove him once more through the forests into the hands of his enemies. The chief who had been born a Huron finally became a warrior among the Mohawks!"

"I had heard something like this before," Cora said, noticing that he stopped to control the emotions that were starting to flare up too intensely as he remembered what he believed were the wrongs done to him.

"Was it Le Renard's fault that his head wasn't made of stone? Who gave him the whiskey? Who turned him into a villain? It was the white men, people of your own race."

"And am I responsible for the fact that thoughtless and unprincipled men exist, whose facial features may resemble mine?" Cora calmly asked the agitated savage.

"No; Magua is a man, and not a fool; people like you never drink the firewater: the Great Spirit has blessed you with wisdom!"

"So what should I do or say about your troubles, not to mention your mistakes?"

"Listen," the Indian repeated, returning to his serious demeanor; "when his English and French fathers took up arms for war, Le Renard joined the Mohawks' war party and turned against his own people. The white men have forced the Native Americans from their hunting territories, and now when they go to battle, a white man commands them. The old chief at Fort William Henry, your father, served as the great leader of our war party. He gave orders to the Mohawks to do this and that, and they obeyed him. He established a rule that if a Native American drank alcohol and entered the tents of his soldiers, it would not be overlooked. Magua foolishly drank, and the strong liquor led him into Munro's quarters. What did the gray-haired man do? Let his daughter tell the story."

"He didn't forget his promise and delivered justice by punishing the wrongdoer," said the fearless daughter.

"Justice!" the Indian repeated, shooting a sideways look of fierce hatred at her unwavering face. "Is it justice to create evil and then punish someone for it? Magua was not in control of himself; it was the alcohol that spoke and acted through him! But Munro believed otherwise. The Huron chief was bound in front of all the white soldiers and beaten like a dog."

Cora stayed quiet, because she didn't know how to soften her father's reckless harshness in a way that would make sense to an Indian.

"Look!" Magua continued, ripping away the thin cotton fabric that barely covered his painted chest; "these are scars from knives and bullets—wounds a warrior can proudly display before his people; but the old man left marks on the Huron chief's back that must be hidden like a woman's shame, beneath this decorated cloth from the white men."

"I thought," Cora continued, "that an Indian warrior was patient, and that his spirit didn't feel or know the pain his body endured."

"When the Chippewas bound Magua to the stake and made this cut," said the other, placing his finger on a deep scar, "the Huron laughed at them and declared, Women hit so weakly! His spirit soared high then! But when he experienced Munro's strikes, his spirit was crushed beneath the birch. A Huron's spirit never becomes intoxicated; it remembers everything forever!"

"But it can be calmed. If my father has wronged you, show him how an Indian can forgive a wrong, and take back his daughters. You have heard from Major Heyward—"

Magua shook his head, refusing to let them repeat offers he found so contemptible.

"What do you want?" Cora continued after an extremely painful silence, as the realization dawned on her that the overly optimistic and noble Duncan had been ruthlessly tricked by the craftiness of the savage.

"What a Huron loves—good for good; bad for bad!"

"So you want to get back at Munro for the harm he caused his defenseless daughters. Wouldn't it be more honorable to confront him directly and settle this like a warrior?"

"The white men have long reach, and their blades are sharp!" the savage replied with a cruel laugh. "Why should Le Renard walk among his warriors' guns when he holds the old man's soul in his grasp?"

"Tell us what you want, Magua," Cora said, fighting to keep her voice calm and steady. "Are you planning to take us as prisoners into the forest, or do you have something even worse in mind? Isn't there some reward we could offer, some way to make up for the wrong done to you and soften your heart? At the very least, let my gentle sister go free and take out all your hatred on me instead. You could gain riches by ensuring her safety and satisfy your need for revenge with just one victim. If the old man loses both his daughters, it might kill him, and then what satisfaction would Le Renard have?"

"Listen," the Indian said again. "The one with light eyes can return to Lake George and tell the old chief what happened, if the dark-haired woman will swear by the Great Spirit of her ancestors to speak only the truth."

"What do I need to promise?" Cora asked, still keeping her mysterious control over the savage warrior through her calm and graceful feminine presence.

"When Magua left his people, his wife was given to another chief. He has now become allies with the Hurons and will return to the burial grounds of his tribe on the shores of the great lake. Let the daughter of the English chief come with him and live in his home forever."

However disgusting such a proposal might be to Cora, she maintained enough self-control, despite her strong revulsion, to respond without revealing her vulnerability.

"And what joy would Magua find in sharing his home with a wife he didn't love; someone who would belong to a different nation and race than his own? It would be wiser to accept Munro's gold and use his wealth to win the affection of some Huron woman."

The Indian remained silent for nearly a minute, fixing his fierce gaze on Cora's face with such unsettling looks that her eyes dropped in shame, feeling for the first time that she had met an expression no virtuous woman should have to bear. As she recoiled inwardly, fearing her ears might be assaulted by some suggestion even more appalling than what had come before, Magua's voice responded with tones of profound malice:

"When the blows burned the back of the Huron, he would know where to find a woman to feel the pain. Munro's daughter would draw his water, tend his corn, and cook his venison. The gray-haired man's body would sleep among his cannons, but his heart would lie within reach of Le Subtil's knife."

"Monster! You truly deserve that treacherous name," Cora shouted in an uncontrollable outburst of filial rage. "Only a demon could plan such revenge. But you're overestimating your power! You'll discover that you really do hold Munro's heart, and that it will resist your worst cruelty!"

The Indian responded to this bold challenge with a chilling smile that revealed his unchanged intentions, while he gestured for her to leave, as if to end their conversation permanently. Cora, already regretting her hasty words, had no choice but to obey, since Magua immediately departed from the spot and walked toward his greedy companions. Heyward rushed to the distressed woman's side and asked about the outcome of the conversation he had been watching from a distance with such keen interest. However, not wanting to frighten Alice, she avoided giving a direct answer, revealing her concern only through her worried glances fixed on every slight movement of their captors. When her sister repeatedly and urgently asked about where they were likely being taken, she gave no response other than pointing toward the dark group with uncontrollable agitation, whispering as she pulled Alice close to her chest.

"There, there; read our fortunes in their faces; we shall see; we shall see!"

The gesture and Cora's strangled words conveyed more meaning than any speech could have, immediately capturing her companions' attention and directing it to the same place where her own gaze was fixed with an intensity that only the critical importance of what was at stake could produce.

When Magua reached the group of lounging warriors, who had stuffed themselves with their revolting feast and now lay sprawled on the ground in crude satisfaction, he began to speak with the authority of an Indian chief. The first words he spoke immediately caused his listeners to sit up in postures of respectful attention. Since the Huron spoke in his native tongue, the captives, despite the fact that their guards had kept them close enough to be within striking distance of their tomahawks, could only guess at the meaning of his speech from the expressive hand movements and gestures that Indians always use to accompany their words.

At first, Magua's language and actions seemed calm and thoughtful. Once he had successfully captured his companions' attention, Heyward noticed that his frequent gesturing toward the great lakes suggested he was speaking about their ancestral homeland and their distant tribe. The listeners frequently showed their approval, uttering the expressive "Hugh!" while looking at each other with admiration for the speaker. Le Renard was too clever to waste this opportunity. He then spoke about the long and difficult journey they had taken from those vast lands and peaceful villages to come and fight against the enemies of their Canadian allies. He listed the warriors in their group, describing each one's individual qualities, their repeated service to the nation, their battle wounds, and the number of scalps they had claimed. Whenever he mentioned anyone present (and the cunning Indian overlooked no one), that flattered person's dark face lit up with pride, and he didn't hesitate to confirm the truth of these words through gestures of approval and agreement. Then the speaker's voice dropped and lost the loud, spirited tones of victory with which he had recounted their successful deeds and triumphs. He described Glenn's waterfall, the unassailable position of its rocky island with its caves and countless rapids and whirlpools; he spoke the name "La Longue Carabine" and waited until the forest below had echoed back the final sound of the loud and prolonged yell that greeted this despised name. He pointed toward the young military prisoner and described the death of a beloved warrior who had been thrown into the deep canyon by his hand. He not only told of the fate of the one who, suspended between heaven and earth, had created such a horrifying sight for the entire group, but he reenacted the terror of his situation, his bravery, and his death using the branches of a young tree; and finally, he quickly retold how each of their friends had died, always emphasizing their courage and their most recognized virtues. When this account of events was finished, his voice changed once again, becoming sorrowful and even melodic in its low, throaty tones. He now spoke of the wives and children of the dead; their poverty; their suffering, both physical and emotional; their isolation; and finally, their unresolved grievances. Then suddenly raising his voice to a pitch of terrible intensity, he concluded by demanding:

"Are the Hurons dogs to endure this? Who will tell the wife of Menowgua that the fish have claimed his scalp, and that his people have failed to seek revenge! Who will dare face the mother of Wassawattimie, that proud woman, with clean hands! What will we say to the elders when they demand scalps from us, and we don't have a single hair from a white man's head to offer them! The women will mock us with pointed fingers. There is a dark stain on the honor of the Hurons, and it must be washed away with blood!" His voice could no longer be heard above the explosion of fury that erupted into the air, as if the forest, rather than holding such a small group, was filled with the entire nation. Throughout the preceding speech, those most invested in his success could clearly read the speaker's impact through the expressions on the faces of the men he addressed. They had responded to his sorrow and mourning with understanding and grief; his declarations with confirming gestures; and his boasting with savage triumph. When he spoke of bravery, their expressions became steady and supportive; when he referred to their wounds, their eyes blazed with anger; when he mentioned the women's mockery, they hung their heads in disgrace; but when he outlined their path to revenge, he touched something that never failed to stir within an Indian's heart. At the first hint that vengeance was within their grasp, the entire group leaped to their feet as one; expressing their rage through wild screams, they charged at their captives together with drawn knives and raised tomahawks. Heyward positioned himself between the sisters and the leader, wrestling with him using desperate strength that momentarily stopped his attack. This unexpected resistance gave Magua the opportunity to step in, and with quick speech and lively gestures, he redirected the group's attention back to himself. Using the persuasive tone he had mastered so well, he turned his companions away from their immediate goal and convinced them to extend their victims' suffering. His suggestion was met with enthusiastic approval and carried out with lightning speed.

Two powerful warriors threw themselves at Heyward, while another focused on capturing the less combative singing-master. Neither prisoner gave up without a desperate, though futile, fight. Even David managed to knock his attacker to the ground; Heyward wasn't subdued until the Indians had defeated his companion and could combine their efforts against him. He was then tied and bound to the trunk of the young tree where Magua had performed his mime of the dying Huron. When the young soldier came back to his senses, he faced the agonizing reality that the same fate awaited their entire group. To his right sat Cora, imprisoned just as he was, pale and shaken, but her steady gaze still tracked their captors' movements. To his left, the rope bindings that secured Alice to a pine tree supported her trembling body when her own strength failed, keeping her delicate frame from collapsing. Her hands were pressed together in prayer, but rather than looking up toward the only power that could save them, her unfocused eyes drifted toward Duncan's face with childlike dependence. David had fought back, and the strangeness of his situation left him quiet, pondering whether his unusual behavior had been appropriate.

The Hurons' desire for revenge had now shifted in a new direction, and they began preparing to carry it out with the savage creativity that centuries of practice had made second nature to them. Some warriors searched for knots to build up the blazing fire; one was splitting pine wood into sharp pieces so he could stab their prisoners with the burning splinters; and others were bending the tops of two young trees down to the ground so they could hang Heyward by his arms between the springing branches. But Magua's thirst for vengeance craved a more profound and vicious satisfaction.

While the cruder members of the group prepared their familiar and common methods of torture in full view of those who would endure them, he moved closer to Cora and indicated, with the most malicious expression on his face, the swift doom that lay ahead of her:

"Ha!" he added, "what does Munro's daughter say? Her head is too valuable to rest on a pillow in Le Renard's wigwam; will she prefer it when it rolls around this hill as a toy for the wolves? Her chest cannot feed the children of a Huron; she will watch it be spat upon by Indians!"

"What does this monster mean!" demanded the astonished Heyward.

"Nothing!" came the resolute answer. "He is a savage, a barbarous and ignorant savage, and doesn't know what he's doing. Let us find time, with our dying breath, to ask for his repentance and forgiveness."

"Forgive you!" the fierce Huron repeated angrily, misunderstanding what she meant; "an Indian's memory lasts no longer than a white man's reach; his mercy is shorter than their sense of justice! Tell me; should I send the blonde woman to her father, and will you come with Magua to the great lakes, to bring him water and feed him corn?"

Cora waved him away, unable to hide the disgust she felt.

"Leave me alone," she said, with such seriousness that it momentarily stopped the Indian's cruelty; "you're adding bitterness to my prayers; you're standing between me and my God!"

The small impact made on the savage was quickly forgotten, however, and he kept pointing toward Alice with mocking sarcasm.

"Look! The child is crying! She's too young to die! Send her to Munro, to comb his gray hair, and keep the old man's heart alive."

Cora couldn't resist the urge to look at her young sister, whose eyes met hers with a pleading expression that revealed her natural yearnings.

"What did he say, dearest Cora?" asked Alice in a trembling voice. "Did he mention sending me to our father?"

For several moments, the older sister gazed at the younger one, her face showing the struggle of intense and conflicting emotions. Finally she spoke, though her voice had lost its rich and calm depth, taking on an expression of tenderness that seemed motherly.

"Alice," she said, "the Huron is offering both of us our lives, and actually more than that; he's offering to return Duncan, our precious Duncan, along with you, to our friends—to our father— to our heartbroken, childless father, if I will set aside this defiant, stubborn pride of mine, and agree—"

Her voice became choked, and clasping her hands together, she looked upward, as if searching in her anguish for understanding from an infinite wisdom.

"Keep talking," Alice exclaimed; "to what, dearest Cora? Oh! if only that offer were made to me! To save you, to comfort our elderly father, to bring Duncan back, how gladly I would die!"

"Die!" Cora repeated, her voice now calmer and steadier, "that would be easy! Perhaps the other choice might not be any less difficult. He wants me," she continued, her voice dropping as she became deeply aware of how degrading his proposal was, "to follow him into the wilderness; to go live among the Hurons; to stay there; in other words, to become his wife! Speak then, Alice; child of my heart! sister of my love! And you too, Major Heyward, help my confused mind with your advice. Should life be bought with such a sacrifice? Will you, Alice, accept it from me at such a cost? And you, Duncan, guide me; help me decide between you both; because I belong completely to you!"

"Would I!" the young man echoed, his voice filled with indignation and shock. "Cora! Cora! you're making light of our suffering! Don't mention that terrible option again; the very idea is worse than dying a thousand times."

"I knew that would be your response!" Cora exclaimed, her cheeks turning red and her dark eyes sparkling again with the intense emotions of a woman. "What does my Alice say? I'll accept her decision without any further complaint."

Although both Heyward and Cora listened with anxious suspense and complete attention, they heard no sounds in response. Alice's delicate and sensitive figure seemed to withdraw into itself as she listened to this suggestion. Her arms had dropped to her sides, her fingers twitching in small spasms; her head fell forward onto her chest, and her entire body appeared to lean against the tree, resembling a beautiful symbol of her wounded feminine dignity, lifeless yet acutely aware. After a few moments, however, her head began to move slowly from side to side, expressing deep, unwavering disapproval.

"No, no, no; it's better that we die as we have lived, together!"

"Then die!" Magua screamed, hurling his tomahawk with brutal force at the defiant speaker, grinding his teeth in fury that could no longer be contained at this unexpected display of courage from the one he had considered the weakest of the group. The axe sliced through the air in front of Heyward, cutting through some of Alice's flowing curls before embedding itself in the tree above her head. The scene drove Duncan into a frenzy of desperation. Gathering all his strength in one explosive effort, he broke free from the twigs that bound him and lunged at another warrior who was preparing, with wild shouts and more careful aim, to strike again. They collided, wrestled, and crashed to the ground together. His opponent's bare skin gave Heyward nothing to grip, and the man slipped from his hold, rising again to pin Duncan down with one knee on his chest, pressing him to the earth with tremendous weight. Duncan could already see the blade flashing in the air when a whistling sound rushed past him, accompanied—or perhaps followed—by the sharp report of a rifle. He felt the crushing weight lift from his chest; he watched as his enemy's savage expression transformed into a look of empty confusion, and then the Indian collapsed dead onto the withered leaves beside him.

---

# Chapter XII.

"Clo.—I am gone, sire,
And anon, sire, I'll be with you again."
—Twelfth Night

The Hurons were stunned by this sudden death that struck one of their group. However, as they considered the deadly precision of a shot that had dared to kill an enemy while risking a friend's life, the name "La Longue Carabine" erupted from every mouth at once, followed by a wild and mournful howl. The cry was met by a loud shout from a small thicket where the careless group had stacked their weapons; and in the next moment, Hawkeye, too impatient to reload the rifle he had recovered, could be seen charging toward them, swinging the clubbed weapon and slicing through the air with wide and powerful strokes. As bold and swift as the scout's advance was, it was surpassed by that of a light and energetic figure that bounded past him, leaping with incredible agility and boldness into the very heart of the Huron group, where it stood spinning a tomahawk and waving a gleaming knife with terrifying threats in front of Cora. Faster than thoughts could follow these unexpected and daring movements, a figure armed in the symbolic armor of death glided before their eyes and took a menacing position at the other's side. The savage torturers fell back before these warlike intruders and voiced, as they appeared in such rapid succession, the frequently repeated and distinctive cries of surprise, followed by the well-known and feared names of:

"The Agile Stag! The Great Serpent!"

However, the cautious and alert Huron leader wasn't easily thrown off balance. Sweeping his sharp gaze across the small clearing, he instantly understood the nature of the attack, and while rallying his men with both his voice and his actions, he drew his long and deadly knife and charged with a fierce war cry toward the anticipated Chingachgook. This served as the signal for an all-out battle. Neither side carried guns, and the fight would be settled in the most lethal way possible, in close combat, using only weapons meant to kill, with no means of protection.

Uncas responded to the war cry, and jumping onto an enemy, he split the man's skull to the brain with a single, perfectly aimed strike of his tomahawk. Heyward grabbed Magua's weapon from the young tree and charged eagerly into the battle. Since the fighters were now equal in number, each one picked an opponent from the opposing group. The attack and strikes came with the violence of a tornado and the speed of lightning. Hawkeye quickly brought another enemy within range of his arm, and with one swing of his powerful weapon he knocked down his opponent's weak and crude defenses, smashing him to the ground with the blow. Heyward dared to throw the tomahawk he had grabbed, too eager to wait for the right moment to get closer. It hit the Indian he had chosen in the forehead and stopped his forward charge for a moment. Motivated by this small advantage, the reckless young man kept attacking and jumped on his enemy with bare hands. A single moment was enough to show him how foolish this action was, because he immediately found himself completely occupied, using all his energy and bravery, trying to block the desperate stabs made with the Huron's knife. No longer able to outsmart an enemy so quick and watchful, he wrapped his arms around him and managed to trap the other man's limbs against his side with a grip like iron, but one that was far too draining for him to maintain for long. In this desperate situation he heard a voice near him, calling out:

"Wipe out those scoundrels! Show no mercy to a cursed enemy!"

At the next moment, Hawkeye's rifle butt struck the bare head of his opponent, whose muscles seemed to collapse under the impact as he slipped from Duncan's arms, limp and still.

When Uncas had killed his first opponent, he turned like a starving lion to find another. The fifth and only remaining Huron who had broken away during the initial attack had stopped for a moment, and then seeing that everyone around him was engaged in deadly combat, he had tried, with evil revenge in mind, to finish the failed work of vengeance. Letting out a triumphant shout, he lunged toward the helpless Cora, hurling his sharp axe as the terrible herald of his attack. The tomahawk scraped her shoulder, and cutting through the ropes that tied her to the tree, left the young woman free to escape. She avoided the savage's grip, and without regard for her own safety, threw herself onto Alice's chest, struggling with shaking and clumsy fingers to tear apart the branches that held her sister captive. Anyone other than a monster would have shown mercy at such an act of selfless devotion to the deepest and most pure love; but the Huron's heart knew no compassion. Grabbing Cora by the beautiful hair that fell in disorder around her body, he pulled her away from her desperate grip and forced her down with savage brutality to her knees. The savage ran the flowing locks through his hand, and lifting them high with an extended arm, he moved the knife around the perfectly shaped head of his victim, with a mocking and triumphant laugh. But he paid for this moment of cruel satisfaction with the loss of the deadly chance. It was exactly then that the scene caught Uncas's attention. Leaping from where he stood, he appeared for an instant flying through the air and dropping like a cannonball, he landed on his enemy's chest, hurling him many yards away, headfirst and flat on the ground. The force of the effort threw the young Mohican down beside him. They got up together, fought, and bled, each taking turns. But the battle was quickly settled; Heyward's tomahawk and Hawkeye's rifle struck the Huron's skull at the exact same moment that Uncas's knife pierced his heart.

The battle had now completely ended except for the prolonged fight between "Le Renard Subtil" and "Le Gros Serpent." These fierce warriors clearly proved they deserved those meaningful names they had earned through their actions in previous wars. When they first clashed, some time passed as they dodged the swift and powerful strikes aimed at their lives. Suddenly lunging at each other, they grappled and fell to the ground, intertwined like coiling serpents in flexible and cunning embraces. When the victors found themselves with nothing left to do, the area where these skilled and desperate fighters lay could only be identified by a swirling cloud of dust and leaves that drifted from the center of the small clearing toward its edge, as if stirred up by a passing tornado. Driven by different feelings of family love, friendship, and thankfulness, Heyward and his companions rushed together toward the spot, surrounding the small dome of dust that hovered over the warriors. Uncas circled the cloud uselessly, hoping to plunge his knife into his father's enemy's heart; Hawkeye's menacing rifle was lifted and held without purpose, while Duncan tried to grab the Huron's limbs with hands that seemed to have lost their strength. Covered in dust and blood as they were, the rapid movements of the fighters seemed to merge their bodies into one. The deathly appearance of the Mohican and the dark shape of the Huron flashed before their eyes in such rapid and chaotic sequence that the allies of the former couldn't tell where to deliver a helping blow. There were indeed brief and passing moments when Magua's blazing eyes could be seen gleaming like the legendary eyes of the basilisk through the dusty haze that surrounded him, and he could read from those quick and lethal looks the outcome of the fight in front of his enemies; before any enemy hand could strike his doomed head, however, his position was taken by Chingachgook's fierce face. In this way, the scene of combat moved from the center of the small clearing to its edge. The Mohican now found a chance to deliver a forceful stab with his knife; Magua suddenly released his hold and fell backward motionless, apparently lifeless. His opponent jumped to his feet, making the forest canopy echo with sounds of victory.

"Excellent work by the Delawares! Victory belongs to the Mohicans!" shouted Hawkeye, raising the stock of his long and deadly rifle once again. "A final strike from a man of pure blood will never damage his honor or deny him his rightful claim to the scalp."

But at the exact moment when the deadly weapon was about to strike, the clever Huron quickly rolled away from the danger, over the edge of the cliff, and landing on his feet, was seen jumping with a single leap into the middle of a cluster of low bushes that grew along the cliff's sides. The Delawares, who had thought their enemy was dead, cried out in surprise and were chasing after him with speed and noise, like hunting dogs in clear sight of a deer, when a sharp and distinctive call from the scout immediately changed their plan and brought them back to the top of the hill.

"That's just like him!" shouted the stubborn frontiersman, whose deep-seated prejudices greatly clouded his natural sense of fairness in all matters involving the Mingoes. "He's nothing but a lying and deceitful scoundrel. An honest Delaware warrior, after being fairly defeated, would have stayed down and accepted death, but these treacherous Maquas hang onto life like wildcats. Let him go—let him go; he's just one man, without a rifle or bow, many miles away from his French allies; and like a rattlesnake that's lost its fangs, he can't cause any more harm until we—and he too—have traveled far across the sandy plains, leaving only our moccasin tracks behind. Look, Uncas," he continued, speaking in Delaware, "your father is already taking the scalps. It might be wise to check on the remaining scoundrels to make sure they're dead, or we might have another one of them running through the forest, shrieking like a wounded blue jay."

The honest but relentless scout spoke these words as he moved around the dead bodies, plunging his long knife into their lifeless chests with the same detachment as if they were nothing more than animal carcasses. However, the older Mohican had already beaten him to it, having stripped the scalps from the defenseless heads of the fallen as trophies of their victory.

But Uncas, going against his usual habits—we might even say his very nature—rushed with natural sensitivity, joined by Heyward, to help the women, and after quickly freeing Alice, he placed her in Cora's arms. We won't try to describe the gratitude to the Almighty Controller of Events that burned in the hearts of the sisters, who were so unexpectedly brought back to life and reunited with each other. Their prayers of thanks were deep and quiet; the offerings of their gentle souls glowing brightest and most purely on the hidden altars of their hearts; and their renewed and more worldly emotions showing themselves in long and passionate yet wordless embraces. As Alice stood up from her knees, where she had fallen beside Cora, she threw herself against her sister's chest and cried out their elderly father's name, while her soft, gentle eyes sparkled with rays of hope.

"We're saved! We're saved!" she whispered; "we can return to our beloved father's arms, and his heart won't be shattered by grief. And you too, Cora, my sister, more than a sister to me, like a mother; you too have been spared. And Duncan," she added, glancing at the young man with a smile of pure innocence, "even our own courageous and noble Duncan has come through without injury."

Cora responded to these passionate and almost innocent words only by pulling the young woman close to her heart, bending over her with overwhelming tenderness. Heyward felt no shame in his tears as he witnessed this display of loving emotion; and Uncas stood there, still fresh and bloodstained from the fight, appearing calm and seemingly unmoved as he watched, but his eyes had already lost their fierce intensity and now shone with a compassion that lifted him far beyond the understanding of his people and placed him probably centuries ahead of his nation's customs.

During this display of emotions that was so natural given their circumstances, Hawkeye, whose careful suspicion had convinced him that the Hurons who had marred the peaceful scene no longer had the ability to disrupt its tranquility, walked over to David and freed him from the restraints he had endured with remarkable patience up to that point.

"There," declared the scout, throwing the last binding behind him, "you're free to move again, though you don't seem to use your freedom with much better sense than when you were first created. If advice from someone who isn't older than you, but who has spent most of his life in the wilderness and could be said to have experience beyond his years, won't offend you, then you're welcome to hear my thoughts. Here's what I think: get rid of that little musical instrument in your jacket—sell it to the first fool you come across, and use the money to buy some weapon, even if it's just the barrel of a cavalry pistol. Through hard work and careful attention, you might actually advance yourself in life. By now, I would think your own eyes should clearly show you that a scavenging crow is a better bird than a mockingbird. At least the crow removes disgusting sights from human view, while the mockingbird only creates chaos in the forest by deceiving the ears of everyone who hears it."

"Weapons and battle trumpets are for fighting, but songs of thanksgiving are for victory!" replied the freed David. "Friend," he continued, extending his thin, delicate hand toward Hawkeye in friendship, while his eyes sparkled and became moist, "I thank you that the hair on my head still grows where Providence first planted it; for though other men's hair may be shinier and more curled, I have always found my own well suited to the brain it protects. That I did not join the battle was due less to unwillingness than to being bound by the heathens. You have proven yourself brave and skilled in the fight, and I thank you here before I go on to fulfill other and more important duties, because you have shown yourself truly worthy of a Christian's praise."

"It's really nothing special, and you'd see this kind of thing often if you stayed with us long enough," the scout replied, his attitude toward the singing man considerably warmer after this clear show of appreciation. "I've gotten my old companion 'Killdeer' back," he continued, patting the stock of his rifle, "and that alone counts as a victory. These Iroquois are clever, but they outsmarted themselves when they put their guns where they couldn't reach them. If Uncas or his father had just shown typical Indian patience, we would have attacked those scoundrels with three loaded rifles instead of one, and that would have finished off the entire group, including that running coward and his companions. But everything was predetermined, and it's all for the best."

"You speak well," David replied, "and you've grasped the true spirit of Christianity. Those who are meant to be saved will be saved, and those who are predestined to be damned will be damned. This is the doctrine of truth, and it is most consoling and refreshing to the true believer."

The scout, who had now taken a seat and was checking his rifle with the careful attention of a devoted parent, looked up at the other man with obvious displeasure that he made no effort to hide, abruptly cutting off any further conversation.

"Whether there's religious teaching or not," said the tough woodsman, "it's what dishonest people believe, and it's a burden on honest folks. I can accept that the Huron over there was meant to die by my hand, because I saw it happen with my own eyes; but nothing less than witnessing it myself will make me believe he received any kind of reward, or that Chingachgook there will face judgment on the final day."

"You have no guarantee for such a bold teaching, nor any promise to back it up," shouted David, who was heavily influenced by the complex theological distinctions that, during his era, and particularly in his region, had been constructed around the pure simplicity of divine revelation. These distinctions came from attempts to understand the mysterious nature of God, replacing faith with human arrogance, and consequently trapping those who relied on such human-made beliefs in contradictions and uncertainty. "Your foundation is built on sand, and the first storm will sweep away what supports it. I want to know your sources for such an unloving claim." (Like other defenders of a belief system, David wasn't always precise in how he used words.) "Give me Chapter and verse; in which of the sacred texts do you find words that support your position?"

"Book!" Hawkeye repeated, with unmistakable and poorly hidden contempt; "do you think I'm some whimpering child clinging to one of your old women's apron strings; and that this fine rifle on my knee is nothing more than a goose feather, my powder horn just a bottle of ink, and my leather pouch merely a checkered handkerchief for carrying my lunch? Book! What would someone like me, a warrior of the wilderness, though a man without religious faith, want with books? I've only ever read from one book, and the words written there are so simple and clear that they don't require much education to understand; though I can proudly say I've learned this through forty long and hard years of experience."

"What do you call the book?" said David, misunderstanding what the other person meant.

"It's right there in front of you," the scout replied, "and whoever created it doesn't hold back from showing it. I've heard people say there are men who read books to convince themselves that God exists. I don't know, but maybe people have so damaged His works in civilized places that what's crystal clear out here in the wilderness becomes something traders and preachers argue about. If there are such people, and one of them follows me from sunrise to sunset through these winding forest paths, he'll see enough to learn that he's a fool, and that his greatest foolishness is trying to reach the level of Someone he can never match, whether in goodness or in power."

The moment David realized he was arguing with someone who drew his beliefs from natural reasoning alone, avoiding all complex religious teachings, he gladly gave up a debate that he felt would bring neither benefit nor honor. While the scout was talking, David had also taken a seat, and pulling out his small, well-worn book and wire-rimmed glasses, he prepared to fulfill a responsibility that only the unexpected challenge to his religious beliefs could have delayed for so long. He was, in fact, a singer of the American continent—certainly from a much more recent time than those talented poets who once sang about the worldly fame of nobles and royalty, but he followed the spirit of his own era and nation; and he was now ready to use his artistic skills in celebration of, or more accurately in gratitude for, the recent victory. He waited patiently for Hawkeye to finish speaking, then raising both his eyes and his voice, he spoke aloud:

"I invite you, friends, to join me in praising this remarkable rescue from the hands of savages and non-believers, to the comforting and reverent melody of the hymn tune called 'Northampton'."

He then announced the page and verse where the selected hymns could be found, and brought the pitch-pipe to his lips with the same solemn dignity he had always shown in church. This time, however, he performed without any musical accompaniment, since the sisters were at that moment expressing those heartfelt displays of love that have already been mentioned. Undaunted by his small audience, which actually consisted of only the unhappy scout, he lifted his voice and began the sacred song, completing it from start to finish without any mishap or interruption whatsoever.

Hawkeye listened while he calmly adjusted his flint and reloaded his rifle, but the sounds, lacking the additional support of setting and emotional connection, failed to stir his dormant feelings. No musician, or whatever more appropriate title David deserved, ever performed before a more unresponsive audience; yet considering the pure and genuine nature of his purpose, it's likely that no singer of worldly songs ever produced melodies that rose so close to that sacred place where all honor and worship belong. The scout shook his head, and mumbling some unclear words, among which only "throat" and "Iroquois" could be heard, he walked away to gather and inspect the condition of the seized weapons belonging to the Hurons. In this task he was soon joined by Chingachgook, who discovered his own rifle, as well as his son's, among the collection of arms. Even Heyward and David were provided with weapons, and there was no shortage of ammunition to make them all effective.

When the foresters had made their choices and handed out their rewards, the scout announced that the time had come when they needed to leave. By now Gamut's singing had stopped, and the sisters had learned to control the display of their feelings. With help from Duncan and the younger Mohican, the two women made their way down the steep slopes of the hill they had climbed so recently under very different circumstances, and whose peak had almost become the site of their slaughter. At the bottom they found the Narragansett horses grazing on the vegetation among the bushes, and after mounting up, they followed the movements of a guide who had proven himself their friend so many times in the most dangerous situations. The journey was brief, however. Hawkeye left the hidden trail that the Hurons had taken, turned sharply to his right, and entering the thick woods, he crossed a gurgling stream and stopped in a narrow valley beneath the shade of several water elms. Their distance from the base of the deadly hill was only a few yards, and the horses had been useful only for crossing the shallow creek.

The scout and the Native Americans seemed to know this hidden spot well. They leaned their rifles against the trees and began brushing away the dried leaves, clearing the blue clay beneath. Soon, a clear and sparkling spring of bright, shimmering water bubbled up from the ground. The white man then looked around, as if searching for something that wasn't as easy to find as he had anticipated.

"Those careless troublemakers, the Mohawks, along with their Tuscarora and Onondaga brothers, have been here quenching their thirst," he grumbled, "and the rascals have discarded the gourd! This is what happens with good deeds when they're given to such ungrateful dogs! Here the Lord has intervened, in the middle of this wild wilderness, for their benefit, and created a spring of water from the depths of the earth that could surpass the finest apothecary shop in all the colonies; and look! the scoundrels have trampled in the mud and ruined the purity of this place, as if they were wild animals rather than civilized human beings."

Uncas quietly handed him the gourd he wanted, which Hawkeye's bad mood had kept him from noticing hanging on an elm branch. After filling it with water, he moved a short distance away to a spot where the ground was more solid and dry; there he calmly sat down, and after taking a long and seemingly refreshing drink, he began carefully examining the scraps of food the Hurons had left behind, which he carried in a pouch on his arm.

"Thank you, young man!" he went on, handing the empty gourd back to Uncas. "Now we'll see how these rampaging Hurons lived when they were camped out in ambush. Look at this! These scoundrels know the best cuts of deer, and you'd think they could carve and roast a saddle as well as the finest cook in the country! But everything is raw, because the Iroquois are complete savages. Uncas, take my flint and steel and start a fire; a bite of tender grilled meat will give nature a helping hand after such a long journey."

Heyward noticed that their guides were now seriously focused on preparing their meal, so he helped the ladies dismount and positioned himself beside them, quite ready to enjoy a few moments of welcome rest after the violent encounter he had just experienced. While the cooking was underway, curiosity prompted him to ask about the circumstances that had brought about their timely and unexpected rescue:

"How is it that we see you so soon, my generous friend," he asked, "and without help from Edward's garrison?"

"If we had gone to the bend in the river, we might have arrived in time to rake the leaves over your dead bodies, but too late to save your scalps," the scout replied calmly. "No, no; rather than wasting our strength and opportunity by crossing to the fort, we stayed hidden under the bank of the Hudson, waiting to observe the movements of the Hurons."

"So you witnessed everything that happened?"

"Not everyone; Indian eyesight is too sharp to be easily fooled, and we stayed hidden. It was also difficult to keep this Mohican boy quiet in our hiding place. Ah! Uncas, Uncas, you acted more like a curious woman than a warrior tracking his prey."

Uncas allowed his gaze to rest briefly on the determined face of the man speaking, but he remained silent and showed no signs of regret. Instead, Heyward believed the young Mohican's demeanor appeared scornful, perhaps even somewhat hostile, and that he was holding back emotions ready to burst forth, doing so as much out of respect for those listening as from the courtesy he typically showed his white companion.

"You witnessed our capture?" Heyward asked next.

"We heard it," came the meaningful reply. "An Indian war cry speaks clearly to men who have spent their lives in the wilderness. But when you came ashore, we were forced to crawl like snakes beneath the foliage; and then we completely lost track of you, until we spotted you again tied to the trees, bound and prepared for an Indian slaughter."

"Our rescue was an act of divine intervention. It was almost miraculous that you didn't lose your way, since the Hurons had split up, and each group had their own horses."

"Yes! That's where we lost the trail and might have given up completely if it hadn't been for Uncas. We decided to take the path that headed into the wilderness because we figured—and we were right—that the natives would go that way with their captives. But after we'd traveled many miles along it without finding even one broken branch, as I had suggested we look for, I started to have doubts, especially since all the footprints showed moccasin marks."

"Our captors were careful to make sure we wore the same kind of shoes they did," Duncan said, lifting his foot to show the buckskin footwear he had on.

"Yes, it was clever and typical of them; though we were too experienced to be thrown off a trail by such a common trick."

"What, then, do we owe our safety to?"

"To what, as a white man with no trace of Indian blood, I should be embarrassed to admit; to the judgment of the young Mohican, in matters that I should understand better than he does, but which I can now barely believe to be true, even though my own eyes tell me it is so."

"This is extraordinary! Won't you tell me the reason?'"

"Uncas was brave enough to point out that the animals the ladies were riding," Hawkeye went on, casting his gaze with obvious curiosity toward the women's horses, "put both legs on one side down at the same time, which goes against how every four-legged creature I know moves when trotting, except for bears. And yet here we have horses that always travel this way, as I've witnessed myself, and as their tracks have proven for twenty long miles."

"It's the quality of the animal! They come from the shores of Narragansett Bay, in the small province of Providence Plantations, and are famous for their toughness and the ease of this distinctive gait; though other horses are often trained to do the same."

"It could be—it could be," said Hawkeye, who had been listening with unusual attention to this explanation; "although I am a man with pure white blood, my expertise with deer and beaver is better than with pack animals. Major Effingham owns many fine horses, but I have never seen one move with such a sideways manner of walking."

"That's true; he would appreciate the animals for completely different qualities. Even so, this is a breed that's highly valued and, as you can see, greatly honored by the heavy loads it's often meant to carry."

The Mohicans had stopped what they were doing around the flickering fire to listen carefully; and when Duncan finished speaking, they exchanged meaningful looks with each other, the father letting out his characteristic expression of amazement. The scout pondered thoughtfully, like someone processing this new information he had just learned, and once again cast a quick glance toward the horses.

"I dare to say there are even stranger sights to be seen in the settlements!" he said, at length. "Nature is sadly mistreated by man, when he once gains control. But, whether moving sideways or straight ahead, Uncas had spotted the movement, and their trail led us to the broken bush. The outer branch, near the footprints of one of the horses, was bent upward, like a lady picking a flower from its stem, but all the rest were jagged and broken down, as if a man's strong hand had been tearing at them! So I concluded that the cunning creatures had noticed the bent twig, and had torn the rest, to make us believe a deer had been rubbing the branches with his antlers."

"I really think your sharp judgment didn't mislead you, because something like that actually happened!"

"That was obvious," the scout added, completely unaware that he had shown any remarkable insight. "It was completely different from a lumbering horse! It occurred to me then that the Mingoes would head straight for this spring, since those scoundrels know perfectly well how valuable these waters are!"

"Is it really that famous?" Heyward asked, studying the hidden valley more carefully, taking in the bubbling spring surrounded by deep, dark brown earth.

"Few Native Americans who travel south and east of the great lakes haven't heard of its qualities. Will you taste it for yourself?"

Heyward accepted the gourd, and after drinking a small amount of the water, tossed it away with expressions of displeasure. The scout chuckled in his quiet but genuine way, and nodded his head with great satisfaction.

"Ah! You want the flavor that comes from habit; there was a time when I disliked it just as much as you do; but I've developed a taste for it, and now I crave it like a deer craves salt licks. Your fancy spiced wines aren't enjoyed any more than a Native American enjoys this water, especially when his body needs healing. But Uncas has built his fire, and it's time we think about eating, since our journey is long and lies entirely ahead of us."[1]

[1] Many animals in American forests are drawn to areas where natural salt springs can be found. These locations are known as "licks" or "salt licks" in local terminology, named this way because four-legged animals frequently must lick the ground to get the salt particles they need. These salt licks serve as popular gathering spots for hunters, who set up ambushes along the trails that animals use to reach these areas.

Breaking off the conversation with this sudden shift, the scout immediately turned to the scraps of food that had survived the ravenous appetite of the Hurons. A quick and simple cooking process finished the basic preparation, and then he and the Mohicans began their modest meal, eating with the quiet and focused determination of men who consumed food purely to sustain themselves for the demanding and relentless work ahead.

When this necessary and, fortunately, appreciated duty had been completed, each of the woodsmen bent down and took a long, final drink from that isolated and quiet spring, around which and its neighboring fountains, within fifty years, the riches, beauty and talent of half the world would gather in crowds, seeking health and enjoyment. Then Hawkeye declared his intention to continue. The sisters got back on their horses; Duncan and David grabbed their rifles, and followed behind; the scout led the way, and the Mohicans brought up the rear. The entire group moved quickly through the narrow trail, heading north, leaving the healing waters to flow unnoticed into the nearby streams and the bodies of the dead to decay on the surrounding mountain, without proper burial; a destiny all too familiar to the warriors of the wilderness to inspire either pity or remark.

The events described above took place where the village of Ballston now stands, which is one of America's two main spa destinations.

---

# Chapter XIII.

"I'll seek a readier path."
—Parnell

Hawkeye's path led across the same sandy plains, broken up by occasional valleys and rolling hills, that their group had crossed earlier that morning with the frustrated Magua as their guide. The sun had dropped low toward the far-off mountains, and since their journey took them through the endless forest, the heat was no longer unbearable. As a result, they moved much faster, and well before dusk settled around them, they had covered many difficult miles on their way back.

The hunter, like the native whose position he had taken, appeared to choose among the faint traces of their wilderness trail with an almost instinctive ability, rarely slowing his pace and never stopping to think things through. A quick sideways glance at the moss growing on tree trunks, an occasional upward look toward the setting sun, or a brief but focused examination of the direction of the many streams he crossed were enough to guide his way and solve his most challenging problems. Meanwhile, the forest started to transform its colors, losing the vibrant green that had decorated its canopy in favor of the more subdued light that typically signals the approach of evening.

While the sisters tried to catch glimpses through the trees of the flood of golden light that formed a glittering halo around the sun, adding ruby streaks here and there, or creating narrow borders of bright yellow around a mass of clouds piled not far above the western hills, Hawkeye suddenly turned and pointed upward toward the magnificent heavens as he spoke:

"Over there is the signal given to humans to seek their food and natural rest," he said; "it would be better and wiser if people could understand nature's signs and learn from the birds in the sky and the animals in the fields! Our night, however, will soon be over, because we must be up and moving again when the moon rises. I remember fighting the Mohawks around here during the first war where I ever shed human blood; and we built a fortification of logs to keep those savage creatures from taking our scalps. If my landmarks don't deceive me, we should find the place a few yards further to our left."

Without waiting for agreement or any response, the experienced hunter boldly pushed into a thick grove of young chestnut trees, pushing through the branches of the vigorous new growth that almost completely covered the ground, moving like someone who anticipated discovering something familiar at every step. The scout's memory proved accurate. After forcing his way through the tangled brush, thick with thorns, for several hundred feet, he emerged into a clearing that encircled a small, grass-covered mound topped by the crumbling blockhouse they sought. This crude and abandoned structure was one of those forsaken fortifications that had been hastily constructed during an emergency, then left behind when the threat passed, and now quietly deteriorated in the forest's isolation, neglected and almost forgotten, much like the events that had led to its construction. Such remnants of human presence and conflict still dot the vast wilderness barrier that once divided the warring territories, creating ruins that are deeply connected to colonial memories and perfectly match the somber mood of the surrounding landscape. The bark roof had long ago collapsed and mixed with the earth, but the massive pine logs that had been quickly assembled still maintained their original arrangement, though one corner of the structure had collapsed under the weight and threatened to bring down the rest of the rough building soon. While Heyward and his group hesitated to approach such a deteriorated structure, Hawkeye and the Indians walked through the low walls without hesitation and with clear fascination. As the former examined the ruins both inside and out with the interest of someone whose memories were awakening moment by moment, Chingachgook told his son in the Delaware language, with a victor's pride, the short account of the battle that had taken place in his younger days at this remote location. A note of sadness, however, mixed with his sense of triumph, making his voice soft and melodious as always.

In the meantime, the sisters happily got down from their horses and prepared to enjoy their rest in the cool evening air, feeling safe and believing that only wild animals from the forest could threaten their security.

"Wouldn't our resting place have been more secluded, my good friend," asked the more cautious Duncan, noticing that the scout had already completed his brief examination, "if we had picked a location that was less familiar and not visited as often as this one?"

"Not many people alive today know that the blockhouse was ever built," came the slow and thoughtful reply. "Books aren't often written, and stories aren't usually told about the kind of battle that took place here between the Mohicans and the Mohawks, fighting their own private war. I was young then, and I joined up with the Delawares because I knew they were a people who had been wronged and treated badly. For forty days and forty nights, those warriors tried to get our blood around this pile of logs that I designed and helped build, being, as you'll recall, not an Indian myself, but a man of mixed heritage. The Delawares helped with the construction, and we held our ground, ten against twenty, until our numbers were almost even, and then we charged out at those dogs, and not one of them made it back to report what happened to his war party. Yes, yes; I was young then, and new to seeing bloodshed; and not liking the idea that beings who had souls like mine should lie on the bare earth, to be ripped apart by wild animals, or to turn white in the rain, I buried the dead with my own hands, under that small hill where you've made yourselves comfortable; and it makes a decent resting place too, even though it's built on the bones of mortal men."

Heyward and the sisters immediately stood up from the grassy burial ground; despite the horrifying scenes they had recently endured, the two women couldn't completely suppress a natural feeling of dread when they realized they were in such close contact with the grave of the dead Mohawks. The dim light, the somber little patch of dark grass surrounded by its border of brush, beyond which the pine trees rose in breathing silence, seemingly reaching into the very clouds, and the deathlike quiet of the vast forest all combined to intensify such feelings. "They are gone, and they are harmless," Hawkeye continued, gesturing with his hand and offering a melancholy smile at their obvious fear; "they'll never cry out the war-whoop or strike a blow with the tomahawk again! And of all those who helped place them where they now rest, Chingachgook and I are the only ones still alive! The brothers and family of the Mohican made up our war party; and you see before you all that remains of his people."

The listeners' eyes naturally turned toward the Indians, feeling genuine sympathy for their tragic circumstances. Their dark figures could still be seen in the shadows of the blockhouse, with the son listening to his father's account with the kind of deep attention that comes from hearing a story that brings such honor to those whose names he had long respected for their bravery and fierce virtues.

"I believed the Delawares were a peaceful people," Duncan said, "and that they never fought wars themselves, instead relying on those very Mohawks you killed to defend their territory!"

"That's partly true," the scout replied, "but deep down, it's a wicked lie. Such a treaty was made long ago, through the scheming of the Dutch, who wanted to disarm the natives that had the best claim to the land where they had settled. The Mohicans, though part of the same nation, had to deal with the English and never agreed to that foolish bargain, but maintained their dignity; just as the Delawares did, when they finally saw through their mistake. You see before you a chief of the great Mohican leaders! Once his family could hunt their deer across stretches of land wider than what belongs to the Albany landowner, without crossing any stream or hill that wasn't theirs; but what remains for their descendant? He might find his six feet of earth when God decides, and keep it in peace, perhaps, if he has a friend willing to bury him so deep that the plows cannot disturb it!"

"Enough!" said Heyward, worried that the topic might spark an argument that would disturb the peace so essential for protecting his female companions; "we have traveled a long distance, and few of us are fortunate enough to possess a physique like yours, which appears to experience neither exhaustion nor frailty."

"The muscles and bones of a man carry me through everything," said the hunter, examining his strong limbs with a straightforwardness that revealed the genuine satisfaction the praise gave him; "there are bigger and heavier men to be found in the settlements, but you could travel for many days in a city before you would find someone capable of walking fifty miles without stopping to catch their breath, or who has kept the dogs within earshot during a hunt lasting hours. Still, since everyone's strength and endurance are not the same, it makes perfect sense to assume that the ladies are ready to rest, after everything they have witnessed and experienced today. Uncas, clean out the spring, while your father and I construct a shelter for their delicate heads from these chestnut branches, and a bed of grass and leaves."

The conversation stopped as the hunter and his companions got busy preparing for the comfort and safety of those under their care. A spring that had convinced the local people many years earlier to choose this spot for their temporary fortress was quickly cleared of leaves, and crystal-clear water bubbled up from the ground, spreading across the green hillside. One corner of the structure was then covered to keep out the thick dew that was common in this climate, and heaps of fragrant bushes and dried leaves were placed underneath for the sisters to rest on.

While the hardworking woodsmen continued their tasks, Cora and Alice ate the food that duty demanded more than their appetites desired. They then went inside the walls, and after first giving thanks for past blessings and asking for God's continued protection through the coming night, they lay down on the sweet-smelling bed, and despite their memories and fears, soon fell into the deep sleep that nature urgently required, made peaceful by hopes for tomorrow. Duncan had prepared to spend the night keeping watch near them, just outside the ruins, but the scout, noticing his plan, gestured toward Chingachgook as he calmly settled himself on the grass, and said:

"A white man's eyes are too tired and too clouded for this kind of watch duty! The Mohican will stand guard for us, so let's get some sleep."

"I showed myself to be lazy at my post last night," Heyward said, "and I need less rest than you, who brought more honor to what it means to be a soldier. Let everyone in the group get some sleep, then, while I stand guard."

"If we were camped among the white tents of the Sixtieth Regiment, facing an enemy like the French, I couldn't ask for a better guard," the scout replied; "but in this darkness and surrounded by the signs of the wilderness, your judgment would be like a child's foolishness, and your watchfulness would be wasted. So then, like Uncas and myself, sleep, and sleep safely."

Heyward noticed that the younger Indian had indeed stretched out on the side of the small hill while they were speaking, like someone trying to make the most of their allotted rest time, and that David had followed his lead, his voice literally sticking to his throat due to the fever from his wound, which had been made worse by their exhausting journey. Not wanting to continue a pointless argument, the young man pretended to agree by leaning his back against the logs of the blockhouse in a half-lying position, though he was firmly resolved in his mind not to close his eyes until he had safely delivered his precious charge into Munro's own arms. Hawkeye, believing he had won the argument, soon drifted off to sleep, and a silence as profound as the wilderness in which they had discovered it settled over the secluded location.

For many minutes Duncan managed to stay alert and aware of every mournful sound that came from the forest. His sight grew sharper as the evening shadows fell over the area, and even after the stars began twinkling overhead, he could make out the lying forms of his companions as they stretched out on the grass, and observe Chingachgook, who sat upright and still as one of the trees that created the dark wall surrounding them. He continued to hear the soft breathing of the sisters, who rested just a few feet away from him, and his ear caught the whispered sound of every leaf stirred by the passing breeze. Eventually, though, the sad calls of a whip-poor-will mixed with the hooting of an owl; his tired eyes occasionally looked toward the bright starlight, and he then imagined he could see the stars through his closed eyelids. During brief moments when he stirred awake, he mistook a bush for his fellow guard; his head then dropped onto his shoulder, which in turn leaned toward the ground for support; and finally, his entire body became loose and limp, and the young man fell into a deep sleep, dreaming that he was a knight from ancient times of chivalry, keeping his midnight watch outside the tent of a rescued princess, whose affection he still hoped to win through such a display of dedication and vigilance.

Duncan never knew how long he remained unconscious in his exhausted state, but his sleeping dreams had long faded into complete oblivion when a gentle tap on his shoulder woke him up. Despite how light the touch was, this signal immediately brought him to his feet with a jumbled memory of the responsibility he had taken upon himself at the beginning of the night.

"Who's there?" he called out, reaching for his sword where it normally hung at his side. "Answer me! Are you friend or foe?"

"Friend," responded Chingachgook in his quiet voice, gesturing toward the moon that cast its gentle light through the gap in the trees directly above their camp, then immediately continued in his broken English: "Moon rises and white man's fort is far—very far away; time to go, when sleep closes both eyes of the Frenchman!"

"You're absolutely right! Gather your friends and get the horses ready while I prepare my own companions for the journey!"

"We're awake, Duncan," came Alice's gentle, melodious voice from inside the building, "and we're ready to travel at great speed after such a refreshing sleep; but you've kept watch through the long, wearisome night on our behalf, after enduring so much exhaustion throughout the entire day!"

"Instead, I should say that I intended to keep watch, but my unreliable eyes failed me; I have now shown twice that I am not worthy of the responsibility I carry."

"No, Duncan, don't deny it," interrupted Alice with a smile, stepping from the building's shadows into the moonlight, radiating all the beauty of her refreshed appearance. "I know you're careless when it comes to taking care of yourself, yet far too watchful when it comes to others. Can't we stay here a bit longer while you get the rest you need? Cora and I will gladly, most gladly, keep watch while you and all these brave men try to get some sleep!"

"If shame could cure my drowsiness, I would never close my eyes again," said the restless young man, looking at Alice's innocent face, where he saw nothing in her gentle concern to confirm his half-formed suspicion. "It's all too true that after leading you into danger through my carelessness, I don't even have the honor of protecting your sleep as a soldier should."

"Only Duncan himself should accuse Duncan of such weakness. Go ahead and sleep; trust me, neither of us, weak girls though we may be, will abandon our watch."

The young man was spared the embarrassment of having to make any more declarations about his own shortcomings by an exclamation from Chingachgook and the posture of intense focus that his son adopted.

"The Mohicans sense an enemy!" Hawkeye whispered, having awakened along with the rest of the group, all of them now alert and moving. "They can smell danger in the air!"

"God forbid!" Heyward exclaimed. "Surely we've had enough of bloodshed!"

While he was speaking, the young soldier grabbed his rifle and moved toward the front lines, ready to make up for his minor negligence by willingly risking his life to defend those under his protection.

"It's some forest creature prowling around us looking for food," he whispered, as soon as the quiet and seemingly distant sounds that had startled the Mohicans reached his ears.

"Listen!" replied the alert scout; "it's a man; even I can now recognize his footsteps, weak as my senses are compared to an Indian's! That fleeing Huron has encountered one of Montcalm's advance patrols, and they have discovered our trail. I wouldn't want to shed more human blood in this place myself," he added, glancing around with worry evident in his expression, at the shadowy shapes surrounding him; "but what has to happen, has to happen! Take the horses into the blockhouse, Uncas; and, friends, you should follow to the same refuge. Worn down and old as it is, it provides protection, and has echoed with the sound of rifle fire before tonight!"

He was immediately obeyed, with the Mohicans guiding the Narragansetts into the ruins, where the entire group gathered in complete silence.

The sound of approaching footsteps was now too clear to leave any doubt about what was interrupting them. Soon the footsteps mixed with voices calling to each other in a Native American language, which the hunter whispered to Heyward was the Huron tongue. When the group reached the spot where the horses had entered the dense brush surrounding the blockhouse, they were clearly confused, having lost the trail markers that had guided their chase up to that point.

It sounded like twenty men had quickly gathered at that single location, mixing their various opinions and suggestions in a loud, chaotic uproar.

"The scoundrels know our weakness," whispered Hawkeye, who stood beside Heyward in the deep shadows, peering through a gap in the logs, "or they wouldn't give in to their laziness with such a woman's pace. Listen to those snakes! every man among them seems to have two tongues, and only one leg."

Duncan, brave as he was in battle, couldn't respond to the scout's calm and typical comment during such a tense moment of waiting. He simply gripped his rifle tighter and fixed his gaze on the narrow gap through which he watched the moonlit scene with growing worry. The deeper voice of someone who clearly held authority could be heard next, surrounded by a silence that showed the respect his commands, or more accurately his suggestions, received. After this, the rustling of leaves and snapping of dry branches made it clear that the savages were spreading out to search for the lost trail. Luckily for those being hunted, the moonlight, though it cast a gentle glow over the small clearing around the ruins, wasn't bright enough to reach into the forest's deep shadows, where everything remained hidden in misleading darkness. The search came up empty; the travelers' quick and sudden move from the faint path into the dense undergrowth had been so brief that all signs of their footprints vanished in the woods' darkness.

It wasn't long, however, before the restless warriors could be heard beating through the undergrowth, slowly moving closer to the inner edge of the thick border of young chestnut trees that surrounded the small clearing.

"They're coming," Heyward muttered, trying to push his rifle through the gap in the logs. "Let's fire as they approach."

"Keep everything hidden," the scout replied; "the striking of a flint, or even the scent of a single grain of gunpowder, would bring those hungry scoundrels down on us all at once. If God wills that we must fight for our lives, rely on the experience of men who understand the ways of the natives, and who rarely hesitate when the war cry sounds."

Duncan looked behind him and saw the frightened sisters huddled in the far corner of the building, while the Mohicans stood in the shadows like two upright pillars, prepared and seemingly ready to attack when the moment called for it. Restraining his eagerness, he peered out at the open area again and waited quietly for what would happen next. Just then the bushes parted, and a tall, armed Huron stepped several paces into the clearing. As he stared at the quiet blockhouse, moonlight illuminated his dark face, revealing his astonishment and interest. He made the sound that typically goes with such surprise among Indians, and speaking quietly, quickly brought another warrior to join him.

These forest dwellers stood together for several moments, pointing at the crumbling structure and speaking in their tribe's incomprehensible language. They then moved closer, though with slow and careful steps, stopping every moment to stare at the building, like frightened deer whose curiosity battled fiercely with their sudden fears for control. One of them suddenly stepped onto the mound and paused to examine what it was made of. At that moment, Heyward noticed that the scout loosened his knife in its sheath and lowered his rifle's muzzle. Following these actions, the young man prepared himself for the fight that now seemed unavoidable.

The hostile warriors were so close that the slightest movement from one of the horses, or even breathing louder than usual, would have exposed the fleeing party. However, upon recognizing the nature of the burial mound, the Hurons seemed to focus their attention on something entirely different. They spoke among themselves in hushed, reverent tones, as though filled with a deep respect mixed with fear. Then they carefully retreated, their eyes fixed on the ancient structure, as if they anticipated seeing spirits of the dead emerge from its quiet stone walls, until they reached the edge of the clearing and slowly melted back into the dense forest, vanishing from sight.

Hawkeye lowered the back end of his rifle to the ground, and taking a long, deep breath, said in a loud whisper:

"Yes! They respect the dead, and this time it has saved their own lives, and perhaps the lives of better men as well."

Heyward briefly focused his attention on his companion, but without responding, he turned back toward those who currently interested him more. He heard the two Hurons emerge from the bushes, and it quickly became clear that all the pursuers had gathered around them, listening intently to their report. After several minutes of serious and solemn conversation, completely different from the loud commotion with which they had initially assembled at the location, the sounds became quieter and more distant, and eventually disappeared entirely into the depths of the forest.

Hawkeye waited until Chingachgook, who had been listening carefully, gave him a signal confirming that all sounds from the departing group had been completely absorbed by the distance. Then he gestured to Heyward to bring forward the horses and help the sisters mount their saddles. As soon as this was accomplished, they moved through the damaged gateway and slipped away in a direction opposite to the one they had used when entering. They left the location while the sisters stole quick, secretive looks at the quiet, solemn, and crumbling ruins as they departed from the gentle moonlight to hide themselves in the darkness of the forest.

---

# Chapter XIV.

"Guard.—Who goes there?
Puc. —Peasants, poor people of France."
—King Henry VI

During the quick escape from the blockhouse, and until the group was deep within the forest, everyone was too focused on getting away to risk speaking even in whispers. The scout took his position at the front again, though his steps, after he had put a safe distance between himself and his enemies, were more careful than during their earlier march, because he had no knowledge of the surrounding woodland areas. Several times he stopped to discuss with his allies, the Mohicans, pointing up at the moon and carefully examining the bark of the trees. During these short breaks, Heyward and the sisters listened, with their senses made twice as sharp by the danger, trying to detect any signs that might reveal how close their enemies were. At these moments, it felt as if a huge expanse of land lay in endless sleep; not the slightest sound came from the forest, except for the distant and barely audible trickling of a stream. Birds, animals, and humans all seemed to be sleeping, if indeed any people could be found in that vast stretch of wilderness. But the sounds of the small stream, weak and soft as they were, immediately freed the guides from a significant problem, and they headed straight toward it.

When they reached the banks of the small stream, Hawkeye stopped once more and removed the moccasins from his feet, motioning for Heyward and Gamut to do the same. He then stepped into the water, and for nearly an hour they walked through the streambed, leaving no trace behind them. The moon had already disappeared behind a massive wall of dark clouds that loomed over the western horizon when they emerged from the shallow, winding waterway and climbed back up to the sandy but forested plain. Here the scout appeared to be in familiar territory again, as he continued forward with the confidence and purpose of someone moving through well-known ground. The trail soon became more rugged, and the travelers could clearly see that mountains were closing in on both sides, indicating they were truly approaching one of the mountain passes. Without warning, Hawkeye stopped and waited for the entire group to gather around him before speaking in such hushed and careful tones that his words carried even greater weight in the stillness and darkness surrounding them.

"It's easy to learn the trails and locate the salt licks and streams in the wilderness," he said; "but who could look at this place and dare to claim that a powerful army was camped among those quiet trees and empty mountains?"

"So we're not very far from William Henry?" Heyward asked, moving closer to the scout.

"The path ahead is still long and exhausting, and figuring out when and where to take action is our biggest challenge right now. Look," he said, pointing through the trees toward a spot where a small pool of water mirrored the stars on its calm surface, "there is the 'bloody pond'; and I'm standing on ground that I have not only traveled many times, but where I have fought the enemy from sunrise to sunset."

"Ha! So that stretch of dark and gloomy water is the burial place of the brave men who died in the battle. I've heard it mentioned before, but I've never stood on its shores until now."

"We fought three battles with the Dutch-Frenchman in a single day," Hawkeye went on, following his own line of thinking rather than responding to Duncan's comment. "He encountered us nearby during our outward march to ambush his advancing forces, and he scattered us like startled deer through the narrow pass, all the way to the shores of Lake George. Then we regrouped behind our fallen trees and mounted a counterattack under Sir William—who earned his knighthood for that very action; and we certainly made him pay for the morning's humiliation! Hundreds of Frenchmen saw their last sunrise that day; and even their commander, Dieskau himself, fell into our hands, so badly wounded by musket balls that he returned to his homeland, no longer capable of military service."[1]

> [1] Baron Dieskau, a German officer serving France, had been defeated by Sir William Johnson of Johnstown, New York, on the shores of Lake George a few years before the events of this story.

"That was a noble defeat!" exclaimed Heyward, in the heat of his youthful enthusiasm; "word of it reached us early, in our southern army."

"Yes! but that wasn't the end of it. Major Effingham sent me, on Sir William's direct orders, to circle around the French and carry news of their defeat across the portage to the fort on the Hudson. Right here, where you can see the trees rising into a mountain slope, I encountered a group coming down to help us, and I guided them to where the enemy was eating their meal, never suspecting that they hadn't completed the bloody work of the day."

"And you surprised them?"

"If death can catch men off guard when they're focused only on satisfying their desires. We allowed them just a brief moment to rest, since they had pressed us hard during the morning battle, and nearly everyone in our group had lost a friend or family member to their violence."

"When everything was finished, the dead, and some say the dying, were thrown into that small pond. These eyes have witnessed its waters stained with blood, as natural water has never flowed from the depths of the earth."

"It was a convenient, and I trust it will prove to be a peaceful grave for a soldier. You have seen much service on this frontier then?"

"Yes!" said the scout, straightening his tall frame with an air of military pride; "there aren't many echoes among these hills that haven't rung with the crack of my rifle, nor is there a square mile between Horican and the river where 'Killdeer' hasn't dropped a living body, whether it be an enemy or a wild animal. As for the grave being as quiet as you mention, that's another matter entirely. There are those in the camp who say and believe that a man, to lie still, should not be buried while there's still breath in his body; and it's certain that in the rush of that evening, the doctors had little time to determine who was living and who was dead. Listen! Do you see anything moving on the shore of the pond?"

"It's unlikely that anyone else is as homeless as we are in this gloomy forest."

"Someone like him probably doesn't worry much about having a house or shelter, and the night dew can't really soak a body that spends its days in the water," the scout replied, gripping Heyward's shoulder with such intense, trembling force that the young soldier could painfully feel how much supernatural fear had taken control of a man who was normally so fearless.

"Good heavens, there's a human figure, and it's coming closer! Get ready to defend yourselves, my friends, because we don't know who we're dealing with."

"Who goes there?" demanded a stern, sharp voice that sounded like a challenge from another world, emerging from that lonely and solemn place.

"What is it saying?" whispered the scout; "it's speaking neither Indian nor English."

"Who goes there?" the same voice repeated, quickly followed by the clatter of weapons and a threatening stance.

"France!" shouted Heyward, stepping forward from the shadows of the trees toward the edge of the pond, coming within just a few yards of the guard.

"Where are you coming from—or where are you going, so early in the morning?" demanded the grenadier, speaking in the language and with the accent of a man from old France.

"I have just come from making a discovery, and I am going to bed."

"Are you an officer of the king?"

"Of course, my comrade; do you take me for a provincial! I am a captain of chasseurs (Heyward well knew that the other was of a regiment in the line); I have here, with me, the daughters of the commander of the fortification. Aha! you have heard of it! I took them prisoner near the other fort, and I am conducting them to the general."

"My word! Ladies, I'm sorry for you," exclaimed the young soldier, gracefully touching his cap; "but—fortune of war! You'll find our general to be a good man, and very polite with the ladies."

"That's the nature of soldiers," said Cora, with admirable self-control. "Goodbye, my friend; I wish you had a more pleasant duty to fulfill."

The soldier gave a quiet and respectful acknowledgment of her politeness, and Heyward added a "Bonne nuit, mon camarade" as they moved carefully forward, leaving the guard walking along the shores of the quiet pond, never suspecting an enemy with such boldness, and humming to himself those words that came to his mind at the sight of women, and perhaps from memories of his own faraway and beautiful France:[2]

[2] "Long live wine, long live love," and so on, and so forth.

"Good thing you understood that scoundrel!" the scout whispered once they had moved a short distance away, lowering his rifle back into the crook of his arm. "I could tell right away he was one of those restless Frenchmen, and it's lucky for him that he spoke in a friendly manner and had good intentions, or he might have ended up buried alongside his fellow countrymen."

He was interrupted by a long, heavy groan that rose from the small basin, as if the spirits of the dead truly lingered around their watery grave.

"It was definitely made of flesh," the scout continued; "no ghost could hold its weapons so firmly."

"It was flesh and blood; but whether that poor soul is still among the living is highly questionable," Heyward said, scanning their surroundings and noticing that Chingachgook was no longer with their small group. Another groan, weaker than the previous one, was followed by a heavy and dull splash into the water, and then everything fell silent again, as if the edges of the gloomy pond had never been disturbed from the quiet that had existed since the beginning of time. While they still stood there uncertain, they saw the Indian's figure emerging from the dense brush. As the chief returned to join them, he fastened the bloody scalp of the unfortunate young Frenchman to his belt with one hand, while with the other he put away the knife and tomahawk that had been stained with the man's blood. He then resumed his usual position, carrying himself like someone who believed he had performed an honorable act.

The scout lowered one end of his rifle to the ground and rested his hands on the other end, standing lost in deep thought and complete silence. Then, shaking his head sadly, he whispered:

"It would have been a cruel and inhuman act for a white person; but it's the natural way and character of an Indian, and I suppose it shouldn't be criticized. I could wish, though, that it had happened to a cursed Mingo, rather than that spirited young boy from the old countries."

"Enough!" said Heyward, worried that the unaware sisters might understand what was causing the delay, and overcoming his revulsion through a series of thoughts very similar to those of the hunter; "it's finished; and though it would have been better left undone, it cannot be changed now. You can see we are clearly within the enemy's guard posts; what plan do you suggest we follow?"

"Yes," said Hawkeye, stirring himself once more; "it's just as you say, too late to dwell on it any further. Indeed, the French have surrounded the fort in earnest and we have a tricky path to navigate in getting past them."

"And we have very little time to accomplish it," Heyward added, looking up toward the layer of mist that hid the setting moon.

"And we don't have much time to do it!" the scout said again. "This can be accomplished in two ways, with the help of

Providence—without which it cannot be done at all."

"Name them quickly because time is running out."

"One option would be to have the peaceful ones get off their horses and let the animals roam freely across the field. By sending the Mohicans ahead of us, we could then carve a path through their guards and enter the fort by stepping over the dead bodies."

"This won't work—this won't work!" interrupted the generous Heyward; "a soldier might force his way through like this, but never with such a convoy."

"It would certainly be a dangerous path for such delicate feet to travel," replied the equally hesitant scout; "but I felt it was proper for my manhood to mention it. We must then reverse our trail and get beyond the range of their sentries, when we will turn sharply to the west and enter the mountains; where I can conceal you so that all the devil's hounds in Montcalm's service would lose the trail for months to come."

"Let it be done, and that instantly."

No more words were needed; Hawkeye simply gave the command to "follow" and began moving along the same route they had used to enter their current perilous and dangerous predicament. They moved carefully and silently, just as their recent conversation had been; none of them knew when a passing patrol or a hidden enemy sentry might suddenly appear on their path. As they made their quiet way along the edge of the pond, Heyward and the scout once again cast secretive glances at its terrifying bleakness. They searched unsuccessfully for the figure they had so recently observed moving silently along these shores, while the gentle, steady lapping of small waves served as a chilling reminder that the waters had not yet receded and provided a horrifying memento of the violent act they had just witnessed. Like everything else in that fleeting and somber scene, the shallow basin soon disappeared into the darkness and merged with the mass of dark shapes behind the travelers.

Hawkeye soon turned away from their retreat path, heading toward the mountains that formed the western edge of the narrow plain, leading his companions with quick steps deep into the shadows cast by the high and jagged peaks. The route became difficult now, crossing ground littered with rocks and cut through with ravines, making their progress much slower. Dark and barren hills surrounded them on all sides, offering some compensation for the extra effort of the march through the sense of safety they provided. Eventually the group began slowly climbing a steep and rocky slope, following a path that wound cleverly among rocks and trees, avoiding one while using the other for support, in a way that showed it had been created by people with long experience in wilderness skills. As they gradually climbed from the valley floor, the thick darkness that usually comes before dawn began to fade, and objects became visible in the clear and vivid colors that nature had given them. When they emerged from the stunted woods that clung to the barren mountainsides onto a flat and moss-covered rock that formed the summit, they encountered the morning as it came glowing above the green pines of a hill that lay on the far side of the Horican valley.

The scout instructed the sisters to get down from their horses. He removed the bridles from the mouths and the saddles from the backs of the exhausted animals, then set them free to forage for whatever meager food they could find among the bushes and sparse vegetation of that high mountain area.

"Go," he said, "and find your food where nature provides it for you; and be careful that you don't become food for hungry wolves yourselves, among these hills."

"Don't we need them anymore?" Heyward asked.

"Look and see for yourself," said the scout, moving toward the eastern edge of the mountain as he motioned for the entire group to follow him. "If it were as simple to see into a person's heart as it is to observe the exposed weaknesses of Montcalm's camp from this location, hypocrites would become rare, and the cleverness of a Mingo might turn out to be a losing strategy when compared to the honesty of a Delaware."

When the travelers reached the edge of the cliffs, they immediately saw that the scout's statement was true, and they recognized the excellent foresight he had shown in leading them to this commanding position.

The mountain where they stood, rising perhaps a thousand feet into the air, was a tall cone that jutted out slightly ahead of the mountain range stretching for miles along the lake's western shores, until it joined its neighboring peaks miles beyond the water and continued toward Canada in scattered and broken masses of rock, sparsely covered with evergreen trees. Directly below the group, the southern shore of the Horican curved in a wide semicircle from mountain to mountain, forming a broad beach that gradually rose into an uneven and somewhat elevated plain. To the north stretched the clear waters of what appeared from that dizzying height to be the narrow expanse of the "holy lake," carved with countless bays, decorated with striking headlands, and scattered with numerous islands. A few miles away, the lake's surface disappeared among the mountains or became hidden in masses of mist that drifted slowly along the mountainsides, carried by a gentle morning breeze. However, a narrow gap between the hilltops revealed the passage through which the waters continued their journey north, spreading their pure and expansive surface once more before flowing into the distant Champlain. To the south lay the narrow pass, or rather the broken plain, mentioned so frequently. For several miles in that direction, the mountains seemed reluctant to give up their control, but within sight they separated and eventually merged into the flat and sandy lands across which we have followed our travelers on their round trip. Along both mountain ranges that bordered the opposite sides of the lake and valley, wisps of light mist rose in spiraling columns from the uninhabited forests, resembling smoke from hidden cabins, or drifted lazily down the slopes to blend with the fog of the lower ground. A single, isolated, snow-white cloud hung above the valley, marking the spot beneath which lay the quiet waters of the "bloody pond."

Directly on the shore of the lake, positioned closer to its western edge than to its eastern boundary, stood the massive earthen fortifications and low structures of William Henry. Two of the curved defensive walls seemed to rest directly on the water that lapped at their foundations, while a deep trench and sprawling marshlands protected its remaining sides and corners. The surrounding land had been stripped of trees for a considerable distance around the fortress, but everywhere else the landscape wore nature's green clothing, except where the clear water softened the scenery, or where stark rocks pushed their dark and bare surfaces above the rolling outline of the mountain ridges. In front of the fort could be seen the scattered guards, who maintained a tiresome watch against their many enemies; and within the walls themselves, the travelers gazed down upon soldiers still groggy from a night of standing guard. Toward the southeast, but directly connected to the fort, stood a fortified camp positioned on a rocky height that would have been a much better location for the main fortress itself, where Hawkeye pointed out the presence of those supporting regiments that had so recently departed the Hudson in their company. From the forest, a bit further to the south, rose many dark and ominous columns of smoke that could easily be told apart from the cleaner vapors rising from the springs, and which the scout also indicated to Heyward as proof that the enemy was gathered in large numbers in that direction.

But the sight that most captured the young soldier's attention was on the western shore of the lake, though quite close to its southern end. On a strip of land that appeared from his position too narrow to hold such an army, but which actually stretched many hundreds of yards from the shores of the Horican to the base of the mountain, the white tents and military equipment of a camp housing ten thousand men could be seen. Artillery positions had already been constructed in front of them, and even while the observers above watched from their vantage point, each experiencing very different feelings as they gazed down at a scene that spread out like a map below them, the thunder of cannon fire rose from the valley and echoed across the eastern hills.

"Morning is just beginning to reach them down there," said the thoughtful and contemplative scout, "and the guards intend to wake up those who are sleeping with the sound of cannons. We've arrived a few hours too late! Montcalm has already filled the forest with his cursed Iroquois."

"The place is definitely under siege," Duncan replied; "but isn't there some way we could get inside? Being captured within the fortifications would be much better than falling back into the hands of wandering Indians."

"Look!" shouted the scout, without thinking drawing Cora's attention to her father's quarters, "see how that shot sent stones flying from the side of the commandant's house! Yes! these Frenchmen will tear it apart faster than it was built, even though it's solid and thick!"

"Heyward, it makes me sick to see danger that I can't face alongside you," said the fearless but worried daughter. "Let's go to Montcalm and demand he let us in: he wouldn't dare refuse a child this request."

"You'd hardly find the Frenchman's tent with your hair still on your head," said the straightforward scout. "If I had just one of the thousand boats lying empty along that shore, it could be done! Look! The shooting will end soon, because there's a fog coming that will turn day into night and make an Indian arrow more dangerous than a cast cannonball. Now, if you're up for the task and will follow me, I'll make an attempt; I'm eager to get down into that camp, even if it's just to scatter some Mingo dogs I see hiding at the edges of that birch grove."

"We are equals," Cora said with determination; "on a mission like this, we will follow you into any danger."

The scout turned to her with a smile of genuine and warm approval as he replied:

"I wish I had a thousand men with strong bodies and sharp eyes who feared death as little as you do! I'd send those chattering Frenchmen back to their hideout before the week was over, making them howl like chained dogs or starving wolves. But listen," he said, turning away from her to address the rest of the group, "the fog is rolling in so quickly that we'll barely have enough time to reach it on the plain and use it for cover. Remember, if anything happens to me, keep the wind blowing on your left cheeks—or better yet, follow the Mohicans; they can find their way by scent, whether it's day or night."

He gestured for them to follow and threw himself down the steep slope, moving with confident but cautious steps. Heyward helped the sisters make their way down, and within minutes they had all descended far down a mountain whose sides they had climbed with such great effort and difficulty.

The path Hawkeye chose quickly led the travelers down to the flat ground of the plain, positioning them almost directly across from a sally-port in the fort's western wall, which stood roughly half a mile away from where he stopped to let Duncan catch up with his group. In their enthusiasm, and helped by the favorable terrain, they had moved ahead of the fog that was slowly rolling down across the lake, making it necessary to wait until the mist had completely covered the enemy's camp in its thick, white blanket. The Mohicans used this waiting time to slip quietly out of the forest and examine the area around them. The scout followed them at a short distance, hoping to benefit quickly from what they discovered and to gain some basic understanding of the immediate surroundings for himself.

In just a few moments he came back, his face flushed red with frustration, while he grumbled his disappointment in words that were far from polite.

"The clever Frenchman has positioned a guard post right in our way," he said; "Indians and white men; and we're just as likely to stumble right into them as we are to slip past them in this fog!"

"Can't we take a detour to avoid the danger," Heyward asked, "and get back on our path once it's behind us?"

"Anyone who strays from their path once they're lost in fog can never tell when or how they'll find their way back! The mists of Lake George aren't like the gentle curls rising from a peace pipe, or the smoke that hovers above a fire lit to ward off mosquitoes."

He was still speaking when a loud crashing sound echoed through the air, and a cannonball flew into the thicket, hitting the trunk of a young tree before bouncing to the ground, its power greatly reduced by the obstacles it had already encountered. The Indians immediately followed like eager servants of this deadly projectile, and Uncas began speaking urgently and with animated gestures in the Delaware language.

"That might be true, boy," the scout murmured when he had finished speaking; "because serious fevers can't be treated like a simple toothache. Come on, then, the fog is closing in."

"Stop!" Heyward shouted; "first explain what you expect."

"It's quickly done, and it's a small hope; but it's better than nothing. This cannonball that you see," added the scout, kicking the harmless iron with his foot, "has plowed the earth on its path from the fort, and we shall hunt for the furrow it has made, when all other signs may fail. No more words, but follow, or the fog may leave us in the middle of our path, a mark for both armies to shoot at."

Heyward realized that they had reached a critical moment where action mattered more than words, so he positioned himself between the sisters and quickly guided them forward, keeping his eyes on the shadowy outline of their guide. It quickly became clear that Hawkeye hadn't exaggerated the fog's intensity, because after they had walked only twenty yards, the members of the group could barely make each other out through the thick mist.

They had completed their small loop to the left and were already turning back toward the right, having covered what Heyward estimated to be nearly half the distance to the allied fortifications, when his ears were struck by a fierce challenge, seemingly coming from just twenty feet away:

"Who goes there?"

"Keep moving!" the scout whispered, leaning to the left again.

"Keep moving!" Heyward repeated; when the command was called out again by a dozen voices, each one seeming to carry a threat.

"It's me," Duncan shouted, dragging rather than guiding the people he was helping as he moved quickly forward.

"Bête!—qui?—moi!"

"Friend of France."

"You look more like an enemy of France to me; stop or by God I'll make you a friend of the devil. No! Fire, comrades, fire!"

The command was immediately followed, and the mist was disturbed by the blast of fifty rifles. Fortunately, the marksmanship was poor, and the bullets sliced through the air in a direction slightly different from the path taken by the escapees; though still close enough that to the inexperienced ears of David and the two women, it sounded as if the shots whizzed just inches from their heads. The shouting resumed, and the command not only to fire again but to give chase was clearly heard. When Heyward quickly explained what the words they heard meant, Hawkeye stopped and spoke with swift determination and great resolve.

"Let's unleash our attack," he said; "they'll think it's a sudden assault and retreat, or they'll hold their position and wait for backup."

The plan was well thought out, but it didn't work as intended. The moment the French heard the gunshots, it looked as though the entire plain was swarming with soldiers, with musket fire crackling across its full length, from the lake's shoreline to the farthest edge of the forest.

"We'll draw their entire army toward us and trigger a full-scale attack," Duncan said. "Lead the way, my friend, for the sake of your life and ours."

The scout appeared ready to follow through, but in the rush of the moment and with the shift in position, he had lost his sense of direction. He tried turning each side of his face toward the gentle breeze, but both felt equally cool. In this predicament, Uncas discovered the groove carved by the cannon ball, where it had sliced through the earth across three neighboring ant-hills.

"Tell me the distance!" said Hawkeye, leaning down to get a quick look at the direction, and then immediately moving forward.

Shouts, curses, voices calling out to one another, and the crack of musket fire were now rapid and continuous, seemingly coming from all directions around them. Suddenly a brilliant flash of light blazed across the landscape, the fog swirled upward in dense clouds, and several cannons thundered across the field, their roar echoing powerfully off the rumbling mountainsides.

"It's from the fort!" Hawkeye shouted, spinning around abruptly; "and here we were, like panicked idiots, running straight into the woods and right into the hands of the Mohawks."

The moment their mistake was corrected, the entire group hurried back to fix their error with complete urgency. Duncan gladly gave up supporting Cora to Uncas's arm, and Cora willingly accepted the welcome help. Men, heated and furious in their chase, were clearly following their trail, and every moment threatened their capture, if not their complete destruction.

"No mercy for the scoundrels!" shouted an eager pursuer, who appeared to be directing the enemy's operations.

"Hold your ground and stay alert, my brave Sixtieths!" a voice suddenly called out from above them. "Wait until you can see the enemy, aim low, and clear the slope."

"Father! Father!" a sharp cry rang out through the mist. "It's me! Alice! Your own Elsie! Please, spare us! Save your daughters!"

"Stop!" shouted the previous speaker, his voice filled with the terrible anguish of a father, the sound carrying all the way to the woods and echoing back solemnly. "It's her! God has given me back my children! Open the sally-port; to the field, Sixtieths, to the field; don't fire a single shot, or you might kill my daughters! Drive away these French dogs with your bayonets."

Duncan heard the harsh scraping of rusty hinges, and rushing toward the sound, he encountered a long column of dark red-uniformed soldiers moving quickly toward the glacis. He recognized them as his own battalion of the Royal Americans, and racing to join them at the front, he quickly cleared away all signs of his pursuers from the area around the fortifications.

For a moment, Cora and Alice stood trembling and confused by this sudden abandonment; but before either had time to speak, or even think, an officer of enormous build, whose hair had turned white with age and military service, but whose commanding military presence had been mellowed rather than diminished by time, burst out of the thick fog, and pulled them into his arms, while large burning tears streamed down his pale and lined face, and he cried out, in the distinctive accent of Scotland:

"For this I thank you, Lord! Let danger come as it will, your servant is now prepared!"

---

# Chapter XV.

"Then let's go inside to learn what his message is; I could probably guess what it's about before the French even say a word."
—King Henry V

A few days that followed were spent enduring the hardships, chaos, and threats of the siege, which was aggressively conducted by an enemy force that Munro had no adequate means to defend against. It seemed as though Webb, with his army resting idly along the Hudson River banks, had completely forgotten about the desperate situation his fellow countrymen faced. Montcalm had positioned his warriors throughout the woods of the portage, and every cry and war whoop they made echoed through the British camp, striking fear into the hearts of soldiers who were already inclined to overestimate the threat they faced.

The situation was entirely different for those under siege, however. Inspired by their leaders' words and motivated by their examples, the defenders had discovered their bravery and upheld their longstanding reputation with an enthusiasm that honored their commander's resolute character. Though he was a skilled general, the French commander seemed content with the effort of marching through the wilderness to face his enemy, and he failed to capture the nearby mountains. From these heights, the besieged could have been destroyed without risk, and in the more contemporary warfare of that region, such an oversight would not have been tolerated for even an hour. This kind of disregard for high ground, or perhaps fear of the effort required to climb it, could be considered the persistent flaw in the military tactics of that era. This weakness stemmed from the straightforward nature of Indian warfare, where the type of fighting and the thick forests made fortresses uncommon and artillery nearly useless. The negligence that developed from these practices carried over into the Revolutionary War and cost the States the crucial fortress of Ticonderoga, creating a path for Burgoyne's army into what was then the heart of the nation. We now look back at this ignorance, or delusion, whatever we might call it, with amazement, understanding that neglecting a high position whose challenges, like those of Mount Defiance, have been so greatly overstated, would today destroy the reputation of either the engineer who designed the fortifications at its base or the general responsible for defending them.

The tourist, the person seeking better health, or the lover of natural beauty who now travels comfortably in his horse-drawn carriage through the landscapes we have tried to describe, searching for knowledge, health, or enjoyment, or glides smoothly toward his destination on those man-made waterways that have been created under the leadership of a politician who has been bold enough to risk his political reputation on this uncertain venture, should not assume that his ancestors crossed those hills or battled the same currents with the same ease. Moving a single heavy cannon was often considered as significant as winning a battle; that is, if the challenges of the journey had not separated it so far from its essential companion, the ammunition, that it became nothing more than a useless tube of cumbersome iron.[1]

[1] Evidently the late De Witt Clinton, who died as governor of New York in 1828.

The problems created by this situation weighed heavily on the determined Scottish commander who was now defending Fort William Henry. Although his enemy had ignored the surrounding hills, he had strategically positioned his artillery on the flat ground and ensured they were operated with energy and expertise. To counter this attack, the defenders could only rely on the incomplete and rushed fortifications of a stronghold built in the untamed frontier.

It was on the afternoon of the fifth day of the siege, and the fourth day of his own service in it, that Major Heyward took advantage of a truce that had just been called by going to the ramparts of one of the water bastions to breathe the cool air from the lake and to observe the progress of the siege. He was alone, except for the solitary guard who walked back and forth on the mound; the artillery crews had also hurried to take advantage of the temporary break from their demanding duties. The evening was wonderfully calm, and the light breeze from the clear water was fresh and refreshing. It seemed as if, with the end of the thundering cannons and the crash of cannonballs, nature had also seized the moment to display her gentlest and most enchanting appearance. The sun cast its farewell splendor on the scene, without the harsh intensity of those burning rays that characterized the climate and the season. The mountains appeared green, fresh, and beautiful, softened by the gentler light or mellowed in shadow as thin mists drifted between them and the sun. The many islands lay on the surface of Lake Horican, some low and sunken as if set into the waters, and others seeming to float above the surface like small hills covered in green velvet; among these, the fishermen of the besieging army peacefully rowed their boats or drifted at rest on the smooth, mirror-like surface as they quietly went about their work.

The scene was both lively and peaceful at the same time. Everything that belonged to the natural world was either beautiful or simply magnificent, while the parts that depended on human mood and activity were energetic and lighthearted.

Two small, pristine flags flew in the open air—one positioned on a protruding corner of the fort, and the other on the forward battery of the attacking forces; these served as symbols of the truce that applied not only to military actions, but apparently also to the hostility between the opposing sides.

Behind these, the rival banners of England and France swayed back and forth, their heavy silk fabric opening and closing in graceful folds.

A hundred cheerful and carefree young Frenchmen were pulling a net toward the rocky shore, dangerously close to the grim but quiet cannons of the fort, while the eastern mountain echoed back the loud calls and joyful laughter that accompanied their activity. Some were rushing eagerly to enjoy the water sports on the lake, and others were already making their way up the nearby hills, driven by the restless curiosity typical of their people. Yet all these games and activities were merely watched by idle but interested spectators—both the enemy forces observing the besieged and the besieged defenders themselves. Here and there a guard post had indeed started a song or joined in a dance, which had drawn the dark-skinned natives from their hiding places in the forest to gather around them. In short, everything looked more like a day of entertainment than an hour stolen from the dangers and hardships of a brutal and vengeful war.

Duncan had been standing thoughtfully, observing this scene for several minutes, when the sound of approaching footsteps drew his attention to the glacis in front of the sally-port he had noticed earlier. He moved to a corner of the bastion and saw the scout being escorted by a French officer toward the main part of the fort. Hawkeye's face looked worn and exhausted, and he appeared dejected, as if he felt deeply humiliated by falling into enemy hands. He was missing his beloved weapon, and his arms were tied behind his back with leather strips made from deerskin. The arrival of flags to protect messengers delivering demands had become so common recently that when Heyward first glanced casually at this group, he expected to see another enemy officer carrying out a similar duty, but the moment he recognized the tall figure and the still strong yet downcast features of his friend, the woodsman, he was startled with surprise and turned to climb down from the bastion into the heart of the fortification.

The sounds of other voices caught his attention and momentarily made him forget what he had come to do. At the inner corner of the earthwork, he encountered the sisters walking along the defensive wall, seeking fresh air and escape from being cooped up indoors, just as he was. They hadn't seen each other since that distressing moment when he had left them on the open ground, concerned only with ensuring their safety. When he had departed from them, he was exhausted by worry and worn down by fatigue; now he saw them looking rested and radiant, though still fearful and worried. Given such circumstances, it's no wonder that the young man temporarily forgot about everything else in order to speak with them. However, the voice of the sincere and young Alice spoke first.

"Oh! You tyrant! You cowardly knight! You who abandons your ladies right in the arena," she cried; "here we have been for days, no, for what feels like forever, waiting for you to come to us, begging for mercy and forgiveness for your cowardly retreat, or I should say, your cowardly escape—because you truly ran away in a way that no wounded deer, as our good friend the scout would put it, could match!"

"You know that Alice expresses our gratitude and our blessings," added the more serious and thoughtful Cora. "Honestly, we're a bit puzzled about why you would so strictly keep yourself away from a place where the daughters' appreciation could be reinforced by a father's thanks."

"Your father could tell you himself that even though I've been away from you, I haven't forgotten about your safety," the young man replied. "Control of that village of huts over there," he said, gesturing toward the nearby fortified camp, "has been fiercely contested. Whoever controls it will surely possess this fort and everything in it. I've spent all my days and nights there since we parted ways because I believed duty required me to be there. But," he continued, with a look of disappointment that he tried but failed to hide, "if I had known that what I considered proper soldier's behavior could be interpreted differently, shame would have been another reason to add to my list."

"Heyward! Duncan!" Alice cried out, leaning forward to study his face as he turned away, until a strand of her golden hair fell against her flushed cheek and almost hid the tear that had begun to form in her eye. "If I thought my thoughtless words had hurt you, I would never speak again. Cora could tell you, if she chose to, how much we have valued everything you've done for us, and how profound—I almost said, how passionate—our gratitude truly is."

"And will Cora confirm this is true?" Duncan exclaimed, letting his troubled expression give way to a smile of genuine delight. "What does our more serious sister say? Will she find a way to excuse the knight's neglect in favor of his duty as a soldier?"

Cora didn't respond right away, but instead turned to face the water, gazing out at the surface of Lake George. When she finally looked back at the young man with her dark eyes, they were filled with such anguish that it immediately pushed every thought from his mind except concern for her wellbeing.

"You're not feeling well, dearest Miss Munro!" he exclaimed; "we've been fooling around while you're suffering!"

"It's nothing," she replied, declining his help with feminine modesty. "The fact that I cannot see the bright side of life's picture, like this innocent but passionate optimist," she continued, placing her hand gently but lovingly on her sister's arm, "is the price of experience, and perhaps the curse of my temperament. Look," she went on, as if determined to overcome weakness through a sense of duty; "look around you, Major Heyward, and tell me what kind of future this presents for the daughter of a soldier whose greatest joy lies in his honor and his military reputation."

"Neither should nor will be tarnished by circumstances beyond his control," Duncan replied warmly. "But your words remind me of my own duty. I'm going now to your brave father to hear his final decisions regarding the defense. May God bless you in whatever comes, noble—Cora—I may and must call you that." She openly offered him her hand, though her lip trembled, and her cheeks slowly turned ashen pale. "Whatever happens, I know you will bring honor and distinction to your gender. Alice, farewell"—his voice shifted from admiration to tenderness—"farewell, Alice; we'll meet again soon; as victors, I hope, and celebrating!"

Without waiting for a response from either of them, the young man hurled himself down the grass-covered steps of the fortification, and moving swiftly across the parade ground, he quickly found himself in their father's presence. Munro was walking back and forth in his cramped quarters with an agitated manner and enormous steps when Duncan entered.

"You've anticipated what I was hoping for, Major Heyward," he said; "I was just about to ask you for this favor."

"I'm sorry to see, sir, that the messenger I recommended so highly has come back under French guard! I hope there's no reason to question his loyalty?"

"I'm well aware of 'The Long Rifle's' loyalty," Munro replied, "and it's beyond question; though his usual good luck appears to have finally run out. Montcalm has captured him, and with the cursed courtesy typical of his people, he has sent him back with a sorrowful story, claiming 'knowing how much I valued the man, he couldn't bear to keep him.' That's a cunning way, Major Duncan Heyward, of informing a person about his troubles!"

"But what about the general and his reinforcements?"

"Did you look to the south when you entered, and couldn't you see them?" said the old soldier, laughing bitterly. "Come now! You're an impatient young man, sir, and you can't give the gentlemen time for their march!"

"They are coming, then? The scout has said as much?"

"When? And by what path? The fool has failed to tell me this. There appears to be a letter as well; and that is the only pleasant part of this situation. As for the usual courtesies of your Marquis of Montcalm—I assure you, Duncan, that the Marquis of Lothian could purchase a dozen such titles—but if the news in the letter were bad, the politeness of this French gentleman would certainly require him to inform us of it."

"So he keeps the letter but lets the messenger go?"

"Yes, he certainly does, and all for the sake of what you call your 'good nature.' I would bet, if the truth were known, that fellow's grandfather taught the noble art of dancing."

"But what does the scout say? He has eyes and ears, and a tongue. What spoken report does he give?"

"Oh! sir, he has all his natural faculties, and he's free to share everything he has seen and heard. The whole story comes down to this: there's one of his majesty's forts on the banks of the Hudson River, called Edward, named in honor of his gracious highness of York, as you know; and it's well stocked with armed soldiers, as such a fortification should be."

"But wasn't there any movement, no signs of any intention to advance to help us?"

"There were the morning and evening parades; and when one of the provincial fools—you'll understand, Duncan, since you're half Scottish yourself—when one of them spilled his gunpowder over his porridge, if it hit the coals, it simply caught fire!" Then, abruptly shifting from his harsh, sarcastic tone to something more serious and contemplative, he went on: "and yet there could, and should be, something in that letter that would be important to discover!"

"We need to make our decision quickly," Duncan said, taking advantage of this shift in mood to focus on the more critical matters they needed to discuss. "I can't hide from you, sir, that we won't be able to hold the camp much longer. And I'm sorry to say that conditions in the fort aren't any better—more than half of our cannons have exploded."

"And how could it be any different? Some were pulled up from the bottom of the lake; some have been rusting away in the woods since the country was first discovered; and some were never real guns at all—just toys that privateers played with! Do you think, sir, that you can have a Woolwich Arsenal in the middle of a wilderness, three thousand miles away from Great Britain?"

"The walls are falling down around us, and our supplies are running low," Heyward continued, ignoring the fresh outburst of anger; "even the soldiers are showing signs of unrest and fear."

"Major Heyward," Munro said, turning to his younger colleague with the dignity that came from his years and higher rank, "I would have served his majesty for fifty years and earned these gray hairs for nothing if I didn't understand everything you're telling me and the urgent nature of our situation. Still, we owe everything to the honor of the king's forces, and something to ourselves as well. As long as there's hope of rescue, I will defend this fortress, even if I have to do it with stones picked up from the lake shore. What we need is to see that letter, so we can understand the intentions of the man the Earl of Loudon left here to take his place."

"And can I be of service in the matter?"

"Sir, you can; the Marquis of Montcalm has, along with his other courtesies, invited me to a personal meeting between the fortifications and his own camp, in order to share some additional information, as he puts it. Now, I believe it wouldn't be wise to appear overly eager to meet with him, and I would use you, an officer of rank, as my representative; for it would hardly be fitting with Scotland's honor to let it be said that one of her gentlemen was surpassed in courtesy by a native of any other country on earth."

Without taking on the unnecessary task of debating the relative merits of national politeness, Duncan cheerfully agreed to take the veteran's place in the upcoming meeting. A lengthy and private conversation followed, during which the young man gained further understanding of his responsibilities from his commander's experience and natural sharp judgment, and then Duncan departed.

As Duncan could only serve as the fort commandant's representative, the formal ceremonies that typically accompanied meetings between opposing military leaders were naturally omitted. The ceasefire remained in effect, and accompanied by the roll and beat of drums under the protection of a small white flag, Duncan departed through the sally-port within ten minutes of receiving his final instructions. The French officer stationed at the forward position received him with standard military courtesies and immediately escorted him to the distant tent of the distinguished soldier who commanded the French forces.

The enemy general welcomed the young messenger, flanked by his top officers and a dark-skinned group of native chiefs who had accompanied him to battle with warriors from their various tribes. Heyward stopped abruptly when his eyes swept quickly across the shadowy gathering of tribal leaders and he spotted Magua's malicious face watching him with the quiet yet brooding focus that characterized that cunning savage's expression. A brief cry of shock escaped from the young man's mouth, but immediately remembering his mission and the company he was in, he stifled any sign of feeling and turned toward the enemy commander, who had already stepped forward to greet him.

The Marquis de Montcalm was, during the time we are describing, in the prime of his life and at the height of his success. Yet even in this fortunate position, he remained approachable and was known as much for his careful attention to proper etiquette as for the gallant bravery that would lead him to sacrifice his life on the Plains of Abraham just two years later. Duncan, looking away from Magua's hostile expression, found his gaze settling with satisfaction on the cheerful and refined face and the dignified military bearing of the French general.

"Sir," said the latter, "I have great pleasure in—bah!—where is that interpreter?"

"I believe, sir, that it will not be necessary," Heyward modestly replied; "I speak a little French."

"Ah! I am very pleased about that," said Montcalm, taking Duncan familiarly by the arm and leading him deep into the marquee, a little out of earshot; "I detest those scoundrels; one never knows where one stands with them. Well then! sir," he continued, still speaking in French; "though I should have been proud of receiving your commandant, I am very happy that he has seen fit to employ an officer so distinguished, and who, I am sure, is so amiable, as yourself."

Duncan bowed deeply, gratified by the praise, despite his heroic resolve to resist any manipulation that might make him forget his duty to his prince; and Montcalm, after pausing briefly as if gathering his thoughts, continued:

"Your commander is a brave man, and well qualified to fight off my attack. But, sir, isn't it time to start listening more to humanity, and less to your courage? One quality defines a hero just as strongly as the other."

"We believe these qualities go hand in hand," Duncan replied with a smile, "but while we see in your excellency's strength every reason to encourage one quality, we don't yet see any specific need to put the other into practice."

Montcalm, for his part, gave a slight bow, but he carried himself like someone too experienced to be swayed by flattering words. After thinking for a moment, he continued:

"My telescope might have misled me, and perhaps your fortifications can withstand our artillery better than I initially thought. Are you aware of our military strength?"

"Our reports differ," Duncan said casually, "but the highest estimate hasn't gone beyond twenty thousand men."

The Frenchman bit his lip and fixed his eyes intently on the other man as if trying to read his thoughts; then, with the quick adaptability that was characteristic of him, he went on as if agreeing with the accuracy of a count that essentially doubled the size of his army:

"It doesn't say much for how alert we soldiers are, sir, that no matter what we do, we can never hide how many of us there are. If it could be done anywhere, you'd think it might work in these woods. Even though you think it's too early to listen to what compassion tells us," he added with a sly smile, "I might be allowed to think that someone as young as you hasn't forgotten what it means to be chivalrous. The commandant's daughters, I understand, have made it into the fort since the siege began?"

"That's true, sir; but rather than weakening our efforts, they show us what courage looks like through their own strength. If nothing more than determination were needed to fight off such a skilled soldier as M. de Montcalm, I would happily entrust the defense of William Henry to the older of those ladies."

"We have a wise law in our Salic code, which states, 'The crown of France shall never lower the spear to the spinning wheel'," said Montcalm, curtly, and with a touch of arrogance; but immediately adding, with his previous open and relaxed manner: "since all the finer qualities are passed down through bloodlines, I can easily believe you; though, as I mentioned before, bravery has its boundaries, and compassion must not be overlooked. I trust, sir, you come with authority to negotiate the surrender of this fortress?"

"Has your excellency found our defense so weak that you believe this action is necessary?"

"I would hate to see this defense drag on in a way that would anger my Native American allies over there," Montcalm continued, looking toward the group of serious and watchful Indians, while ignoring the other man's questions. "Even now, I'm finding it hard to keep them following the rules of warfare."

Heyward remained quiet, as painful memories of the dangers he had just escaped flooded his thoughts, bringing back images of those helpless people who had endured all his hardships alongside him.

"Those gentlemen," said Montcalm, pressing the advantage he believed he had gained, "are most dangerous when they've been thwarted; and I don't need to tell you how hard it is to control them when they're angry. Well then, sir! Shall we discuss the terms?"

"I'm afraid your excellency has been misled about the strength of William Henry and the resources available to its garrison!"

"I haven't positioned my forces outside Quebec, but rather before an earthwork that's defended by twenty-three hundred brave men," came the brief response.

"Our fortifications are made of earth, that's true—and they're not positioned on the rocky cliffs of Cape Diamond; but they're built on the same shoreline that proved so devastating to Dieskau and his forces. There's also a strong military force just a few hours' march from our position, which we're counting on as part of our resources."

"About six or eight thousand men," Montcalm replied with obvious indifference, "whose leader wisely believes they're safer behind their fortifications than on the battlefield."

Now it was Heyward's turn to bite his lip in frustration as the other man so casually referred to a military force that the young officer knew was being exaggerated. Both men reflected quietly for a moment, until Montcalm resumed their conversation in a manner that revealed he believed his guest's visit was purely to discuss surrender terms. Meanwhile, Heyward began presenting various incentives to the French general, hoping to trick him into revealing what he had learned from the intercepted letter. Neither man's strategy worked, however, and after a lengthy and unsuccessful meeting, Duncan departed, having formed a favorable impression of his enemy commander's politeness and abilities, but remaining just as uninformed about what he had come to discover as when he first arrived. Montcalm accompanied him to the tent entrance, continuing to invite the fort's commandant to meet with him immediately on the open field between the two armies.

There they parted ways, and Duncan went back to the French advance position with the same escort as before. From there, he immediately headed to the fort and to his commanding officer's quarters.

---

# Chapter XVI.

"EDG.—Before you fight the battle open this letter."
—King Lear

Major Heyward discovered Munro with only his daughters for company. Alice was sitting on his lap, gently running her delicate fingers through the gray hair on the old man's forehead; and whenever he pretended to scowl at her playfulness, she would soothe his feigned irritation by tenderly pressing her rosy lips against his wrinkled brow. Cora sat nearby, watching calmly and with amusement; she observed her younger sister's capricious behavior with the kind of maternal affection that defined her love for Alice. Not only the perils they had already endured, but also those that still threatened them, seemed temporarily forgotten in the comforting pleasure of such a family reunion. It appeared as though they had taken advantage of the brief ceasefire to dedicate a moment to the purest and finest love; the daughters setting aside their fears, and the old soldier his worries, in the safety of the present moment. Duncan, who had entered without announcement in his eagerness to report his arrival, stood for several minutes as an unnoticed and enchanted observer of this scene. But Alice's quick and lively eyes soon caught sight of his reflection in a mirror, and she jumped up from her father's knee with a blush, crying out:

"Major Heyward!"

"What about the boy?" her father demanded. "I've sent him to have a brief conversation with the Frenchman. Ha, sir, you are young, and you're quick! Get out of here, you troublemaker; as if there weren't enough problems for a soldier, without having his camp filled with such chattering women as yourself!"

Alice followed her sister with a laugh, as her sister immediately led them away from a room where she could tell they were no longer welcome. Rather than asking about the outcome of the young man's mission, Munro walked back and forth across the room for several minutes, his hands clasped behind his back and his head tilted downward, like someone deep in thought. Finally, he lifted his eyes, which sparkled with a father's love, and called out:

"They are a pair of excellent girls, Heyward, and such as anyone may boast of."

"You don't need to hear my opinion of your daughters now, Colonel Munro."

"That's right, son, that's right," the impatient old man cut in. "You were about to share your thoughts more completely on that subject the day you arrived, but I didn't think it was proper for an old soldier to be discussing marriage blessings and wedding humor when the king's enemies might show up uninvited to the celebration. But I was mistaken, Duncan, my boy, I was mistaken about that; and I'm now ready to listen to what you have to say."

"Despite the pleasure your assurance brings me, dear sir, I have just received a message from Montcalm—"

"Let the Frenchman and his entire army go to hell, sir!" shouted the impatient veteran. "He hasn't conquered William Henry yet, and he never will, as long as Webb proves himself to be the man he ought to be. No, sir, thank God we're not in such desperate circumstances that anyone could say Munro is too overwhelmed to handle the simple family matters of his own household. Your mother was the only child of my dearest friend, Duncan; and I'll give you a proper hearing, even if all the knights of St. Louis were gathered together at the gate, with the French saint leading them, demanding to have a word. What a fine example of knighthood that is, sir—one that can be purchased with barrels of sugar! And then there are your cheap little marquisates. The thistle is the true order of dignity and ancient heritage; the genuine 'nemo me impune lacessit' of chivalry. You had ancestors who held that honor, Duncan, and they brought distinction to the nobility of Scotland."

Heyward noticed that his commanding officer was taking spiteful satisfaction in showing his disdain for the French general's message, so he felt compelled to indulge this irritation that he knew wouldn't last long; therefore, he responded with as much detachment as he could manage regarding such a matter:

"My request, as you know, sir, went so far as to presume to the honor of being your son."

"Yes, boy, you found the words to make yourself very clearly understood. But let me ask you, sir, have you been as clear to the girl?"

"I swear, absolutely not," Duncan declared passionately; "it would have been a betrayal of the trust placed in me if I had used my position for such a purpose."

"Your ideas are those of a gentleman, Major Heyward, and they're perfectly appropriate in their proper context. But Cora Munro is a young woman too wise, and possesses a mind too refined and cultivated, to require protection even from a father."

"Cora!"

"Yes—Cora! We are discussing your romantic intentions toward Miss Munro, are we not, sir?"

"I—I—I wasn't aware that I had mentioned her name," said Duncan, stammering.

"And who exactly did you want my permission to marry, Major Heyward?" the old soldier demanded, straightening himself with the dignity of wounded pride.

"You have another child, and she is just as beautiful."

"Alice!" the father cried out, his astonishment matching the surprise Duncan had just shown when repeating her sister's name.

"That's exactly what I was hoping for, sir."

The young man waited quietly for the outcome of the remarkable impact created by news that, as it now seemed, was completely unexpected. For several minutes, Munro walked back and forth across the room with long, quick steps, his stern face twitching uncontrollably, and all his attention apparently focused on his own thoughts. Finally, he stopped directly in front of Heyward, and fixing his gaze on the other man's eyes, he spoke with a trembling lip:

"Duncan Heyward, I have loved you because of the man whose blood runs through your veins; I have loved you for your own admirable qualities; and I have loved you because I believed you would bring happiness to my daughter. But all this love would transform into hatred if I were certain that what I fear so deeply is actually true."

"God forbid that any action or thought of mine should cause such a change!" the young man declared, his gaze never wavering under the intense look he faced. Without considering how impossible it would be for the other man to understand the feelings hidden within his own heart, Munro allowed himself to be calmed by the unchanged expression he saw before him, and speaking in a noticeably gentler voice, he went on:

"You would be my son, Duncan, but you don't know the history of the man you want to call your father. Sit down, young man, and I'll reveal to you the wounds of a scarred heart, in as few words as possible."

By this point, both the messenger and the person who was supposed to receive Montcalm's message had completely forgotten about it. Each man pulled up a chair, and while the older soldier spent a few moments lost in his own thoughts, clearly feeling melancholy, the young man controlled his eagerness and maintained a respectful, attentive posture. Finally, the older man began to speak:

"You already know, Major Heyward, that my family was both ancient and honorable," the Scotsman began, "though it may not have been blessed with the wealth that should match its standing. I was perhaps someone like yourself when I pledged my love to Alice Graham, the only daughter of a neighboring landowner of considerable property. But her father disapproved of our union for reasons beyond just my lack of money. So I did what any honest man should do—I released the young woman from her promise and left the country to serve my king. I traveled to many places and spilled much blood in foreign lands before duty brought me to the West Indies. There I met someone who eventually became my wife and Cora's mother. She was the daughter of a gentleman from those islands and a lady who had the misfortune, if you choose to see it that way," the old man said with pride, "of being distantly descended from that unfortunate group of people who are so shamefully enslaved to serve the needs of a wealthy society. Yes, sir, that is a curse that Scotland inherited through its unnatural alliance with a foreign nation of merchants. But if I ever found a man among them who dared to speak ill of my daughter, he would face a father's wrath! Indeed, Major Heyward, you yourself were born in the south, where these unfortunate people are viewed as belonging to a race beneath your own."

"It's unfortunately true, sir," said Duncan, unable to keep his eyes from dropping to the floor in embarrassment.

"And you throw this at my child like an insult! You refuse to mix the Heyward family blood with someone you consider so beneath you—even though she's beautiful and good?" the jealous parent demanded fiercely.

"God save me from such an unworthy bias!" Duncan replied, even as he recognized that very feeling within himself, embedded as deeply as if it were part of his very nature. "The charm, the beauty, the enchanting quality of your younger daughter, Colonel Munro, could account for my actions without attributing such unfairness to me."

"You're right, sir," the old man replied, once again shifting his tone to one of gentleness, or perhaps tenderness; "the girl looks exactly like her mother did at that age, before she had experienced sorrow. When death took my wife from me, I returned to Scotland, having gained wealth through the marriage; and can you believe it, Duncan! that suffering angel had remained unmarried for twenty long years, all for the sake of a man who had forgotten her! She did even more than that, sir; she forgave my lack of faithfulness, and with all obstacles now cleared away, she accepted me as her husband."

"And became Alice's mother?" Duncan exclaimed, with an intensity that could have been risky at a time when Munro's mind wasn't so preoccupied with other matters.

"She certainly did," the old man said, "and she paid a heavy price for the blessing she gave. But she's a saint in heaven now, sir; and it's wrong for someone whose foot is on the edge of the grave to grieve for such a blessed fate. I only had her for one year, though; such a brief period of happiness for someone who had watched her youth slip away in hopeless longing."

There was something so powerful and overwhelming in the old man's anguish that Heyward didn't dare speak a single word of comfort. Munro sat completely unaware of anyone else being there, his face exposed and contorting with the pain of his remorse, while heavy tears streamed from his eyes and rolled down his cheeks to the floor without him noticing. Eventually he stirred, as if suddenly remembering where he was; then he stood up, took a single walk across the room, and approached his companion with the bearing of a military commander, demanding:

"Don't you have some message for me from the Marquis de Montcalm, Major Heyward?"

Duncan began speaking in turn, immediately starting the half-remembered message in an awkward voice. There's no need to elaborate on the evasive yet courteous way the French general had avoided every effort by Heyward to extract the true meaning of the communication he had intended to deliver, or on the firm but still refined message through which he now made it clear to his enemy that unless he decided to receive it personally, he wouldn't receive it at all. As Munro listened to Duncan's account, the stirred emotions of the father slowly yielded to the duties of his position, and when Duncan finished, he saw before him only the seasoned officer, filled with the hurt pride of a soldier.

"You've said enough, Major Heyward," the angry old man burst out; "enough to fill an entire book commenting on French politeness. This gentleman here invited me to a meeting, and when I send him a qualified representative—because that's exactly what you are, Duncan, even though you're still young—he responds to me with a puzzle."

"He might have had a less favorable opinion of the replacement, my dear sir; and you should remember that the invitation he's now extending again was meant for the commander of the fortifications, not for his deputy."

"Well, sir, isn't a representative given all the authority and status of the person who sends him? He wants to meet with Munro! Honestly, sir, I'm quite tempted to humor the man, if only to let him see how steadfast we remain despite his forces and his demands. There could be some good strategy in such a move, young man."

Duncan, who believed it was extremely important that they quickly learn what was written in the letter carried by the scout, gladly supported this suggestion.

"There's no question that seeing how indifferent we were wouldn't give him any confidence," he said.

"You've never spoken truer words. I wish, sir, that he would attack our fortifications in broad daylight, leading a direct assault; that's the most reliable way to see an enemy's true intentions, and it would be far better than the siege tactics he's using. The honor and courage of warfare has been greatly corrupted, Major Heyward, by the methods of your Monsieur Vauban. Our forefathers were far above such calculated cowardice!"

"That might be completely true, sir; but now we have no choice but to fight skill with skill. What would you like to do about this meeting?"

"I will meet with the Frenchman, and I'll do so without fear or hesitation; immediately, sir, as befits a servant of my royal master. Go, Major Heyward, and have them play a musical flourish; send out a messenger to inform them who is approaching. We will follow with a small guard, for such respect is owed to someone who holds his king's honor in his care; and listen, Duncan," he added in a half whisper, even though they were alone, "it might be wise to have some assistance ready, in case there's treachery behind all of this."

The young man took advantage of this command to leave the room, and since the day was quickly drawing to an end, he hurried without hesitation to make the required preparations. Only a few minutes were needed to assemble several rows of soldiers and to send a messenger with a flag to announce the arrival of the fort's commanding officer. After Duncan had completed both tasks, he led the guard to the sally-port, where he discovered his superior already waiting for him. Once the standard ceremonies of a military departure had been performed, the veteran and his younger companion departed from the fortress, accompanied by their escort.

They had walked only a hundred yards from the fortifications when the small group accompanying the French general to the meeting could be seen emerging from the sunken path that formed the bed of a stream running between the attackers' artillery positions and the fort. From the moment Munro left his own fortifications to appear before his enemy, his bearing had been dignified, and his stride and expression distinctly military. The instant he caught sight of the white feather that fluttered in Montcalm's hat, his eyes brightened, and age no longer seemed to have any effect over his large and still powerful frame.

"Tell the men to stay alert, sir," he said quietly to Duncan, "and make sure their weapons are ready, because you can never trust one of King Louis's men. At the same time, we need to appear completely confident and unworried. You understand what I mean, Major Heyward!"

He was interrupted by the sound of a drum from the approaching French soldiers, which received an immediate response. Both sides then sent forward an orderly carrying a white flag, and the cautious Scottish commander stopped with his guard positioned closely behind him. Once this brief formal greeting had taken place, Montcalm approached them with quick yet elegant steps, removing his hat before the experienced officer and lowering his pristine plume almost to the ground as a gesture of respect. While Munro's bearing was more authoritative and masculine, it lacked both the natural grace and persuasive refinement that characterized the Frenchman's manner. Neither man spoke for several moments, each studying the other with curious and attentive gazes. Then, as befitted his higher rank and the purpose of their meeting, Montcalm broke the silence. After speaking the customary words of greeting, he turned to Duncan and continued with a smile of recognition, speaking entirely in French:

"I'm delighted, sir, that you've given us the pleasure of your company on this occasion. There will be no need to use a regular interpreter, because with you handling things, I feel as confident as if I were speaking your language myself."

Duncan acknowledged the compliment, and then Montcalm turned to his guard, who had pressed close around him in imitation of their enemies, and continued:

"Step back, my children—it's hot—move away a little."

Before Major Heyward would follow this example of trust, he looked around the plain and saw with anxiety the many dark groups of Native Americans who watched from the edge of the surrounding woods as curious observers of the meeting.

"General Montcalm will easily understand the difference in our circumstances," he said, somewhat awkwardly, gesturing toward the threatening enemies who could be seen in nearly every direction. "If we were to send away our guards, we would be left here completely at the mercy of our foes."

"Sir, you have the sworn word of a French gentleman for your safety," Montcalm replied, placing his hand solemnly on his heart; "that should be enough."

"It will. Move back," Duncan told the officer leading the escort; "move back, sir, out of earshot, and wait for orders."

Munro watched this movement with obvious discomfort, and he immediately demanded an explanation.

"Isn't it in our best interest, sir, to show no signs of suspicion?" Duncan replied. "Monsieur de Montcalm has given his word that we'll be safe, and I've instructed the men to pull back a bit to demonstrate how much we trust his promise."

"It might be fine, sir, but I don't have much confidence in the trustworthiness of these marquesses, or marquis, as they call themselves. Their titles of nobility are too easily obtained to be sure they carry the mark of genuine honor."

"You're forgetting, my dear sir, that we're speaking with an officer who has earned distinction both in Europe and America through his actions. From a soldier with his reputation, we have nothing to fear."

The old man made a gesture showing he was giving up, though his stiff facial expression still revealed his stubborn commitment to distrust, which came from a kind of inherited scorn for his enemy, rather than from any current evidence that might justify such an unforgiving attitude. Montcalm waited patiently until this quiet conversation was finished, when he moved closer and began discussing the topic of their meeting.

"I requested this meeting with your commanding officer, sir," he said, "because I believe he can be convinced that he has already done everything necessary to uphold his prince's honor, and will now be willing to listen to what humanity demands. I will always testify that his resistance was brave and continued as long as there was any hope."

When this proposal was explained to Munro, he responded with dignity while maintaining proper courtesy:

"However much I may value such praise from Monsieur Montcalm, it will be more meaningful when it has been better earned."

The French general smiled when Duncan told him what the reply meant, and he remarked:

"What is now so generously granted to recognized bravery might be denied to pointless stubbornness. Would the gentleman like to visit my camp and see for himself our forces, and how impossible it would be for him to resist them successfully?"

"I know that the king of France is well served," replied the unshaken Scotsman as soon as Duncan finished his translation, "but my own royal master has just as many and just as loyal troops."

"Luckily for us, they're not nearby," Montcalm said, his enthusiasm making him speak without waiting for the interpreter. "War has its own fate, and a courageous man learns to accept it with the same bravery he shows when confronting his enemies."

"If I had known that Monsieur Montcalm spoke English, I wouldn't have bothered with such a clumsy translation," Duncan said irritably, immediately recalling his recent exchange with Munro.

"Excuse me, sir," the Frenchman replied, a faint blush appearing on his dark cheek. "There's a huge difference between understanding and speaking a foreign language; you will therefore please continue to help me." Then, after a brief pause, he added: "These hills give us every chance to scout your fortifications, gentlemen, and I'm probably as familiar with their weakened state as you are yourselves."

"Ask the French general if his telescope can see all the way to the Hudson," said Munro with pride; "and find out if he knows when and where to expect Webb's army."

"Let General Webb speak for himself," replied the shrewd Montcalm, suddenly holding out an open letter toward Munro as he spoke; "you will discover there, sir, that his actions are unlikely to cause any trouble for my army."

The veteran grabbed the paper that was offered to him, not waiting for Duncan to translate what had been said, and with an eagerness that revealed how crucial he believed its contents to be. As his eyes quickly scanned the words, his expression shifted from one of military pride to deep disappointment; his lip started to tremble; and letting the paper drop from his hand, his head fell onto his chest, like a man whose hopes had been crushed in an instant. Duncan picked up the letter from the ground, and without apologizing for taking such liberty, he read its harsh message at a glance. Their commanding officer, rather than encouraging them to fight back, recommended they surrender quickly, stating in the clearest terms that it would be completely impossible for him to send even a single soldier to help them.

"There's no trickery here!" Duncan declared, studying the note thoroughly on both sides; "this bears Webb's signature and must be the intercepted letter."

"The man has betrayed me!" Munro finally exclaimed with bitterness. "He has brought dishonor to the home of someone who had never known disgrace before, and he has piled shame heavily upon my gray hairs."

"Don't say that," Duncan shouted; "we still control the fort, and we still have our honor. Let us make our enemies pay such a high price for our lives that they'll think the cost was too steep."

"Boy, I thank you," the old man exclaimed, shaking himself from his daze; "you have, for once, reminded Munro of his duty. We will go back, and dig our graves behind those ramparts."

"Gentlemen," said Montcalm, stepping forward with genuine concern, "you don't really know Louis de St. Veran if you think he would use this letter to humiliate brave men or to build a false reputation for himself. Hear my terms before you go."

"What does the Frenchman say?" the veteran demanded sternly. "Is he trying to take credit for capturing a scout carrying a message from headquarters? Sir, he would be better off abandoning this siege and going to lay siege to Edward instead, if he thinks he can intimidate his enemies with mere words."

Duncan clarified what the other person meant.

"Monsieur de Montcalm, we will hear you," the veteran added, more calmly, as Duncan finished speaking.

"Holding the fort is now impossible," said his generous enemy; "my master's interests require that it be destroyed; but as for you and your brave companions, no privilege valued by a soldier will be withheld."

"Our colors?" Heyward demanded.

"Take them to England and present them to your king."

"Our arms?"

"Keep them; no one can use them better."

"Our march; the surrender of the place?"

"Everything shall be carried out in a manner that brings you the greatest honor."

Duncan now turned to explain these proposals to his commander, who listened with amazement and deep emotion, profoundly moved by such extraordinary and unexpected generosity.

"Go ahead, Duncan," he said. "Go with this marquess—and he truly deserves that title. Go to his tent and work everything out. In my old age, I've witnessed two things I never thought I'd live to see: an Englishman too afraid to stand by a friend, and a Frenchman too honorable to take advantage of his position."

So saying, the veteran lowered his head to his chest once more and walked slowly back toward the fort, his dejected manner signaling to the anxious garrison that he brought bad news.

From the shock of this unexpected blow, Munro's proud spirit never recovered; but from that moment, a transformation began in his resolute character that would follow him to an early grave. Duncan stayed behind to negotiate the terms of surrender. He was observed returning to the fortifications during the early hours of the night, and shortly after a private meeting with the commanding officer, he departed once more. It was then publicly declared that fighting must end—Munro having signed an agreement by which the fortress would be surrendered to the enemy at dawn; the garrison would keep their weapons, their flags and their personal belongings, and therefore, according to military standards, their honor.

---

# Chapter XVII.

"Weave we the woof.
The thread is spun.
The web is wove.
The work is done."—Gray

The opposing armies, positioned in the wilderness around Lake George, spent the night of August 9th, 1757, much as they would have if they had met on any battlefield in Europe. While the defeated remained quiet, bitter, and downcast, the winners celebrated their victory. However, both sorrow and celebration have their boundaries, and well before the morning watch arrived, the silence of those vast forests was interrupted only by a cheerful shout from some triumphant young French soldier on the forward guard posts, or a threatening challenge from the fort, which strictly prohibited any enemy approach before the agreed-upon time. Even these sporadic intimidating sounds stopped during that quiet hour before dawn, when anyone listening would have found no trace of the armed forces that were then sleeping along the shores of the sacred lake.

During these moments of profound quiet, the canvas covering the entrance to a large tent in the French camp was pushed aside, and a man emerged from beneath the fabric into the open air. He wore a cloak that might have been meant to protect him from the cold dampness of the forest, but it also served perfectly to hide his identity. The grenadier who stood guard over the sleeping French commander allowed him to pass without challenge, offering the standard salute that shows military respect as the figure moved quickly through the small city of tents toward William Henry. Whenever this mysterious person came across any of the countless sentries who crossed his path, his response was immediate and apparently acceptable, since he was consistently permitted to continue without further questioning.

With the exception of these repeated but brief interruptions, he had moved silently from the center of the camp to its most advanced outposts, when he approached the soldier who was standing guard closest to the enemy's fortifications. As he came near, he was met with the usual challenge:

"Who goes there?"

"France," came the response.

"What's the password?"

"Victory," said the other, drawing so close as to be heard in a loud whisper.

"That's fine," replied the guard, shifting his musket from ready position to his shoulder; "you're out walking quite early this morning, sir!"

"It is necessary to be vigilant, my child," the other observed, letting a fold of his cloak fall as he looked the soldier directly in the face while passing him, continuing on his way toward the British fortification. The man jumped; his weapons clanged loudly as he thrust them forward in the deepest and most respectful salute; and after he had recovered his rifle, he turned to walk his patrol route, mumbling under his breath:

"We must stay alert, truly! I believe we have here a corporal who never sleeps!"

The officer continued forward, ignoring the words that slipped from the surprised sentinel, and didn't stop again until he reached the low shoreline in a somewhat risky position near the fort's western water bastion. The faint moonlight provided just enough illumination to make objects visible in outline, though they remained dim. He therefore took care to position himself against a tree trunk, where he stood for several minutes, appearing to study the dark and quiet mounds of the English fortifications with intense focus. His examination of the ramparts wasn't that of a casual or idle observer; instead, his eyes moved systematically from one point to another, revealing his understanding of military practices and showing that his inspection was accompanied by suspicion. Eventually he seemed satisfied, and after glancing impatiently upward toward the peak of the eastern mountain, as though expecting dawn's arrival, he was about to retrace his steps when a soft sound from the nearest corner of the bastion reached his ears and caused him to stay put.

Just then a figure appeared at the edge of the fortification, where it stood, seemingly studying the distant tents of the French camp. The person's head turned toward the east, as if equally eager for daybreak to arrive, when the form leaned against the earthwork and appeared to stare at the smooth surface of the water, which sparkled with countless reflected stars like an underwater sky. The somber mood, the early hour, along with the large frame of the man who leaned there, lost in thought, against the English fortifications, left no question about his identity in the mind of the watching observer. Both courtesy and caution now compelled him to withdraw; and he had carefully moved around the trunk of the tree for this purpose, when another sound caught his attention and once again stopped him in his tracks. It was a quiet and barely audible stirring of the water, followed by the scraping of pebbles against each other. In an instant he saw a dark shape emerge, as if rising from the lake itself, and move silently to shore, landing within just a few feet of where he stood. A rifle then slowly appeared between his eyes and the watery surface; but before it could be fired his own hand was on the trigger mechanism.

"Hugh!" shouted the warrior, whose deceitful shot was so strangely and so suddenly disrupted.

Without saying a word, the French officer placed his hand on the Indian's shoulder and led him in complete silence away from the area, where their upcoming conversation could have been dangerous, and where it appeared that at least one of them was looking for someone to harm. Then he opened his cloak wide to reveal his uniform and the cross of St. Louis hanging from his chest, and Montcalm demanded sternly:

"What does this mean? Doesn't my son know that the hatchet is buried between the English and his Canadian Father?"

"What can the Hurons do?" the Native American replied, also speaking in French, though not perfectly.

"Not a single warrior has taken a scalp, and the white men are making peace!"

"Ha, The Cunning Fox! I think this shows too much enthusiasm for a friend who was recently an enemy! How many days have passed since The Cunning Fox struck the war-post of the English?"

"Where is that sun?" the brooding warrior demanded. "It's behind the hill, and everything is dark and cold. But when it returns, it will be bright and warm again. Le Subtil is the sun of his people. There have been clouds and many mountains separating him from his nation, but now he shines and the sky is clear!"

"I'm well aware that Le Renard holds influence over his people," Montcalm said. "Yesterday he was out hunting for their scalps, and today they're listening to him at the council fire."

"Magua is a great chief."

"Let him prove it by teaching his people how to behave toward our new allies."

"Why did the leader of the Canadians bring his warriors into the forest and fire his cannons at the fort?" asked the cunning Indian.

"To conquer it. My master owns the land, and your father was commanded to remove these English settlers. They have agreed to leave, and now he no longer calls them enemies."

"That's good. Magua took the hatchet to stain it with blood. It is now bright; when it turns red, it will be buried."

"But Magua has promised not to dishonor the purity of France. The enemies of the great king beyond the ocean are his enemies; his friends are the friends of the Hurons."

"Friends!" the Indian repeated with contempt. "Let his father give Magua a hand."

Montcalm understood that his control over the warrior tribes he had assembled depended more on making compromises than on using force, so he reluctantly agreed to the other man's request. The native warrior pressed the French commander's fingers against a deep scar on his chest, and then triumphantly asked:

"Does my father know that?"

"What warrior doesn't? That's where a lead bullet has cut."

"And this?" the Indian continued, having turned his bare back toward the other man, his body now without its customary cotton wrap.

"This! My son has been badly hurt here; who did this to him?"

"Magua slept restlessly in the English camps, and their beatings have left their scars," the warrior replied with a bitter laugh that couldn't hide the rage burning inside him. Then, remembering himself and drawing upon his natural dignity, he continued: "Go; tell your young men that we are at peace. Le Renard Subtil knows how to address a Huron warrior."

Without bothering to say another word or wait for any response, the warrior slung his rifle into the crook of his arm and moved quietly through the camp toward the forest where his tribe was camped. Every few steps as he walked, the guards called out to him; but he continued forward stubbornly, completely ignoring the soldiers' commands, who only let him live because they recognized the bearing and stride as well as the defiant boldness of a Native American.

Montcalm remained on the shore for a long time, feeling deeply troubled after his companion had left him there, thinking heavily about the temperament his uncontrollable ally had just revealed. His good reputation had already been damaged by one terrible incident, and the circumstances were frighteningly similar to those he now faced. As he reflected, he became acutely aware of the serious responsibility taken on by those who ignore proper methods to achieve their goals, and of all the risks involved in setting something in motion that no human has the power to control. Then, pushing away these thoughts that he considered a sign of weakness at such a moment of victory, he walked back toward his tent, giving orders as he went to make the signal that would wake the army from sleep.

The first beat of the French drums echoed from within the fort, and soon the valley filled with the sounds of military music, rising long, thrilling and lively above the rattling accompaniment. The horns of the victors played merry and cheerful flourishes, until the last straggler of the camp reached his position; but the moment the British fifes had blown their sharp signal, they fell silent. Meanwhile the day had broken, and when the line of the French army was ready to receive its general, the rays of a brilliant sun were gleaming along the glittering formation. Then that victory, which was already so well known, was officially announced; the chosen band who were selected to guard the gates of the fort were assigned, and marched before their commander;

the signal of their approach was given, and all the usual preparations for a change of masters were ordered and carried out directly under the guns of the disputed fortification.

A completely different scene unfolded within the ranks of the Anglo-American army. The moment the warning signal sounded, it displayed all the characteristics of a rushed and reluctant withdrawal. The grim soldiers hoisted their empty muskets and took their positions, like men whose blood had been stirred by the recent battle, and who craved only the chance to avenge a humiliation that continued to sting their pride, hidden though it was beneath the formalities of military protocol.

Women and children rushed from one spot to another, some carrying the meager remains of their belongings, while others searched through the ranks looking for the familiar faces of those they depended on for safety.

Munro emerged among his quiet soldiers, appearing resolute yet downcast. It was clear that the unforeseen setback had wounded him deeply, even as he fought to bear his adversity with the dignity of a man.

Duncan was moved by the quiet and powerful display of the old man's sorrow. He had completed his own responsibilities, and now he hurried to the elderly man's side to learn how he might be of service to him.

"My daughters," was the brief but expressive reply.

"Good heavens! Haven't arrangements already been made for their convenience?"

"Today I am only a soldier, Major Heyward," said the veteran. "All that you see here, claim alike to be my children."

Duncan had heard enough. Without wasting any of those moments that had become so precious, he rushed toward Munro's quarters, searching for the sisters. He found them at the entrance of the low building, already ready to leave, and surrounded by a loud and weeping crowd of women who had gathered around the place, with a kind of instinctive awareness that it was the spot most likely to be protected. Though Cora's cheeks were pale and her face showed worry, she had lost none of her strength; but Alice's eyes were red and swollen, revealing how long and bitterly she had been crying. Both of them, however, welcomed the young man with obvious pleasure; Cora, unusually, being the first to speak.

"The fort is lost," she said, with a melancholy smile; "though our good name, I trust, remains."

"It's brighter than ever. But, dearest Miss Munro, it is time to think less of others, and to make some provision for yourself. Military custom—pride—that pride on which you so much value yourself, demands that your father and I should for a little while continue with the troops. Then where to seek a proper protector for you against the confusion and chances of such a scene?'"

"None is necessary," Cora replied; "who would dare to harm or insult the daughter of such a father at a time like this?"

"I wouldn't leave you by yourself," the young man continued, glancing around nervously, "not even for command of the finest regiment in the king's service. Remember, our Alice doesn't have your strength of character, and only God knows what fear she might suffer."

"You might be right," Cora responded, smiling once more, though with much greater sadness than before. "Listen! fate has already brought us a friend just when we need one most."

Duncan listened carefully and immediately understood what she meant. The quiet, solemn sounds of the sacred music, familiar throughout the eastern provinces, reached his ears and drew him toward a room in a nearby building that had been abandoned by its usual occupants. There he discovered David, expressing his devout emotions through the only form of expression he ever allowed himself. Duncan waited until the movement of David's hand stopped, indicating that the musical piece had concluded, then touched his shoulder to get his attention and briefly explained what he wanted.

"Even so," replied the devoted follower of the King of Israel, when the young man had finished speaking; "I have discovered much that is beautiful and harmonious in the young women, and it is proper that we who have shared in so much danger should remain together in peace. I will accompany them, once I have finished my morning prayers, which need only the closing hymn of praise. Will you join in, friend? The rhythm is familiar, and the melody is 'Southwell'."

Then, holding out the small book and carefully setting the pitch of the tune once more with thoughtful attention, David began again and completed his hymn with such focused determination that it would have been difficult to interrupt him. Heyward had no choice but to wait until the verse was finished; when he saw David removing his spectacles and putting the book away, he continued speaking.

"Your responsibility will be to ensure that no one dares to approach the ladies with any crude intentions, or to insult them or mock the misfortune of their courageous father. The servants of their household will assist you in this duty."

"Even so."

"Enemy Indians and scattered soldiers might show up, and if they do, you'll need to remind them about the surrender agreement and warn them that you'll report any bad behavior to Montcalm. That should be enough to handle the situation."

"If not, I have something here that will," David replied, showing his book with an attitude that uniquely combined humility and assurance. Here are words that, when spoken—or rather proclaimed with proper emphasis and in rhythmic cadence—will calm even the most turbulent disposition:

"Why do the nations rage furiously'?"

"Enough," said Heyward, cutting off the outpouring of his melodic prayer; "we understand each other; it's time we should take on our individual responsibilities."

Gamut happily agreed, and together they went to find the women. Cora welcomed her new and rather unusual protector politely, at the very least; and even Alice's pale face brightened once more with some of her natural playfulness as she expressed gratitude to Heyward for his protection. Duncan made sure to reassure them that he had done everything possible under the circumstances, and he believed it was quite sufficient to ease their concerns; there was no real danger. He then spoke enthusiastically about his plan to return to them as soon as he had guided the advance party a few miles toward the Hudson, and he immediately said his goodbyes.

By this time the signal for departure had been given, and the front of the English column was moving. The sisters jumped at the sound, and looking around, they saw the white uniforms of the French grenadiers, who had already seized control of the fort's gates. At that moment a massive cloud appeared to pass suddenly overhead, and when they looked up, they realized they were standing beneath the broad folds of the French flag.

"Let's go," said Cora; "this is no longer a suitable place for the children of an English officer."

Alice held tightly to her sister's arm, and together they departed from the parade, surrounded by the flowing crowd that moved alongside them.

As they walked through the gates, the French officers, who had discovered their rank, bowed frequently and deeply, yet they held back from offering attention that they sensed, with remarkable sensitivity, might not be welcome. Since every wagon and pack animal was being used to carry the sick and wounded, Cora had chosen to endure the hardships of walking rather than take away from their comfort. In fact, many injured and weakened soldiers were forced to drag their worn-out bodies behind the marching columns because there weren't enough ways to transport people in that remote area. Everyone was moving forward though; the weak and wounded were moaning in pain; their fellow soldiers marched in grim silence; and the women and children were frightened, though they didn't know exactly what they should fear.

As the bewildered and frightened crowd left the protective earthworks of the fort and emerged onto the open plain, the entire scene spread out before them. A short distance to the right and slightly behind them, the French army stood ready with weapons in hand, as Montcalm had gathered his forces as soon as his guards had taken control of the fortifications. They watched the proceedings of the defeated with careful attention but remained silent, maintaining all the agreed-upon military courtesies and offering no mockery or insults to their less fortunate enemies in their moment of victory. Living masses of English soldiers, numbering nearly three thousand in total, moved slowly across the plain toward a common gathering point, gradually drawing closer to each other as they converged on their destination—a pathway cut through the towering trees where the road to the Hudson entered the forest. Along the curving edges of the woods hung a dark mass of native warriors, watching their enemies pass and lurking at a distance like vultures held back from diving on their prey only by the presence and control of a superior army. A few had wandered among the defeated columns, where they moved with sullen displeasure, remaining watchful yet still passive observers of the moving crowd.

The advance, with Heyward leading it, had already reached the narrow pass and was slowly vanishing from sight, when Cora's attention was caught by a group of stragglers amid sounds of conflict. A wayward colonial soldier was paying the price for his disobedience by being robbed of the very possessions that had caused him to abandon his position in the formation. The man had a strong build and was too greedy to give up his belongings without a fight. People from both sides got involved; one group trying to stop the theft and the other helping to carry it out. Voices became loud and angry, and a hundred warriors appeared, as if by magic, where only a dozen had been visible just a minute earlier. It was then that Cora spotted Magua's figure moving among his fellow tribesmen, speaking with his deadly and cunning persuasiveness. The crowd of women and children came to a halt and clustered together like frightened and nervous birds. But the greed of the Indian was quickly satisfied, and the different groups began moving slowly forward once again.

The warriors now pulled back and appeared willing to let their enemies move forward without further interference. However, as the group of women approached them, the bright colors of a shawl caught the attention of a wild and uncivilized Huron. He moved forward to grab it without any hesitation. The woman, driven more by fear than by attachment to the decoration, wrapped her child in the desired item and held both more tightly against her chest. Cora was about to speak, intending to advise the woman to give up the trivial object, when the warrior released his grip on the shawl and snatched the screaming baby from her arms. Giving up everything to the eager hands of those surrounding her, the mother rushed forward with desperation written across her face to get her child back. The Indian grinned menacingly and held out one hand as a sign that he was willing to make a trade, while with the other hand he waved the baby above his head, gripping it by the feet as if to increase the value of the ransom.

"Here—here—there—all—any—everything!" cried the breathless woman, frantically pulling the lighter pieces of clothing from her body with shaking, unsteady hands; "take it all, but give me my baby!"

The savage rejected the worthless rags, and seeing that the shawl had already been claimed by someone else, his mocking yet grim smile transformed into a flash of savage fury as he smashed the infant's head against a rock and threw its trembling body at her feet. For a moment the mother stood frozen like a statue of despair, staring wildly down at the horrific sight of what had so recently rested against her chest and smiled up at her; then she lifted her eyes and face toward heaven, as if calling upon God to curse the one who committed this terrible act. She was spared from the sin of such a prayer because, driven mad by his frustration and aroused by the sight of blood, the Huron mercifully buried his tomahawk in her own skull. The mother collapsed from the blow and fell, reaching for her child in death with the same all-consuming love that had made her treasure it in life.

At that dangerous moment, Magua cupped his hands around his mouth and let out the deadly and terrifying war cry. The scattered Indians reacted to the familiar call like racehorses leaping forward at the starting signal, and immediately such a shriek rose across the plain and echoed through the forest arches as had rarely escaped from human throats before. Those who heard it felt their blood freeze with horror, a terror almost as great as the dread one might feel upon hearing the trumpets of the final judgment.

More than two thousand frenzied warriors burst from the forest at the signal and hurled themselves across the deadly plain with natural speed. We will not focus on the horrifying atrocities that followed. Death was present everywhere, appearing in its most terrifying and repulsive forms. Fighting back only made the killers more violent, as they continued their savage attacks long after their victims could no longer feel their rage. The flow of blood could be compared to a bursting flood; and as the natives became excited and driven mad by what they saw, many of them actually knelt on the ground and drank eagerly, triumphantly, wickedly, from the red stream.

The well-trained soldiers quickly formed tight formations, trying to intimidate their attackers with the impressive sight of an organized military line. This strategy worked to some extent, although far too many soldiers allowed their unloaded rifles to be ripped from their grasp, foolishly hoping this would calm the hostile forces.

In such chaos, no one had time to notice the passing moments. It might have been ten minutes (though it felt like an eternity) that the sisters had remained frozen in place, paralyzed by horror and nearly powerless to act. When the first strike landed, their screaming companions had crowded around them in a mass, making escape impossible; and now that terror or death had driven most, if not all, away from their vicinity, they could see no clear path except those that led directly to their enemies' tomahawks. From all directions came screams, moans, desperate pleas and angry curses. At that moment, Alice caught sight of her father's imposing figure moving swiftly across the field toward the French forces. He was indeed heading to Montcalm, unafraid of any danger, to demand the delayed protection he had previously negotiated. Fifty gleaming axes and sharp-pointed spears threatened his life without acknowledgment, but the warriors respected his authority and composure, even in their rage. The deadly weapons were swept away by the veteran's still-steady arm, or dropped on their own after threatening an action that apparently no one had the nerve to carry out. Luckily, the vengeful Magua was hunting for his target among the very group the veteran had just left behind.

"Father—father—we are here!" Alice screamed as he walked by, not far away, without seeming to notice them. "Come to us, father, or we die!"

The cry rang out again, delivered in words and tones that could have softened even the hardest heart, but no response came. At one point, the elderly man seemed to hear the sound, as he stopped and strained to listen; however, Alice had collapsed unconscious to the ground, and Cora had fallen beside her, watching over her motionless sister with unwavering devotion. Munro shook his head in frustration and continued forward, focused on the important responsibilities of his position.

"Lady," said Gamut, who, despite being helpless and useless, had never considered abandoning his duty, "this is a celebration of devils, and this is no proper place for Christians to remain. Let us get up and flee."

"Go," said Cora, still looking at her unconscious sister; "save yourself. You can't help me anymore."

David understood the unwavering nature of her decision through the simple yet meaningful gesture that went along with her words. He looked for a moment at the shadowy figures performing their demonic rituals all around him, and his tall frame straightened while his chest rose and fell, and every part of his face expanded and appeared to express the strength of the emotions that controlled him.

"If the Jewish boy could calm the mighty spirit of Saul with the sound of his harp and the words of sacred song, it might not be wrong," he said, "to test the power of music here."

Then raising his voice to its highest pitch, he poured out a melody so powerful that it could be heard even above the noise of that bloody battlefield. More than one warrior rushed toward them, planning to strip the defenseless sisters of their clothing and take their scalps; but when they discovered this strange and unmoved figure fixed firmly in his position, they stopped to listen. Amazement quickly turned to respect, and they moved on to other and less brave victims, openly showing their approval of the courage with which the white warrior sang his death song. Encouraged and misled by his success, David used all his strength to spread what he believed was such a sacred influence. The unusual sounds reached the ears of a distant warrior, who came charging angrily from group to group, like someone who, refusing to bother with ordinary prey, searched for some victim more deserving of his reputation. It was Magua, who let out a cry of delight when he saw his former prisoners once again at his mercy.

"Come," he said, placing his dirty hands on Cora's dress, "the Huron's wigwam is still open. Isn't it better than this place?"

"Get away!" Cora shouted, covering her eyes to avoid looking at his disgusting appearance.

The Indian laughed mockingly as he raised his blood-stained hand and replied: "It is red, but it flows from white veins!"

"Monster! There is blood, oceans of blood, upon your soul; your spirit has caused this scene."

"Magua is a great chief!" the triumphant warrior replied, "will the dark-haired woman come to his tribe?"

"Never! Strike me if you want to, and finish your revenge." He paused for a moment, then scooped up Alice's limp and unconscious body in his arms, and the cunning Indian quickly moved across the open ground toward the forest.

"Stop!" screamed Cora, chasing frantically after him; "let the child go! monster! what are you doing?"

But Magua was deaf to her voice; or rather, he knew his power and was determined to maintain it.

"Wait—lady—wait," Gamut called out to the unconscious Cora. "The sacred power is starting to take effect, and soon you'll see this terrible chaos calmed."

Noticing that he too was being ignored, the loyal David followed the distraught sister, lifting his voice once more in holy song and sweeping his long arm through the air in careful rhythm to accompany the melody. In this way they crossed the field, moving past those who fled, the injured, and the fallen. The fierce Huron was always capable of handling both himself and the captive he carried; though Cora would have collapsed more than once beneath the strikes of her brutal attackers, if not for the remarkable figure who walked behind her, and who now seemed to the amazed natives to be blessed with the protective power of insanity.

Magua, who understood how to dodge the most immediate threats and escape from those chasing him, entered the forest through a shallow valley, where he quickly discovered the Narragansett horses that the travelers had left behind just moments earlier, waiting for his arrival under the watch of a savage whose expression was as fierce and malicious as his own. Placing Alice on one of the horses, he gestured for Cora to climb onto the other.

Despite the terror caused by her captor's presence, Cora felt some immediate relief in getting away from the violent scene unfolding on the plain below, and she couldn't help but be aware of this feeling. She sat down and reached out her arms toward her sister with a look of pleading and affection that even the Huron couldn't refuse. After placing Alice on the same horse as Cora, he grabbed the reins and began his journey by heading deeper into the forest. David, realizing he had been left behind and completely ignored as someone too insignificant to even bother killing, swung his long leg over the saddle of the horse they had abandoned and made whatever progress he could in following them, given the challenging nature of the trail.

They quickly started climbing upward, but since the movement was beginning to awaken her sister's unconscious state, Cora found her attention split between her deepest concern for her sister and listening to the screams that could still be heard too clearly from the valley below to pay attention to which direction they were traveling. However, when they reached the flat surface at the top of the mountain and came near the eastern cliff, she recognized the place where she had been brought once before under the more welcoming guidance of the scout. At this location, Magua allowed them to get down from their horses, and despite being prisoners themselves, the curiosity that seems to go hand in hand with terror compelled them to stare at the disturbing scene below.

The brutal slaughter continued unchecked. On all sides, the captured fled before their merciless pursuers, while the armed forces of the Christian king remained motionless in a state of indifference that has never been explained, and which has left a permanent stain on the otherwise honorable reputation of their commander. The killing did not stop until greed overcame the desire for revenge. Only then did the screams of the wounded and the cries of their killers become less frequent, until finally, the sounds of terror faded from their hearing, or were overwhelmed by the loud, prolonged, and piercing war cries of the victorious warriors.

---

# Chapter XVIII.

"Why, anything;
An honorable murderer, if you will;
For naught I did in hate, but all in honor."
—Othello

The brutal and inhumane scene briefly mentioned rather than fully described in the previous Chapter stands out in colonial history records under the well-deserved name of "The Massacre of William Henry." This event further darkened the stain that an earlier and very similar incident had already left on the French commander's reputation, a stain that his early and heroic death could not completely wash away. Time is now beginning to obscure these events; thousands who know that Montcalm died heroically on the plains of Abraham still need to learn how much he lacked in moral courage, without which no person can be truly great. Entire pages could be written using this distinguished example to demonstrate the flaws in human excellence; to show how easily generous feelings, refined manners, and noble bravery can lose their power under the cold influence of selfishness, and to present to the world a man who excelled in all the lesser qualities of character but fell short when it became necessary to prove that principle matters more than strategy. However, such a task would go beyond our authority; and since history, like love, tends to surround her heroes with an aura of false glory, it seems likely that future generations will remember Louis de Saint Veran only as the brave defender of his homeland, while his heartless indifference on the shores of the Oswego and of the Horican will be forgotten. While deeply regretting this failing of a fellow discipline, we shall immediately withdraw from her sacred domain and return to the proper boundaries of our own modest calling.

The third day since the fort's capture was coming to an end, but the story must keep the reader focused on the shores of the "holy lake." When we last observed it, the area around the fortifications was filled with violence and chaos. Now it was overtaken by silence and death. The bloodstained victors had left; and their camp, which had recently echoed with the cheerful celebrations of a triumphant army, now lay as a quiet and abandoned city of shelters. The fortress was a smoking ruin; burned beams, pieces of destroyed cannons, and torn stonework scattered across its earthen hills in chaotic disarray.

A terrifying transformation had also taken place in the weather. The sun had hidden its warmth behind an impenetrable wall of clouds, and hundreds of human bodies, which had turned black under the brutal heat of August, were now growing rigid in their twisted forms before the winds of an early November. The swirling and pristine mists that had been seen drifting above the hills toward the north were now returning as an endless dark sheet, driven forward by the violence of a storm. The smooth mirror-like surface of Lake George had vanished; and in its place, the green and furious waters struck the shores, as if angrily throwing back its contamination to the polluted beach. The clear spring still maintained some of its magical power, but it reflected only the dark gloom that descended from the threatening sky above. That moist and pleasant atmosphere that usually enhanced the landscape, hiding its roughness and smoothing its harsh edges, had vanished, the northern air swept across the expanse of water so severe and pure that nothing remained for the eye to imagine or for the mind to create.

The harsh elements had stripped away the green vegetation from the plain, making it look as if it had been burned by destructive lightning. However, scattered throughout the barren landscape, dark green patches emerged from the devastation—the first growth from soil that had been enriched with human blood. The entire scene, which had appeared so beautiful when viewed in favorable light and pleasant weather, now resembled a painted allegory of life itself, where everything was displayed in its most severe yet honest colors, without any softening shadows to provide comfort.

The isolated and dry grass blades swayed from the passing winds in a way that felt unsettling; the stark and rocky mountains stood out too clearly in their emptiness, and the eye searched for relief without success by trying to look into the endless expanse of sky, which was blocked from view by the dark blanket of torn and moving clouds.

The wind blew unevenly, sometimes sweeping heavily across the ground, appearing to whisper its sorrowful sounds into the cold ears of the dead, then rising in a sharp and mournful whistling as it rushed into the forest, filling the air with the leaves and branches it scattered along its way. Within this unnatural downpour, a few starving ravens fought against the strong wind; but as soon as they had passed over the green ocean of woods that stretched below them, they eagerly landed wherever they could to begin their gruesome feast.

In short, it was a scene of wildness and desolation; and it looked as if everyone who had disrespectfully entered it had been struck down instantly by the merciless hand of death. But the ban had ended; and for the first time since those who committed the terrible acts that had helped to mar the scene were gone, living people had now dared to approach the place.

About an hour before sunset on the day we've already described, five men could be seen emerging from the narrow opening between the trees where the path to the Hudson River entered the forest, moving toward the destroyed fortifications. Initially, they moved slowly and carefully, as if they were reluctant to enter this place of horrors or feared experiencing its terrible events again. A nimble figure led the group ahead of the others, showing the caution and skill of a native warrior; he climbed every small hill to scout the area and used hand signals to show his companions the route he thought would be safest to take. The men following behind also used every careful strategy and planning technique known in forest combat. One of them, who was also an Indian, moved slightly to one side and kept watch on the edge of the woods with eyes that had long experience reading even the smallest signs of danger. The other three men were white, though they wore clothing suited in both material and color to their current dangerous mission—following at a distance behind a retreating army through the wilderness.

The horrifying scenes that constantly appeared along their path to the lake shore affected each member of the group differently, reflecting their individual characters. The young man leading the way cast serious but secretive glances at the mutilated bodies as he moved quickly across the open ground, reluctant to show his emotions, yet too inexperienced to completely suppress their sudden and overwhelming impact. His Native American companion, however, was above such vulnerability. He walked past the clusters of corpses with unwavering determination and such composed eyes that only extensive and deeply ingrained experience could have allowed him to maintain such control. The reactions stirring in the minds of even the white men varied, though all were uniformly filled with grief. One man, whose gray hair and lined features, combined with a military bearing and stride, revealed—despite his disguise in a frontiersman's clothing—someone long familiar with the scenes of battle, felt no shame in groaning openly whenever a particularly horrific sight met his eyes. The younger man beside him trembled, but seemed to hold back his emotions out of consideration for his companion. Among them all, the straggler bringing up the rear seemed to be the only one who revealed his true thoughts without fear of being watched or concern for the consequences. He stared at the most terrifying sights with eyes and muscles that never wavered, but with curses so harsh and profound that they showed how deeply he condemned his enemies' crimes.

The reader will immediately recognize these characters as the Mohicans and their white companion, the scout, along with Munro and Heyward. It was indeed the father searching for his daughters, accompanied by the young man who had such a deep personal interest in their well-being, and those courageous and reliable woodsmen who had already demonstrated their expertise and loyalty throughout the challenging events that had been described.

When Uncas, who was walking ahead of the group, reached the middle of the plain, he let out a cry that brought his companions rushing to where he stood. The young warrior had stopped beside a cluster of women who lay together in a confused pile of bodies. Despite the horrifying sight before them, Munro and Heyward rushed toward the decaying heap, driven by a love so strong that no gruesome scene could diminish it, as they tried to see if any trace of those they were looking for could be found among the torn and multicolored clothing. Both the father and the lover felt immediate relief as they searched, though each was forced once again to endure the agony of uncertainty that was almost as unbearable as the most shocking truth would have been. They stood quietly and pensively around the tragic pile when the scout came near. Looking at the sorrowful scene with an expression of anger, the tough frontiersman spoke clearly and loudly for the first time since entering the plain:

"I have been on many terrible battlefields, and have followed trails of blood for exhausting miles," he said, "but never have I seen the devil's work so clearly displayed as it is here! Revenge is a Native feeling, and all who know me understand that there is no Native blood in my veins; but this much I will say—here, before heaven itself, and with the Lord's power so evident in this wild wilderness—that should these French ever dare to come within range of a rough bullet again, there is one rifle that will do its duty as long as flint will spark or gunpowder will burn! I leave the tomahawk and knife to those who have a natural talent for using them. What do you say, Chingachgook," he added, in Delaware; "will the Hurons brag about this to their women when the deep snows arrive?"

A flash of anger crossed the dark features of the Mohican chief; he loosened his knife in its sheath; and then turning calmly away from the scene, his expression settled into a composure as profound as if he had mastered the stirring of emotion.

"Montcalm! Montcalm!" the deeply bitter and unrestrained scout went on; "they say there will come a time when all actions taken in life will be revealed in a single glance, seen by eyes freed from human limitations. Pity the poor soul who must witness this battlefield with divine judgment weighing upon him! Wait—as sure as I have white man's blood, there lies a Native American warrior, scalped clean where his hair once grew! Take a look at him, Delaware; he might be one of your lost tribe members, and he deserves a proper warrior's burial. I can see it in your expression, Sagamore; a Huron will pay for this before the autumn winds carry away the smell of spilled blood!"

Chingachgook walked over to the mutilated body and turned it over, discovering the identifying marks of one of those six allied tribes, or nations as they were known, who fought alongside the English forces while remaining deadly enemies to his own people. He kicked the disgusting corpse with his foot and turned away from it with the same indifference he would show when leaving behind a dead animal. The scout understood what he was doing and very deliberately continued on his own path, though he kept up his angry complaints against the French commander in the same bitter tone.

"Only vast wisdom and unlimited power should dare to destroy men in large numbers," he continued; "because only wisdom can understand when such judgment is necessary, and what else besides unlimited power could replace the Lord's creatures? I believe it's wrong to kill a second deer before you've eaten the first one, unless you're planning to march ahead or set up an ambush. It's different when a few warriors are fighting openly in rough terrain, because it's their nature to die with a rifle or tomahawk in their hands, depending on whether they happen to be white or red. Uncas, come over here, boy, and let the ravens feed on the Mingo. I know from seeing it many times that they crave the flesh of an Oneida, and it's just as well to let the bird follow its natural appetite."

"Hugh!" shouted the young Mohican, rising up on his toes and staring intensely ahead, scaring the ravens away to find other prey with his voice and movement.

"What is it, boy?" the scout whispered, lowering his tall frame into a crouching position, like a panther preparing to pounce. "God, let it be some slow-moving Frenchman sneaking around looking for loot. I truly believe 'Killdeer' would have exceptional range today!'"

Uncas didn't respond with words but instead leaped away from where he stood, and moments later he appeared pulling something from a bush, triumphantly waving a piece of Cora's green riding veil. His sudden movement, this discovery, and the cry that once again escaped from the young Mohican's lips immediately brought the entire group rushing toward him.

"My child!" said Munro, speaking rapidly and frantically; "give me my child!"

"Uncas will try," was the brief and moving response.

The father missed the simple yet meaningful reassurance entirely, grabbing the piece of gauze and crushing it in his fist, while his gaze darted anxiously through the bushes, as though he both feared and longed for whatever secrets they might hold.

"There are no dead here," said Heyward; "the storm seems not to have passed this way."

"That's obvious; clearer than the sky above us," replied the calm scout; "but either she, or whoever took her, has gone past the bushes; I remember the cloth she used to cover a face that everyone loved to see. Uncas, you're right; the dark-haired woman has been here, and she has run like a scared deer into the woods; no one who could escape would stay to be killed. Let's look for the signs she left behind; sometimes I think that to Indian eyes, even a hummingbird leaves its path in the air."

The young Mohican rushed off at the suggestion, and the scout had barely finished speaking when the young man called out triumphantly from the edge of the forest. When the worried group reached the location, they discovered another piece of the veil hanging from a low branch of a beech tree.

"Easy now, easy," the scout said, holding his long rifle out to block the eager Heyward. "We understand what we need to do, but we can't mess up this perfect trail. One step too early could cause us hours of problems. But we've got them cornered—there's no doubt about that."

"Bless you, bless you, good man!" exclaimed Munro; "where then have they fled, and where are my children?"

"The route they've taken depends on many random factors. If they've traveled alone, they're just as likely to have wandered in circles as to have gone straight, and they could be within twelve miles of us. However, if the Hurons or any of the French Indians have captured them, they're probably now near the Canadian borders. But what does that matter?" the calm scout continued, noticing the intense worry and disappointment his listeners displayed. "The Mohicans and I are here at one end of the trail, and you can count on us to find the other end, even if they're a hundred leagues apart! Easy, easy, Uncas, you're as restless as someone from the settlements. You're forgetting that quick feet leave only faint tracks!"

"Hugh!" Chingachgook exclaimed, having been busy examining an opening that had clearly been cut through the low undergrowth bordering the forest; he now stood upright, pointing downward with the posture and expression of a man who had just spotted a revolting snake.

"Here's the clear impression of a man's footprint," Heyward exclaimed, leaning over the spot that had been pointed out; "he stepped at the edge of this pool, and there's no mistaking the mark. They are prisoners."

"It's better than leaving them to starve in the wilderness," the scout replied; "and they'll leave a clearer trail to follow. I'd bet fifty beaver pelts against the same number of flints that the Mohicans and I will be inside their camps within a month! Get down there, Uncas, and see what you can figure out from that moccasin; it's definitely a moccasin, not a regular shoe."

The young Mohican leaned down over the trail, brushing away the scattered leaves from the area around it, and studied it with the kind of careful examination that a banker today, in our era of financial uncertainty, would give to a questionable promissory note. Finally, he stood up from his crouched position, satisfied with what his inspection had revealed.

"Well, boy," the alert scout asked, "what does it say? Can you figure out anything from the evidence?"

"The Cunning Fox!"

"Ha! That raging devil is back! There will never be an end to his running around until 'killdeer' has a friendly conversation with him."

Heyward reluctantly acknowledged that this information was accurate, and now voiced his hopes rather than his doubts by saying:

"One moccasin looks so much like another that there's probably some mistake."

"One moccasin is just like another! You might as well claim that one foot is identical to another, even though we all understand that some are long while others are short, some are wide and others narrow, some have high arches while others have low ones, some turn inward and some turn outward. One moccasin resembles another no more than one book resembles another, yet those who can interpret one are rarely capable of understanding the distinguishing features of the other. All of this is arranged for the greater good, providing each person with their inherent strengths. Let me attend to this matter, Uncas; neither book nor moccasin suffers from having two perspectives rather than just one." The scout bent down to begin the work and immediately continued:

"You're right, boy; here's the footprint we saw so many times during that other pursuit. And this man will drink whenever he gets the chance; an Indian who drinks always learns to walk with his toes spread wider than a natural savage, since it's the nature of a drunkard to stagger, whether he's white or red-skinned. It's exactly the same length and width, too! Look at it, Sagamore; you measured these tracks more than once when we chased those scoundrels from Glenn's to the health springs."

Chingachgook agreed; and after completing his brief inspection, he stood up, and with a calm manner, he simply said the word:

"Magua!"

"Yes, it's certain; the dark-haired one and Magua have passed through here."

"And not Alice?" Heyward demanded.

"We haven't seen any trace of her yet," the scout replied, carefully examining the trees, bushes, and ground around them. "What's that over there? Uncas, go get whatever you see hanging from that thorn bush."

When the Indian had followed through, the scout took the reward, and raising it up high, he laughed in his quiet but genuine way.

"That's the musician's horn! Now we'll have a path that even a priest could follow," he said. "Uncas, look for footprints from a shoe long enough to support six feet two inches of unsteady human body. I'm starting to have some hope for this fellow, since he's stopped his wailing to pursue some better occupation."

"At least he has remained loyal to his duty," said Heyward. "And Cora and Alice are not without a friend."

"Yes," said Hawkeye, lowering his rifle and leaning on it with obvious contempt, "he can handle their singing. But can he kill a deer for their meal, navigate using the moss on birch trees, or cut down a Huron warrior? If he can't, then the first mockingbird he encounters would be more useful than him. Well, boy, do you see any evidence of such skills?"[1]

[1] The abilities of the American mockingbird are widely recognized. However, the true mockingbird doesn't range as far north as New York state, where it has two less

impressive replacements: the catbird, which the scout frequently mentions, and the bird commonly known as the ground-thresher. Both of these birds surpass the nightingale or the lark in their musical abilities, although American birds are typically less melodious than their European counterparts.

"Here is something that looks like the footprint of someone who has worn a shoe; could it belong to our friend?"

"Touch the leaves gently or you'll disturb the pattern. There! That's a footprint, but it belongs to the dark-haired one; and it's quite small too, for someone of such impressive height and commanding presence. The singer could easily cover it with his heel."

"Where! Let me see my child's footprints," said Munro, pushing the bushes aside and leaning tenderly over the nearly erased mark. Although the step that had left the impression had been light and quick, it was still clearly visible. The elderly soldier studied it with eyes that grew misty as he stared; he didn't straighten up from his bent position until Heyward noticed that he had moistened the trace of his daughter's path with a burning tear. Wanting to redirect a grief that threatened at any moment to break through his composed appearance by giving the veteran something to occupy himself with, the young man spoke to the scout:

"Now that we have these reliable signs, let's begin our journey. A single moment, at a time like this, will feel like an eternity to the prisoners."

"The fastest running deer doesn't always provide the longest hunt," Hawkeye replied, keeping his eyes fixed on the various signs he had spotted; "we know the fierce Huron has come through here, along with the dark-haired one and the singer, but where is the one with blonde hair and blue eyes? Though small in stature and not nearly as brave as her sister, she's beautiful to look at and delightful to talk with. Doesn't she have anyone who cares about her welfare?"

"God forbid she should ever need hundreds! Aren't we already searching for her? As for me, I will never stop looking until she is found."

"In that case, we might need to take separate routes, since she hasn't come this way—even though her footsteps would be light and barely noticeable."

Heyward pulled back, all his eagerness to continue appearing to disappear immediately. Without paying attention to this sudden shift in the other man's mood, the scout paused thoughtfully for a moment and then went on:

"No woman in this wilderness could leave a footprint like that except the dark-haired one or her sister. We know the first one has been here, but where are the signs of the other? Let's follow the trail deeper, and if we find nothing, we'll have to go back to the plain and pick up another trail. Keep moving, Uncas, and watch the dried leaves carefully. I'll keep an eye on the bushes while your father tracks close to the ground. Keep moving, friends; the sun is setting behind the hills."

"Isn't there anything I can do?" asked the worried Heyward.

"You?" the scout repeated, already moving forward with his Indian companions in the formation he had ordered; "yes, you can stay behind us and make sure not to cross our path."

Before they had traveled very far, the Indians stopped and seemed to examine some marks on the ground with greater intensity than usual. Both father and son spoke rapidly and loudly, alternately looking at what had captured their shared attention and then at each other with unmistakable delight.

"They found the little footprint!" the scout shouted, moving forward without paying any more attention to his own part of the job. "What do we have here? Someone set up an ambush in this spot! No, by the most accurate rifle on the frontier, those one-sided horses have been here again! Now the whole mystery is solved, and everything is as clear as the north star at midnight. Yes, this is where they got on their horses. Over there the animals were tied to a young tree, waiting; and there runs the wide trail heading north, going straight toward Canada."

"But there are still no signs of Alice, the younger Miss Munro," Duncan said.

"Unless that shiny trinket Uncas just picked up from the ground turns out to be one. Hand it over here, boy, so we can take a look at it."

Heyward immediately recognized it as a piece of jewelry that Alice loved to wear, and which he remembered, with the persistent memory of someone in love, having seen on the terrible morning of the massacre, hanging from the delicate neck of his beloved. He grabbed the precious jewel; and as he announced this discovery, it disappeared from the sight of the amazed scout, who searched for it on the ground in vain, long after it was pressed warmly against Duncan's pounding heart.

"Nonsense!" said the frustrated Hawkeye, stopping his search through the leaves with the butt of his rifle. "It's a sure sign of getting old when your eyesight starts to fail. Such a shiny trinket, and I can't even spot it! Well, I can still aim down a cloudy gun barrel, and that's all I need to settle any arguments between me and the Mingoes. I'd really like to find that thing, though, if only to return it to its rightful owner. That would tie together both ends of what I consider a very long journey, because by now the wide St. Lawrence River, or maybe even the Great Lakes themselves, lie between us."

"That gives us even more reason not to delay our march," Heyward replied; "let's move forward."

"Young blood and hot blood, they say, are much the same thing. We're not about to go on a squirrel hunt or chase a deer into the Horican, but to camp out for days and nights, and to travel across a wilderness where human feet rarely tread, and where book learning won't keep you safe. A Native American never begins such a journey without deliberating around his council fire; and though I'm a white man, I respect their customs in this matter, since they are thoughtful and wise. We will, therefore, go back and light our fire tonight in the ruins of the old fort, and in the morning we'll be refreshed and ready to tackle our task like men, not like chattering women or impatient boys."

Heyward could tell from the scout's behavior that arguing would be pointless. Munro had once again fallen into the kind of listlessness that had gripped him ever since his recent devastating misfortunes, and it seemed he could only be stirred from this state by some fresh and compelling event. Making the best of the situation, the young man took the veteran by the arm and followed behind the Indians and the scout, who had already started retracing the path that led them back to the plain.

---

# Chapter XIX.

"Salar.—Why, I am sure, if he forfeit, thou wilt not take his flesh; what's that good for?
  Shy.—To bait fish withal; if it will feed nothing else, it will feed my revenge."
—The Merchant of Venice

Evening shadows had fallen, making the place even more gloomy, when the group entered the ruins of Fort William Henry. The scout and his companions quickly began preparing to spend the night there, but their serious and somber behavior revealed how deeply the terrible scenes they had just witnessed had affected even their experienced hearts. A few broken pieces of roof beams were propped against a charred wall, and after Uncas had lightly covered them with brush, these makeshift shelters were considered adequate. When his work was finished, the young Indian gestured toward his crude shelter, and Heyward, understanding what the silent motion meant, gently encouraged Munro to go inside. Leaving the grieving old man alone with his grief, Duncan immediately went back outside, too agitated himself to seek the rest he had suggested to his older companion.

While Hawkeye and the Indians lit their fire and ate their evening meal, a simple dinner of dried bear meat, the young man walked over to the crumbling wall of the ruined fort that overlooked Lake George. The wind had died down, and the waves were now washing onto the sandy shore below him in a steadier, gentler rhythm. The clouds, as though exhausted from their wild race across the sky, were starting to break apart; the thicker masses gathered in dark clusters along the horizon, while lighter wisps still rushed over the water or swirled around the mountaintops like scattered flocks of birds circling their nesting places. Occasionally, a red and blazing star pushed through the drifting mist, casting an eerie glow across the dim expanse of sky. Deep within the surrounding hills, complete darkness had already fallen; and the valley stretched out like an enormous and abandoned graveyard, without any sign or sound to disturb the sleep of its countless and unfortunate inhabitants.

Duncan stood for many minutes as a captivated observer of this scene, which matched the past in such a chilling way. His eyes moved from the center of the mound, where the woodsmen sat around their flickering fire, to the dim light that still remained in the sky, and then focused long and anxiously on the thick darkness that spread like a gloomy emptiness on the side where the dead lay buried. Soon he imagined that mysterious sounds came from that place, though they were so faint and fleeting that he couldn't be sure of their nature or even whether they actually existed. Embarrassed by his fears, the young man turned toward the water and tried to focus his attention on the reflected stars that faintly sparkled on its rippling surface. Still, his overly alert ears continued their unwelcome task, as if warning him of some hidden danger. Finally, what sounded like rapid footsteps seemed to rush clearly across the darkness. No longer able to calm his anxiety, Duncan spoke quietly to the scout, asking him to climb the mound to where he was standing. Hawkeye slung his rifle over his arm and agreed, but with such a relaxed and peaceful manner that it showed how confident he was in the safety of their position.

"Listen!" Duncan said as the other man positioned himself deliberately at his side. "There are muffled sounds coming from the plain that might indicate Montcalm hasn't completely abandoned what he's conquered."

"Then ears are better than eyes," said the calm scout, who had just placed a piece of bear meat between his teeth and spoke in a thick, slow manner, like someone whose mouth was busy with two tasks at once. "I saw him trapped in Ty myself, along with his entire army; because you French, when you've accomplished something clever, like to return home and celebrate with dancing or festivities with the women to mark your victory."

"I don't know. An Indian rarely sleeps during wartime, and the possibility of plunder might keep a Huron here even after his tribe has moved on. It would be wise to put out the fire and post a guard—listen! you hear that sound I'm talking about!"

"A Native American rarely lingers around burial sites. While prepared to kill and not particularly concerned about the methods used, he typically settles for taking the scalp, except when his blood runs hot and his temper flares; however, once the spirit has truly departed, he sets aside his hatred and allows the deceased to rest in peace naturally. Speaking of spirits, major, do you believe that the afterlife of a Native American and that of us white people will be one and the same?"

"Absolutely—absolutely. I thought I heard it once more! Or was it just the rustling of leaves in the crown of the beech tree?"

"As for me," Hawkeye continued, glancing briefly in the direction Heyward had pointed out, though his expression remained distant and indifferent, "I believe that paradise is meant for happiness, and that people will enjoy it based on their nature and abilities. So I think a Native American isn't wrong when he believes he'll find those magnificent hunting grounds his traditions speak of. And honestly, I don't think it would be beneath a white man to spend his time—"

"You hear it again?" Duncan interrupted.

"Yes, yes; whether food is scarce or plentiful, a wolf becomes bold," said the calm scout. "There would be good pickings among the skins of those devils too, if we had light and time for such sport. But regarding the afterlife, major; I've heard preachers say in the settlements that heaven was a place of rest. Now, people's minds differ when it comes to their ideas of enjoyment. As for myself, and I say this with respect for Providence's plan, it wouldn't be much of a reward to be locked up in those mansions they preach about, having a natural desire for movement and the hunt."

Duncan, who now understood what had caused the noise he had heard, responded with greater focus on the topic the scout had humorously decided to discuss:

"It's hard to explain the emotions that might come with life's final great transformation."

"It would certainly be quite a change for a man who has spent his days outdoors," replied the straightforward scout, "and who has so frequently eaten his morning meal near the source of the Hudson River, to now sleep within hearing distance of the thundering Mohawk. But it brings comfort to know that we serve a compassionate God, even though we each do so in our own way, and with vast stretches of untamed land separating us—what's happening over there?"

"Isn't that the sound of the wolves rushing that you mentioned?"

Hawkeye slowly shook his head and motioned for Duncan to follow him to a place where the firelight couldn't reach. After taking this precaution, the scout positioned himself with intense focus and listened carefully for a long time, hoping to hear again the faint sound that had so suddenly alarmed him. His watchfulness, however, appeared to be pointless; after waiting without success, he whispered to Duncan:

"We need to call for Uncas. The young man has Native American instincts, and he might detect what we're missing; after all, being white, I won't pretend my nature is otherwise."

The young Mohican, who had been speaking quietly with his father, suddenly tensed when he heard an owl's mournful cry, and jumping to his feet, he gazed toward the dark hills as if trying to locate where the sound was coming from. The scout made the call again, and within moments, Duncan spotted Uncas moving carefully along the fortification toward where they were standing.

Hawkeye explained what he wanted in just a few words, speaking in the Delaware language. As soon as Uncas understood why he had been called, he threw himself flat on the grass, where he appeared to Duncan to lie still and motionless. Surprised by the young warrior's unmoving position and curious to see how he was using his skills to gather the information they needed, Heyward took a few steps forward and leaned over the dark shape he had been watching. It was then that he realized Uncas had disappeared, and he was looking only at the dark outline of a bump in the embankment.

"What happened to the Mohican?" he asked the scout, stepping back in shock. "This is where I saw him fall, and I could have sworn he was still lying here."

"Listen! Keep your voice down; we don't know who might be listening, and the Mingoes are a clever people. As for Uncas, he's out on the plain, and the Maquas, if there are any around us, will meet their match."

"You think that Montcalm has not called off all his Indians? Let us give the alarm to our companions, that we may stand to our arms. Here are five of us, who are not unused to meet an enemy."

"Do you think Montcalm hasn't recalled all his Indians? Let's alert our companions so we can prepare for battle. There are five of us here who have experience fighting enemies."

"Don't say a word to either of them if you value your life. Look at the Sagamore, sitting by the fire like a magnificent Indian chief. If there are any lurkers hiding out there in the darkness, they'll never be able to tell from his expression that we suspect danger is near."

"But they might find him, and that would mean his death. The firelight makes his figure too clearly visible, and he'll become the first and most certain victim."

"There's no denying you're speaking the truth now," the scout replied, showing more worry than he typically displayed; "but what options do we have? One suspicious glance could trigger an attack before we're prepared to handle it. He understands from the signal I sent to Uncas that we've picked up a trail; I'll inform him that we're tracking the Mingoes; his Indian instincts will guide him on what to do."

The scout pressed his fingers to his lips and made a soft hissing noise that initially startled Duncan, who thought he was hearing a snake. Chingachgook had been sitting alone with his head resting on his hand, lost in thought, but the instant he heard the warning call of the creature whose name he carried, he straightened up, his dark eyes scanning quickly and sharply in all directions. After this sudden and perhaps instinctive reaction, all signs of surprise or concern disappeared. His rifle remained untouched and seemingly ignored within arm's reach. The tomahawk he had loosened from his belt for comfort was allowed to drop from its normal position to the ground, and his body appeared to relax like that of someone whose muscles and nerves were being allowed to rest. Cleverly returning to his previous pose, though switching hands as if the movement had simply been to ease his arm, the native waited for what would happen next with a composure and steadiness that only an Indian warrior could have demonstrated.

But Heyward noticed that while the Mohican chief seemed to be sleeping to someone less observant, his nostrils were flared, his head was tilted slightly to one side as if to help his hearing, and his sharp, quick eyes constantly scanned everything he could see.

"Look at that noble man!" Hawkeye whispered, gripping Heyward's arm; "he understands that even a glance or the slightest movement could ruin our plans and leave us completely at the mercy of those devils—"

He was interrupted by the flash and crack of a rifle. The air filled with sparks of fire around the spot where Heyward's eyes remained fixed, filled with admiration and wonder. A second glance revealed that Chingachgook had vanished in the chaos. Meanwhile, the scout had raised his rifle, ready for action, and waited impatiently for an enemy to come into view. But after that single, unsuccessful attempt on Chingachgook's life, the attack seemed to have ended. Once or twice the listeners thought they heard the distant rustling of bushes as unknown figures rushed through them; it wasn't long before Hawkeye pointed out the "scampering of the wolves" as they fled hastily before some intruder entering their territory. After an impatient and breathless pause, they heard a splash in the water, immediately followed by the crack of another rifle.

"There goes Uncas!" said the scout; "that boy carries a fine rifle! I know the sound of its shot as well as a father knows his child's voice, because I carried that gun myself until I found a better one."

"What could this possibly mean?" Duncan demanded. "We're being watched, and it appears we've been marked for destruction."

"That scattered fire over there can prove that no harm was meant, and this Indian will confirm that no damage has been done," the scout replied, lowering his rifle across his arm once more and following Chingachgook, who had just emerged back into the circle of light, toward the center of the fortification. "What's the situation, Sagamore? Are the Mingoes attacking us for real, or is it just one of those cowards who follow behind a war party to scalp the dead, sneak around, and then brag to the women back home about the brave acts they supposedly performed against the white men?"

Chingachgook calmly returned to his seat and remained silent until he had inspected the burning stick that had been hit by the bullet which had almost killed him. After examining it, he simply held up one finger and responded with a single English word:

"One."

"I thought so," Hawkeye replied, sitting down. "Since he reached the cover of the lake before Uncas could shoot him, it's very likely the scoundrel will spread his lies about some great ambush, claiming he was tracking two Mohicans and a white hunter—because the officers might as well be considered useless in a fight like that. Well, let him talk. There are always some honest men in every nation, though God knows they're rare among the Maquas, who will put down a braggart when he boasts against common sense. That villain sent his bullet close enough to your ears that you could hear it whistle, Sagamore."

Chingachgook calmly looked toward the spot where the bullet had hit, showing no curiosity, then returned to his previous position with a composure that such a minor event couldn't shake. At that moment, Uncas slipped into the circle and sat down by the fire, displaying the same indifferent manner that his father maintained.

Heyward watched these various moments with deep interest and amazement. It seemed to him that the forest dwellers possessed some secret method of communication that had gone unnoticed by his own senses. Instead of the eager and talkative storytelling that a white young man would have used to share, and likely embellish, what had happened in the darkness of the plain, the young warrior appeared satisfied to let his actions speak for themselves. This was, indeed, neither the right time nor the proper situation for a Native American to brag about his achievements; and it's likely that if Heyward had failed to ask questions, not another word would have been spoken about the matter at that moment.

"What happened to our enemy, Uncas?" Duncan asked. "We heard your rifle shot and hoped you didn't miss your target."

The young chief pulled back a section of his hunting shirt and silently revealed the deadly lock of hair that he carried as a trophy of his triumph. Chingachgook placed his hand on the scalp and examined it for a moment with intense focus. Then he let it fall, with revulsion clearly visible on his weathered face, and exclaimed:

"Oneida!"

"Oneida!" the scout repeated, his interest in the scene rapidly fading into an indifference that nearly matched that of his Native American companions. However, he now stepped forward with unusual urgency to examine the bloody trophy. "Good Lord, if the Oneidas are positioned along our trail, we'll find ourselves surrounded by enemies on all sides! To white men's eyes, there's no distinction between this piece of skin and that of any other Indian, yet the Sagamore claims it came from the head of a Mingo. He even identifies the specific tribe of the unfortunate victim as easily as if the scalp were a page from a book and each strand of hair a written letter. What right do Christian white men have to pride themselves on their education when a savage can decipher a language that would baffle even the most learned among them? Tell me, young man, what tribe did this scoundrel belong to?"

Uncas lifted his gaze to look at the scout's face and replied in his gentle voice:

"Oneida."

"Oneida, once more! When a single Indian makes a statement, it's usually true; but when his people back him up, you can take it as absolute fact!"

"The poor man has mistaken us for French," said Heyward; "otherwise he wouldn't have tried to kill a friend."

"He mistook a Mohican in his war paint for a Huron! You might as well mistake Montcalm's white-coated grenadiers for the scarlet jackets of the Royal Americans," the scout replied. "No, no, the serpent knew what he was doing; there wasn't any real mistake in the matter, because there's little love between a Delaware and a Mingo, regardless of which tribes they fight for in a white man's war. For that matter, even though the Oneidas serve his sacred majesty, who is my sovereign lord and master, I wouldn't have hesitated long before firing 'Killdeer' at that devil myself, if luck had put him in my path."

"That would have violated our agreements and been beneath your dignity."

"When a man spends a lot of time with a people," Hawkeye continued, "if they were honest and he was no scoundrel, love will develop between them. It's true that white cunning has managed to throw the tribes into great confusion when it comes to friends and enemies; so that the Hurons and the Oneidas, who speak the same language, or what may be called the same, take each other's scalps, and the Delawares are divided among themselves; a few lingering around their great council-fire on their own river, and fighting on the same side with the Mingoes while the majority are in the Canadas, out of natural hatred for the Maquas—thus throwing everything into disorder, and destroying all the harmony of warfare. Yet a red man's nature is not likely to change with every shift of policy; so that the love between a Mohican and a Mingo is much like the regard between a white man and a serpent."

"I'm sorry to hear that; I had believed the native people living within our territory found us fair and generous enough to fully support our cause."

"Well, I think it's natural to care more about your own fights than those of strangers. As for me, I do love justice, so I won't say I hate a Mingo, since that wouldn't be right for someone of my race and faith. Still, I'll say again that it might have been because of the darkness that 'Killdeer' played no part in killing this sneaking Oneida."

Then, as if pleased with the strength of his own arguments, regardless of how they might affect his opponent's views, the honest but stubborn woodsman turned away from the fire, willing to let the debate rest. Heyward retreated to the defensive wall, too anxious and too inexperienced in forest warfare to feel comfortable knowing such sneaky attacks were possible. The scout and the Mohicans, however, felt differently. Their sharp and well-trained senses, which possessed abilities that often surpassed what most people would believe possible, had not only spotted the danger but had also determined how serious it was and how long it might last. None of the three seemed to have any doubt about their complete safety, as shown by the preparations they quickly made to gather and discuss their next steps.

The confusion among nations, and even among tribes, that Hawkeye mentioned existed in its strongest form during that time. The great bond of language, and naturally of shared ancestry, had been broken in many places; one result of this was that the Delaware and the Mingo (as the Six Nations people were known) found themselves fighting side by side, while the Mingo sought to take the scalp of the Huron, even though the Huron were believed to be from the same ancestral line. The Delawares were split even within their own people. While love for the land that had belonged to his forefathers kept the Sagamore of the Mohicans with a small group of followers who were serving at Edward under the flags of the English king, the vast majority of his nation was known to be fighting in the field as allies of Montcalm. The reader likely understands, if enough information hasn't already been gathered from this story, that the Delaware, or Lenape, claimed to be the ancestors of that large group of people who had once controlled most of the eastern and northern states of America, and the Mohican community was an ancient and greatly respected member of this group.

It was, naturally, with a complete grasp of the complex and detailed interests that had turned friend against friend, and brought natural enemies to fight alongside one another, that the scout and his companions now prepared themselves to discuss the plans that would guide their future actions, surrounded by so many conflicting and fierce tribes of men. Duncan understood enough about Indian traditions to comprehend why the fire was built up, and why the warriors, including Hawkeye, took their places within the circle of its smoke with such solemnity and formality. Positioning himself at a corner of the fortifications, where he could observe the scene from outside, he waited for the outcome with as much patience as he could manage.

After a brief and striking pause, Chingachgook lit a pipe with a bowl that had been skillfully carved from one of the region's soft stones and a wooden stem, then began to smoke. Once he had breathed in enough of the calming tobacco's aroma, he handed the pipe to the scout. The pipe circulated among them three complete times in complete silence before anyone spoke a word. Then the Sagamore, being the eldest and highest in authority, calmly and with dignity introduced the topic they needed to discuss. The scout responded to him, and Chingachgook replied when the scout disagreed with his views. Meanwhile, young Uncas remained a quiet and respectful observer until Hawkeye, out of courtesy, asked for his thoughts. From watching how each person spoke, Heyward could tell that the father and son supported one position on the disputed matter, while the white man argued for the opposite side. The discussion gradually became more heated, and it became clear that the speakers were becoming emotionally invested in the argument.

Despite the growing intensity of the friendly debate, even the most proper Christian gathering, including those where respected ministers come together, could have learned a valuable lesson in restraint from the patience and politeness shown by these debaters. Uncas's words received the same careful attention as those that came from his father's more experienced wisdom; and rather than showing any sign of impatience, neither man responded immediately, but instead appeared to spend several moments in quiet reflection, carefully considering what had already been spoken.

The Mohican language came with gestures that were so straightforward and natural that Heyward found it quite easy to follow what they were discussing. The scout, however, was harder to understand because his lingering racial pride made him adopt the cold and artificial manner that characterizes all Anglo-Americans when they're not emotionally stirred. From how often the Indians pointed out signs of a forest trail, it was clear they were pushing for a pursuit by land, while Hawkeye's repeated sweeping gestures toward Lake George showed that he favored crossing the water instead.

The latter appeared to be rapidly losing ground, and the decision was about to go against him, when he rose to his feet and shook off his indifference, suddenly taking on the manner of an Indian and employing all the techniques of native eloquence. Raising his arm, he pointed out the path of the sun, repeating the gesture for each day that would be needed to accomplish their goals. Then he outlined a long and difficult journey through rocks and waterways. The age and frailty of the sleeping and unaware Munro were shown through signs too clear to be misunderstood. Duncan realized that even his own abilities were being spoken of dismissively, as the scout extended his palm and referred to him by the name "Open Hand"—a title his generosity had earned him among all the friendly tribes. Then came a demonstration of the light and graceful movements of a canoe, placed in sharp contrast to the unsteady steps of someone weakened and exhausted. He finished by pointing to the scalp of the Oneida, and apparently emphasizing the need for them to leave quickly, and in a way that would leave no trace.

The Mohicans listened seriously, their faces showing they understood what the speaker was saying. Gradually, they became convinced by his words, and by the end of Hawkeye's speech, they were making the usual sounds of approval. In essence, Uncas and his father came around to his way of thinking, giving up their earlier opinions with such openness and honesty that, if they had been leaders of some major civilized nation, it would have certainly destroyed their political careers by ruining their reputation for being consistent forever.

The moment the issue they were discussing was settled, the argument and everything related to it seemed to be forgotten, except for the outcome. Hawkeye didn't bother looking around to see his victory reflected in admiring eyes, but instead calmly stretched his tall body in front of the fading embers and closed his eyes to sleep.

Now left largely to themselves, the Mohicans, who had spent so much time focused on the needs of others, took this opportunity to turn their attention to their own concerns. Immediately abandoning the serious and stern bearing of an Indian chief, Chingachgook began speaking to his son in the gentle and tender tones of a loving father. Uncas warmly responded to his father's familiar manner; and before the heavy breathing of the scout indicated that he had fallen asleep, a complete transformation had taken place in the behavior of his two companions.

It's impossible to capture the musical quality of their language during these moments of laughter and affection in a way that would make sense to anyone who has never heard its melody. The range of their voices, especially the young man's, was remarkable—spanning from the deepest bass notes to tones so gentle they seemed almost feminine. The father watched his son's graceful and clever movements with obvious joy, always responding with a smile to the young man's infectious yet quiet laughter. When influenced by these tender and natural emotions, no hint of savagery could be detected in the Sagamore's softened expression. His elaborate war paint and symbols of death appeared more like a costume worn as a joke than a fierce declaration of his intent to bring destruction wherever he went.

After an hour spent enjoying these better emotions, Chingachgook suddenly declared his intention to sleep by wrapping his head in his blanket and lying down on the bare ground. Uncas immediately stopped his cheerful behavior; and carefully arranging the coals so they would provide warmth to his father's feet, the young man found his own place to rest among the debris of the location.

Drawing fresh confidence from the safety provided by these seasoned woodsmen, Heyward quickly followed their lead; and well before the night had passed, those who rested within the shelter of the destroyed fortification appeared to sleep as deeply as the unaware masses whose bones were already starting to whiten on the surrounding field.

---

# Chapter XX.

"Land of Albania! let me bend mine eyes
On thee; thou rugged nurse of savage men!"
—Childe Harold

The sky was still filled with stars when Hawkeye came to wake up those who were sleeping. Throwing off their cloaks, Munro and Heyward got to their feet while the woodsman was still making his quiet calls at the entrance of the rough shelter where they had spent the night. When they emerged from under its cover, they found the scout waiting for them nearby, and the only greeting between them was the meaningful gesture for silence made by their wise leader.

"Think over your prayers," he whispered as they came closer to him, "because the One you're praying to understands every language—the language of the heart just as much as the words from your mouth. But don't say a word out loud; it's unusual for a white person's voice to carry properly through the forest, as we've learned from that wretched fool, the singer. Come on," he said, turning toward a barrier of the fortifications, "let's get down into the trench on this side, and make sure to step only on the stones and pieces of wood as you move."

His companions followed his instructions, although two of them still didn't understand why such unusual caution was necessary. When they entered the shallow depression that encircled the earthen fortress on three sides, they discovered the pathway was almost completely blocked by debris. Through careful and patient effort, however, they managed to climb over the obstacles following the scout's lead, until they finally arrived at the sandy shoreline of Lake Horican.

"That's a trail that only a nose could follow," said the pleased scout, glancing back along their challenging path; "grass makes a dangerous surface for a group on the run to walk on, but wood and stone don't hold impressions from a moccasin. If you had worn your heavy boots, there might have been real cause for concern; but with properly prepared deerskin, a person can usually trust himself on rocks safely. Push the canoe closer to shore, Uncas; this sand will hold a mark as easily as the butter of the Germans on the Mohawk. Gently, boy, gently; it must not touch the beach, or those scoundrels will know which way we left this place."

The young man followed the precaution carefully, and the scout placed a plank from the debris to the canoe, gesturing for the two officers to get in. Once they were aboard, everything was carefully returned to its previous state of disarray, and then Hawkeye managed to reach his small birch bark boat without leaving any of the traces he seemed so concerned about. Heyward remained quiet until the Indians had carefully paddled the canoe a good distance from the fort and into the wide, dark shadows cast by the eastern mountain across the smooth surface of the lake; then he asked:

"Why do we need this secretive and rushed escape?"

"If the blood of an Oneida could stain a sheet of pure water like the one we're floating on," the scout replied, "your own two eyes would answer your question. Have you forgotten the sneaking snake that Uncas killed?"

"Absolutely not. But they said he was by himself, and dead men don't give anyone reason to be afraid."

"Yes, he was alone in his evil deeds! But an Indian whose tribe has so many warriors rarely needs to worry that his blood will be spilled without the death cry quickly coming from some of his enemies."

"But our presence—the authority of Colonel Munro—would provide enough protection against the anger of our allies, especially in a situation where the wretch so clearly deserved his fate. I trust to Heaven you haven't strayed even a single foot from the direct path of our route for such a trivial reason!"

"Do you think that scoundrel's bullet would have changed course, even if the king himself had been standing in its way?" the stubborn scout replied. "Why didn't the French commander, the one who's the governor-general of Canada, make the Hurons put down their tomahawks, if a white man's words can have such a powerful effect on an Indian's nature?"

Heyward's response was cut short by a groan from Munro, but after pausing briefly out of respect for his elderly friend's grief, he continued with the topic.

"The marquis of Montcalm can only settle that error with his God," the young man said solemnly.

"Yes, yes, now your words make sense, because they're based on religion and honesty. There's a huge difference between putting a regiment of soldiers in white uniforms between the tribes and the prisoners, and persuading an angry warrior to forget he's carrying a knife and rifle, using words that must start by calling him your son. No, no," the scout continued, glancing back at the fading shore of William Henry, which was now quickly disappearing, and laughing in his own quiet but sincere way; "I've put a trail of water between us; and unless those devils can make friends with the fish, and learn who has paddled across their lake this beautiful morning, we'll put the entire length of Lake George behind us before they've decided which path to follow."

"With enemies ahead of us and enemies behind us, our journey is likely to be dangerous."

"Danger!" Hawkeye repeated calmly. "No, not exactly danger. With sharp ears and keen eyes, we can stay a few hours ahead of those scoundrels. And if we need to use our rifles, the three of us know how to handle them as well as anyone you'll find on the frontier. No, it's not really danger. But we'll likely face what you might call a tough fight, and there could be a skirmish, a battle, or some other excitement like that. The good news is we'll always have good cover and plenty of ammunition."

It's possible that Heyward's assessment of the danger was somewhat different from the scout's, because instead of responding, he remained quiet while the canoe moved across several miles of water. Just as dawn broke, they reached the narrow part of the lake, and moved quickly and carefully among the countless small islands. This was the route Montcalm had used to retreat with his army, and the adventurers couldn't be sure whether he had positioned some of his Indians in hiding to guard the rear of his forces and gather any stragglers. They therefore approached the passage with the usual silence that their cautious habits demanded.[1]

> [1] The beauties of Lake George are well known to every American tourist. While it may not match the towering heights of the mountains that encircle it or the man-made features found at the most spectacular Swiss and Italian lakes, it stands as their complete equal in terms of shoreline contours and crystal-clear waters. When it comes to the quantity and arrangement of its islands and smaller islets, it far surpasses all of them combined. People say there are several hundred islands scattered across this body of water that stretches less than thirty miles in length. The narrow passages that link what could truly be considered two separate lakes are so densely packed with islands that the waterways between them often measure only a few feet across. The lake's width ranges from one to three miles throughout its expanse.

Chingachgook set down his paddle while Uncas and the scout pushed the lightweight boat through winding and complex waterways, where every foot of progress put them at risk of someone suddenly appearing to block their path. The Sagamore's eyes moved cautiously from small island to small island, and from grove to grove, as the canoe moved forward; and when a more open stretch of water allowed it, his sharp eyesight scanned the bare rocks and overhanging forests that loomed menacingly over the narrow passage.

Heyward, who found himself deeply engaged as an observer for two reasons—both the stunning beauty of the location and the anxiety that naturally came with his circumstances—was just starting to think he had allowed his fears to get the better of him without good cause, when the paddle stopped moving in response to a signal from Chingachgook.

"Hugh!" Uncas shouted, almost at the exact moment his father's light tap on the side of the canoe warned them that danger was nearby.

"What now?" asked the scout; "the lake is as calm as if the wind had never stirred its surface, and I can see across its expanse for miles; there isn't even the dark head of a loon visible on the water."

The Native American solemnly lifted his paddle and pointed toward where his unwavering gaze was fixed. Duncan's eyes followed the gesture. A short distance ahead of them lay another of the forested small islands, but it looked as tranquil and serene as if its isolation had never been broken by human presence.

"I don't see anything," he said, "except land and water; and it's a beautiful sight."

"Listen!" the scout interrupted. "Yes, Sagamore, there's always a reason behind your actions. It's just a shadow, but it doesn't look natural. You can see the mist, major, that's rising above the island; you can't really call it fog, because it looks more like a thin strip of cloud—"

"It is vapor from the water."

"Any child could see that. But what about that strip of darker smoke hanging along the bottom edge, the one you can follow down into the hazel thicket? It's from a fire, but one that I believe has been allowed to burn low."

"Let's head to that spot and put our doubts to rest," said the impatient Duncan. "Any group camping on such a small piece of land can't be very large."

"If you measure Indian cleverness by the standards you read about in books, or by white man's wisdom, they will mislead you, possibly even to your death," Hawkeye replied, studying the tracks and markings of the area with the sharp perception that set him apart. "If I'm allowed to offer my opinion on this situation, I'd say we have only two options to consider: one is to turn back and abandon any idea of pursuing the Hurons—"

"Never!" Heyward shouted, his voice much too loud for their situation.

"Well, well," Hawkeye continued, making a quick gesture to control his impatience, "I share your opinion; though I felt it was appropriate given my experience to explain everything. We must then make our move, and if the Indians or French are in the narrow passages, we'll have to run the gauntlet through these towering mountains. Does what I'm saying make sense, Sagamore?"

The Indian gave no response other than dipping his paddle into the water and pushing the canoe forward. Since he was responsible for steering their direction, his decision was clearly shown by this action. The entire group now worked their paddles energetically, and within just a few moments they had arrived at a position where they could see the complete northern shoreline of the island, the side that had been hidden from view until now.

"There they are, as clear as any sign could be," whispered the scout, "two canoes and smoke. Those scoundrels haven't spotted us through the mist yet, or we'd be hearing their cursed war cry. Stay together, friends! We're getting away from them, and we're almost beyond rifle range."

The familiar crack of a rifle shot rang out, its bullet bouncing across the calm surface of the waterway, followed by a piercing scream from the island that cut short his words and revealed that their crossing had been spotted. Within moments, several warriors could be seen charging toward canoes, which were quickly skimming across the water in hot pursuit. These ominous signs of an approaching battle caused no visible change in the expressions or actions of his three guides, as far as Duncan could tell, except that their paddle strokes became longer and more synchronized, making the small vessel surge forward like a living creature driven by its own will.

"Keep them right there, Sagamore," said Hawkeye, glancing calmly back over his left shoulder while continuing to work his paddle; "hold them in that exact position. Those Hurons don't have a single weapon in their entire tribe that can reach this far; but 'Killdeer' has a barrel that a man can rely on."

The scout, having confirmed that the Mohicans were capable of maintaining the necessary distance on their own, carefully set down his paddle and picked up the deadly rifle. Three separate times he brought the weapon to his shoulder, and when his companions expected to hear the shot, he just as often lowered it to ask the Indians to let their enemies come a little closer. Finally his precise and demanding eye appeared satisfied, and, extending his left arm along the barrel, he was slowly raising the muzzle when a cry from Uncas, who was sitting in the bow, once again made him hold back the shot.

"What's this now, boy?" Hawkeye demanded. "You just saved a Huron from his death cry with that word. Do you have a good reason for what you're doing?"

Uncas gestured toward a rocky shoreline just ahead of them, where another war canoe was shooting straight across their path. Their dangerous situation was now so clear that no words were needed to confirm it. The scout set down his rifle and picked up his paddle again, while Chingachgook angled the front of the canoe slightly toward the western shore to put more distance between them and this fresh enemy. Meanwhile, wild and triumphant shouts from behind reminded them of their pursuers closing in from the rear. The intense scene even roused Munro from his indifference.

"Let's head for the rocks on the mainland," he said, looking like a weary soldier, "and fight the savages. God forbid that I, or anyone connected to me and my family, should ever trust again in the word of any servant of Louis!"

"Anyone who wants to succeed in fighting Indians," the scout replied, "shouldn't be too proud to learn from a native's cleverness. Keep her closer to the shore, Sagamore; we're circling back on those scoundrels, and they might try to pick up our trail if they think ahead."

Hawkeye was right; when the Hurons realized their path would put them behind their quarry, they made it less direct, gradually angling more and more sideways until the two canoes were soon gliding on parallel courses within two hundred yards of each other. Now it became purely a test of speed. The light boats moved so rapidly that the lake formed small waves in front of them, and their motion became rolling due to their own speed. This situation, combined with the need to keep every hand busy with the paddles, probably explained why the Hurons didn't immediately use their guns. The escaping party's efforts were too intense to last long, and their pursuers had the advantage of greater numbers. Duncan noticed with worry that the scout was starting to look around anxiously, as if searching for some additional way to help their escape.

"Move her a bit farther from the sun, Sagamore," said the determined woodsman; "I can see those scoundrels are assigning a man to the rifle. One broken bone could cost us our scalps. Move farther from the sun and we'll position the island between us."

The strategy proved useful. A long, low island stretched out a short distance ahead of them, and as they approached it, the pursuing canoe was forced to take the opposite side from where those being chased had passed. The scout and his companions made full use of this advantage, and the moment they were hidden from view by the bushes, they doubled their efforts that had already seemed extraordinary. The two canoes rounded the final low point like two racehorses at full speed, with the fugitives in the lead. This maneuver had brought them closer to each other, though it had changed their positions relative to one another.

"You demonstrated skill in selecting a birch bark canoe, Uncas, when you picked this one from among the Huron vessels," the scout said with a smile, appearing more pleased with their advantage in the race than with the possibility of ultimate escape that was starting to seem within reach. "Those devils have put all their power back into paddling, and now we must fight for our lives with pieces of flattened wood instead of with loaded rifle barrels and accurate aim. Take long strokes, and stay together, friends."

"They're getting ready to fire," Heyward said, "and since we're directly in their line of sight, they can hardly miss."

"Get down to the bottom of the canoe then," the scout replied; "you and the colonel; it will make you that much smaller as targets."

Heyward smiled as he replied:

"It would set a terrible example for those in the highest positions to avoid danger while their soldiers were facing enemy fire."

"Lord! Lord! That's what you call a white man's courage!" the scout exclaimed. "And like many of his ideas, it can't be backed up with logic. Do you think the Sagamore, or Uncas, or even myself—a man without mixed blood—would hesitate to find cover during a fight when staying in the open wouldn't help anyone? Why do you think the French built up their Quebec if all fighting was supposed to happen out in the open?"

"Everything you're saying is absolutely true, my friend," Heyward responded; "however, our customs must prevent us from doing what you want."

A burst of gunfire from the Hurons cut short their conversation, and as bullets whizzed around them, Duncan noticed Uncas turn his head to look back at him and Munro. Despite being so close to the enemy and facing serious personal danger, the young warrior's face showed no emotion other than what Duncan could only interpret as surprise at finding men willing to face such pointless risk. Chingachgook probably understood white men's thinking better, since he didn't even glance away from his focused gaze on the landmark that guided their path. A musket ball quickly struck the lightweight, smooth paddle from the chief's hands and sent it flying through the air far ahead of them. The Hurons let out a shout, seizing the chance to fire another round. Uncas swept his own paddle in a wide curve through the water, and as their canoe sped forward, Chingachgook retrieved his paddle, raised it high above his head, released the war cry of the Mohicans, and then put his strength and expertise back into their crucial task.

The loud shouts of "Le Gros Serpent!" "La Longue Carabine!" "Le Cerf Agile!" erupted all at once from the canoes behind them, and appeared to inspire fresh enthusiasm in their pursuers. The scout grabbed "killdeer" with his left hand, and raising it above his head, he waved it triumphantly at his enemies. The natives responded to this provocation with a fierce cry, and immediately another round of gunfire followed. The bullets splashed across the lake's surface, and one even penetrated the bark of their small boat. No visible emotion could be detected in the Mohicans during this dangerous moment, their stern faces showing neither hope nor fear; but the scout once again turned his head, and, chuckling in his own quiet way, he spoke to Heyward:

"The fools love to hear the sounds of their weapons firing; but you won't find an eye among the Mingoes that can calculate an accurate shot from a rocking canoe! You can see the silent devils have assigned a man to load the gun, and by the smallest measurement that can be allowed, we move three feet to their two!"

Duncan, who wasn't quite as comfortable with this careful calculation of distances as his companions, was relieved to discover that thanks to their superior skill and the confusion among their enemies, they were clearly gaining the upper hand. The Hurons fired again soon after, and a bullet hit the blade of Hawkeye's paddle without causing any damage.

"That's enough," said the scout, studying the small dent with an inquisitive gaze; "it wouldn't have scratched the skin of a baby, let alone men like us, who have been weathered by the fury of the elements. Now, major, if you'll try using this piece of flattened wood, I'll let 'killdeer' join the discussion."

Heyward grabbed the paddle and threw himself into the work with enthusiasm that made up for his lack of skill, while Hawkeye was busy checking the priming of his rifle. Hawkeye then took quick aim and fired. The Huron at the front of the lead canoe had stood up with the same intention, and he now tumbled backward, letting his gun slip from his hands into the water. Within moments, though, he got back on his feet, even though his movements were erratic and confused. At the same time, his companions stopped paddling, and the pursuing canoes gathered together and came to a halt. Chingachgook and Uncas used this break to catch their breath, while Duncan kept working with relentless determination.

The father and son now exchanged calm but questioning looks to see if either had been hurt by the gunfire; both understood that no cry or shout would be allowed to reveal such an injury during such a critical moment. A few large drops of blood were running down the Sagamore's shoulder, and when he noticed that Uncas was staring at the wound too long, he cupped some water in his hand and washed away the blood, showing in this simple way that the injury was minor.

"Easy there, major," said the scout, who had by now reloaded his rifle; "we're already a bit too far out for a rifle to show what it can really do, and you can see those devils over there are having a meeting. Let them get close enough for a good shot—you can trust my judgment on something like this—and I'll track those scoundrels all the way along Lake George, promising you that their shots won't do anything worse than scratch the surface, while my 'Killdeer' will find its mark at least two times out of three."

"We're forgetting our mission," replied the dutiful Duncan. "For God's sake, let's take advantage of this opportunity and put more distance between us and the enemy."

"Give me my children," Munro said in a rough, strained voice; "don't toy with a father's suffering any longer, but return my babies to me."

Years of consistently following orders from his commanding officers had instilled in the scout a deep respect for obedience. Taking one final, longing look at the far-off canoes, he set down his rifle and took over from the exhausted Duncan, picking up the paddle, which he handled with muscles that seemed never to grow weary. The Mohicans supported his efforts, and within just a few minutes they had created such a wide expanse of water between themselves and their pursuers that Heyward could finally breathe easily again.

The lake started to widen, and their path followed a broad stretch of water that was bordered, just as before, by tall and jagged mountains. However, the islands were scarce and easily navigated around. The paddle strokes became more steady and rhythmic, while those who wielded them kept working after the intense and dangerous pursuit they had just escaped from, with as much composure as if their speed had been tested in a game, rather than under such urgent, indeed almost hopeless, conditions.

Instead of following the western shore, where their mission was taking them, the cautious Mohican steered his course more toward those hills behind which Montcalm was known to have led his army into the imposing fortress of Ticonderoga. Since the Hurons had apparently given up the chase, there seemed to be no clear reason for this extra caution. Nevertheless, this careful approach was kept up for hours, until they reached a bay near the northern end of the lake. Here the canoe was pushed onto the beach, and everyone got out. Hawkeye and Heyward climbed a nearby cliff, where the former, after studying the stretch of water below him, pointed out to the latter a small dark object floating beneath a headland, several miles away.

"Do you see it?" the scout asked urgently. "Now, what would you make of that spot if you were left alone with only your limited experience to find your way through this wilderness?"

"If it weren't so far away and so large, I would think it's a bird. Could it possibly be something alive?"

"It's a canoe made of good birch bark, and it's being paddled by fierce and cunning Mingoes. Although Providence has given those who live in the woods eyesight that would be unnecessary for men in the settlements, where there are devices to help with vision, no human eyes can see all the dangers that surround us right now. These scoundrels pretend to be focused mainly on their evening meal, but the moment darkness falls they will be following our trail, as surely as hounds follow a scent. We must shake them off, or we'll have to abandon our pursuit of Le Renard Subtil. These lakes can be useful sometimes, especially when prey takes to the water," the scout continued, looking around with a worried expression; "but they offer no protection, except perhaps for the fish. God only knows what this country would become if the settlements ever spread far from the two rivers. Both hunting and warfare would lose their appeal."

"Let's not waste a single moment without a clear and valid reason."

"I don't like that smoke you can see curling up along the rock above the canoe," interrupted the distracted scout. "I'd bet my life that other eyes besides ours are watching it and understand what it means. Well, talking won't fix the situation, and it's time we took action."

Hawkeye stepped away from his observation point and walked down to the shore, deep in thought. He shared what he had seen with his companions in the Delaware language, and they held a brief but intense discussion. As soon as their conversation ended, all three immediately began carrying out their new plans.

The canoe was lifted from the water and carried on the shoulders of the group as they moved into the woods, deliberately creating as wide and obvious a trail as they could manage. They quickly reached the stream, which they crossed before continuing forward until they arrived at a large, bare rock. At this location, where their footprints would no longer be visible, they carefully retraced their steps back to the brook, walking backward with extreme caution. They then followed the streambed down to the lake, where they immediately launched their canoe once more. A low point of land hid them from the headland, and the lake's shoreline was bordered for quite a distance with thick, overhanging bushes. Protected by these natural features, they worked their way forward with steady determination until the scout declared that he believed it would be safe to come ashore again.

The halt continued until evening made objects unclear and hard to see. Then they resumed their journey, and helped by the darkness, moved quietly and energetically toward the western shore. Although the rough outline of the mountain they were heading toward showed no distinctive features to Duncan's eyes, the Mohican entered the small harbor he had chosen with the confidence and precision of an experienced pilot.

The boat was lifted once more and carried into the woods, where it was carefully hidden beneath a pile of brush. The adventurers picked up their weapons and packs, and the scout informed Munro and Heyward that he and the Indians were finally ready to move forward.

---

# Chapter XXI.

"If you find a man there, he shall die a flea's death."
—The Merry Wives of Windsor

The group had arrived at the edge of a territory that remains, even today, less familiar to Americans than the deserts of Arabia or the steppes of Tartary. This was the barren and harsh landscape that divides the waterways flowing into Lake Champlain from those feeding the Hudson River, the Mohawk River, and the St. Lawrence River. Since the time of our story, the enterprising nature of the nation has encircled this area with a ring of prosperous and flourishing communities, yet even now only hunters or Native Americans are known to venture into its untamed wilderness.

Since Hawkeye and the Mohicans had frequently traveled through the mountains and valleys of this enormous wilderness, they didn't hesitate to venture deep into it with the confidence of men who were used to its hardships and challenges. For many hours the travelers worked their way along the difficult path, guided by a star or following the course of some stream, until the scout called for a stop, and after holding a brief discussion with the Indians, they lit their fire and made the typical preparations to spend the rest of the night at their current location.

Following the example and drawing courage from their more seasoned companions, Munro and Duncan slept without fear, though not without some restlessness. They allowed the morning dew to evaporate, and the sun had cleared away the mist, casting bright and clear light through the forest, when the travelers continued their journey.

After traveling a few miles, Hawkeye, who was leading the group, began moving more carefully and cautiously. He frequently paused to study the trees, and he wouldn't cross a stream without carefully examining how much water was flowing, how fast it moved, and what color it was. Since he wasn't entirely confident in his own assessment, he often turned to Chingachgook for advice, seeking his opinion with genuine concern. During one of these discussions, Heyward noticed that Uncas stood quietly and patiently nearby, appearing to listen with interest despite his silence. Heyward felt a strong urge to speak directly to the young chief and ask what he thought about their journey's progress, but Uncas's composed and dignified manner made Heyward think that, like himself, the young man was completely relying on the wisdom and experience of the older members of their group. Finally, the scout began speaking in English and immediately clarified why their situation was so troubling.

"When I discovered that the Hurons' homeward route runs north," he said, "it didn't take years of experience to figure out that they would follow the valleys and stay between the Hudson and Lake George waters until they could reach the headwaters of the Canadian streams, which would lead them into the heart of French territory. Yet here we are, within a short distance of the Scaroon Mountains, and we haven't crossed a single trail! Human nature is fallible, and it's possible we may not have picked up the right trail."

"God save us from making such a mistake!" Duncan cried out. "Let's go back the way we came and look more carefully as we search. Doesn't Uncas have any advice to give us in this difficult situation?"

The young Mohican glanced at his father, but he kept his calm and reserved expression and remained silent. Chingachgook had noticed the look, and with a gesture of his hand, he told him to speak. The instant this permission was given, Uncas's face transformed from its serious composure to a flash of intelligence and joy. Leaping forward like a deer, he bounded up the slope of a small hill just a few yards ahead and stood triumphantly over a patch of fresh earth that appeared to have been recently disturbed by the passage of some large animal. The eyes of the entire group followed his sudden movement, and they could see their success in the triumphant manner the young man displayed.

"That's the trail!' the scout exclaimed, moving toward the spot. 'The boy has sharp eyes and a quick mind for someone his age.'"

"It's extraordinary that he should have kept his knowledge to himself for so long," Duncan muttered at his elbow.

"It would have been more impressive if he had spoken without being asked. No, no; your young white man, who gets his education from books and can measure what he knows by the page, may think that his knowledge, like his legs, surpasses that of his fathers', but when experience is the teacher, the student learns to understand the value of years, and respects them accordingly."

"Look!" said Uncas, pointing north and south at the clear signs of the wide trail on both sides of him, "the dark-haired one has headed toward the forest."

"No hound ever followed a more beautiful trail," the scout replied, immediately rushing forward along the path they had found. "We're incredibly lucky and can track them easily with our heads held high. Yes, here are both of your clumsy horses: this Huron moves around like a white general. The man has lost his judgment and gone crazy! Keep an eye out for wheel tracks, Sagamore," he added, glancing back and laughing with his newfound confidence. "Soon we'll have that fool traveling in a carriage, with three of the sharpest pairs of eyes on the frontier following right behind him."

The scout's high spirits and the remarkable success of their pursuit, which had covered a winding distance of more than forty miles, managed to give the entire group a sense of hope. They moved forward quickly and with as much confidence as a traveler walking along a main road. Whenever a rock, stream, or patch of unusually hard ground broke the trail they were following, the scout's keen eye would pick it up again in the distance, rarely requiring even a moment's delay. Their progress was greatly helped by the certainty that Magua had been forced to travel through the valleys, which made the general direction of his route predictable. The Huron hadn't completely abandoned the tactics that natives typically used when retreating from an enemy. He frequently created false trails and made sudden changes in direction wherever a stream or the landscape made such deception possible, but his pursuers were seldom fooled and never failed to recognize their mistake before losing any time or ground on the misleading path.

By mid-afternoon they had passed the Scaroons and were following the path of the setting sun. After going down a hill to a low valley where a fast-moving stream flowed, they suddenly came upon a place where Le Renard's group had stopped to rest. Cold ashes from dead fires lay scattered around a spring, the remains of a deer were spread about the area, and the trees showed clear signs of having been eaten by horses. A short distance away, Heyward found and looked upon with deep feeling the small shelter where he desperately hoped Cora and Alice had rested. But while the ground was trampled and the footprints of both people and animals were clearly visible all around the spot, the trail seemed to have suddenly disappeared.

It was simple to track the Narragansetts' trail, but they appeared to have wandered aimlessly without any guides or purpose other than searching for food. Eventually Uncas, who along with his father had been trying to follow the horses' path, discovered a sign of their presence that was quite fresh. Before pursuing this lead, he shared his discovery with his companions; and while they were discussing this development, the young man returned, bringing the two young mares with their saddles damaged and their coverings dirty, as if they had been allowed to roam freely for several days.

"What is this supposed to prove?" Duncan said, his face turning pale as his eyes darted around nervously, as though he expected the surrounding brush and leaves to reveal some terrible secret.

"Our journey has come to an abrupt end, and we find ourselves in enemy territory," the scout replied. "If the scoundrel had been under pressure, and the ladies had needed horses to keep pace with the group, he might have taken their scalps; but without an enemy pursuing him, and with such sturdy animals as these, he wouldn't harm a single hair on their heads. I understand your concerns, and it's shameful for our race that you have good reason to think this way; but anyone who believes that even a Mingo would mistreat a woman, except to kill her with a tomahawk, understands nothing about Indian nature or the laws of the wilderness. No, no; I've heard that the French Indians have come into these hills to hunt moose, and we're getting close enough to catch the scent of their camp. Why wouldn't they be here? The morning and evening cannon fire from Fort Ticonderoga can be heard on any given day throughout these mountains, since the French are establishing a new boundary line between the king's provinces and Canada. It's true that the horses are here, but the Hurons have departed; let us therefore search for the trail they took when they left."

Hawkeye and the Mohicans now focused on their task with serious determination. They drew a circle several hundred feet around, and each member of the group took responsibility for searching a section. The examination, however, led to no discovery. There were numerous footprint impressions, but they all looked like those of men who had wandered around the area without any intention of leaving it. Once again the scout and his companions walked around the resting place, each slowly following behind the other, until they gathered in the center again, no more knowledgeable than when they had begun.

"That kind of cleverness has something wicked about it," Hawkeye declared when he saw the frustrated expressions on his companions' faces.

"We need to get to work, Sagamore, starting from the beginning and examining every inch of the ground carefully. That Huron will never be able to boast to his tribe that he can walk without leaving any tracks."

Leading by example, the scout threw himself into the search with fresh enthusiasm. Every leaf was carefully examined. Sticks were moved aside, and stones were lifted; they knew that Indian cleverness often used these natural objects as hiding places, working with incredible patience and skill to hide every footprint as they traveled. Yet they still found nothing. Eventually Uncas, whose energy had allowed him to finish his section of the search first, scraped away the earth around the muddy little stream that flowed from the spring, and redirected its flow into a different path. As soon as the narrow streambed below the makeshift dam had dried out, he bent over it with sharp and eager eyes. A shout of triumph immediately revealed that the young warrior had succeeded. The entire group rushed to the spot where Uncas pointed out the print of a moccasin in the wet soil.

"This young man will bring honor to his people," said Hawkeye, studying the trail with the same admiration a scientist would show when examining a mammoth's tusk or a mastodon's rib. "Yes, and he'll be a constant threat to the Hurons. But that's not an Indian's footprint! There's too much weight on the heel, and the toes are square-shaped, as if one of those French dancers had come through here, showing off his fancy steps to his tribe! Go back, Uncas, and get me the measurement of the singer's foot. You'll find a perfect impression of it right across from that rock, against the hillside."

While the young man was busy with this task, the scout and Chingachgook were carefully examining the footprints. The measurements matched, and the scout confidently declared that the footprint belonged to David, who had once again been forced to trade his shoes for moccasins.

"I can now read all of it as clearly as if I had witnessed Le Subtil's techniques," he continued; "since the singer was a man whose talents were mainly in his voice and movement, he was made to go first, and the others have followed in his footsteps, copying how he moved."

"But," Duncan exclaimed, "I don't see any signs of—"

"The gentle ones," the scout interrupted; "the scoundrel has found a way to carry them, until he thought he had thrown any pursuers off the trail. I'd bet my life on it, we'll see their delicate little footprints again, before we've gone much further."

The entire group continued forward, following the stream's path while keeping watchful eyes on the consistent tracks. The water quickly returned to its normal channel, but by monitoring the ground on both sides, the woodsmen moved ahead satisfied that they knew the trail ran underneath. They traveled more than half a mile before the stream bubbled closely around the bottom of a large, barren rock formation. At this point they stopped to confirm that the Hurons hadn't left the water.

It was lucky they made that choice. The swift and alert Uncas quickly discovered a footprint pressed into a clump of moss, where it appeared a Native American had accidentally stepped. Following the path indicated by this find, he went into the nearby undergrowth and picked up the trail, as clear and evident as it had been before they arrived at the spring. Another cry proclaimed the young man's success to his companions, and immediately ended their search.

"Yes, it has been planned with Indian wisdom," said the scout, when the group was gathered around the location, "and would have fooled white men's eyes."

"Should we continue?" Heyward asked.

"Quietly, quietly, we know our way; but it's wise to study how things are formed. This is my education, major; and if someone ignores the book, there's little opportunity to learn from the vast wilderness of Providence. Everything is clear except for one thing, which is how the scoundrel managed to lead the innocent ones along the hidden path. Even a Huron would be too proud to let their delicate feet touch the water."

"Will this help explain the problem?" said Heyward, pointing toward the pieces of what looked like a makeshift stretcher that had been roughly built from tree branches and tied together with flexible twigs, and which now appeared to have been carelessly thrown aside as no longer needed.

"It's all clear now!" exclaimed the thrilled Hawkeye. "If those scoundrels passed by just a minute ago, they've spent hours trying to create a false ending to their trail! Well, I've seen them waste an entire day doing the same thing with just as little success. Here we can see three pairs of moccasins, and two sets of small feet. It's incredible that any human beings can travel on legs so tiny! Hand me that strip of buckskin, Uncas, and let me measure the length of this footprint. Good Lord, it's no bigger than a child's, and yet these young women are tall and beautiful. That Providence distributes its gifts unevenly for its own wise purposes is something even the best and most satisfied among us must acknowledge."

"My daughters' delicate bodies aren't strong enough for these harsh conditions," Munro said, watching his children's light footsteps with a father's love; "we'll find them collapsed and exhausted in this wilderness."

"There's little reason to worry about that," the scout replied, slowly shaking his head. "This footprint shows a firm and straight step, though light, and the stride isn't too long. Look, the heel barely touched the ground, and over there the dark-haired person made a small leap from root to root. No, no—I'm certain neither of them was close to collapsing around here. Now, the singer was starting to get sore feet and tired legs, as his trail clearly shows. There, you can see where he slipped; here he walked unsteadily and wobbled; and over there it looks like he was walking on snowshoes. Yes, indeed, a man who uses his voice for everything can hardly give his legs proper exercise."

From this undeniable evidence, the experienced woodsman reached the truth with almost as much certainty and accuracy as if he had personally witnessed all the events that his skill so easily explained. Encouraged by these confirmations and convinced by reasoning that was both obvious and straightforward, the group continued their journey after a brief stop to eat a quick meal.

When the meal was finished, the scout looked up at the setting sun and moved forward with such speed that Heyward and the still strong Munro had to use all their strength to keep up. Their path now followed the valley floor that had been mentioned before. Since the Hurons had stopped trying to hide their tracks, the pursuers no longer had to slow down because of uncertainty. Within an hour, though, Hawkeye's pace clearly slowed, and his head, rather than staying focused straight ahead as before, started turning warily from side to side, as if he sensed approaching danger. He stopped again soon after and waited for the entire group to catch up.

"I can smell the Hurons," he said, speaking to the Mohicans; "there's open sky visible through the treetops over there, and we're getting too close to their camp. Sagamore, you'll take the hillside to the right; Uncas will follow along the brook to the left, while I'll try the trail. If anything goes wrong, the signal will be three caws of a crow. I saw one of those birds circling in the air just beyond the dead oak—another sign that we're approaching a camp."

The Indians went their separate ways without saying a word, while Hawkeye carefully moved forward with the two gentlemen. Heyward quickly moved to walk beside their guide, anxious to get an early look at those enemies he had chased with such effort and worry. His companion instructed him to quietly move to the edge of the forest, which was bordered by dense undergrowth as usual, and wait for him to return, since he wanted to investigate some questionable signs a short distance away. Duncan followed these instructions and soon positioned himself where he could see a view that he found both remarkable and completely new to him.

Trees covering many acres had been cut down, and the soft glow of a mild summer evening had settled over the clearing, creating a beautiful contrast with the gray light of the forest. A short distance from where Duncan stood, the stream appeared to have widened into a small lake, covering most of the low-lying land from mountain to mountain. The water flowed out of this broad basin in a waterfall so steady and gentle that it seemed more like the work of human hands than something shaped by nature. A hundred earthen homes stood along the edge of the lake, and even in its waters, as if the lake had overflowed its usual boundaries. Their rounded roofs, expertly shaped to protect against the weather, showed more skill and planning than the natives typically put into their permanent homes, let alone those they used temporarily for hunting and warfare. In short, the entire village or town, whatever it might be called, displayed more organization and careful construction than white men had grown accustomed to believing was typical of Indian customs. However, it appeared to be abandoned. At least, that's what Duncan thought for several minutes; but eventually, he imagined he saw several human figures moving toward him on hands and knees, apparently dragging behind them something heavy, and as he quickly realized, something threatening. Just then a few dark-looking heads appeared from the dwellings, and the place suddenly seemed alive with beings who nevertheless moved from shelter to shelter so quickly that there was no chance to examine their moods or activities. Alarmed by these suspicious and mysterious movements, he was about to try the signal of the crows when the rustling of leaves nearby drew his attention in another direction.

The young man jumped back and instinctively retreated several steps when he realized he was within a hundred yards of an unfamiliar Native American. Quickly regaining his composure, rather than raising an alarm that could endanger his own life, he stayed perfectly still and carefully watched the other person's movements.

A moment of quiet observation convinced Duncan that he remained unnoticed. The native, like Duncan himself, appeared to be studying the low buildings of the village and watching the secretive movements of the people living there. It was impossible to make out the expression on his face through the strange mask of paint that covered his features, though Duncan thought it seemed more sad than fierce. His head was shaved in the typical fashion, except for the crown, where three or four worn feathers from a hawk's wing hung loosely from a small tuft of hair. A tattered calico cloak was wrapped halfway around his body, while his lower clothing consisted of an ordinary shirt, with sleeves that had been adapted to serve a purpose usually handled by a much more practical garment. His legs, however, were covered with a pair of well-made deerskin moccasins. Overall, the man's appearance was pitiful and wretched.

Duncan continued to study his neighbor with curious interest when the scout quietly and carefully moved to his side.

"You can see we've reached their settlement or encampment," the young man whispered; "and here's one of the natives himself, in a very awkward position for our next moves."

Hawkeye jumped and let his rifle fall when his companion pointed out the stranger who had come into sight. After lowering the threatening barrel, he craned his long neck forward, as though trying to help with an examination that was already extremely focused.

"That devil isn't a Huron," he said, "or from any of the Canadian tribes; but you can tell by his clothing that the scoundrel has been robbing a white man. Yes, Montcalm has scoured the forests for his attack, and he's assembled a howling, murderous band of criminals. Can you see where he's placed his rifle or his bow?"

"He doesn't appear to have any arms, and he doesn't seem to be aggressive either. As long as he doesn't alert his companions, who you can see are moving around in the water, we don't have much to worry about from him."

The scout turned to Heyward and looked at him for a moment with obvious amazement. Then he opened his mouth wide and let out genuine, uncontrolled laughter, though he did so in that quiet and distinctive way that years of danger had taught him to use.

"Fellows who are dodging about the water!" he repeated, then continued, "That's what comes from getting an education and spending your childhood in the settlements! The scoundrel has long legs, though, and can't be trusted. Keep your rifle trained on him while I sneak up behind him through the bushes and capture him alive. Don't shoot under any circumstances."

Heyward had already allowed his companion to hide part of his body in the dense bushes when he reached out his arm and stopped him to ask:

"If I see you in danger, may I not risk a shot?"

Hawkeye looked at him for a moment, like someone who didn't know how to interpret the question; then, nodding his head, he replied, still laughing, though silently:

"Fire a whole platoon, major."

In the next moment, the leaves hid him from view. Duncan waited several minutes with anxious impatience before catching another glimpse of the scout. Then Hawkeye reappeared, crawling along the ground, his clothing barely distinguishable from the earth itself, moving directly behind his intended target. When he had gotten within a few yards of the man, he rose to his feet silently and slowly. At that instant, several loud splashes echoed across the water, and Duncan turned his gaze just in time to see a hundred dark shapes diving together into the disturbed little lake. Gripping his rifle, he focused his attention back on the Indian nearby. Rather than becoming alarmed, the unaware warrior stretched his neck forward, as if he too was watching the activity around the dark lake with a kind of foolish curiosity. Meanwhile, Hawkeye's raised hand hovered above him. But for no apparent reason, he pulled it back and indulged in another long, though still silent, bout of amusement. When Hawkeye's distinctive and hearty laughter had finished, instead of grabbing his victim by the throat, he tapped him gently on the shoulder and called out loudly:

"What's this, friend! Do you really think you can teach beavers to sing?"

"Even so," came the quick reply. "It would appear that the Being who granted them the ability to enhance His gifts so effectively would not refuse them voices to declare His praise."

---

# Chapter XXII.

"Bottom—Are we all here?
Quince—Exactly, exactly; and this is a wonderfully convenient place for our rehearsal."
—A Midsummer Night's Dream

The reader can better imagine than we can describe Heyward's astonishment. His hidden Indians had suddenly transformed into four-legged animals; his lake had become a beaver pond; his waterfall had turned into a dam built by those hardworking and clever creatures; and a suspected enemy had revealed himself to be his trusted friend, David Gamut, the psalm teacher. The appearance of David sparked so many unexpected hopes about the sisters that the young man immediately abandoned his hiding place without hesitation and rushed forward to join the two main figures in the scene.

Hawkeye's amusement wasn't easily satisfied. Without any formality and using rough hands, he spun the flexible Gamut around on his heel, repeatedly declaring that the Hurons had brought themselves great honor in how they had dressed him. Then, grabbing the other man's hand, he squeezed it with such force that it brought tears to the calm David's eyes, and congratulated him on his new situation.

"You were about to start your singing practice among the beavers, weren't you?" he said. "Those clever creatures already know half the skill, since they keep rhythm with their tails, as you just heard; and it was perfect timing too, or 'killdeer' might have been the first sound they made. I've known bigger fools who could read and write than a seasoned old beaver; but when it comes to making noise, these animals are naturally silent! What do you think of a song like this?"

David covered his delicate ears, and even Heyward, despite being aware of what the sound really meant, glanced up searching for the bird when the harsh cawing of a crow echoed through the air around them.

"Look!" the scout continued with a laugh, pointing toward the rest of their group, who were already coming closer in response to his signal. "Now that's the kind of music that actually works—it brings two good rifles right to my side, not to mention all the knives and tomahawks. But we can see you're safe now; tell us what happened to the young women."

"They are prisoners of the pagans," said David; "and, although deeply distressed in their souls, they find comfort and safety for their bodies."

"Both!" demanded the breathless Heyward.

"Even so. Though our journey has been difficult and our food scarce, we have had little other reason to complain, except for the harm done to our emotions by being led as captives into a distant land."

"Thank you for those very words!" cried the shaking Munro; "I will then receive my daughters, pure and angelic, just as I lost them!"

"I don't know if their rescue is coming soon," replied the doubtful David; "the leader of these savages is controlled by an evil spirit that only God's power can control. I have tried reaching him when he was asleep and awake, but neither sounds nor words seem to affect his soul."

"Where is the scoundrel?" the scout interrupted bluntly.

"He hunts the moose today, with his young men; and tomorrow, as I hear, they pass further into the forests, and closer to the borders of Canada. The older maiden is taken to a neighboring people, whose lodges are located beyond that black pinnacle of rock; while the younger is held among the women of the Hurons, whose dwellings are only two short miles from here, on a plateau, where the fire had done the work of the axe, and prepared the place for their settlement."

"Alice, my sweet Alice!" Heyward whispered; "she no longer has the comfort of her sister being with her!"

"That's true. But as long as praise and thanksgiving in psalm-singing can soothe the spirit during times of suffering, she has not truly suffered."

"Does she have a love for music then?"

"Of a more serious and solemn nature; though I must admit that, despite all my efforts, the young woman cries more often than she smiles. During such times I refrain from insisting on the sacred songs; but there are many pleasant and comforting periods of meaningful communication, when the ears of the natives are amazed by the raising of our voices."

"And why are you allowed to roam freely, without supervision?"

David arranged his facial expression to convey modest humility before he humbly responded:

"I deserve little praise, being as lowly as a worm. But while the power of singing psalms was interrupted during the terrible violence of that bloody battlefield we just crossed, it has regained its influence even over the souls of non-believers, and I am now allowed to move about freely."

The scout laughed, and tapping his forehead meaningfully, he perhaps provided a more satisfactory explanation for the unusual tolerance when he said:

"The Indians never harm someone who isn't a composer. But why, when the path was clearly visible in front of you, didn't you turn around and follow your own trail back (it's not so faint that even a squirrel couldn't follow it), and bring the news to Edward?"

The scout, thinking only of his own tough and unyielding character, had likely demanded something that David could never have accomplished under any circumstances. However, without completely abandoning his gentle demeanor, David was satisfied to respond:

"Although my soul would be filled with joy to visit the Christian lands once more, my feet would rather follow the gentle souls entrusted to my care, even into the idol-worshipping territory of the Jesuits, than take a single step backward while they suffered in captivity and grief."

Although David's symbolic language wasn't very clear, the genuine and unwavering expression in his eyes, along with the warmth of his honest face, were hard to misinterpret. Uncas moved closer to him and looked at the speaker with approval, while his father showed his satisfaction with his typical brief exclamation of praise. The scout shook his head as he responded:

"The Lord never meant for a man to put all his efforts into his voice while ignoring other and better talents! But he has fallen under the influence of some foolish woman, when he should have been getting his education under the open sky, surrounded by the beauty of the forest. Here, friend; I was planning to start a fire with this little whistle of yours; but since you value it, take it back and play your best tune on it."

Gamut accepted his pitch-pipe with as much visible delight as he felt was appropriate for someone in his solemn position. After testing it several times against his own voice and confirming that none of its musical quality had been damaged, he made a determined effort to perform a few verses from one of the lengthiest compositions in the small book that has been referenced so frequently.

Heyward quickly cut short his religious intentions by asking more questions about the past and current situation of his fellow prisoners, approaching the matter more systematically than his emotions had allowed during the beginning of their conversation. David, though he gazed longingly at his precious instrument, felt compelled to respond, particularly since the respected elder participated in the questioning with an authority that couldn't be ignored. The scout also made sure to add relevant questions whenever the right moment arose. Through this process, despite frequent interruptions filled with ominous sounds from the restored instrument, the pursuers gathered the essential information that would likely help them achieve their primary and all-consuming goal—rescuing the sisters. David's account was straightforward, and the facts were limited.

Magua had waited on the mountain until a safe opportunity to retreat presented itself, then he had descended and taken the route along the western side of the Horican toward the Canadas. Since the cunning Huron was familiar with the paths and knew well there was no immediate danger of pursuit, their progress had been steady and far from exhausting. It appeared from David's straightforward account that his own presence had been tolerated rather than welcomed; though even Magua had not been completely free from that reverence with which the Indians regard those whom the Great Spirit had touched in their minds. At night, the greatest care had been taken of the captives, both to prevent harm from the dampness of the woods and to guard against an escape. At the spring, the horses were set free, as has been seen; and, despite the distance and length of their trail, the tricks already mentioned were used in order to eliminate every trace to their place of refuge. Upon their arrival at the encampment of his people, Magua, following a policy seldom abandoned, separated his prisoners. Cora had been sent to a tribe that temporarily occupied a nearby valley, though David was far too unfamiliar with the customs and history of the natives to be able to say anything definitive concerning their name or character. He only knew that they had not participated in the recent expedition against William Henry; that, like the Hurons themselves, they were allies of Montcalm; and that they maintained a friendly, though watchful relationship with the warlike and savage people whom chance had, for a time, brought into such close and unpleasant contact with themselves.

The Mohicans and the scout listened to his broken and incomplete story with growing interest as he continued speaking; and it was while he was trying to explain what the community that was holding Cora captive was doing, that she suddenly asked:

"Did you notice the style of their knives? Were they made in the English or French fashion?"

"My thoughts weren't focused on such trivial matters, but instead found comfort by joining with the thoughts of the young women."

"There might come a time when you won't think a savage's knife is such a worthless trinket," the scout replied, clearly showing his contempt for the other man's lack of understanding. "Did they hold their corn feast—or can you tell me anything about the tribe's totems?"

"We enjoyed many abundant feasts of corn, since the grain in its milky stage was both sweet to taste and easy on the stomach. As for totem, I don't understand its meaning; but if it relates in any way to the practice of Indian music, there's no need to ask them about it. They never raise their voices together in worship, and it appears they are among the most irreverent of those who practice idolatry."

"In saying that, you misrepresent the true nature of an Indian. Even the Mingo worships only the one true and loving God. It's a wicked lie created by white people, and I say this to the shame of my own race, that would claim the warrior bows down before idols of his own making. It's true, they try to make peace with the evil one—as anyone would with an enemy they cannot defeat! But they look up for favor and help to the Great and Good Spirit alone."

"That might be true," David said, "but I've seen strange and bizarre images created with their paint, and their admiration and attention to these works seemed to reflect spiritual pride; particularly one image, which was actually a disgusting and repulsive subject."

"Was it a snake?" the scout asked urgently.

"Pretty much the same. It looked like a pathetic, crawling turtle."

"Hugh!" both alert Mohicans exclaimed simultaneously, while the scout shook his head like someone who had made a significant but far from welcome discovery. The father then spoke in the Delaware language, with such composure and dignity that he immediately captured the attention of even those who couldn't understand his words. His gestures were compelling and sometimes forceful. At one point he raised his arm high, and as it came down, the motion swept aside the folds of his light cloak, with one finger resting on his chest as if to emphasize his meaning through his posture. Duncan's gaze followed this movement, and he noticed that the creature he had just mentioned was beautifully, though faintly, tattooed in blue ink on the dark chest of the chief. Everything he had ever learned about the violent division of the great Delaware tribes flooded through his thoughts, and he waited for the right moment to speak, with an anxiety made almost unbearable by how much depended on the outcome. His desire to speak, however, was forestalled by the scout, who turned away from his Native American companion and said:

"We have discovered what could bring us either good fortune or trouble, depending on how fate decides. The Sagamore comes from the noble bloodline of the Delawares and serves as the great chief of their Turtle clan! It's clear from his words that some of his people are among those the singer described to us, and if he had used half the energy asking smart questions instead of wasting his breath boasting loudly, we might have learned how many warriors they have. Overall, we're traveling a treacherous route; often a friend who has turned against you harbors more murderous intentions than an enemy who openly seeks to kill you."

"Explain," said Duncan.

"It's a long and sorrowful tradition, and one I don't like to think about; for it cannot be denied that the harm has been mainly caused by white men. But it has resulted in turning the tomahawk of brother against brother, and brought the Mingo and the Delaware to travel in the same path."

"So you think it might be part of the group that Cora is living with?"

The scout nodded in agreement, though he appeared eager to avoid further discussion of a topic that seemed distressing. The restless Duncan then made several hurried and reckless proposals to attempt rescuing the sisters. Munro appeared to cast off his indifference and listened to the young man's wild plans with a respect that his gray hair and advanced age should have refused to grant. However, the scout, after allowing the passionate lover's enthusiasm to burn itself out somewhat, managed to persuade him that haste was foolish, explaining that their situation would demand their clearest thinking and greatest courage.

"It would be wise," he continued, "to let this man go back in as he normally does, and have him stay in the cabins, warning the peaceful ones that we're coming, until we signal for him to come out so we can talk with him. You know the difference between a crow's call and a whip-poor-will's whistle, don't you, friend?"

"It's a pleasant bird," David replied, "and it has a soft and melancholy song! Though the timing is rather quick and poorly measured."

"He's talking about the whip-poor-will," said the scout; "well, since you like its call, that will be your signal. Remember, then, when you hear the whip-poor-will's call three times in a row, you need to come into the bushes where the bird would likely be—"

"Stop," interrupted Heyward; "I will go with him."

"You!" Hawkeye exclaimed in astonishment. "Are you tired of watching the sun rise and set?"

"David is living proof that the Hurons can be merciful."

"Yes, but David can use his voice, as no sensible person would misuse such a gift."

"I can also play the madman, the fool, the hero; in short, anything and everything to save the woman I love. Don't voice your objections anymore: my mind is made up."

Hawkeye stared at the young man for a moment, completely speechless with amazement. But Duncan, who had previously followed the other man's orders somewhat obediently out of respect for his expertise and help, now took charge with an authority that was hard to oppose. He gestured with his hand to show he didn't want to hear any objections, and then, speaking in a calmer tone, he went on:

"You have the tools to disguise me; transform my appearance; paint my face as well, if you want; in other words, change me into anything—even a fool."

"Someone like me shouldn't say that a person already shaped by such a powerful force as Providence needs to be changed," grumbled the unhappy scout. "When you send your groups out during war, you at least find it wise to set up the signals and locations of camp, so that those who fight alongside you know when and where to expect an ally."

"Listen," Duncan interrupted, "you've heard from this loyal follower of the prisoners that the Indians belong to two different tribes, possibly even separate nations. The woman you call 'dark-hair' is with one group, which you believe to be connected to the Delawares, while the other lady, the younger one, is definitely being held by our sworn enemies, the Hurons. My youth and position make it my duty to take on the more dangerous mission. So while you negotiate with your allies for one sister's freedom, I'll secure the other's release or die trying."

The young soldier's awakened spirit shone brightly in his eyes, and his entire bearing became commanding under its influence. Hawkeye, though far too experienced with Indian tricks not to anticipate the danger of this plan, wasn't sure how to counter this sudden determination.

Perhaps there was something about the proposal that appealed to his tough character, and that hidden love of risky adventure, which had grown stronger through his experiences, until uncertainty and danger had become somewhat essential to his enjoyment of life. Rather than continuing to resist Duncan's plan, his attitude suddenly changed, and he committed himself to carrying it out.

"Come on," he said with a good-natured smile, "a deer that heads for the water needs to be cut off at the pass, not chased from behind. Chingachgook has just as many different paints as that engineer officer's wife who sketches nature on pieces of paper, making the mountains look like piles of old hay and putting the blue sky within arm's reach. The Sagamore knows how to use them too. Sit down on that log, and I'll bet my life he can quickly make you look like a real Indian, and you'll be pleased with the result."

Duncan agreed, and the Mohican, who had been listening carefully to the conversation, willingly took on the task. Having long experience with all the intricate skills of his people, he drew with remarkable skill and speed the elaborate design that his tribe traditionally viewed as proof of a peaceful and good-natured attitude. He carefully avoided every mark that might possibly be seen as a hidden desire for conflict, while instead focusing on those symbols that could be understood as signs of friendship.

In short, he completely gave up any appearance of being a warrior to put on the act of a fool. Such displays were not unusual among the Indians, and since Duncan was already well disguised in his clothing, there was certainly some reason to believe that, with his knowledge of French, he could pass for an entertainer from Ticonderoga, wandering among the allied and friendly tribes.

When they decided he was sufficiently disguised, the scout offered him plenty of friendly guidance, established signals they would use to communicate, and designated where they should meet if both of their missions succeeded. The farewell between Munro and his young friend carried more sadness; even so, the older man accepted their separation with a detachment that his caring and sincere character would never have allowed in a healthier frame of mind. The scout pulled Heyward to one side and informed him of his plan to leave the veteran in a secure camp under Chingachgook's protection, while he and Uncas continued their search among the people they had good reason to believe were Delawares. After repeating his warnings and counsel once more, he finished by speaking with such seriousness and depth of emotion that Duncan felt deeply moved:

"And now, God bless you! You have shown a spirit that I admire; for it is the gift of youth, especially one with warm blood and a brave heart. But believe the warning of a man who has reason to know that everything he says is true. You will need your best courage, and sharper intelligence than what can be learned from books, before you can outsmart the cunning or overcome the bravery of a Mingo. God bless you! If the Hurons take your scalp, rely on the promise of one who has two strong warriors to support him. They shall pay for their victory, with a life for every hair it contains. I say, young gentleman, may Providence bless your undertaking, which is entirely for good; and remember, that to outsmart these villains it is acceptable to use methods that may not come naturally to a white man."

Duncan warmly shook hands with his worthy but hesitant companion, once again entrusting his elderly friend to the man's care, and after exchanging good wishes, he signaled for David to move forward. Hawkeye watched the spirited and daring young man for several moments with obvious admiration; then, shaking his head with uncertainty, he turned and guided his own group into the hidden depths of the forest.

The path that Duncan and David followed led straight across the beaver clearing and along the edge of their pond.

When he found himself alone with someone so inexperienced and so poorly equipped to help in dire situations, he began to truly understand the challenges of what he had taken on. The dimming light made the harsh and wild landscape that extended endlessly around him seem even more ominous, and there was something frightening about the silence of those small shelters, which he knew were filled with inhabitants. As he looked at the impressive structures and the remarkable defenses created by their clever occupants, it occurred to him that even the wild animals of these vast territories possessed instincts that nearly matched his own intelligence; and he couldn't help but feel worried about the uneven battle he had so recklessly invited. Then the vivid image of Alice came to mind; her suffering; her immediate danger; and all thoughts of his own perilous circumstances vanished. Encouraging David, he continued forward with the quick and energetic stride of youth and determination.

After traveling nearly halfway around the pond, they turned away from the waterway and started climbing toward a small hill that rose from the valley floor they were crossing. Within thirty minutes, they reached the edge of another clearing that showed clear evidence of beaver construction, which these intelligent creatures had likely abandoned due to some mishap in favor of the better location they currently inhabited. A completely natural feeling made Duncan pause for a moment, reluctant to leave the protection of their tree-lined trail, much like a person stops to gather his strength before attempting any dangerous undertaking where he knows deep down that all his abilities will be required. He used this brief stop to collect whatever information he could from his quick and hurried observations.

On the opposite side of the clearing, near the point where the brook tumbled over some rocks from a still higher level, about fifty or sixty lodges could be seen, roughly built from logs, brush, and earth mixed together. They were arranged without any order and seemed to be constructed with very little attention to neatness or beauty. Indeed, they were so much inferior in these two aspects compared to the village Duncan had just seen that he began to expect a second surprise, no less astonishing than the first. This expectation was not diminished at all when, in the uncertain twilight, he saw twenty or thirty figures rising alternately from the cover of the tall, coarse grass in front of the lodges, and then sinking again from sight, as if burrowing into the earth. From the brief and hurried glimpses he caught of these figures, they seemed more like dark, flickering specters or some other supernatural beings than creatures made of ordinary flesh and blood. A thin, naked form was seen for a single moment, throwing its arms wildly in the air, and then the spot it had occupied was empty; the figure appearing suddenly in some other distant place, or being replaced by another with the same mysterious character. David, noticing that his companion was hesitating, followed the direction of his gaze and somewhat brought Heyward back to his senses by speaking.

"There's a lot of fertile land that hasn't been farmed here," he said; "and I can say, without the sinful pride of boasting about myself, that during my brief stay in these godless places, much good seed has been planted along the way."

"The tribes prefer hunting over the skills of working men," replied Duncan, unaware of the implications, still staring at the things that amazed him.

"It brings more joy than effort to the spirit to raise one's voice in praise; but these boys sadly misuse their talents. I have rarely encountered anyone their age upon whom nature has so generously bestowed the fundamentals of psalm singing; and certainly, there are none who ignore these gifts more completely. I have now stayed here for three nights, and three separate times I have gathered these children to participate in sacred song; and each time they have answered my attempts with shouts and wails that have frozen my soul!"

"Who are you talking about?"

"Those children of the devil waste precious moments with their pointless antics over there. The healthy discipline and restraint that comes from proper guidance is barely understood among these people who have given up on themselves. In a land full of birch trees, you never see a disciplinary rod being used, so it shouldn't surprise me that the greatest gifts from God are squandered on such worthless behavior as this."

David shut out the sounds of the young war party, whose piercing cries echoed sharply through the woods at that moment; and Duncan, allowing his lip to twist in a sneer that mocked his own superstitious fears, spoke with determination:

"We will proceed."

Without taking the protective coverings from his ears, the master musician agreed, and together they continued their journey toward what David sometimes liked to call the "tents of the Philistines."

---

# Chapter XXIII.

"But though the wild animal we hunt
May claim the privilege of being chased;
Though we give the stag space and legal protection
Before we release the hound, or draw our bow;
Who ever cared where, how, or when
The prowling fox was trapped or killed?"
—Lady of the Lake.

It's uncommon to discover a Native American camp that, like those of more educated white settlers, is protected by armed guards. Being well aware of any approaching threat while it's still far away, the Indian typically feels safe relying on his understanding of forest signs and the long, challenging trails that keep him separated from those he has the greatest reason to fear. However, an enemy who, through some fortunate combination of circumstances, has managed to avoid the watchful eyes of the scouts will rarely encounter sentries closer to the settlement to raise an alert. Beyond this common practice, the tribes allied with the French understood too clearly the severity of the blow that had just been delivered to worry about any immediate threat from the hostile nations that served under the British crown.

When Duncan and David found themselves in the middle of the children who were playing the games already described, they had received no warning of their arrival. As soon as the children noticed them, the entire group of youngsters let out a sharp, piercing cry of alarm in unison, then seemed to vanish from sight as if by magic. The bare, brown-skinned bodies of the crouching children blended so perfectly with the dried grass at that time of day that it initially appeared as though the ground had actually swallowed them whole. However, when Duncan's surprise subsided enough for him to examine the area more carefully, he discovered dark, alert, and darting eyes watching him from every direction.

Receiving no comfort from this alarming preview of the kind of examination he would probably face from the seasoned wisdom of the men, there was a moment when the young soldier almost turned back. However, it was too late to seem uncertain. The shouts of the children had brought a dozen warriors to the entrance of the closest lodge, where they gathered in a dark and fierce group, solemnly waiting for the closer approach of those who had suddenly appeared among them.

David, having become somewhat accustomed to the scene, led the way with a confidence that no minor obstacle could easily shake, into this very building. It was the main structure of the village, though crudely built from tree bark and branches; it served as the lodge where the tribe conducted its councils and public gatherings during their temporary stay on the borders of the English province. Duncan found it challenging to maintain the required appearance of indifference as he passed by the dark and powerful forms of the natives who crowded its entrance; however, aware that his survival depended on keeping his composure, he relied on the judgment of his companion, following closely in his footsteps while trying to gather his thoughts for what lay ahead. His blood ran cold when he found himself in direct contact with such fierce and relentless enemies; yet he managed to control his emotions enough to continue his way into the center of the lodge, maintaining an outward appearance that did not reveal his inner turmoil. Following the example of the composed Gamut, he pulled a bundle of sweet-smelling brush from beneath a pile that filled the corner of the hut, and sat down in silence.

As soon as their visitor had walked by, the watchful warriors stepped back from the entrance and positioned themselves around him, appearing to wait patiently for the moment when it would be appropriate for the stranger to speak. Most of them stood leaning in relaxed, casual poses against the vertical posts that held up the rickety building, while three or four of the eldest and most respected chiefs sat on the ground slightly closer to the front.

A blazing torch burned in the space, casting its red glow from one face to another and from figure to figure as it flickered in the air currents. Duncan used its light to try to understand the likely nature of his welcome by studying the expressions of his hosts. However, his cleverness served him poorly against the calculated deceptions of the people he had met. The chiefs standing in front barely glanced at him, keeping their gaze fixed on the ground with a manner that might have been meant to show respect, but could easily be interpreted as suspicion. The men standing in the shadows were less restrained. Duncan quickly noticed their probing yet secretive glances that carefully examined his appearance and clothing inch by inch, missing no facial expression, no movement, no detail of his war paint, nor even the style of his garments, leaving nothing unobserved and without silent judgment.

Eventually, a man whose hair was starting to show streaks of gray, but whose muscular body and steady walk showed he was still capable of handling a man's responsibilities, stepped forward from the shadows of a corner where he had likely positioned himself to watch without being noticed, and began to speak. He spoke in the language of the Wyandots, or Hurons; his words were therefore incomprehensible to Heyward, though they appeared, based on the hand movements that went along with them, to be spoken more out of politeness than hostility. Heyward shook his head and made a motion showing his inability to respond.

"Don't any of my brothers speak French or English?" he asked in French, looking around from face to face, hoping to see someone nod in agreement.

Though several people had turned around, as if trying to understand what he meant, no one responded to his words.

"It would sadden me to think," Duncan continued, speaking slowly and using the most basic French he could manage, "that no one from this wise and courageous nation understands the language that the 'Grand Monarque' speaks when he addresses his children. His heart would be heavy if he believed his red warriors showed him so little respect!"

A long and serious silence followed, during which no movement of a limb or expression in anyone's eyes revealed the impact his comment had made. Duncan, who understood that silence was considered a virtue among his hosts, was happy to follow this custom as it gave him time to organize his thoughts. Finally, the same warrior who had spoken to him earlier responded by curtly asking, in the language of the Canadas:

"When our Great Father speaks to his people, does he use the language of a Huron?"

"He doesn't distinguish between his children based on whether their skin is red, black, or white," Duncan replied evasively, "though he's particularly pleased with the brave Hurons."

"How will he respond," asked the cautious chief, "when the messengers tell him about the scalps that were taken from the heads of the English just five nights ago?"

"They were his enemies," Duncan said, shuddering involuntarily, "and no doubt he will say it is good; my Hurons are very brave."

"Our Canadian father doesn't see it that way. Instead of looking ahead to reward his Indians, he's looking backward. He sees the dead Americans, but no Huron. What could this mean?"

"A great chief, like him, has more thoughts than tongues. He looks to see that no enemies are on his trail."

"A dead warrior's canoe won't float on Lake George," the Native American replied darkly. "He listens to the Delawares, who aren't our allies, and they're filling his head with lies."

"That's impossible. Look; he has commanded me, a man who understands the healing arts, to visit his children, the red Hurons of the great lakes, and find out if any of them are ill!"

Another silence followed this announcement of the role Duncan had taken on. Every eye turned toward him at the same time, as if trying to determine whether his claim was true or false, with such sharp intelligence and intensity that the person under their examination began to worry about what they might conclude. However, he was once again rescued by the previous speaker.

"Do the clever men of Canada paint their skin?" the Huron continued coldly; "we have heard them boast that their faces were pale."

"When an Indian chief visits his white fathers," Duncan replied with unwavering composure, "he sets aside his buffalo robe to wear the shirt they offer him. My brothers have given me paint and I wear it."

A quiet murmur of approval indicated that the tribe had received the compliment well. The elderly chief made a gesture of praise, which his companions echoed by extending their hands and voicing short expressions of satisfaction. Duncan started to breathe more easily, thinking that the most difficult part of his questioning was over; and since he had already crafted a straightforward and believable story to back up his false identity, his chances of eventual success seemed more promising.

After a few moments of silence, as if gathering his thoughts to give a proper response to what their guests had just declared, another warrior stood up and positioned himself to speak. Just as his lips were beginning to part, a low but terrifying sound rose from the forest, immediately followed by a high, piercing scream that stretched out until it matched the longest and most mournful howl of a wolf. The sudden and horrible interruption made Duncan jump from his seat, aware of nothing except the impact of such a frightening cry. At that same moment, the warriors moved as one group out of the lodge, and the outside air filled with loud shouts that nearly overwhelmed those dreadful sounds, which continued to echo through the forest canopy. No longer able to control himself, the young man broke away from his position and soon found himself standing in the middle of a chaotic crowd that included nearly every living thing within the boundaries of the camp. Men, women, and children; the elderly, the weak, the energetic, and the strong, were all outside, some crying out loudly, others clapping their hands with what seemed like wild joy, and everyone expressing their fierce delight in some unexpected occurrence. Though initially shocked by the commotion, Heyward was soon able to understand its cause from the scene that unfolded.

There was still enough light in the sky to reveal the bright openings among the treetops, where various trails left the clearing and disappeared into the deep wilderness. Under one of these openings, a line of warriors emerged from the woods and moved slowly toward the houses. The one in front carried a short pole, which, as it later became clear, had several human scalps hanging from it. The shocking sounds that Duncan had heard were what white people have fittingly called the "death-hallo," and each time the cry was repeated, it was meant to tell the tribe about the fate of an enemy. This much of Heyward's knowledge helped him understand what was happening, and now that he knew the disturbance was caused by the unexpected return of a victorious war party, all his unpleasant feelings were replaced by quiet relief, grateful for the timely distraction and how it made his own situation seem unimportant.

When the newly arrived warriors stopped a few hundred feet away from the lodges, their mournful and terrifying cry came to an end—a sound meant to express both grief for the dead and celebration of victory. One of the warriors then shouted something in words that, while less frightening than their previous howls, were no more understandable to those listening. It would be hard to describe the wild excitement with which this announcement was received. The entire camp instantly erupted into violent activity and chaos. The warriors pulled out their knives and, waving them in the air, formed two lines that created a pathway stretching from the war party to the lodges. The women grabbed clubs, axes, or whatever weapons they could find and rushed forward eagerly to take part in the brutal ritual about to begin. Even the children insisted on joining in; young boys who could barely handle the weapons snatched tomahawks from their fathers' belts and slipped into the ranks, copying the savage behavior they saw in their parents.

Large piles of brush were scattered throughout the clearing, and a cautious, elderly woman was busy lighting as many as needed to illuminate the upcoming spectacle. As the flames rose, their brightness surpassed that of the fading daylight and helped make objects both clearer and more frightening at the same time. The entire scene created a dramatic picture, framed by the dark, towering border of pine trees. The warriors who had just arrived stood as the most distant figures. A little ahead stood two men, who had apparently been chosen from the group as the main participants in what was about to unfold. The light wasn't strong enough to make their features clear, though it was obvious they were experiencing very different emotions. While one stood upright and steady, ready to face his destiny like a hero, the other hung his head, as if paralyzed by fear or overcome with shame. The spirited Duncan felt a strong surge of admiration and sympathy for the former, though no chance presented itself to show his noble feelings. He watched the man's every movement with intense eyes, and as he observed the fine outline of his perfectly proportioned and athletic body, he tried to convince himself that if human strength, supported by such brave determination, could carry someone safely through such a harsh ordeal, the young prisoner before him might have hope for success in the dangerous gauntlet he was about to run. Without realizing it, the young man moved closer to the dark ranks of the Hurons and barely breathed, so absorbed did he become in the spectacle. Just then the signal cry rang out, and the brief silence that had come before it was shattered by an explosion of shouts that far exceeded any heard before. The more dejected of the two victims remained motionless, but the other sprang from his position at the cry with the agility and speed of a deer. Instead of charging straight through the enemy lines as had been expected, he barely entered the dangerous passage, and before time was given for a single strike, he turned sharply and leaped over the heads of a row of children, reaching at once the outer and safer side of the threatening formation. The trick was met by a hundred voices raised in curses, and the entire excited crowd broke from their positions and scattered about the area in wild disorder.

Twelve roaring fires now cast their eerie glow across the area, transforming it into something like a cursed and otherworldly battleground where evil spirits had gathered to perform their violent and chaotic rituals. The figures moving in the shadows appeared like ghostly creatures, drifting past and cutting through the air with wild and senseless movements, while the brutal emotions of those who crossed near the flames became terrifyingly clear in the flickering light that danced across their heated faces.

It's easy to understand that with so many vengeful enemies surrounding him, the fleeing man had no chance to rest. For one brief moment, it looked like he might actually make it to the forest, but his entire group of captors rushed in front of him and forced him back toward the center of his merciless pursuers. Spinning around like a cornered deer, he darted with arrow-like speed through a column of split flames, and racing past the entire crowd unharmed, he emerged on the far side of the clearing. But even there, he was blocked and turned back by some of the older and more cunning Hurons. Once again he plunged into the crowd, as if trying to find safety in the chaos, and then several moments passed during which Duncan was convinced that the agile and brave young stranger was doomed.

Nothing could be seen except a dark mass of human figures thrown together in bewildering chaos. Arms, flashing knives, and threatening clubs rose above the crowd, but the strikes were clearly delivered without aim. The terrifying scene was made worse by the sharp screams of women and the savage howls of warriors. Occasionally Duncan caught sight of a swift figure cutting through the air in some frantic leap, and he hoped rather than truly believed that the prisoner still possessed control of his remarkable agility. Suddenly the crowd surged backward and moved toward the place where he stood. The dense mass at the back pushed against the women and children in front, forcing them to the ground. The stranger appeared again in the chaos. Human strength could not, however, endure such a harsh test much longer. The captive seemed aware of this. Taking advantage of the brief opening, he shot out from among the warriors and made a desperate attempt that appeared to Duncan to be a final effort to reach the forest. As if sensing that no threat came from the young soldier, the fleeing man nearly brushed against him as he passed. A tall and strong Huron, who had conserved his energy, followed closely behind, and with a raised arm threatened a deadly strike. Duncan stuck out his foot, and the impact sent the eager warrior tumbling headfirst many feet beyond his intended target. Thought itself moves no faster than the motion with which the captive seized this opportunity; he spun around, flashed like a shooting star once more before Duncan's eyes, and in the next instant, when Duncan regained his focus and looked around searching for the prisoner, he saw him calmly resting against a small decorated post that stood in front of the main lodge's entrance.

Worried that his role in the escape might cost him his life, Duncan quickly left the area. He joined the crowd moving toward the lodges, their mood dark and bitter, like any group that had been denied the spectacle of an execution they'd expected to witness. Curiosity, or perhaps compassion, drew him toward the stranger. He discovered the man standing with one arm wrapped around the protective post, breathing heavily from his ordeal, yet refusing to show any sign of pain or weakness. Ancient and sacred customs now shielded him from harm until the tribal council could meet and decide his destiny. Still, it wasn't hard to predict what that decision would be, judging by the hostile attitude of those gathering around the place.

There wasn't a single insult in the Huron language that the frustrated women didn't heap upon the successful stranger. They mocked his attempts and told him with harsh ridicule that his feet served him better than his hands, and that he deserved wings since he didn't know how to use an arrow or knife. The captive offered no response to any of this, choosing instead to maintain a bearing that remarkably combined dignity with contempt. Infuriated as much by his calm demeanor as by his success, their words became incomprehensible and gave way to sharp, piercing screams. At that moment, the cunning old woman, who had taken the necessary step of lighting the fires, pushed through the crowd and made space for herself directly in front of the prisoner. The filthy and shriveled appearance of this crone could easily have earned her a reputation for possessing supernatural cleverness. Pulling back her thin garment, she extended her long, bony arm in mockery, and speaking in the Lenape tongue since it would be more understandable to the target of her taunts, she began to speak loudly:

"Listen here, Delaware," she said, snapping her fingers right in front of his face, "your people are nothing but a bunch of women, and you're better suited for farming tools than weapons. Your women give birth to timid creatures like deer, but if something fierce like a bear, wildcat, or snake appeared among you, you'd all run away. The Huron women will sew you some skirts, and we'll help you find a husband."

A burst of wild laughter followed this assault, and the gentle, melodious giggles of the younger women oddly blended with the harsh voice of their older, more spiteful companion. However, the stranger remained unaffected by all their attempts. His head stayed perfectly still, and he showed no sign of awareness that anyone else was there, except when his proud gaze shifted toward the shadowy figures of the warriors, who moved in the background as silent and brooding witnesses to what was happening.

Enraged by the captive's self-control, the woman put her hands on her hips and threw herself into a defiant stance, unleashing a fresh torrent of words that no skill of ours could successfully capture on paper. Her efforts were wasted, however, because even though she was known throughout her tribe as an expert in the art of verbal abuse, she was allowed to work herself into such a rage that she actually foamed at the mouth, without causing a single muscle to move in the motionless figure of the stranger. The impact of his indifference began to spread to the other onlookers, and a young man who was just leaving boyhood behind to enter manhood tried to help the fierce woman by waving his tomahawk in front of their victim and adding his hollow threats to the women's taunts. At that moment, the captive did turn his face toward the light and looked down at the youth with an expression that went beyond contempt. The next moment he returned to his calm and relaxed position against the post. But the shift in posture had allowed Duncan to make eye contact with the steady and penetrating eyes of Uncas.

Breathless with shock and deeply troubled by his friend's dangerous situation, Heyward stepped back from that look, shaking with fear that its meaning might somehow speed up the prisoner's doom. However, there wasn't any immediate reason for such worry. At that moment, a warrior pushed his way through the angry crowd. With a harsh gesture, he waved the women and children aside, grabbed Uncas by the arm, and guided him toward the entrance of the council lodge. All the chiefs and most of the prominent warriors followed them there, and among this group, the worried Heyward managed to slip inside without drawing any threatening attention to himself.

A few minutes passed as everyone present was positioned according to their status and power within the tribe. The arrangement closely resembled the one used in the previous meeting; the elderly and high-ranking chiefs took their places in the main area of the large room, illuminated by the bright glow of a blazing torch, while the younger and lower-ranking members were positioned in the shadows behind them, creating a dark silhouette of weathered and distinctive faces. In the exact center of the lodge, directly beneath an opening that let in the flickering light of one or two stars, stood Uncas, composed, dignified, and self-possessed. His proud and noble bearing did not go unnoticed by his captors, who frequently turned their gaze toward him with eyes that, while maintaining their unwavering determination, clearly revealed their respect for the stranger's courage.

The situation was entirely different for the individual Duncan had noticed standing with his friend before the desperate race began. Rather than participating in the chase, this person had remained motionless throughout all the chaotic noise, resembling a cowering statue that embodied shame and humiliation. Although no one had reached out to welcome him, and not a single eye had bothered to observe his actions, he too had entered the lodge, as if driven by destiny whose commands he appeared to accept without resistance. Heyward took the first chance he got to study the man's face, secretly worried he might recognize the features of someone else he knew. However, the face belonged to a stranger, and what made it even more puzzling was that this person displayed all the characteristic features of a Huron warrior. Rather than mixing with his tribe, though, he sat by himself, isolated among the crowd, his body hunched in a submissive and degraded posture, as if he wanted to occupy as little room as he could. Once everyone had found their appropriate place and quiet settled over the area, the gray-haired chief who has already been introduced to the reader began speaking loudly in the language of the Lenni Lenape.

"Delaware," he said, "even though you belong to a nation of women, you have shown yourself to be a man. I would offer you food, but anyone who shares a meal with a Huron must become his friend. Rest peacefully until the morning sun rises, when we will speak our final words."

"I've gone without food for seven nights and just as many summer days while tracking the Hurons," Uncas replied coldly; "the children of the Lenape know how to follow the righteous path without stopping to eat."

"Two of my young warriors are chasing your friend," the other continued, seeming to ignore his prisoner's boastful words; "when they return, then our wise leader will decide whether you live or die."

"Doesn't a Huron have ears?" Uncas asked scornfully. "Twice since he's been your prisoner, this Delaware has heard a gun he recognizes. Your young men will never return!"

A brief and gloomy silence followed this daring statement. Duncan, who realized the Mohican was referring to the scout's deadly rifle, leaned forward to carefully watch what impact it might have on the victors; but the chief was satisfied with merely responding:

"If the Lenape are so skillful, why is one of their bravest warriors here?"

"He followed in the footsteps of a fleeing coward and walked straight into a trap. Even the clever beaver can be caught."

As Uncas responded in this way, he pointed his finger toward the lone Huron, but he didn't bother to give any other attention to such an unworthy target. His words and his manner created a powerful reaction among those listening. Every eye turned menacingly toward the person he had indicated with that simple gesture, and a low, threatening rumble moved through the crowd. These ominous sounds carried to the outer door, and as the women and children pushed into the gathering, every space between shoulder and shoulder was now filled with the dark features of some eager and curious human face.

In the meantime, the older chiefs in the center spoke to each other in brief and fragmented sentences. Every word they spoke conveyed the speaker's meaning in the simplest and most powerful way possible. Once again, a long and deeply solemn silence followed. Everyone present understood this to be the courageous sign of a significant and important decision to come. Those who formed the outer circle of faces stood on their toes to see better; even the accused momentarily forgot his shame in a deeper feeling, and revealed his dejected features to cast a worried and anxious look at the dark gathering of chiefs. The silence was finally broken by the elderly warrior who had been mentioned so often. He rose from the ground, and walking past the motionless figure of Uncas, positioned himself in a dignified stance before the wrongdoer. At that moment, the withered woman already mentioned entered the circle in a slow, sideways kind of dance, carrying the torch and mumbling the unclear words of what could have been a type of incantation. Though her presence was completely an interruption, it went unnoticed.

Walking toward Uncas, she held the flaming torch in a way that cast its red light across his body and revealed even the smallest change in his facial expression. The Mohican kept his proud and dignified posture, and his eyes, rather than acknowledging her searching gaze, remained fixed on the distance, as if they could see through the barriers blocking the view and peer into the future. Content with what she had observed, she moved away from him with a hint of satisfaction and went on to conduct the same challenging test on her fellow tribesman who had committed the offense.

The young Huron warrior wore his war paint, and his well-built physique was barely hidden by his clothing. The firelight made every muscle and joint clearly visible, and Duncan looked away in disgust when he realized they were twisting in unbearable pain. The woman began a quiet, mournful wailing at this tragic and disgraceful sight, but the chief reached out his hand and carefully moved her to one side.

"Reed-that-bends," he said, speaking directly to the young offender by name in his own language, "although the Great Spirit has blessed you with good looks, it would have been better if you had never been born. Your voice carries loudly throughout the village, but when it comes to battle, you fall silent. None of my warriors drive the tomahawk deeper into the war-post—none of them strike so lightly against the English. The enemy recognizes the shape of your retreating back, but they have never looked into your eyes. Three times they have challenged you to fight, and each time you failed to respond. Your name will never be spoken again among your people—it has already been erased from memory."

As the chief spoke these words slowly, pausing dramatically between each sentence, the guilty man lifted his face out of respect for the other's position and age. Shame, terror, and pride battled across his features. His eye, which was tight with inner torment, fixed on the people whose opinion determined his reputation; and for a moment, pride won out. He stood up, and exposing his chest, stared steadily at the sharp, gleaming knife that his relentless judge already held high. As the blade slowly entered his heart he even smiled, as though pleased to discover that death was less frightening than he had expected, and collapsed heavily face-down at the feet of the stern and unbending figure of Uncas.

The woman let out a loud and mournful cry, threw the torch to the ground, and plunged everything into darkness. The entire trembling group of onlookers slipped away from the lodge like restless spirits, and Duncan realized that he and the still-breathing body of the victim of an Indian trial had now become its only occupants.

---

# Chapter XXIV.

"Thus spoke the sage: the kings without delay
Dissolve the council, and their chief obey."
—Pope's Iliad

A single moment was enough to show the young man that he was wrong. A hand gripped his arm with strong pressure, and Uncas's quiet voice whispered in his ear:

"The Hurons are cowards. Seeing a coward's blood could never make a warrior shake with fear. The 'Gray Head' and the Sagamore are protected, and Hawkeye's rifle remains ready. Leave—Uncas and the 'Open Hand' are no longer allies. That's all there is to say."

Heyward would have been happy to hear more, but a gentle push from his friend urged him toward the door and warned him of the danger that could come from being discovered together. Slowly and reluctantly giving in to necessity, he left the place and blended in with the crowd that lingered nearby. The dying fires in the clearing cast a dim and uncertain light on the shadowy figures that were silently moving back and forth; and occasionally a brighter flash than usual shone into the lodge, revealing the figure of Uncas still standing upright near the dead body of the Huron.

A group of warriors soon entered the place again, and coming back out, they carried the lifeless body into the nearby woods. After this conclusion of the scene, Duncan wandered among the lodges, unquestioned and unnoticed, trying to find some trace of her for whose sake he had taken the risk he was running. In the current mood of the tribe it would have been easy to escape and rejoin his companions, had such a thought crossed his mind. But, in addition to his constant worry about Alice, a newer though weaker concern for the fate of Uncas helped to keep him tied to the spot. He continued, therefore, to wander from hut to hut, looking into each only to meet with additional disappointment, until he had made the complete circuit of the village. Giving up a type of search that proved so useless, he retraced his steps to the council-lodge, determined to seek and question David, in order to put an end to his doubts.

When they reached the building that had served as both courtroom and execution site, the young man discovered that the commotion had already died down. The warriors had gathered again and were now peacefully smoking while they spoke seriously about the main events of their recent journey to the head of Lake Horican. Although Duncan's return would likely remind them of his reputation and the questionable reasons for his visit, it caused no noticeable reaction. So far, the horrific scene that had just taken place worked in his favor, and he needed no encouragement other than his own instincts to realize it would be wise to take advantage of such an unexpected opportunity.

Without any apparent hesitation, he entered the lodge and sat down with a serious demeanor that perfectly matched the behavior of his hosts. A quick but thorough look was enough to show him that while Uncas remained in the same spot where he had left him,

David was nowhere to be seen. The only restriction placed on Uncas was the watchful gaze of a young Huron warrior who had positioned himself nearby, though an armed guard leaned against the post that formed one side of the narrow entrance. In all other ways, the prisoner appeared to be free; however, he was kept out of any conversation and looked much more like a beautifully carved statue than a living, breathing person with his own thoughts and will.

Heyward had just witnessed a terrifying example of how quickly these people punished those who crossed them, so he wasn't about to risk exposing himself through any reckless boldness. He would have much rather stayed quiet and kept his thoughts to himself than speak, especially when revealing his true situation could prove immediately deadly. Unfortunately for this careful plan, his hosts seemed to have other ideas. He hadn't been sitting long in the shaded spot he had wisely chosen when another of the older warriors, who could speak French, spoke to him:

"My Canadian father does not forget his children," said the chief; "I thank him. An evil spirit lives in the wife of one of my young men. Can the clever stranger frighten him away?"

Heyward had some understanding of the theatrical rituals that Indians performed during these supposed supernatural encounters. He immediately recognized that this situation could potentially be used to advance his own goals. At that moment, it would have been hard to suggest anything that would have pleased him more. However, knowing he needed to maintain the dignity of his fictional role, he controlled his emotions and responded with appropriate mystery:

"Spirits differ; some yield to the power of wisdom, while others are too strong."

"My brother is a great medicine," said the cunning savage; "he will try?"

A nod showed agreement. The Huron felt satisfied with this confirmation and, picking up his pipe again, waited for the right time to make his move. Heyward, growing restless and silently cursing the rigid traditions of these native people that demanded such attention to proper appearances, had to pretend he was just as calm and unbothered as the chief, who was actually a close family member of the sick woman. Time dragged on, and what felt like an hour to this inexperienced adventurer was really just minutes, when the Huron finally set down his pipe and pulled his robe across his chest, as though he was ready to lead the way to the sick person's dwelling. At that very moment, a powerfully built warrior appeared in the doorway, and moving quietly through the focused group, he sat down on one end of the low pile of branches that supported Duncan. Duncan shot an irritated glance at this newcomer, and felt his skin crawl with overwhelming dread when he realized he was actually sitting next to Magua.

The unexpected arrival of this cunning and feared leader caused the Huron departure to be postponed. Multiple pipes that had been put out were relit, while the newcomer, without uttering a single word, pulled his tomahawk from his belt and filled the bowl at its head, then began breathing in the smoke from the tobacco through the hollow handle with complete composure, as though he hadn't been away for two exhausting days on a lengthy and demanding hunt. Ten minutes passed in this way, feeling like countless hours to Duncan, and the warriors found themselves completely surrounded by a thick cloud of white smoke before anyone among them said anything.

"Welcome!" one of them finally said; "has my friend found the moose?"

"The young men are struggling under their heavy loads," Magua replied. "Let 'Reed-that-bends' go on the hunting trail; he will find them."

317

A profound and terrible silence followed the speaking of the forbidden name. Every pipe fell from its owner's lips as if all had breathed in something poisonous at the exact same moment. The smoke swirled above their heads in small whirlwinds, and twisting in a spiral shape it rose quickly through the opening in the lodge's roof, leaving the space below free of its vapors, and making each dark face clearly visible. Most of the warriors kept their eyes fixed on the ground; though a few of the younger and less experienced members of the group allowed their wild and staring eyes to turn toward a white-haired savage who sat between two of the tribe's most respected chiefs. Nothing about this Indian's manner or clothing seemed to justify such an honored position. His bearing was more humble than impressive compared to the other natives; and his dress was the same as commonly worn by ordinary men of the nation. Like most around him, for more than a minute his gaze was also directed at the ground; but, finally allowing his eyes to glance sideways, he noticed that he was becoming the focus of everyone's attention. Then he stood up and raised his voice in the prevailing silence.

"It was a lie," he said. "I never had a son. The one who bore that name is forgotten now. His blood was weak, and it didn't flow from Huron veins. Those treacherous Chippewas deceived my wife. The Great Spirit has declared that the family of Wiss-entush must come to an end. Blessed is the man who knows that his family's curse dies with him. I have spoken."

The speaker, who was the father of the disloyal young Indian, glanced around at those present, as though looking for approval of his composure from the audience. However, the harsh traditions of his tribe had demanded too much from the frail elderly man. The look in his eyes betrayed his symbolic and proud words, while every muscle in his weathered face twisted with pain. After standing for just a moment to savor his painful victory, he turned away, as if disgusted by the stares of others, and covering his face with his blanket, he left the lodge with the silent footsteps of an Indian, seeking in the solitude of his own home the understanding of someone like himself—old, abandoned, and without children.

The Native Americans, who believed that character traits—both virtues and flaws—were passed down through generations, allowed him to leave without saying a word. Then, displaying a level of refinement that many people in more civilized societies could learn from, one of the chiefs redirected the young men's attention away from the weakness they had just observed by speaking in a cheerful tone, courteously addressing Magua as the most recent arrival:

"The Delawares have been like bears going after honey pots, prowling around my village. But who has ever found a Huron asleep?"

The dark cloud that comes before a thunderclap wasn't any blacker than Magua's furrowed brow as he shouted:

"The Delawares of the Lakes!"

"That's not true. Those who dress like women are on their own territory. One of them has been moving through the tribe."

"Did my young men take his scalp?"

"His legs were strong, though his arm is better suited for farming tools than weapons," replied the other, gesturing toward the motionless figure of Uncas.

Instead of showing any feminine curiosity to satisfy his eyes with the sight of a captive from a people he was known to have such good reason to despise, Magua kept smoking with the thoughtful manner he typically maintained when there was no immediate need for his cunning or his speaking skills. Though secretly astonished by the information revealed in the old father's words, he allowed himself to ask no questions, saving his inquiries for a more appropriate time. Only after enough time had passed did he shake the ashes from his pipe, put back the tomahawk, tightened his belt, and stood up, casting for the first time a look toward the prisoner, who stood slightly behind him. The cautious, though apparently distracted Uncas, noticed the movement, and turning quickly toward the light, their eyes met. For nearly a minute these two bold and wild spirits stood looking at each other steadily in the eye, neither backing down in the slightest before the intense stare he faced. Uncas's form expanded, and his nostrils flared like those of a cornered tiger; but his stance was so stiff and unbending that he could easily have been transformed by the imagination into a perfect and flawless representation of his tribe's warrior god. The features of Magua's trembling face proved more flexible; his expression gradually lost its defiant character and took on a look of savage joy, and drawing a breath from the very depths of his chest, he spoke aloud the fearsome name of:

"The Agile Stag!"

Every warrior jumped to his feet when they heard that familiar name, and for a brief moment, the natural composure of the natives was completely overwhelmed by shock. The despised yet admired name echoed as if spoken by a single voice, the sound carrying far beyond the walls of the lodge. The women and children who waited near the entrance picked up the words in an echo, followed by another sharp and mournful cry. Before this cry had finished, the excitement among the men had completely died down. Each person present sat down again, as if embarrassed by their hasty reaction; however, many minutes passed before their intense gazes stopped turning toward their prisoner, studying with curiosity a warrior who had so frequently demonstrated his skill against the finest and most distinguished members of their tribe. Uncas savored his victory, but was satisfied with simply displaying his triumph through a quiet smile—a symbol of contempt that transcends all eras and cultures.

Magua noticed the look on his face, and lifting his arm, he shook it at the prisoner, the bright silver decorations on his bracelet jingling as his limb trembled with rage, while he shouted in English with a voice full of revenge:

"Mohican, you die!"

"The healing waters will never bring the dead Hurons back to life," Uncas replied in the melodious language of the Delawares. "The rushing river carries away their bones; their men have become like women, and their women like screeching owls. Go! Gather the Huron cowards so they can see what a true warrior looks like. My nose is disgusted by their presence; I can smell the blood of cowards on them."

The reference hit home deeply, and the insult festered. Many of the Hurons could understand the foreign language the prisoner was speaking, and Magua was among them. This crafty warrior saw his opportunity and immediately seized upon it. Letting the lightweight animal skin fall from his shoulder, he extended his arm and launched into a display of his formidable and calculated oratory. Though his standing among his people had suffered due to his recurring personal failings and his abandonment of the tribe, his bravery and reputation as a speaker could not be questioned. He never addressed a crowd without gaining listeners, and seldom failed to win people over to his viewpoint. In this moment, his natural abilities were fueled by his desire for vengeance.

He once again told the story of the attack on the island at Glenn's, the death of his companions and the escape of their most dangerous enemies. Then he explained the nature and location of the hill where he had taken the prisoners they had captured. He made no mention of his own violent plans for the young women, or of his frustrated hatred, but quickly moved on to describe how "La Longue Carabine" had surprised their group and the deadly outcome that followed. Here he stopped and looked around, pretending to show respect for the dead, but actually wanting to see how his opening story was affecting his audience. As always, every eye was fixed on his face. Each dark figure looked like a living statue, so still were their positions, so focused was each person's attention.

Then Magua lowered his voice, which until that moment had been clear, strong, and commanding, and began speaking about the qualities of the deceased. He didn't overlook any trait that might earn the compassion of a Native American. One man had never failed in hunting; another had been relentless in tracking their enemies. This one was courageous, that one was generous. In essence, he crafted his references so skillfully that in a tribe made up of so few families, he managed to touch every emotional chord that could resonate within someone's heart.

"Are the bones of my young men," he concluded, "in the burial place of the Hurons? You know they are not. Their spirits have gone toward the setting sun, and are already crossing the great waters to the happy hunting grounds. But they left without food, without guns or knives, without moccasins, naked and poor as they were born. Should this be? Are their souls to enter the land of the just like hungry Iroquois or unmanly Delawares, or should they meet their friends with weapons in their hands and robes on their backs? What will our fathers think the tribes of the Wyandots have become? They will look upon their children with a dark eye, and say, 'Go! A Chippewa has come here with the name of a Huron.' Brothers, we must not forget the dead; a red-skin never stops remembering. We will load the back of this Mohican until he staggers under our generosity, and send him after my young men. They call to us for help, though our ears are not open; they say, 'Do not forget us.' When they see the spirit of this Mohican struggling after them with his burden, they will know we are of that mind. Then they will go on happy; and our children will say, 'This is what our fathers did for their friends, so must we do for them.' What is a Yengee? We have killed many, but the earth is still pale. A stain on the name of Huron can only be hidden by blood that comes from the veins of an Indian. Let this Delaware die."

The impact of such a speech, delivered in the forceful language and with the passionate style of a Huron speaker, could hardly be misunderstood. Magua had so skillfully combined the natural emotions with the religious beliefs of his listeners, that their minds, already conditioned by tradition to offer a sacrifice to the spirits of their fallen people, abandoned every trace of compassion in their desire for vengeance. One warrior in particular, a man with a wild and savage appearance, had been notable for the attention he had paid to the speaker's words. His expression had shifted with each emotion that passed through him, until it settled into a look of murderous hatred. As Magua finished speaking he stood up and, releasing the scream of a devil, his polished small axe could be seen flashing in the firelight as he spun it over his head. The movement and the scream were too quick for words to stop his violent purpose. It seemed as if a bright flash shot from his hand, which was intercepted at the same instant by a dark and strong line. The first was the tomahawk in its flight; the second was the arm that Magua thrust forward to redirect its path. The swift and alert movement of the chief was not completely too late. The sharp weapon sliced the war feather from the scalp lock of Uncas, and went through the thin wall of the lodge as though it had been thrown from some powerful machine.

Duncan witnessed the threatening move and jumped to his feet, his heart racing as it pounded in his throat, yet filled with the most noble determination to help his friend. One look showed him that the strike had missed, and his fear transformed into admiration. Uncas remained motionless, staring his opponent directly in the eyes with an expression that appeared beyond any emotion. Stone could not have been more cold, composed, or unwavering than the face he displayed in response to this sudden and spiteful assault. Then, as if feeling sorry for the lack of ability that had turned out so lucky for him, he smiled and spoke a few scornful words in his native language.

"No!" Magua declared, once he had confirmed the prisoner was secure; "the sun must witness his humiliation; the women must watch his body shake with fear, or our vengeance will be nothing more than children's games. Go! Take him somewhere quiet; let's find out if a Delaware can rest through the night and face death come morning."

The young men responsible for guarding the prisoner immediately bound his arms with strips of bark and escorted him from the lodge, surrounded by a deep and foreboding silence. Only when Uncas appeared in the doorway did his steady stride falter. At that moment, he turned and cast a sweeping, proud gaze around the circle of his enemies, and Duncan glimpsed an expression that he was relieved to interpret as a sign that hope had not completely abandoned him.

Magua was satisfied with his success, or perhaps too preoccupied with his hidden plans to pursue his questioning any further. He adjusted his cloak and wrapped it around his chest, then left the area as well, abandoning a topic that could have proven deadly to the person standing beside him. Despite his growing anger, his natural courage, and his concern for Uncas, Heyward felt noticeably relieved when such a dangerous and cunning enemy departed. The tension created by the speech slowly faded away. The warriors returned to their places and thick clouds of smoke filled the lodge once again. For nearly thirty minutes, no one spoke a word or even glanced around much; a serious and thoughtful quiet typically followed every episode of conflict and disturbance among these people, who were equally passionate yet remarkably disciplined.

When the chief, who had asked for Duncan's help, finished smoking his pipe, he made one last successful attempt to leave. He signaled with a finger for the supposed doctor to follow him; and walking through the thick smoke, Duncan was happy, for several reasons, to finally breathe the clean air of a cool and refreshing summer evening.

Instead of following his path among those lodges where Heyward had already conducted his fruitless search, his companion turned away and headed straight toward the base of a nearby mountain that loomed over the temporary village. A dense thicket of brush bordered its base, making it necessary to travel through a winding and narrow trail. The boys had returned to their games in the clearing and were acting out a mock chase to the post among themselves. To make their games as realistic as possible, one of the most daring among them had carried several burning sticks to some piles of treetops that had so far avoided the flames. The blaze from one of these fires lit the way for the chief and Duncan and added an extra sense of wildness to the rough landscape. A short distance from a bare rock, and directly in front of it, they entered a grassy clearing that they prepared to cross. Just then more fuel was thrown onto the fire, and a strong light reached even to that far-off place. It struck the white surface of the mountain and reflected downward onto a dark and mysterious-looking creature that appeared suddenly in their path. The Indian stopped, as if uncertain whether to continue, and allowed his companion to come to his side. A large black mass, which at first appeared motionless, now began to move in a way that was puzzling to the latter. Once again the fire grew brighter and its light fell more clearly on the object. Then even Duncan recognized it, by its restless and sideways movements that kept the upper part of its body in constant motion while the animal itself seemed to be sitting, as a bear. Though it snarled loudly and fiercely, and there were moments when its gleaming eyes could be seen, it showed no other signs of aggression. The Huron, at least, appeared confident that the intentions of this unusual intruder were peaceful, for after giving it a careful look, he calmly continued on his way.

Duncan, who knew that these animals were often tamed by the Indians, followed his companion's lead, thinking that some beloved pet of the tribe had wandered into the bushes looking for food. They walked past it without being bothered. Although they had to come almost close enough to touch the creature, the Huron, who had initially been so careful in identifying his strange visitor, was now satisfied with moving forward without spending any time on further inspection; but Heyward couldn't stop himself from glancing back, keeping a cautious watch for any attacks from behind. His anxiety only grew when he noticed the beast moving along their trail, tracking their steps. He was about to say something, but at that moment the Indian pushed aside a door made of bark and stepped into a cave carved into the mountainside.

Taking advantage of such a simple escape route, Duncan followed him and was relieved to be closing the narrow entrance behind them, when he felt it pulled from his grasp by the creature, whose hairy body immediately blocked the passageway. They found themselves in a straight and lengthy corridor, carved into a crevice in the rock, where turning back without facing the animal was out of the question. Making the most of their situation, the young man pushed ahead, staying as near as he could to his guide. The bear snarled repeatedly behind him, and several times its massive paws touched his body, as though it wanted to stop him from going deeper into the cave.

How long Heyward's nerves could have endured this extraordinary situation would be hard to determine, since fortunately, he soon discovered relief. A faint light had been visible ahead of them the entire time, and they now reached the source from which it came.

A large hollow in the rock had been roughly adapted to serve the functions of multiple rooms. The divisions were basic yet clever, made from a mixture of stone, sticks, and bark. Openings overhead let in daylight, and during the night, fires and torches took the place of the sun. The Hurons had brought most of their treasures here, particularly those that belonged specifically to the tribe; and here, as it now became clear, the ill woman, who was thought to be suffering from supernatural forces, had also been moved, believing that her tormentor would have greater difficulty attacking through stone walls than through the leafy roofs of the lodges. The room that Duncan and his guide entered first had been set aside entirely for her care. His companion moved toward her bed, which was encircled by women, and in their midst Heyward was astonished to discover his missing friend David.

A single glance was enough to tell the fake doctor that the sick woman was far beyond any hope of recovery. She lay in a kind of paralyzed state, unaware of the things that filled her vision, and fortunately unconscious of any pain. Heyward felt relieved that his pretense would be performed on someone who was too ill to care whether he succeeded or failed. The small pang of guilt he had felt about the planned deception immediately disappeared, and he started to gather his thoughts to play his role convincingly, when he discovered that someone was about to test the healing power of music before he could demonstrate his supposed medical skills.

Gamut, who had been ready to pour out his soul in song when the visitors arrived, paused for a moment, then drew a melody from his pipe and began a hymn that could have performed a miracle, if faith in its power had been worth anything. He was permitted to continue until the end, with the Indians showing respect for his supposed disability, and Duncan too grateful for the delay to risk even the smallest interruption. As the fading notes of his music reached Duncan's ears, he jerked aside upon hearing them echoed behind him in a voice that was half human and half ghostly. Turning around, he saw the hairy beast sitting upright in a shadowy part of the cave, where, while its restless body swayed in the uneasy way of the creature, it repeated in a kind of low rumble sounds, if not actual words, that bore some faint similarity to the singer's melody.

The impact of such an extraordinary echo on David was beyond description and could only be imagined. His eyes widened as though he questioned what he was seeing, and his voice fell completely silent from overwhelming amazement. A carefully planned strategy to share crucial information with Heyward vanished from his mind, replaced by a feeling that closely resembled fear, though he preferred to think of it as wonder. Under this powerful influence, he cried out: "She expects you, and is at hand"; then hastily fled the cavern.

---

# Chapter XXV.

"Snug.—Do you have the lion's part written down? Please, if you do, give it to me, because I'm slow at memorizing lines.

Quince.—You can do it on the spot, since it's nothing but roaring."
—A Midsummer Night's Dream.

The scene contained an odd mixture of the absurd and the serious. The creature kept up its rolling, seemingly tireless movements, though its comical effort to copy David's melody stopped the moment David left the area. Gamut's words were, as we have seen, spoken in his own language; to Duncan they appeared filled with some secret meaning, though nothing around him helped him figure out what they were referring to. All speculation about this matter was quickly ended, however, by the chief's behavior, as he walked over to the sick person's bedside and motioned for the entire group of female attendants who had gathered there to watch the stranger's abilities to leave. They obeyed without question, though unwillingly; and when the faint echo that traveled through the hollow, natural corridor from the distant closing door had faded away, he pointed toward his unconscious daughter and said:

"Now let my brother show his power."

Clearly called upon to perform the duties of the role he had taken on, Heyward worried that even the slightest hesitation could be dangerous. Trying to gather his thoughts, he prepared to carry out the kind of mystical ritual and strange ceremonies that Indian medicine men typically use to hide their lack of knowledge and power. It's quite likely that, given how confused his mind was, he would have quickly made some mistake that would arouse suspicion or even prove deadly, if his early attempts hadn't been interrupted by a fierce growl from the four-legged creature. Three separate times he tried again to continue, and each time he encountered the same mysterious resistance, with each interruption appearing more wild and menacing than the one before.

"The clever ones are envious," the Huron said; "I'm leaving. Brother, this woman is married to one of my most courageous young warriors; treat her fairly. Quiet!" he added, gesturing to the restless animal to settle down; "I'm going."

The chief kept his promise, and Duncan found himself alone in that wild and desolate dwelling with the helpless sick man and the fierce and dangerous bear. The animal listened to the Indian's movements with the kind of intelligence that bears are known to have, until another echo indicated that he too had left the cave. Then it turned and came shuffling toward Duncan, sitting down in front of him in its natural position, upright like a human being. The young man looked around anxiously for some weapon he could use to defend himself against the attack he now genuinely expected.

It appeared, though, that the creature's mood had suddenly shifted. Rather than continuing its unhappy growling or showing any other signs of rage, its entire furry body began shaking violently, as though seized by some peculiar internal spasm. The massive and clumsy claws fumbled awkwardly around the snarling snout, and while Heyward watched its movements with anxious attention, the fierce head tilted to one side and was replaced by the genuine, solid face of the scout, who was enjoying from the depths of his being his own distinctive form of amusement.

"Listen!" said the cautious woodsman, cutting off Heyward's surprised exclamation; "those scoundrels are around this area, and any sounds that don't seem like natural witchcraft would bring them all down on us at once."

"Tell me what this disguise means, and why you've tried such a dangerous scheme?"

"Well, logic and careful planning are often beaten by pure chance," the scout replied. "But since a story should always start at the beginning, I'll tell you everything in the proper order. After we separated, I put the commandant and the Sagamore in an old beaver lodge, where they're much safer from the Hurons than they would be in Edward's fort; you see, those northern Indians from the northwest, who haven't had traders come among them yet, still hold the beaver sacred. After that, Uncas and I headed for the other camp as we had agreed. Have you seen the boy?"

"To my overwhelming sorrow! He has been captured and sentenced to death at sunrise."

"I had a feeling that would be his fate," the scout continued, his voice less confident and cheerful than before. But he quickly recovered his naturally steady tone and went on: "His misfortune is the real reason I'm here, because I could never abandon a boy like that to the Hurons. Those scoundrels would have quite a celebration if they could tie 'The Bounding Elk' and 'The Long Carabine,' as they call me, to the same stake! Though I've never understood why they gave me that name, since there's about as much similarity between the abilities of 'killdeer' and the performance of one of your actual Canada carbines as there is between the nature of pipestone and flint."

"Stick to your story," said the impatient Heyward; "we don't know when the Hurons might come back."

"Don't worry about them. A magician needs his time, just like a wandering priest in the frontier settlements. We're as safe from being interrupted as a missionary would be at the start of a two-hour sermon. Well, Uncas and I encountered a group of those scoundrels heading back; the young man was far too eager for a scout; actually, considering his fiery nature, he wasn't entirely at fault; and in the end, one of the Hurons turned out to be a coward, and while running away led him straight into a trap."

"And he has paid a heavy price for that weakness."

The scout deliberately drew his hand across his throat and nodded, as if to say, "I understand what you mean." Then he went on speaking in a louder voice, though his words were hardly any clearer:

"After losing the boy, I turned against the Hurons, as you can imagine. There were several skirmishes between one or two of their scouts and myself, but that's beside the point. So, after I had shot those devils, I managed to get quite close to their lodges without causing any more disturbance. Then what should fortune do in my favor but bring me to the exact spot where one of the tribe's most famous medicine men was preparing himself, as I well knew, for some great spiritual battle with Satan—though why should I call that fortune, when it now appears to have been a special arrangement of Providence. So a well-placed blow to the head knocked out the lying fraud for a while, and leaving him a piece of walnut for his dinner to prevent any outcry, and tying him up between two young trees, I helped myself to his ceremonial clothing and took on the role of the bear myself, so that the proceedings could continue."

"You played that role brilliantly; even the actual animal would have been embarrassed by how well you portrayed it."

"Lord, major," replied the pleased woodsman, "I would be a poor student for someone who has spent so much time in the wilderness if I didn't know how to demonstrate the movements or nature of such an animal. If it had been a mountain lion, or even a full-grown panther, I would have put on a performance for you worth watching. But it's no great accomplishment to show off the actions of such a sluggish creature; though, for that matter, a bear can also be overacted. Yes, yes; not every imitator understands that nature can be overdone more easily than it can be matched. But all our work still lies ahead of us. Where is the gentle one?"

"God knows. I've searched every lodge in the village without finding the slightest trace of her presence in the tribe."

"You heard what the singer said as he left us: 'She is at hand, and expects you'?"

"I've been forced to believe he was referring to this unfortunate woman."

"The fool was scared and stumbled through his words, but there was a deeper meaning behind them. There are enough walls here to divide the entire settlement. A bear should be able to climb, so I'll take a look over them. There might be honey jars hidden in these rocks, and I'm an animal, you know, that craves sweet things."

The scout glanced back over his shoulder, chuckling at his own cleverness as he climbed up the barrier, copying the awkward movements of the animal he was pretending to be. However, the moment he reached the top, he signaled for quiet and quickly slid back down with urgent haste.

"She's here," he whispered, "and you'll find her by that door. I would have offered some words of comfort to that troubled soul, but the sight of such a monster might disturb her sanity. Though to be honest, major, you're not exactly the most welcoming sight yourself with all that paint on your face."

Duncan, who had already leaned forward eagerly, immediately pulled back upon hearing these disheartening words.

"Am I really that disgusting?" he asked, looking hurt and disappointed.

"You might not startle a wolf, or make the Royal Americans retreat from battle; but I've seen times when you looked much better; your painted faces may impress the Native women, but young white women prefer men of their own race. Look," he added, pointing to a spot where water dripped from a rock, creating a small clear spring before flowing out through the nearby cracks; "you can easily wash off the chief's war paint, and when you return I'll try my skill at creating new decorations. It's as normal for a medicine man to change his paint as it is for a gentleman in the towns to change his fine clothes."

The experienced woodsman didn't need to search for reasons to support his advice. He was still talking when Duncan took advantage of the water. In an instant, every frightening or disgusting mark was wiped away, and the young man appeared once more with the natural features he had been born with. Now ready for a meeting with his beloved, he quickly said goodbye to his companion and vanished through the passage that had been pointed out to him. The scout watched him leave with satisfaction, nodding his head in his direction and murmuring his best wishes; after that, he calmly began examining the condition of the food storage among the Hurons, since the cave served multiple purposes, including as a place to store the results of their hunting expeditions.

Duncan had no guide except for a faint, distant light that nonetheless served as his North Star in his quest for love. With its help, he managed to reach the destination of his hopes, which was simply another chamber within the cave that had been set aside specifically for holding such an important captive as the daughter of the commanding officer of William Henry. The room was abundantly scattered with stolen goods from that unfortunate fort. Amid all this disorder, he discovered the woman he was searching for—pale, worried, and frightened, yet still beautiful. David had prepared her for this kind of visit.

"Duncan!" she cried out, her voice seeming to shake at the very sound of her own words.

"Alice!" he called out, jumping recklessly between trunks, boxes, weapons, and furniture until he reached her side.

"I knew you would never abandon me," she said, looking up with a brief spark of light on her otherwise downcast face. "But you're all by yourself! As grateful as I am to be remembered this way, I wish I could believe you're not completely alone."

Duncan, noticing that she was trembling so much that she could barely stand, gently encouraged her to sit down while he told her about the main events that we have described. Alice listened with intense interest, and although the young man spoke carefully about her father's grief, being mindful not to hurt her feelings, tears flowed freely down her face as if she had never cried before. Duncan's gentle kindness, however, soon calmed her initial outburst of emotion, and she was then able to listen to the rest of his account with complete attention, if not with complete calm.

"And now, Alice," he continued, "you will see how much we still need from you. With the help of our experienced and invaluable friend, the scout, we may find our way away from these savage people, but you will have to show your greatest courage. Remember that you are rushing to the arms of your respected father, and how much his happiness, as well as your own, depends on your efforts."

"Can I do anything else for a father who has done so much for me?"

"And for me as well," the young man continued, softly squeezing the hand he held between both of his own.

The expression of innocence and surprise that he received in response convinced Duncan that he needed to be more direct.

"This isn't the right time or place to burden you with my personal concerns," he continued; "but what person carrying such a heavy heart wouldn't want to unload their troubles? People say that shared hardship creates the strongest bonds; the pain we both endured for your sake left little that needed explaining between your father and me."

"And, dearest Cora, Duncan; surely Cora was not forgotten?"

"Not forgotten! No; she is mourned as few women have ever been mourned before. Your respected father saw no difference between his children; but I—Alice, I hope you won't take offense when I say that to me her true value was somewhat hidden—"

"Then you didn't understand my sister's true worth," Alice said, pulling her hand away. "She always talks about you as someone who is her closest friend."

"I would happily believe her to be that way," Duncan replied quickly. "I could wish for her to be even more than that; but with you, Alice, I have your father's permission to hope for an even closer and more precious bond."

Alice shook violently, and for a moment she turned her face away, giving in to the emotions typical of women; but these feelings quickly faded, leaving her in control of her behavior, if not her emotions.

"Heyward," she said, looking directly into his eyes with a moving expression of innocence and trust, "let me have the blessed presence and sacred approval of that parent before you press me any further."

"Though I should not say more, I could not say less," the young man was about to respond, when a gentle tap on his shoulder interrupted him. Jumping to his feet, he spun around, and facing the intruder, his eyes fell upon Magua's dark figure and malevolent face. The savage's deep, throaty laugh sounded to

Duncan, at that moment, like the demonic mockery of a fiend. If he had followed the sudden and violent impulse of that instant, he would have thrown himself at the Huron and left their fate to the outcome of a fight to the death. However, without any weapons whatsoever, unaware of what assistance his cunning enemy might summon, and responsible for the safety of someone who had just become dearer to his heart than ever before, he no sooner considered the desperate plan than he gave it up.

"What do you want?" Alice asked quietly, crossing her arms over her chest and fighting to hide her terrible fear for Heyward, speaking in the same cold and distant way she always used when her captor came to see her.

The triumphant Indian had returned to his stern expression, though he cautiously stepped back from the threatening look in the young man's blazing eyes. He studied both his prisoners for a moment with an unwavering stare, and then, moving to one side, he placed a wooden log across a doorway that was different from the one Duncan had used to enter. Duncan now understood how he had been caught off guard, and believing he was hopelessly trapped, he pulled Alice close to his chest and stood ready to face a destiny he barely mourned, since he would endure it alongside such cherished company. However, Magua had no plans for immediate harm. His first actions were clearly intended to secure his new prisoner; he didn't even spare a second look at the still figures in the middle of the cave until he had completely blocked any chance of escape through the secret exit he had used himself. Heyward watched his every move, yet remained steadfast, continuing to hold Alice's delicate form against his heart, being both too proud and too despairing to beg mercy from an enemy he had thwarted so many times. Once Magua had accomplished his goal, he walked toward his captives and spoke in English:

"The pale faces trap the clever beavers; but the red-skins know how to capture the Yankees."

"Huron, do your worst!" shouted the agitated Heyward, forgetting that more than just his own life hung in the balance; "I despise both you and your revenge."

"Will the white man say these words when he's tied to the stake?" Magua asked, his sneer revealing just how little he believed in the other man's courage.

"Here; individually to your face, or in front of your entire nation."

"Le Renard Subtil is a great chief!" the Indian replied; "he will go and bring his young men, to see how bravely a pale face can laugh at tortures."

He turned away as he spoke and was about to leave through the same path Duncan had used to arrive, when a growling sound reached his ears and made him pause. The bear figure appeared in the doorway, where it sat swaying back and forth with its usual restless movements. Magua, like the father of the sick woman, watched it carefully for a moment, as if trying to determine what it was. He was far above the common superstitions of his tribe, and as soon as he recognized the familiar costume of the medicine man, he prepared to walk past it with cold disdain. But a louder and more menacing growl made him stop again. Then he seemed to suddenly decide he would waste no more time, and stepped forward with determination.

The mimicking animal, which had moved forward slightly, slowly backed away in front of him until it reached the pass again, where it rose up on its hind legs and clawed at the air with its paws, just like its savage counterpart would do.

"Fool!" the chief shouted in Huron, "go play with the children and women; leave men to their wisdom."

He tried once again to get past the supposed fake doctor, not even bothering with the show of threatening to use the knife or tomahawk hanging from his belt. Suddenly the creature stretched out its arms, or rather legs, and wrapped him in a grip that could have matched the legendary strength of the famous "bear's hug" itself. Heyward had watched the entire sequence involving Hawkeye with intense fascination. First he let go of Alice; then he grabbed a strip of buckskin that had been tied around some package, and when he saw his enemy with both arms pinned to his sides by the scout's iron-strong muscles, he rushed forward and effectively bound them in place. Arms, legs, and feet were wrapped in twenty loops of the leather strip in less time than it takes us to describe what happened. When the dangerous Huron was completely tied up, the scout let go of his grip, and Duncan placed his enemy on his back, completely unable to move.

During this entire sudden and remarkable action, Magua had fought fiercely until he realized he was in the grip of someone whose nerves were much steadier than his own, yet he hadn't made a single sound. However, when Hawkeye removed the beast's shaggy jaws to quickly explain what he had done, revealing his own weathered and serious face to the Huron's eyes, the Indian's composure was so completely shaken that he couldn't help but speak the words he always used:

"Hugh!"

"Yes, you've found your voice," said his calm victor; "now, to make sure you don't use it to destroy us, I'll have to silence you."

Since there was no time to waste, the scout immediately began carrying out this essential safety measure; and once he had gagged the Indian, his enemy could safely have been considered as "hors de combat."

"Where did the devil get in?" asked the diligent scout when he finished his task. "Nobody has come through my area since you left me here."

Duncan pointed toward the door through which Magua had entered, which now offered too many barriers for a swift escape.

"Bring on the gentle one, then," his friend continued; "we need to make a dash for the woods through the other exit."

"It's impossible!" Duncan said. "Fear has overwhelmed her, and she's helpless. Alice! My sweet, my dear Alice, wake up; now is the time to escape. It's no use! She hears me, but she can't respond. Go, noble and worthy friend; save yourself, and leave me to my fate."

"Every trail has its end, and every disaster teaches us something!" the scout replied. "Here, wrap her in those Indian clothes. Cover up her entire small body. No, that foot is unlike any other in the wilderness; it will give her away. Everything, every part of her. Now pick her up in your arms, and follow me. Leave the rest to me."

Duncan, as could be seen from his companion's words, was eagerly following orders; and when the other man finished speaking, he lifted Alice's slender form into his arms and followed behind the scout. They discovered the sick woman exactly as they had left her, still by herself, and moved quickly through the natural corridor toward the entrance. As they neared the small bark door, the sound of hushed voices from outside revealed that the patient's friends and family had assembled around the area, waiting patiently for permission to come back inside.

"If I speak," Hawkeye whispered, "my English, which is the true language of a white man, will reveal to those scoundrels that an enemy is in their midst. You must speak to them in your dialect, major; tell them that we have trapped the evil spirit in the cave, and we are taking the woman into the woods to search for healing roots. Use all your cleverness, for this is a righteous mission."

The door cracked open slightly, as though someone outside was trying to listen to what was happening inside, forcing the scout to stop giving his instructions. A fierce growl drove away whoever was listening, and then the scout boldly pushed open the bark covering and left the place, acting like a bear as he moved. Duncan stayed right behind him, and quickly found himself surrounded by a group of twenty worried relatives and friends.

The crowd stepped back slightly, allowing the father and someone who seemed to be the woman's husband to come forward.

"Has my brother driven away the evil spirit?" the former demanded. "What is he carrying in his arms?"

"Your child," Duncan replied seriously; "the sickness has left her; it is trapped in the rocks. I will take the woman to a distant place, where I will make her stronger against any future attacks. She will be in the young man's lodge when the sun rises again."

When the father had explained what the stranger meant in the Huron language, a quiet murmur showed how pleased everyone was to hear this news. The chief himself gestured for Duncan to continue, speaking out loud in a strong voice and with a dignified bearing:

"Go; I am a man, and I will enter the rock and fight the wicked one."

Heyward had willingly complied and had already moved beyond the small group when these shocking words stopped him in his tracks.

"Is my brother insane?" he shouted; "is he heartless? He will encounter the sickness, and it will take hold of him; or he will force out the illness, and it will pursue his daughter into the forest. No; let my children remain outside, and if the spirit shows itself, strike him down with clubs. He is crafty, and will hide himself in the mountain when he sees how many are prepared to battle him."

This unique warning achieved exactly what was intended. Rather than going into the cave, the father and husband pulled out their tomahawks and positioned themselves ready to unleash their revenge on the supposed tormentor of their ill family member, while the women and children snapped off branches from the shrubs or grabbed pieces of stone with the same purpose in mind. At this perfect moment, the fake medicine men vanished.

Hawkeye, while he had taken such bold advantage of the Indian superstitions, understood that the wisest chiefs tolerated rather than truly believed in them. He was well aware of how precious time was in this urgent situation. No matter how deeply his enemies might deceive themselves, and regardless of how their delusions had helped his plans, the smallest hint of suspicion, working on an Indian's naturally suspicious mind, could easily prove deadly. Therefore, choosing the route least likely to draw attention, he moved around the edges of the village rather than walking directly through it. In the dim glow of the dying fires, warriors could still be seen in the distance, moving from lodge to lodge. However, the children had given up their games and gone to their beds of animal skins, and the peaceful quiet of night was already starting to replace the chaos and excitement of such a busy and significant evening.

Alice recovered under the refreshing influence of the fresh air, and since her physical strength rather than her mental faculties had been weakened, she required no explanation of what had happened.

"Now let me try to walk," she said as they entered the forest, blushing despite being unseen because she hadn't been able to leave Duncan's arms sooner; "I really am feeling better now."

"No, Alice, you are still too weak."

The young woman gently tried to free herself, and Heyward was forced to let go of his treasured burden. The person disguised as a bear had definitely been completely unaware of the delightful feelings of a lover while holding his beloved in his arms; and he was probably also unfamiliar with the nature of that sense of innocent embarrassment that weighed heavily on the trembling Alice. But when he positioned himself at an appropriate distance from the dwellings, he stopped and began speaking about a topic he knew extremely well.

"This path will take you to the stream," he said; "walk along its northern shore until you reach a waterfall; climb the hill to your right, and you'll see the fires of the other people. You need to go there and ask for protection; if they are real Delawares you will be safe. A long journey with that gentle one right now is not possible. The Hurons would track us down and take our scalps before we traveled even twelve miles. Go, and may Providence watch over you."

"And you!" Heyward demanded in surprise; "surely we're not parting ways here?"

"The Hurons have captured the pride of the Delawares; the final descendant of the noble Mohican bloodline is now their prisoner," the scout replied. "I'm going to find out what I can do to help him. If they had taken your scalp, major, I would have killed one enemy for every hair on your head, just as I promised. But if they're planning to burn the young chief at the stake, those Indians will also witness how a white man can face death with courage."

Duncan wasn't offended at all by the rugged woodsman's clear preference for someone who could, to some extent, be considered his adopted child. He kept presenting arguments against such a dangerous attempt. Alice supported him, adding her pleas to Duncan's as they both urged the scout to give up a plan that offered so much risk with so little chance of success. Their persuasive words and clever reasoning accomplished nothing. The scout listened to them carefully but with growing impatience, and eventually ended the conversation by responding in a voice that immediately silenced Alice and made Duncan realize that any further protests would be pointless.

"I have heard," he said, "that there is a feeling in youth which binds man to woman closer than the father is tied to the son. It may be so. I have seldom been where women of my color dwell; but such may be the gifts of nature in the settlements. You have risked life, and all that is dear to you, to bring off this gentle one, and I suppose that some such disposition is at the bottom of it all. As for me, I taught the lad the real character of a rifle; and well has he paid me for it. I have fought at his side in many a bloody skirmish; and so long as I could hear the crack of his piece in one ear, and that of the Sagamore in the other, I knew no enemy was on my back. Winters and summers, nights and days, have we roamed the wilderness in company, eating of the same dish, one sleeping while the other watched; and before it shall be said that Uncas was taken to the torment, and I at hand—There is but a single Ruler of us all, whatever may be the color of the skin; and Him I call to witness, that before the Mohican boy shall perish for the want of a friend, good faith shall depart the earth, and 'Killdeer' become as harmless as the tooting weapon of the singer!"

Duncan let go of the scout's arm, and the scout turned around and walked steadily back toward the lodges. After stopping for a moment to watch him leave, Heyward and Alice, who felt both successful and sad, headed together toward the distant Delaware village.

---

# Chapter XXVI.

"Bot.—Let me play the lion too."
—A Midsummer Night's Dream

Despite Hawkeye's strong determination, he completely understood all the difficulties and dangers he was about to face. As he made his way back to the camp, his sharp and experienced mind was focused entirely on creating strategies to overcome the watchfulness and suspicion of his enemies, which he knew matched his own abilities perfectly. Only the color of his skin had spared the lives of Magua and the medicine man, who would have been the first to die for his own safety, if the scout hadn't believed that such an action, however natural it might be for an Indian, would be completely unworthy of someone who claimed descent from men with pure blood. Therefore, he relied on the ropes and bindings he had used to tie up his prisoners, and headed straight toward the center of the village. As he got closer to the buildings, his steps became more careful, and his alert eyes missed no detail, whether friendly or threatening. An abandoned hut stood slightly ahead of the others, and looked as though it had been left unfinished when only half built—most likely because it lacked some essential requirements, such as wood or water. A dim light flickered through its gaps, though, and showed that despite its incomplete construction, someone was living there. The scout then moved toward that place, like a wise general who tests his enemy's forward positions before risking the main assault.

Positioning himself appropriately for the animal he was pretending to be, Hawkeye crept toward a small opening where he could get a clear view of what was inside. It turned out to be where David Gamut was staying. The devoted singing teacher had brought himself here, along with all his troubles, his fears, and his humble trust in God's protection. At the exact moment when the scout spotted his awkward figure in the way just described, the woodsman himself, even while disguised, was the focus of the lonely man's deep thoughts.

However deep David's faith was in the performance of ancient miracles, he rejected the belief in any direct supernatural intervention in the management of modern morality. In other words, while he had complete faith in the ability of Balaam's donkey to speak, he was somewhat doubtful about the idea of a bear singing; and yet he had been convinced of the latter based on the evidence of his own refined senses. There was something in his appearance and demeanor that revealed to the scout the complete confusion of his mental state. He was sitting on a pile of brush, a few twigs from which occasionally fed his small fire, with his head resting on his arm, in a posture of melancholy contemplation. The clothing of the devotee of music had undergone no other change from what had been so recently described, except that he had covered his bald head with the triangular beaver hat, which had not proven sufficiently attractive to arouse the greed of any of his captors.

The clever Hawkeye, who remembered the hurried way the other man had left his position beside the sick woman's bed, had his doubts about what was causing all this serious thinking. After first walking around the hut and making sure it stood completely alone, and that the nature of the person living there would likely keep visitors away, he stepped through the low doorway into Gamut's presence. Gamut's position placed the fire between them, and after Hawkeye had settled himself nearby, nearly a full minute passed while the two men stared at each other in silence. The unexpected nature of this surprise had almost overwhelmed—we won't call it his philosophy—but rather David's composure and determination. He searched for his pitch-pipe and stood up with the confused idea of trying a musical remedy.

"Dark and mysterious monster!" he cried out, his hands shaking as he put away his glasses and reached for his reliable source of comfort in times of trouble—his treasured book of psalms. "I don't know what you are or what you're planning, but if you're thinking of harming someone who is just a humble servant of the temple, then listen to the inspired words of the young people of Israel, and change your ways."

The bear shook his shaggy sides, and then a familiar voice responded:

"Put away that noisy weapon and learn to speak with restraint. Five words of clear and understandable English are worth more right now than an hour of shouting."

"What are you?" David demanded, completely unable to carry out his original plan and almost gasping for breath.

"A man like yourself; and one whose blood is just as free from any mixing with a bear or an Indian as your own. Have you already forgotten who gave you that foolish weapon you're holding in your hand?"

"Is this really possible?" David replied, breathing more easily as understanding began to come to him. "I've discovered many amazing things during my time with the non-believers, but certainly nothing to surpass this."

"Come on, come on," Hawkeye replied, removing his disguise to reveal his honest face, hoping to reassure his companion's shaky confidence. "You can see my skin, which may not be as white as one of the refined ladies, but has no red coloring except what the winds and sun have naturally given it. Now let's get down to business."

"First tell me about the maiden, and about the young man who so bravely sought her," David interrupted.

"Yes, they are fortunately safe from the tomahawks of these scoundrels. But can you help me find the trail of Uncas?"

"The young man is trapped, and I'm deeply afraid his death has been decided. I'm filled with sorrow that someone with such good intentions should die without understanding, and I've been searching for a worthy hymn—"

"Can you take me to him?"

"The task won't be difficult," David replied, hesitating; "though I'm very worried that your presence would make his unfortunate situation worse rather than better."

"No more talking—let's go," Hawkeye replied, covering his face once more and leading by example as he immediately left the lodge.

As they continued forward, the scout learned that his companion had gained access to Uncas by taking advantage of his pretended disability, helped by the goodwill he had earned from one of the guards. This guard, who spoke some English, had been chosen by David as a target for religious conversion. Whether the Huron truly understood what his new friend intended was questionable, but since focused attention flatters a savage just as much as it does a civilized person, it had achieved the desired result. There's no need to describe in detail the clever way the scout drew these details from the innocent David, nor will we elaborate here on the guidance he provided once he had gathered all the essential information, since everything will be adequately explained to the reader as the story unfolds.

The lodge where Uncas was being held prisoner stood right in the heart of the village, positioned in what was probably the most challenging spot of all to reach or escape from without being noticed. However, Hawkeye had no intention of trying to hide his presence. Confident in his disguise and his skill at playing the role he had taken on, he chose the most straightforward and direct path to the location. The late hour did provide him with some of the protection he seemed to care so little about. The children had already fallen asleep, and all the women, along with most of the warriors, had gone back to their lodges for the night. Only four or five of the warriors remained near the entrance to Uncas's prison, keeping a careful but close watch on how their prisoner was behaving.

When they saw Gamut, along with someone dressed in the familiar costume of their most famous medicine man, they quickly stepped aside to let both men pass. However, they showed no signs of leaving. Instead, they were clearly eager to stay, drawn by their curiosity about the mysterious rituals they naturally expected to witness from such a visit.

Due to the scout's complete inability to speak the Huron language, he had no choice but to rely entirely on David to handle the conversation. Despite David's simple nature, he carried out the instructions he had been given exceptionally well, exceeding even his teacher's highest expectations.

"The Delawares are women!" he shouted, speaking to the warrior who understood a little of the language he was using. "The Americans, my foolish fellow countrymen, have told them to pick up their war axes and attack their fathers in Canada, and they have forgotten they are supposed to be women. Does my brother want to hear 'Le Cerf Agile' beg for his skirts and watch him cry in front of the Hurons at the torture stake?"

The exclamation "Hugh!" delivered with strong approval revealed how much satisfaction the warrior would feel watching such a display of weakness from an enemy he had hated for so long and feared so deeply.

"Then let him step aside, and the cunning man will blow upon the dog. Tell it to my brothers."

The Huron explained what David meant to his companions, who listened to the plan with the kind of pleasure that their wild nature would naturally find in such a sophisticated form of cruelty. They stepped back slightly from the entrance and gestured for the supposed medicine man to come inside. However, the bear, rather than following their instructions, stayed in the position it had assumed and let out a growl:

"The clever man worries that his breath will reach his brothers and drain their courage as well," David continued, building on the suggestion he had received; "they need to move farther away."

The Hurons, who would have considered such a disaster the worst catastrophe that could happen to them, retreated as a group, taking up a position where they were beyond hearing range, while still maintaining a clear view of the lodge entrance. Then, apparently confident in their security, the scout abandoned his post and slowly walked into the place. The interior was quiet and dark, occupied only by the prisoner, and illuminated by the fading coals of a fire that had been used for cooking.

Uncas sat in a far corner, leaning back, his hands and feet tightly bound with strong, painful cords. When the terrifying figure first appeared before the young Mohican, he refused to give the creature even a single look. The scout, who had left David by the entrance to make sure they weren't being watched, decided it was wise to keep up his disguise until he was certain they had privacy. Rather than speaking, he threw himself into performing one of the movements of the animal he was pretending to be. The young Mohican, who initially thought his enemies had brought in a real beast to torture him and test his courage, noticed flaws in those performances that had seemed so convincing to Heyward—imperfections that immediately revealed the fake. If Hawkeye had known how little the skilled Uncas thought of his acting, he probably would have continued the show a bit longer out of spite. But the contemptuous look in the young man's eyes could be interpreted in so many ways that the good scout was saved from the embarrassment of making such a realization. As soon as David gave the agreed-upon signal, a quiet hissing sound echoed through the lodge instead of the fierce growling of the bear.

Uncas had leaned his body back against the hut's wall and shut his eyes, as though he wanted to block out such a despicable and unpleasant sight. However, the instant he heard the serpent's sound, he stood up and looked around on both sides, lowering his head and turning it questioningly in all directions, until his sharp gaze settled on the hairy creature, where it stayed fixed, as if held by some magical force. The same sounds came again, clearly coming from the beast's mouth. Once more the young man's eyes swept across the inside of the lodge, and returning to where they had looked before, he spoke in a deep, muffled voice:

"Hawkeye!"

"Cut his ropes," Hawkeye said to David, who was just approaching them.

The singer followed the command, and Uncas felt his restraints fall away. At that same moment, the dried animal hide rustled, and soon the scout stood upright, revealing his true identity. The Mohican seemed to understand instinctively what his friend had attempted, showing no sign of surprise in his expression or speech. After Hawkeye had removed his rough disguise by simply untying several leather strips, he pulled out a long, gleaming knife and placed it in Uncas's hands.

"The red Hurons are outside," he said; "let us prepare ourselves." At the same time he placed his finger meaningfully on another similar weapon, both being the results of his skill against their enemies during the evening.

"We will go," said Uncas.

"Whither?"

"To the Tortoises; they are the children of my grandfathers."

"Yes, boy," said the scout in English—a language he tended to use when his mind was somewhat distracted; "I believe the same blood flows through your veins; but time and distance have somewhat altered its nature. What should we do about the Mingoes at the door? There are six of them, and this singer is practically useless."

"The Hurons are braggarts," said Uncas, with contempt; "their 'totem' is a moose, and they run like snails. The Delawares are children of the tortoise, and they outrun the deer."

"Yes, young man, there's truth in what you're saying; and I have no doubt that in a sudden dash, you could outrun the entire nation; and in a straight two-mile race, you'd finish and catch your breath again before any one of those scoundrels could get within earshot of the next village. But a white man's strength lies more in his arms than in his legs. As for me, I can strike down a Huron as well as any man; but when it comes to running, those scoundrels would prove too much for me."

Uncas, who had already moved toward the door, ready to lead the way, now stepped back and positioned himself once again at the far end of the lodge. But Hawkeye, who was too absorbed in his own thoughts to notice the movement, kept talking more to himself than to his companion.

"After all," he said, "it's unreasonable to keep one person dependent on another's abilities. So, Uncas, you should take the lead, while I'll put on the disguise again and rely on cleverness since I lack speed."

The young Mohican didn't respond, but calmly crossed his arms and rested his body against one of the vertical posts that held up the hut's wall.

"Well," said the scout looking up at him, "why are you waiting? There will be plenty of time for me, since those scoundrels will chase after you first."

"Uncas will stay," came the calm response.

"For what?"

"To battle against his father's brother, and perish alongside the friend of the Delawares."

"Yes, boy," Hawkeye replied, gripping Uncas's hand firmly between his own strong fingers, "it would have been more like a Mingo than a Mohican if you had abandoned me. But I thought I should make the suggestion, since young people usually value their lives. Well, what cannot be accomplished through direct bravery in warfare must be achieved through clever strategy. Put on the skin; I have no doubt you can act the part of a bear almost as well as I can."

Whatever Uncas might have privately thought about their individual skills in this matter, his serious expression revealed no sense of his own superiority. He quietly and quickly wrapped himself in the animal's hide, then waited for whatever other actions his older companion decided were necessary.

"Listen, friend," Hawkeye said to David, "swapping clothes will really help you out, since you're not used to making do with what you have in the wilderness. Here, take my hunting shirt and cap, and give me your blanket and hat. You'll need to trust me with the book and glasses, plus that little horn of yours too. If we run into each other again when things are better, you'll get everything back, and I'll be mighty grateful on top of that."

David gave up the various items mentioned with such willingness that it would have reflected great generosity on his part, if he hadn't clearly benefited in many ways from the trade. Hawkeye quickly put on the borrowed clothes; and when his restless eyes were hidden behind the spectacles, and his head was topped with the three-cornered hat, since their heights were similar, he could easily have been mistaken for the singer in starlight. Once these arrangements were completed, the scout turned to David and gave him his final instructions.

"Do you tend to be cowardly?" he asked directly, wanting to get a complete understanding of the entire situation before he offered any advice.

"My activities are peaceful, and my temperament, I humbly believe, is deeply inclined toward mercy and love," David replied, somewhat irritated by such a direct challenge to his masculinity; "but no one can claim that I have ever abandoned my faith in the Lord, even in the most desperate circumstances."

"Your greatest danger will come the moment the savages realize they've been tricked. If you don't get killed right then, the fact that you're not a warrior will protect you, and you'll have good reason to hope you'll live to die naturally. If you decide to stay, you'll have to sit here in the shadows and play the role of Uncas until the Indians figure out the deception—and when that happens, as I've already told you, your real test will begin. So make your choice—either make a run for it or stay here."

"Even so," David said firmly, "I will remain in the Delaware's place. He has fought bravely and generously on my behalf, and I will dare this and more in his service."

"You've spoken like a man, and like someone who, with better guidance, could have achieved greater things. Keep your head down and pull in your legs; their shape might reveal the truth too soon. Stay quiet for as long as possible; and it would be smart, when you do speak, to suddenly burst out with one of your yells, which will help remind the Indians that you're not quite as mentally sound as men should be. However, if they do take your scalp, which I trust and believe they won't, you can count on it that Uncas and I won't forget what happened, and we'll get revenge as true warriors and loyal friends should."

"Wait!" David said, realizing they were about to leave him with this promise. "I am an unworthy and humble follower of one who did not teach the damnable principle of revenge. If I should die, therefore, do not seek victims to appease my spirit, but instead forgive those who destroy me; and if you remember them at all, let it be in prayers for the enlightenment of their minds and for their eternal salvation."

The scout paused, seeming lost in thought.

"There's a principle in that," he said, "different from the law of the wilderness; and yet it's fair and noble to think about." Then letting out a heavy sigh, probably among the last he ever drew while longing for a way of life he had abandoned so long ago, he added: "it's what I would want to practice myself, as someone without mixed blood, though it's not always easy to deal with a Native American as you would with a fellow Christian. God bless you, friend; I do believe your instinct isn't far off the mark, when the matter is properly considered, and keeping eternity in mind, though much depends on natural abilities, and the strength of temptation."

So saying, the scout came back and warmly shook David's hand; after this gesture of friendship, he immediately left the lodge, accompanied by the new representative of the beast.

The moment Hawkeye realized the Hurons were watching him, he straightened his tall frame in David's stiff posture, extended his arm as if keeping rhythm, and began what he hoped would pass for an imitation of psalm singing. Fortunately for this risky plan, he was dealing with ears that had little experience with harmonious music, or his terrible attempt would certainly have been discovered. He had to walk dangerously close to the dark cluster of warriors, and the scout's voice grew louder as they approached. When they reached the closest point, the Huron who could speak English reached out his arm and stopped the pretend singing teacher.

"The Delaware dog!" he said, leaning forward and peering through the dim light to catch the expression on the other man's face. "Is he afraid? Will the Hurons hear him groaning?"

A growl, incredibly fierce and realistic, came from the creature, causing the young Indian to let go and jump back, as if to make sure it wasn't a real bear, but rather a fake one, that was rolling in front of him. Hawkeye, who worried his voice might give him away to his clever enemies, happily took advantage of the interruption to burst out again in such an explosion of musical sound that would likely, in a more civilized society, have been called "a grand crash." Among his actual listeners, though, it simply gave him another reason to earn the respect they never deny to those they believe are suffering from mental illness. The small group of Indians stepped back together and allowed what they thought were the magician and his divinely inspired helper to continue.

It took considerable courage for Uncas and the scout to maintain the dignified and deliberate pace they had adopted while passing the lodge, particularly since they immediately noticed that curiosity had overcome fear enough to encourage the watchers to move closer to the hut to observe the results of the magical rituals. Any careless or hasty movement from David could expose them, and time was absolutely essential to ensure the scout's safety. The loud sounds that the scout thought it wise to keep making attracted many curious onlookers to the doorways of various huts as they walked by, and on one or two occasions a menacing-looking warrior crossed their path, driven by superstition and vigilance. They were not interrupted, however, as the darkness of the night and the audacity of their plan proved to be their greatest allies.

The adventurers had escaped from the village and were quickly moving toward the safety of the forest when a loud, prolonged cry echoed from the lodge where Uncas had been held prisoner. The Mohican jumped to his feet and shook off his shaggy disguise, as if the animal he was pretending to be was preparing to make some desperate attempt.

"Wait!" said the scout, grabbing his friend by the shoulder, "let them yell again! It was nothing but amazement."

He had no reason to wait, because in the next moment a sudden eruption of shouts filled the air outside and spread throughout the entire village. Uncas shed his disguise and emerged in his own magnificent form. Hawkeye gave him a gentle tap on the shoulder and moved silently forward.

"Now let the devils pick up our trail!" said the scout, pulling two rifles with all their gear from under a bush and waving "Killdeer" as he passed Uncas his weapon; "at least two of them will pay with their lives."

Then, tossing their equipment onto a lower path, like hunters preparing for their prey, they rushed ahead and quickly disappeared into the dark shadows of the woods.

---

# Chapter XXVII.

"Antony: I shall remember: When Caesar says
Do this, it is performed."
—Julius Caesar

The impatience of the warriors who waited around Uncas's prison, as we have witnessed, had overcome their fear of the medicine man's power. They crept forward carefully, their hearts pounding, toward a crack through which the dim firelight was flickering. For several minutes they mistook David's figure for that of their prisoner; but the very mishap that Hawkeye had predicted took place. Growing tired of keeping his long limbs cramped so close together, the singer gradually allowed his lower legs to stretch out, until one of his awkward feet actually touched and scattered the glowing coals of the fire. At first the Hurons thought the Delaware had been twisted into this shape by magic. But when David, unaware that he was being watched, turned his head and revealed his innocent, gentle face instead of the proud features of their captive, it would have strained the belief of even a native to doubt any longer. They burst into the lodge together, and placing their hands roughly on their prisoner, immediately discovered the deception. Then came the shout that the escaping men first heard. It was followed by the most wild and furious displays of revenge. David, however, steadfast in his resolve to protect his friends' escape, was forced to accept that his own final moment had arrived. Without his book and his pipe, he had to rely on a memory that seldom failed him in such matters; and bursting into a loud and passionate song, he tried to ease his passage into the next world by singing the opening verse of a funeral hymn. The Indians were timely reminded of his condition, and rushing into the open air, they awakened the village in the way already described.

A native warrior fights as he sleeps, without any defensive protection. The alarm sounds had barely been heard before two hundred men were on their feet, ready for battle or pursuit, whichever might be needed. The escape was quickly discovered, and the entire tribe gathered as one around the council lodge, impatiently waiting for direction from their chiefs. In such an urgent situation requiring wisdom, the presence of the clever Magua could hardly be overlooked. His name was called, and everyone looked around in surprise that he had not appeared. Messengers were then sent to his lodge requesting his presence.

In the meantime, some of the fastest and most careful young men were ordered to circle around the clearing, staying hidden in the woods, to make sure that their suspected neighbors, the Delawares, weren't planning any trouble. Women and children rushed back and forth; and, in short, the entire camp showed another scene of wild and savage confusion. Gradually, however, these signs of disorder lessened; and within a few minutes the oldest and most respected chiefs had gathered in the lodge for serious discussion.

The noise of many voices soon revealed that a group was approaching, and they were expected to bring some information that would solve the mystery of this strange surprise. The crowd outside stepped aside, and several warriors entered the area, bringing with them the unfortunate conjurer, who had been left for so long by the scout in captivity.

Despite the fact that this man was viewed very differently among the Hurons, with some having complete faith in his abilities while others considered him a fraud, everyone now listened to him with intense focus. After he finished his short account, the father of the ill woman came forward and, using a few pointed words, shared what he knew about the situation. These two stories provided the right guidance for the follow-up investigation, which was now conducted with the typical shrewdness of indigenous people.

Instead of rushing in a confused and chaotic crowd to the cave, ten of the wisest and most steadfast leaders were chosen to carry out the investigation. Since there was no time to waste, the moment the selection was made, those who had been chosen stood up together and left the area without saying a word. When they reached the entrance, the younger men who were leading stepped aside for their elders, and the entire group moved through the low, dark passage with the determination of warriors prepared to sacrifice themselves for the common good, though they were secretly uncertain about the nature of the force they were about to face.

The outer room of the cave was quiet and dark. The woman lay in her usual spot and position, even though some people there claimed they had seen her carried to the forest by what they believed was the "white men's medicine." This clear and obvious contradiction of the story the father had told made everyone look at him. Irritated by their silent accusation and deeply disturbed by such an inexplicable situation, the chief walked over to the side of the bed and bent down, casting a disbelieving look at her face, as if he couldn't trust what he was seeing. His daughter was dead.

The infallible instinct of nature momentarily took over, and the seasoned warrior covered his eyes in grief. After regaining his composure, he turned to face his companions and, gesturing toward the dead body, spoke in his native tongue:

"My young man's wife has left us! The Great Spirit is angry with his children."

The sad news was received in solemn silence. After a brief pause, one of the older Indians was about to speak when a dark object was seen rolling out of a nearby room into the very center of the space where they stood. Not knowing what kind of beings they were dealing with, the entire group stepped back slightly, and the object, rising upright, revealed the twisted but still fierce and grim features of Magua. The discovery was followed by a collective cry of amazement.

As soon as everyone understood what had really happened to the chief, several knives came out, and his arms and tongue were quickly freed. The Huron stood up and shook himself like a lion leaving its den. He didn't say a word, though his hand moved restlessly on his knife handle, while his dark, threatening eyes looked over the entire group, as if searching for the right target for his first act of revenge.

It was fortunate for Uncas and the scout, and even David, that they were all out of his reach at that moment; for certainly, no elaborate cruelty would have delayed their deaths against the urges of the fierce anger that nearly overwhelmed him. Seeing everywhere faces that he recognized as friends, the savage ground his teeth together like iron files, and suppressed his rage for lack of a victim on whom to release it. This display of fury was observed by everyone present; and from fear of provoking a temper that was already inflamed nearly to the point of madness, several minutes were allowed to pass before another word was spoken. When, however, enough time had gone by, the eldest of the group spoke.

"My friend has found an enemy," he said. "Is he close enough that the Hurons could take their revenge?"

"Let the Delaware die!" shouted Magua in a thunderous voice.

Another long and meaningful silence followed, and once again, it was carefully broken by the same person.

"The Mohican runs fast and can jump great distances," he said, "but my warriors are following his tracks."

"Is he gone?" Magua demanded, his voice so deep and guttural that it seemed to come from the depths of his chest.

"An evil spirit has been among us, and the Delaware has blinded our eyes."

"An evil spirit!" the other repeated mockingly. "It's the spirit that has taken the lives of so many Hurons; the spirit that killed my young men at 'the tumbling river'; that took their scalps at the 'healing spring'; and who has now tied the arms of Le Renard Subtil!"

"Who is my friend talking about?"

"Of the dog who carries the heart and cunning of a Huron under a pale skin—La Longue Carabine."

The mention of such a terrifying name had the expected impact on those listening. However, once they had time to think it over and the warriors realized that their dangerous and bold enemy had actually been inside their own camp causing harm, intense fury replaced their amazement, and all the violent emotions that had been churning within Magua were suddenly felt by his fellow warriors. Some of them ground their teeth in rage, others expressed their emotions through screams, and still others struck at the air wildly as though they were actually hitting the target of their anger. Yet this sudden explosion of anger quickly gave way to the quiet and brooding self-control they typically displayed during periods of rest.

Magua, who had now found time to think things through, changed his approach and took on the bearing of someone who understood how to consider and respond with the seriousness that such an important matter deserved.

"Let's go to my people," he said; "they're waiting for us."

His companions agreed without speaking, and the entire group of warriors left the cave and went back to the council lodge. Once they had taken their seats, everyone looked at Magua, who realized from this attention that they had all agreed he should be the one to tell them what had happened. He stood up and shared his story honestly and completely. The entire deception carried out by both Duncan and Hawkeye was completely exposed, and there was no way left for even the most superstitious members of the tribe to have any doubt about what had really occurred. It was all too clear that they had been insulted, humiliated, and disgracefully tricked. When he finished speaking and sat back down, the assembled tribe—since his listeners essentially included all the warriors of the group—sat looking at each other like men equally amazed by both the boldness and the success of their enemies. Their next concern, however, was finding the ways and chances for revenge.

More pursuers were dispatched to track down the escapees, and then the leaders turned their full attention to the serious matter of planning their next move. Several different strategies were suggested by the senior warriors, one after another, and Magua listened to all of them in silence and with respect. The cunning warrior had regained his composure and strategic thinking, and now moved toward his goal with his usual careful planning and expertise. Only after everyone who wanted to speak had shared their thoughts did he prepare to present his own ideas. His opinions carried extra influence because some of the scouts had already come back and reported that their enemies had been tracked far enough to confirm without doubt that they had sought refuge in the nearby camp of their suspected allies, the Delawares. Armed with this crucial information, the chief carefully presented his plans to his companions, and as could have been expected given his persuasive speaking ability and cleverness, the plans were accepted unanimously. The plans were, in summary, as follows, including both the strategies and the reasoning behind them.

It has already been mentioned that, following a policy they rarely changed, the sisters were separated as soon as they arrived at the Huron village. Magua had quickly realized that by keeping Alice with him, he held the most powerful way to control Cora. When the sisters were separated, he therefore kept Alice close by, while placing the one he valued more in the care of their allies. This arrangement was understood to be only temporary, and was made both to please his neighbors and to follow the unchanging rule of Indian strategy.

While constantly driven by these vengeful urges that rarely rest in a savage, the chief still remained focused on his more lasting personal interests. The foolish mistakes and betrayals of his youth needed to be made right through a long and difficult period of atonement before he could regain the complete trust of his original people; and without trust, there could be no real power within an Indian tribe. In this sensitive and challenging position, the cunning native had used every possible method to grow his influence; and one of his most successful strategies had been how effectively he had won the approval of their powerful and threatening neighbors. The outcome of his approach had met all the goals of his strategy; for the Hurons were not at all free from that basic rule of human nature, which causes people to value their abilities exactly to the extent that others recognize and appreciate them.

While he appeared to be making this obvious sacrifice for broader concerns, Magua never forgot about his personal motivations. These personal goals had been thwarted by the unexpected events that had put all his captives beyond his reach; and he now discovered himself forced into the position of having to ask for favors from those whom he had so recently been trying to accommodate.

Several of the chiefs had suggested elaborate and deceptive plans to catch the Delawares off guard and, by seizing control of their camp, to rescue their prisoners in one decisive strike; for everyone agreed that their honor, their interests, and the peace and happiness of their fallen countrymen urgently demanded that they quickly sacrifice some victims to satisfy their desire for revenge. But Magua had little trouble defeating such dangerous plans that were so risky to carry out and had such uncertain outcomes. He revealed their dangers and flaws with his typical expertise; and only after he had eliminated every obstacle in the form of conflicting advice did he dare to present his own strategies.

He began by appealing to his listeners' pride, a strategy that never fails to capture attention. After listing the numerous occasions when the Hurons had demonstrated their bravery and skill in avenging insults, he launched into an elaborate praise of wisdom as a virtue. He described this quality as the main distinction between beavers and other animals, between animals and humans, and ultimately between the Hurons specifically and all other people. Once he had thoroughly celebrated the value of good judgment, he set out to show how it applied to their tribe's current situation. On one side, he explained, stood their great pale father, the governor of the Canadas, who had viewed his children with disapproval ever since their tomahawks had been stained with so much blood. On the other side was a people as large in number as themselves, who spoke a different tongue, had different concerns, bore them no love, and would welcome any excuse to bring them into disfavor with the great white chief. He then discussed their needs, the gifts they deserved to receive for their previous service, how far they were from their traditional hunting territories and home villages, and why they must rely more on careful thinking and less on their desires in such dangerous times. When he noticed that while the elder men praised his restraint, many of the most fierce and respected warriors were listening to these calculated proposals with dark expressions, he cleverly steered them back to the topic they cherished most. He spoke directly about the rewards of their wisdom, which he confidently declared would result in complete and final victory over their foes. He even suggested mysteriously that their success could be expanded, with appropriate care, to encompass the destruction of everyone they had cause to despise. In essence, he mixed the martial with the clever, the clear with the hidden, in such a way as to appeal to both groups' inclinations and give each side reason for hope, while preventing either from claiming they fully understood his true purpose.

The speaker or politician who can create this kind of situation is usually well-liked by the people of their time, regardless of how history might judge them later. Everyone could sense that there was more being communicated than what was actually said out loud, and each person was convinced that the underlying message was exactly what their own abilities allowed them to grasp, or what their personal desires made them expect to hear.

In this favorable situation, it's not surprising that Magua's leadership won out. The tribe agreed to act thoughtfully, and unanimously they placed the management of the entire matter under the authority of the chief who had proposed such sensible and clear solutions.

Magua had finally achieved the main goal of all his scheming and ambitious efforts. He had completely won back the standing he had lost with his people, and he discovered that he was now positioned as their leader. He was, in reality, their chief; and as long as he could keep their support, no king could wield more absolute power, particularly while the tribe remained in enemy territory. Setting aside, then, any pretense of seeking advice from others, he took on the serious demeanor of command required to uphold the respect his position demanded.

Messengers were sent out to gather information in various directions; scouts were commanded to move close to the Delaware camp and assess the situation; the warriors were sent back to their homes with notice that their services would be required soon; and the women and children were told to withdraw, with a warning that their duty was to remain quiet. After these different preparations were completed, Magua walked through the village, pausing occasionally to make visits where he believed his presence would be pleasing to the person. He strengthened his allies in their trust, steadied those who were uncertain, and pleased everyone. Then he went to his own dwelling. The wife that the Huron chief had left behind when he was driven away from his people was dead. He had no children; and he now lived in a shelter without any companion whatsoever. It was, in reality, the run-down and isolated building where David had been found, and whom he had allowed in his presence on those rare occasions when they encountered each other, with the scornful indifference of arrogant superiority.

Magua withdrew to this place after finishing his political maneuvering. While others slept, he found no rest and didn't even try to find it. If someone had been curious enough to observe the newly chosen chief's actions, they would have seen him sitting in a corner of his dwelling, contemplating his future schemes from the moment he retreated until the time he had set for the warriors to gather once more. From time to time, air drifted through the gaps in the shelter, and the dim flame that danced around the glowing coals cast shifting light across the brooding loner. In those moments, it wouldn't have been hard to imagine the dark-skinned warrior as the Devil himself, dwelling on his perceived injustices and devising wickedness.

Long before dawn broke, however, one warrior after another entered Magua's isolated hut, until twenty of them had gathered. Each carried his rifle and all the other equipment of war, though their war paint showed peaceful intentions. The arrival of these fierce-looking men went unnoticed: some took seats in the shadowy areas of the dwelling, while others stood like motionless statues, until the entire designated group had assembled.

Then Magua stood up and signaled for them to move forward, taking the lead himself. The others followed their leader one by one, maintaining that familiar formation that has earned the distinctive name "Indian file." Unlike other men involved in the exciting business of warfare, they slipped away from their camp quietly and without being noticed, looking more like a group of drifting ghosts than warriors seeking fleeting fame through acts of reckless courage.

Instead of taking the path that led straight to the Delaware camp, Magua guided his group for some distance down the winding stream and along the small artificial lake created by the beavers. Dawn was breaking as they entered the clearing that had been made by those wise and hardworking animals. Although Magua, who had put on his traditional clothing again, wore the outline of a fox on the dressed skin that formed his robe, there was one chief in his group who carried the beaver as his special symbol, or "totem." It would have been a kind of sacrilege if this man had passed by such a powerful community of his imagined relatives without showing some sign of his respect. Therefore, he stopped and spoke in words as gentle and friendly as if he were talking to more intelligent creatures. He called the animals his cousins and reminded them that his protective influence was the reason they remained safe, while many greedy traders were encouraging the Indians to kill them. He promised to continue his protection and warned them to be thankful. After this, he spoke about the mission he was involved in and suggested, though with enough tact and indirect language, that it would be wise for them to give their relative some of that wisdom for which they were so famous.[1]

> [1] These speeches by the beasts were common among the Indians. They would often speak to their victims in this manner, criticizing them for being cowardly or praising their courage, depending on whether they showed bravery or weakness while enduring their suffering.

During this remarkable speech, the speaker's companions remained as serious and attentive to his words as if they were all equally convinced of its appropriateness. Once or twice dark shapes were seen rising to the water's surface, and the Huron showed satisfaction, believing that his words were having an effect. Just as he finished his speech, the head of a large beaver emerged from the entrance of a lodge whose mud walls had been badly damaged, and which the group had assumed, based on its location, to be empty. Such an unusual display of trust was interpreted by the speaker as a very positive sign; and although the animal withdrew somewhat hastily, he was generous with his gratitude and praise.

When Magua decided that enough time had been spent allowing the warrior to enjoy his family reunion, he signaled once more for the group to move forward. As the Indians departed together, walking so quietly that an ordinary person wouldn't have heard their footsteps, the same dignified-looking beaver cautiously poked its head out from hiding again. If any of the Hurons had bothered to glance back, they would have witnessed the creature observing their departure with such keen attention and intelligence that it could easily have been mistaken for human reasoning. The animal's behavior was so remarkably clear and purposeful that even the most skilled observer would have struggled to explain what they were seeing, until the moment when the group disappeared into the forest, at which point everything would have become clear upon seeing the complete animal emerge from its shelter, revealing in the process the solemn face of Chingachgook beneath his furry disguise.

---

# Chapter XXVIII.

"Please be brief, I ask of you; as you can see, this is a busy time for me."
—Much Ado About Nothing.

The Delaware tribe, or more accurately half-tribe, which has been mentioned so frequently and whose current campsite was located so close to the temporary Huron village, could gather roughly the same number of warriors as their neighbors. Like the people around them, they had followed Montcalm into English territory and were launching devastating attacks on Mohawk hunting grounds. However, they had chosen, with the secretive caution so typical of native peoples, to hold back their support precisely when it was needed most. The French had explained this surprising betrayal by their ally in several different ways. The most common belief, though, was that the Delawares had been swayed by respect for an old treaty that had once placed them under the Six Nations' military protection, making them hesitant now to fight against their former protectors. As for the tribe itself, it had simply informed Montcalm through his messengers, with characteristic Native American directness, that their tomahawks had grown dull and they needed time to sharpen them. The shrewd Canadian commander had decided it was smarter to tolerate an inactive ally rather than risk turning him into an active enemy through harsh or poorly considered actions.

On that morning when Magua led his silent group from the beaver settlement into the forests, as previously described, the sun rose over the Delaware camp as though it had suddenly illuminated a bustling community actively engaged in all the typical activities of midday. The women moved quickly from lodge to lodge, some busy preparing their morning meal, a few focused intently on finding the necessities their way of life required, but most stopping to share hurried and whispered conversations with their friends. The warriors gathered in small groups, thinking more than they talked, and when they did speak a few words, they sounded like men who carefully considered their thoughts. Hunting equipment could be seen everywhere throughout the lodges, yet no one left to hunt. Here and there a warrior examined his weapons with a level of attention rarely given to such tools when the only expected enemies are the wild animals of the forest. And from time to time, the eyes of an entire group would turn together toward a large and quiet lodge at the center of the village, as though it held whatever occupied all their minds.

During this scene, a man suddenly appeared at the far end of a rocky platform that formed the village's foundation. He carried no weapons, and his war paint seemed to soften rather than heighten the natural severity of his stern face. When he came into full view of the Delawares, he stopped and made a peaceful gesture by raising his arm toward the sky, then letting it fall meaningfully onto his chest. The village inhabitants responded to his greeting with a quiet murmur of welcome and encouraged him to come forward with similar signs of friendship. Reassured by these welcoming signals, the dark figure left the edge of the natural stone terrace where he had stood for a moment, silhouetted sharply against the rosy morning sky, and walked with dignity straight into the heart of the settlement. As he drew closer, the only sounds were the jingling of the delicate silver ornaments that adorned his arms and neck, and the soft chiming of the small bells that decorated his deerskin moccasins. While he walked forward, he made many polite gestures of greeting to the men he encountered, though he ignored the women entirely, like someone who considered their approval unimportant for his current mission. When he reached the group where it was clear from their proud bearing that the main chiefs had gathered, the stranger stopped, and the Delawares could see that the agile and upright figure standing before them was the famous Huron chief, Le Renard Subtil.

His welcome was serious, quiet, and cautious. The warriors standing in front moved aside, clearing a path through their actions to their most respected speaker, someone who could speak all the languages that were used among the northern native peoples.

"The wise Huron is welcome," said the Delaware, speaking in the language of the Maquas; "he has come to eat his succotash with his brothers of the lakes."[1]

> [1] A dish made from cracked corn and beans. It is also commonly used by white people. By corn, this refers to maize.

"He has arrived," Magua repeated, bowing his head with the dignity of an eastern prince.

The chief extended his arm and grasped the other man by the wrist, and they exchanged friendly greetings once again. The Delaware then invited his guest to come into his lodge and share his morning meal. The invitation was accepted, and the two warriors, accompanied by three or four of the elderly men, walked quietly away, leaving the rest of the tribe consumed with curiosity to understand the reasons for such an unusual visit, yet not showing the slightest impatience through any gesture or word.

During the brief and simple meal that followed, the conversation remained extremely careful, focusing entirely on the events of the hunt in which Magua had recently participated. It would have been impossible for even the most refined manners to appear more natural in treating the visit as an ordinary occurrence than his hosts did, despite the fact that every person present was perfectly aware that it must be connected to some hidden purpose, and probably one of significance to themselves. When everyone's hunger had been satisfied, the women cleared away the wooden plates and bowls, and the two groups began to prepare themselves for a delicate battle of wits.

"Has my great Canadian father turned his attention back to his Huron children?" asked the Delaware speaker.

"When has it ever been any different?" Magua replied. "He calls my people 'most beloved'."

The Delaware man solemnly nodded his agreement to what he knew was untrue, and went on:

"The tomahawks of your young men have been very red."

"That's true; but they are now bright and dull; for the Yankees are dead, and the Delawares are our neighbors."

The other man acknowledged the peaceful compliment with a hand gesture and stayed quiet. Then Magua, as if the reference to the massacre had triggered a memory, asked:

"Is my prisoner causing problems for my brothers?"

"She is welcome."

"The route between the Hurons and the Delawares is short and clear; let her be sent to my women, if she causes trouble for my brother."

"She is welcome," the chief of the other nation replied with even greater emphasis.

The confused Magua remained quiet for several minutes, seemingly unbothered by the rejection he had just received in his first attempt to reclaim Cora.

"Do my young warriors leave the Delawares space in the mountains for their hunting?" he finally continued.

"The Lenape rule their own hills," the other replied with a touch of pride.

"That's good. Justice rules over Native Americans. Why should they polish their tomahawks and sharpen their knives to fight one another? Aren't the white people more numerous than swallows during springtime?"

"Excellent!" shouted two or three of his listeners at the same time.

Magua paused briefly, allowing his words to ease the emotions of the Delawares, before he continued:

"Haven't there been unfamiliar moccasins in the forest? Haven't my brothers caught the scent of white men's tracks?"

"Let my Canadian father come," the other replied evasively; "his children are ready to see him."

"When the great chief arrives, he comes to smoke with the Indians in their homes. The Hurons also say he is welcome. But the English have long reach and legs that never grow weary! My young warriors dreamed they had seen the path of the English near the Delaware village!"

"They will not find the Lenape asleep."

"That's good. A warrior who keeps his eyes open can spot his enemy," Magua said, changing his approach again when he realized he couldn't break through his companion's careful guard. "I've brought presents for my brother. Your people wouldn't join the war because they didn't think it was right, but their allies have remembered where they live."

When he had announced his generous intentions, the cunning chief stood up and solemnly displayed his gifts before the amazed eyes of his hosts. The presents consisted mainly of worthless trinkets that had been stolen from the murdered women of William Henry. In distributing these baubles, the shrewd Huron showed as much skill as he had in choosing them. While he gave the more valuable items to the two most respected warriors, including his host, he accompanied his gifts to the lesser men with such perfectly timed and fitting compliments that they had no reason to feel slighted. In essence, the entire ritual combined profit with flattery so skillfully that the giver could easily see the impact of his cleverly calculated generosity mixed with praise reflected in the eyes of those who received it.

This clever and strategic move by Magua produced immediate results. The Delawares' serious expressions gave way to much more welcoming looks, and their leader, after examining his own generous portion of the loot for several moments with obvious satisfaction, repeated with great emphasis the words:

"My brother is a wise chief. He is welcome."

"The Hurons care deeply for their friends the Delawares," Magua replied. "Why wouldn't they? They share the same sun that colors their skin, and their righteous men will hunt together in the same lands after they die. All red-skinned people should be allies and watch the white men with vigilant eyes. Hasn't my brother detected spies lurking in the forest?"

The Delaware, whose name in English meant "Hard Heart," a title that the French had translated as "le Coeur-dur," abandoned that stubborn determination which had likely earned him such a meaningful name. His expression became noticeably less severe and he now chose to respond more straightforwardly.

"Strange moccasins have been spotted around my camp. Their tracks have been followed right into my lodges."

"Did my brother drive away the dogs?" asked Magua, without referring in any way to the chief's earlier evasive answer.

"That wouldn't be right. The Lenape people always welcome strangers."

"The stranger, but not the spy."

"Would the Americans send their women as spies? Didn't the Huron chief say he captured women in the battle?"

"He spoke the truth. The Americans have sent out their scouts. They have been in my lodges, but they found no one there to greet them. Then they ran to the Delawares—for, they say, the Delawares are our friends; their hearts have turned away from their Canadian father!"

This suggestion hit close to home, and in a more civilized society, it would have earned Magua a reputation as a skilled diplomat. The tribe's recent betrayal had, as they were well aware, exposed the Delawares to considerable criticism from their French allies, and they now realized that their future actions would be viewed with suspicion and mistrust. It didn't take much understanding of cause and effect to see that this situation would likely prove extremely damaging to their future plans. Their remote villages, their hunting territories, and hundreds of their women and children, along with a significant portion of their military strength, were actually located within French-controlled land. As a result, this troubling announcement was received exactly as Magua had hoped—with clear displeasure, if not outright fear.

"Let my father look at my face," said Le Coeur-dur; "he will see no change. It is true, my young men did not go out to war; they had dreams telling them not to do so. But they love and respect the great white chief."

"Will he think the same when he learns that his greatest enemy is being fed in his children's camp? When he discovers that a bloodthirsty Yankee sits at your fire? That the pale-skinned man who has killed so many of his friends moves freely among the Delawares? Go! My great Canada father is no fool!"

"Where is the Englishman that the Delawares fear?" replied the other; "who has killed my young men? Who is the deadly enemy of my Great Father?"

"The Long Rifle!"

The Delaware warriors were startled when they heard the well-known name, and their amazement revealed that they were just now discovering, for the first time, that someone so famous among the Indian allies of France was in their control.

"What does my brother mean?" Le Coeur-dur demanded, his voice carrying a tone of wonder that far surpassed the typical indifference of his people.

"A Huron never lies!" Magua replied coldly, resting his head against the side of the lodge and pulling his thin robe across his bronze chest. "Let the Delawares count their prisoners; they will find one whose skin is neither red nor pale."

A long, thoughtful silence followed. The chief spoke privately with his companions, and messengers were sent out to gather some of the most respected men from the tribe.

As one warrior after another arrived, each was informed about the crucial news that Magua had just shared. They all responded with the same look of astonishment and the characteristic low, deep, throaty sound of surprise. The information passed from person to person until the entire camp was deeply stirred. The women stopped their work to catch whatever words accidentally escaped from the lips of the warriors in discussion. The boys abandoned their games and walked boldly among their fathers, gazing up with fascinated respect as they listened to the brief expressions of amazement that so openly revealed their admiration for their despised enemy's boldness. In essence, every activity was set aside temporarily, and all other concerns seemed forgotten so that the tribe could freely express their emotions in their own distinctive way.

When the excitement had somewhat subsided, the elderly men settled down seriously to consider what their tribe's honor and safety required them to do in such delicate and difficult circumstances. Throughout all these activities, and amid the general chaos, Magua had not only kept his position, but maintained the exact same posture he had first assumed against the side of the lodge, where he remained as motionless and apparently as indifferent as if the outcome meant nothing to him. However, not a single hint of his hosts' future plans escaped his watchful gaze. With his thorough understanding of the nature of the people he was dealing with, he predicted every decision they would make; and it could almost be said that, in many cases, he understood their intentions even before they understood them themselves.

The Delaware council was brief. When it concluded, a flurry of activity indicated that it would be immediately followed by a ceremonial and official gathering of the entire tribe. Since such assemblies were uncommon and only convened for matters of utmost significance, the cunning Huron, who remained seated separately as a shrewd and shadowy observer of the events, now understood that all his schemes had to reach their ultimate conclusion. He therefore departed from the lodge and walked quietly outside to the area in front of the camp, where the warriors were already starting to gather.

About thirty minutes passed before everyone, including the women and children, had taken their designated positions. The delay resulted from the serious preparations considered essential for such a formal and extraordinary gathering. When the sun appeared above the mountain peaks, where the Delawares had established their camp, most people were seated. As the bright sunlight streamed from behind the line of trees crowning the ridge, it illuminated what was likely one of the most solemn, focused, and deeply engaged crowds ever touched by the morning light. The assembly numbered slightly more than a thousand people.

In this gathering of such dignified tribal members, you would never find any eager person seeking early recognition, ready to stir up the listeners toward some rushed and possibly unwise debate just to boost their own reputation. Such reckless and arrogant behavior would permanently destroy any promising young mind. Only the eldest and most seasoned men had the right to present the topic of discussion to the people. Until one of these elders decided to take action, no military achievements, natural talents, or fame as a speaker would justify even the smallest interruption. On this particular occasion, the old warrior who had the privilege to speak remained quiet, apparently overwhelmed by the importance of his topic. The silence had already lasted much longer than the customary thoughtful pause that always came before a meeting; yet not even the youngest child showed any sign of restlessness or confusion. From time to time, someone would lift their gaze from the ground, where most people kept their eyes focused, and glance toward a specific dwelling that was not really different from the others surrounding it, except for the special attention that had been given to shield it from harsh weather conditions.

Eventually, one of those quiet murmurs that tend to ripple through a crowd was heard, and the entire nation rose to their feet as if moved by a single impulse. At that moment, the door of the lodge in question opened, and three men emerged from it, walking slowly toward the place where the council was being held. All three were elderly, even older than the most senior person present, but the one in the middle, who leaned on his companions for support, had lived through so many years that few humans are ever allowed to reach such an age. His body, which had once been tall and straight like a cedar tree, was now bent under the weight of more than a century of life. The quick, graceful stride of an Indian warrior was gone, and instead he was forced to make his slow way across the ground, moving forward inch by inch. His dark, lined face created a striking and remarkable contrast with the long white hair that flowed over his shoulders, so thick that it suggested generations had likely come and gone since it had last been cut.

The clothing of this patriarch—for that's what he could rightfully be called, given his great age combined with his kinship and authority among his people—was elaborate and impressive, though it followed the traditional styles of his tribe. His robe was made from the finest animal skins that had been stripped of their fur to allow for hieroglyphic depictions of various military achievements from past eras. His chest was covered with medals, some made of solid silver and one or two crafted from gold, gifts from different Christian rulers throughout his long lifetime. He also wore bracelets and bands around his ankles, both made from the same precious metal. His head, where all the hair had been allowed to grow since he had long given up the pursuits of war, was crowned with a kind of metal headband that held smaller, more brilliant decorations that gleamed among the shiny colors of three hanging ostrich feathers, dyed deep black, creating a striking contrast against his snow-white hair. His tomahawk was almost completely covered in silver, and the handle of his knife gleamed like it was made from solid gold.

As soon as the initial buzz of excitement and awe that this revered figure's sudden arrival had stirred began to settle down, the name "Tamenund" passed quietly from person to person. Magua had frequently heard about this wise and fair Delaware leader's legendary reputation; his fame had grown so great that people believed he possessed the extraordinary ability to communicate directly with the Great Spirit, and his name had eventually been passed down, with minor changes, to the white settlers who had taken over his ancestral lands, where they regarded him as the mythical guardian saint of their vast territory. The Huron chief, understanding the significance of this moment, quickly pushed forward through the crowd to find a better position where he could get a closer look at the face of the man whose judgment would likely have such a profound impact on his own fate.[2]

> [2] The Americans sometimes referred to their guardian saint as Tamenay, which was a distorted version of the famous chief's name being presented here. Numerous stories exist that tell of Tamenund's character and influence.

The old man's eyes were closed, as if they had grown tired from witnessing the selfish workings of human emotions for so long. His skin color was different from most of those around him, being richer and darker, the latter effect created by delicate and intricate lines forming complex yet beautiful patterns that had been traced across most of his body through tattooing. Despite the Huron's position, he walked past the watchful and silent Magua without acknowledgment, and leaning on his two respected supporters, he made his way to the elevated area where the crowd had gathered, seating himself in the center of his people with the dignity of a king and the bearing of a father.

Nothing could exceed the reverence and love with which this unexpected visit from someone who seemed to belong more to another world than to this one was received by his people. After an appropriate and respectful pause, the leading chiefs stood up, and approaching the patriarch, they placed his hands reverently upon their heads, appearing to seek a blessing. The younger men were satisfied with touching his robe, or even coming near his person, so they could breathe in the presence of someone so aged, so righteous, and so brave. Only the most distinguished among the young warriors even dared to perform this latter ceremony, while the great majority of the crowd considered it sufficient happiness simply to look upon a figure so deeply revered and so well loved. When these acts of love and respect were completed, the chiefs withdrew once more to their respective places, and silence fell over the entire encampment.

After a brief pause, several young men who had received whispered instructions from one of Tamenund's elderly attendants stood up, left the gathering, and went into the lodge that had been the focus of so much attention all morning. Within minutes they emerged again, accompanying the people who had prompted all these ceremonial preparations toward the place of judgment. The crowd parted to create a pathway; and once the group had passed through, it closed back together, forming a wide and compact ring of people arranged in an open circle.

---

# Chapter XXIX.

"The assembly seated, rising o'er the rest,
 Achilles thus the king of men addressed."
—Pope's Iliad

Cora stood at the front of the prisoners, wrapping her arms around Alice's in a display of sisterly affection. Despite the frightening and threatening presence of hostile warriors surrounding them on all sides, the noble-hearted young woman couldn't let concern for her own safety stop her from keeping her gaze fixed on Alice's pale and worried face as her sister trembled with fear. Heyward stood close beside them, caring deeply about both women, though in this moment of intense uncertainty, he could barely determine whether his feelings leaned more toward the one he loved most. Hawkeye had positioned himself slightly behind the others, showing respect for his companions' higher social standing—a courtesy that their shared misfortune couldn't make him abandon. Uncas was not there.

When complete silence returned, and after the customary long, dramatic pause, one of the two elderly chiefs who sat beside the patriarch stood up and called out loudly in very clear English:

"Which of my prisoners is La Longue Carabine?"

Neither Duncan nor the scout responded. Duncan, however, looked around at the dark and quiet gathering, and stepped back when his eyes landed on Magua's hostile face. He immediately realized that this cunning savage was secretly involved in their current trial before the tribe, and he decided to create as many obstacles as possible to prevent his evil schemes from succeeding. He had already seen one example of the Indians' swift justice, and now he feared that his companion would be chosen for a second punishment. Faced with this difficult situation, with little or no time to think, he suddenly decided to protect his precious friend, regardless of any danger to himself. Before he could speak, however, the question was asked again more loudly and more clearly.

"Give us weapons," the young man arrogantly responded, "and put us in those woods over there. Our actions will speak for themselves!"

"This is the warrior whose name we've all been hearing about!" the chief replied, looking at Heyward with the kind of curious fascination that people naturally show when they first encounter someone who has become famous through achievement or chance, good deeds or wrongdoing. "What brings this white man to the Delaware camp?"

"My necessities. I come for food, shelter, and friends."

"That's impossible. The forest is filled with game. A warrior's head needs no shelter other than a clear sky; and the Delawares are enemies, not friends of the English. Go, your mouth has spoken while your heart remained silent."

Duncan, feeling somewhat uncertain about how to proceed, stayed quiet; but the scout, who had been listening carefully to everything that had happened, now moved steadily forward to the front.

"I didn't respond when they called for La Longue Carabine, and it wasn't because of shame or fear," he said, "since neither of those qualities belongs to an honest man. But I don't accept the Mingoes' right to give a name to someone whose friends have already recognized his abilities in this area; especially since their title is false, because 'killdeer' has a grooved barrel and isn't a carbine. I am the man, however, who received the name Nathaniel from my family; the honor of being called Hawkeye from the Delawares, who live along their own river; and whom the Iroquois have taken it upon themselves to call the 'Long Rifle', without any permission from the person who has the most say in the matter."

The eyes of everyone present, which had been seriously studying Duncan's appearance, now instantly turned toward the tall, straight figure of this new person claiming the distinguished title. It wasn't particularly surprising that two people would be willing to claim such a great honor, since impostors, while uncommon, were not unheard of among the natives; but it was absolutely essential to the fair and strict purposes of the Delawares that there be no error in this matter. Some of their elders spoke together privately, and then, it appeared, they decided to question their visitor about the subject.

"My brother has told me that a snake has slipped into my camp," the chief said to Magua. "Which one is he?"

The Huron pointed to the scout.

"Would a wise Delaware trust the howling of a wolf?" Duncan declared, now even more convinced of his old enemy's malicious plans: "a dog never deceives, but when has a wolf ever been known to tell the truth?"

Magua's eyes blazed with fury, but suddenly remembering the importance of keeping his composure, he turned away in silent contempt, confident that the wisdom of the Indians would surely uncover the true facts of the disputed matter. His confidence proved justified, for after another brief discussion, the cautious Delaware approached him once more and conveyed the chiefs' decision, though he expressed it in the most respectful terms.

"My brother has been called a liar," he said, "and his friends are angry. They will demonstrate that he has told the truth. Give my prisoners weapons, and let them prove who is the real man."

Magua pretended to view this suggestion, which he knew full well came from suspicion about his honesty, as a mark of respect, and he nodded his agreement, quite pleased that his truthfulness would be backed up by such an expert shooter as the scout. The weapons were immediately given to the two friendly competitors, and they were told to shoot over the heads of the sitting crowd at a clay pot that happened to be resting on a tree stump about fifty yards away from where they were standing.

Heyward quietly smiled at the thought of competing with the scout, though he decided to continue the deception until he learned what Magua's true intentions were.

Lifting his rifle with extreme care and taking aim three separate times, he fired. The bullet struck the wood just a few inches from the target, and everyone exclaimed with satisfaction, recognizing the shot as evidence of exceptional skill with the weapon. Even Hawkeye nodded his head, as though acknowledging it was better than he had anticipated. However, rather than showing any desire to compete with the skilled marksman, he stood resting against his rifle for over a minute, like someone completely lost in deep thought. He was roused from this contemplation, though, by one of the young Indians who had provided the weapons, who now tapped his shoulder and spoke in heavily broken English:

"Can the pale face beat it?"

"Yes, Huron!" the scout shouted, lifting the short rifle in his right hand and shaking it at Magua with such apparent ease that it might have been a reed. "Yes, Huron, I could kill you right now, and no force on earth could stop me! A hawk swooping down on a dove isn't more certain of its target than I am of you at this moment, if I chose to put a bullet through your heart! Why shouldn't I? Why!—because my nature as a white man forbids it, and I might bring harm to innocent people. If you know anything about God, thank Him in your heart, because you have good reason to!"

The scout's flushed face, furious eyes, and imposing figure filled everyone who heard him with a sense of hidden fear. The Delawares held their breath in anticipation, but Magua himself, even though he doubted his enemy's restraint, stayed motionless and composed where he stood, pressed in by the crowd, as if he had grown from that very spot.

"Get out of here," the young Delaware said again, standing close beside the scout.

"Beat what, you fool—what?" shouted Hawkeye, still waving the weapon angrily above his head, though his eyes no longer searched for Magua.

"If the white man is truly the warrior he claims to be," said the elderly chief, "let him strike closer to the target."

The scout burst into loud laughter—a sound that struck Heyward as unnaturally jarring in their surroundings. Then, letting the object drop heavily into his outstretched left hand, it exploded on impact, sending pieces of the container flying through the air and scattering them in all directions. Almost immediately afterward, the clattering sound of his rifle echoed as he let it fall dismissively to the ground.

The first impression of such an unusual scene was captivating wonder. Then a quiet, but growing murmur, spread through the crowd, and eventually grew into sounds that showed a sharp disagreement in the feelings of the onlookers. While some openly expressed their approval at such extraordinary skill, by far the greater part of the tribe was inclined to believe the success of the shot was the result of luck. Heyward was quick to support an opinion that was so favorable to his own claims.

"It was pure luck!" he shouted; "no one can hit a target without taking aim!"

"Chance!" repeated the agitated woodsman, who was now stubbornly determined to maintain his identity at any cost, and who completely missed Heyward's subtle hints to go along with the deception. "Does that lying Huron over there also think it's chance? Give him another rifle, and put us face to face, without any cover or evasive moves, and let Providence and our own skill decide the matter between us! I'm not making this offer to you, major, because we share the same blood and serve the same master."

"It's obvious that the Huron is lying," Heyward replied calmly; "you heard him yourself claim that you are La Longue Carabine."

It would have been impossible to say what forceful declaration the obstinate Hawkeye would have made next, in his reckless desire to prove his identity, if the elderly Delaware had not intervened once more.

"The hawk that descends from the clouds can come back whenever it chooses," he said; "give them the guns."

This time the scout grabbed the rifle eagerly; and Magua, even though he watched the shooter's movements with suspicious eyes, had no more reason to worry.

"Now let's prove, in front of this group of Delawares, which one of us is the better man," shouted the scout, tapping the stock of his rifle with the same finger that had pulled so many deadly triggers.

"You see that gourd hanging on that tree over there, major; if you're a marksman good enough for the frontier, let me see you break it!"

Duncan spotted the target and got ready to take his turn. The gourd was one of the typical small containers that the Indians used, hanging from a dead branch of a small pine tree by a strip of deerskin, positioned at the full distance of one hundred yards. Self-love creates such strange feelings that the young soldier, even though he knew his savage judges' opinions meant nothing, forgot why the contest had started and simply wanted to do well. We had already seen that his shooting ability was quite respectable, and he now decided to demonstrate his finest skills. Even if his life had been at stake, Duncan could not have aimed more carefully or cautiously. He fired; and three or four young Indians who rushed forward when they heard the shot called out that the bullet had hit the tree, just slightly to one side of the intended target. The warriors made a shared sound of approval, and then looked with curiosity at what his competitor would do next.

"That might work for the Royal Americans!" Hawkeye said, laughing again in his own quiet, genuine way. "But if my rifle had missed the mark that often, many a marten whose fur now warms a lady's muff would still be running through the forest. And many a bloodthirsty Mingo who has gone to meet his maker would still be causing trouble between the colonies to this very day. I hope the woman who owns this gourd has more of them in her lodge, because this one will never hold water again!"

The scout had shaken his priming and cocked his weapon while speaking, and as he finished, he stepped back with one foot and slowly lifted the muzzle from the ground: the movement was steady, uniform, and in one direction. When it reached a perfect level, it remained for a single moment without tremor or variation, as though both man and rifle were carved from stone. During that motionless instant, it discharged its contents in a bright, flashing sheet of flame. Once again the young Indians leaped forward, but their frantic search and disappointed expressions revealed that no traces of the bullet could be found.

"Go!" the old chief said to the scout, his voice filled with strong disgust. "You are a wolf in the skin of a dog. I will speak to the 'Long Rifle' of the Americans."

"Ah! If I had that rifle that gave you the name you're using, I'd promise to cut the strap and drop the water container without breaking it!" Hawkeye replied, completely unruffled by the other man's attitude. "You fools, if you want to find a marksman's bullet in these woods, you need to look at the target itself, not around it!"

The young Native Americans immediately understood what he meant—this time he had spoken in the Delaware language—and pulling the gourd down from the tree, they raised it high with a triumphant cry, showing a hole in its bottom where the bullet had pierced through after first entering the usual opening in the center of its top. At this surprising display, a loud and enthusiastic expression of delight erupted from every warrior who was there.

This settled the matter and firmly established Hawkeye's fearsome reputation. The curious and admiring gazes that had been focused on Heyward were now turned toward the weathered figure of the scout, who immediately became the main focus of attention for the innocent and unspoiled people surrounding him. When the sudden uproar had quieted down somewhat, the elderly chief continued his examination.

"Why did you want to block my ears?" he said, speaking to Duncan; "are the Delawares foolish enough that they couldn't tell the difference between a young panther and a cat?"

"They will discover that the Huron is a singing-bird," said Duncan, trying to use the symbolic language of the natives.

"That's good. We'll find out who can make men stop listening. Brother," the chief continued, turning to look at Magua, "the Delawares are paying attention."

Thus chosen, and directly asked to state his purpose, the Huron stood up; and moving with great care and dignity into the very center of the circle, where he found himself face to face with the prisoners, he positioned himself to speak. Before he began to talk, however, he slowly looked around at the entire living wall of serious faces, as if to adjust his words to match what his listeners could understand. He gave Hawkeye a look of respectful hostility; he looked at Duncan with unmistakable hatred; he barely bothered to acknowledge Alice's cowering figure; but when his gaze fell upon Cora's strong, commanding, yet beautiful form, his eyes paused for a moment, with an expression that would have been hard to interpret. Then, filled with his own sinister plans, he spoke in the language of the Canadas, a dialect that he knew well was understood by most of those listening.

"The Spirit that created people gave them different colors," began the clever Huron. "Some are darker than the lazy bear. These He declared should be slaves; and He commanded them to work without end, like the beaver. You can hear them moan, when the southern wind blows, louder than the bellowing buffalo, along the banks of the great salt water, where the large ships come and go carrying them in groups. Some He created with skin lighter than the white ermine of the woods; and these He commanded to be merchants; servants to their women, and predators to their slaves. He gave this people the character of the pigeon; wings that never grow weary; offspring, more numerous than the leaves on the trees, and hunger to consume the earth. He gave them voices like the deceptive cry of the wildcat; hearts like rabbits; the craftiness of the pig (but not of the fox), and arms longer than the legs of the moose. With his voice he blocks the ears of the Indians; his heart shows him to hire warriors to fight his wars; his craftiness tells him how to gather the riches of the earth; and his arms surround the land from the shores of the salt water to the islands of the great lake. His greed makes him ill. God gave him plenty, and still he desires everything. Such are the pale faces.

"The Great Spirit created some people with skin brighter and redder than that sun up there," Magua continued, pointing dramatically toward the dim orb that was fighting its way through the hazy atmosphere near the horizon. "He shaped these people according to His own vision. He gave them this island just as He had created it, covered with forests and filled with wild animals. The wind cleared their land for them; the sun and rain made their crops grow; and the snows arrived to remind them to give thanks. Why would they need roads for travel! They could see through the mountains! While the beavers labored, they rested in the shade and watched. The breezes kept them cool during summer; in winter, animal hides kept them warm. When they fought each other, it was to prove their manhood. They were courageous; they were fair; they were content."

Here the speaker stopped and looked around once more to see if his story had stirred the emotions of those listening. Everywhere he looked, he saw eyes fixed intently on his own, heads held high and nostrils flared, as if every person there felt capable and ready to single-handedly right the injustices done to his people.

"If the Great Spirit gave different languages to his red children," he continued, in a quiet, deeply sorrowful voice, "it was so that all animals could understand them. Some He placed among the snows, alongside their cousin, the bear. Some he placed near the setting sun, on the path to the happy hunting grounds. Some on the lands surrounding the great fresh waters; but to His greatest, and most beloved, He gave the sands of the salt lake. Do my brothers know the name of this favored people?"

"It was the Lenape!" twenty excited voices shouted all at once.

"It was the Lenni Lenape," Magua replied, pretending to bow his head in respect for their past glory. "It was the tribes of the Lenape! The sun rose from saltwater and set in freshwater, never hiding from their sight. But why should I, a Huron from the forests, tell a wise people their own stories? Why should I remind them of their wounds, their former greatness, their accomplishments, their honor, their joy, their losses, their failures, their suffering? Isn't there someone among you who has witnessed all of this and knows it to be true? I am finished. My voice falls silent because my heart feels heavy as lead. I am listening."

When the speaker's voice suddenly stopped, everyone's faces and eyes turned together toward the respected Tamenund. From the moment he had taken his seat until this very instant, the old leader's lips had remained closed, and barely any sign of life had come from him. He sat hunched over in frailty, and seemed completely unaware of where he was during that entire opening scene, in which the scout's abilities had been so clearly proven. At the carefully modulated sound of Magua's voice, however, he showed some signs of awareness, and once or twice he even lifted his head, as if to listen. But when the cunning Huron mentioned his tribe by name, the old man's eyelids lifted, and he gazed out at the crowd with that kind of vacant, expressionless look that might be expected to appear on the face of a ghost. Then he made an attempt to stand, and being supported by those helping him, he rose to his feet, achieving a posture that commanded respect through its dignity, even as he swayed with frailty.

"Who calls upon the children of the Lenape?" he said, in a deep, throaty voice that became terrifyingly clear in the complete silence of the crowd. "Who speaks of things that are gone? Doesn't the egg become a worm—the worm a fly, and then die? Why tell the Delawares about good things from the past? It's better to thank the Manitou for what we still have."

"He's a Wyandot," said Magua, moving closer to the rough platform where the other man stood; "a friend of Tamenund."

"A friend!" the wise man repeated, his forehead creasing into a dark scowl that brought back some of the harshness that had made his gaze so frightening during his middle years. "Do the Mingoes think they rule the world? What's a Huron doing here?"

"Justice. His prisoners are with his brothers, and he comes for his own."

Tamenund turned his head toward one of his supporters and listened to the brief explanation the man provided.

Then, turning to face the applicant, he looked at him for a moment with intense focus; afterward, he spoke in a quiet and hesitant voice:

"Justice is the law of the great Manitou. My children, give the stranger food. Then, Huron, take thine own and depart."

When this solemn judgment was delivered, the patriarch sat down and closed his eyes once more, appearing more content with the memories of his own mature wisdom than with the physical world around him. No Delaware was bold enough to grumble against such a ruling, let alone openly resist it. The words had barely been spoken when four or five younger warriors stepped behind Heyward and the scout, wrapping leather straps around their arms so skillfully and quickly that both men were immediately bound. Heyward was too focused on his precious and nearly unconscious burden to notice their intentions before they carried them out, while the scout, who regarded even the hostile Delaware tribes as a superior people, offered no resistance. Perhaps, though, the scout's behavior might not have been so compliant if he had fully understood the language in which the earlier conversation had taken place.

Magua looked around the entire gathering with a triumphant expression before he moved forward to carry out his plan. Seeing that the men couldn't put up any fight, he focused his attention on the woman he prized most. Cora looked back at him with such steady, unwavering eyes that his determination faltered for a moment. Then, remembering his earlier scheme, he lifted Alice from the arms of the warrior she had been leaning against, and gestured for Heyward to follow him as he signaled the surrounding crowd to step aside. But instead of responding as he had anticipated, Cora rushed to the patriarch's feet, and raising her voice, she cried out:

"Just and honorable Delaware, we depend on your wisdom and power for mercy! Don't listen to that cunning and ruthless monster over there, who fills your ears with lies to satisfy his bloodthirsty desires. You who have lived a long life and witnessed the world's evils should understand how to ease suffering for those who are miserable."

The old man's eyes opened slowly, and he looked up at the crowd once again. As the urgent tones of the woman pleading reached his ears, his gaze moved gradually toward her, finally resting on her with a steady stare. Cora had dropped to her knees, and with her hands clasped together and pressed against her chest, she remained like a beautiful and living representation of womanhood, gazing up at his weathered but dignified face with a kind of sacred respect. Little by little, the expression on Tamenund's face began to change, and as the emptiness in his eyes gave way to wonder, they brightened with some of that sharp awareness which a hundred years earlier had been known to inspire his youthful passion in the vast tribes of the Delawares. Standing up without help, and apparently without any struggle, he spoke in a voice that surprised those listening with its strength:

"What are you?"

"A woman. One of a hated race, if you wish—a Yankee. But one who has never harmed you, and who cannot harm your people, even if she wanted to; who asks for help."

"Tell me, my children," the patriarch continued in a hoarse voice, gesturing to those gathered around him, though his gaze remained fixed on Cora's kneeling figure, "where have the Delawares set up camp?"

"In the mountains of the Iroquois, beyond the clear springs of the Horican."

"Many scorching summers have passed," the wise man continued, "since I last drank from the waters of my own rivers. The children of Minquon are the most just of all white men, but they were thirsty and they claimed the water for themselves. Are they still pursuing us even this far?"[1]

> [1] William Penn was called Minquon by the Delaware people, and since he never resorted to violence or unfairness in his interactions with them, his reputation for honesty became legendary. Americans rightfully take pride in their nation's founding, which may be unmatched in world history; however, Pennsylvanians and New Jersey residents have greater cause to honor their forebears than people from any other state, because no injustice was committed against the original inhabitants of the land.

"We don't follow anyone, and we don't want anything," Cora replied. "We've been brought here as prisoners against our will, and all we ask is permission to return to our own people in peace.

Are you Tamenund—the father, the judge, I almost said, the prophet—of this people?"

"I am Tamenund of many days."

"It's been about seven years now since one of your people was at the mercy of a white chief on the borders of this province. He claimed to be descended from the good and just Tamenund. 'Go,' said the white man, 'for your parent's sake you are free.' Do you remember the name of that English warrior?"

"I remember when I was a laughing boy," the patriarch said, speaking with the distinctive memory that comes with great age, "I stood on the sandy seashore and watched a large canoe with wings whiter than a swan's and broader than many eagles approaching from the east where the sun rises."

"No, no; I'm not talking about something that happened so long ago, but about kindness shown to your family by one of my people, within the memory of your youngest warrior."

"Was it when the Americans and the Dutch fought for the hunting grounds of the Delawares? Then Tamenund was a chief, and first set aside the bow for the firearms of the white men—"

"Not yet," Cora interrupted, "not by many ages. I'm talking about something that happened just yesterday. Surely you haven't forgotten it."

"It was only yesterday," the old man replied with deep emotion, "that the children of the Lenape ruled the world. The fish in the ocean, the birds, the animals, and the Mengee of the forests recognized them as their chiefs."

Cora lowered her head in disappointment and struggled for a painful moment with her frustration. Then, lifting her beautiful features and bright eyes, she continued in tones almost as piercing as the otherworldly voice of the patriarch himself:

"Tell me, is Tamenund a father?"

The elderly man gazed down at her from his raised platform, a kind smile spreading across his gaunt face, and then slowly sweeping his eyes across the entire gathering, he replied:

"Of a nation."

"I ask for nothing for myself. Like you and your people, respected chief," she went on, pressing her hands desperately against her heart, and letting her head fall until her flushed cheeks were almost hidden in the tangle of dark, shining hair that tumbled messily over her shoulders, "the curse of my forefathers has fallen heavily upon their descendant. But over there is someone who has never felt the burden of Heaven's anger until this moment. She is the daughter of an elderly and weakening man, whose life is approaching its end. She has many, so very many, who love her and take joy in her; and she is too good, far too valuable, to become that scoundrel's victim."

"I know that the white people are a proud and greedy race. I know that they claim not only to own the earth, but that the lowest among them is better than the chiefs of the red man. The dogs and crows of their tribes," the earnest old chief continued, ignoring the hurt feelings of his listener, whose head was nearly pressed to the ground in shame as he went on, "would bark and cry out before they would bring a woman to their homes whose blood was not as white as snow. But let them not boast too loudly before the Great Spirit. They came to this land from the east, and may yet leave when the sun sets in the west. I have often seen locusts strip the leaves from trees, but the season of flowers has always returned."

"That's true," said Cora, taking a deep breath as if awakening from a daze, lifting her face and pushing back her gleaming veil, with eyes that blazed despite the deathly pallor of her face; "but we're not allowed to ask why. There's still one of your own people who hasn't been brought before you; before you let the Huron leave in victory, listen to what he has to say."

Noticing that Tamenund appeared to be looking around with uncertainty, one of his companions said:

"It's a snake—a redskin working for the Yankees. We're keeping him for torture."

"Let him come," the wise man replied.

Then Tamenund settled back into his seat once more, and such a profound silence fell while the young man got ready to follow his straightforward command that the leaves rustling in the gentle morning breeze could be clearly heard throughout the surrounding forest.

---

# Chapter XXX.

"If you deny me, shame on your law!
There is no power in the decrees of Venice:
I stand for judgment: answer, shall I have it?"
—The Merchant of Venice

The silence stretched on without any human sounds for many tense minutes. Then the swaying crowd parted and closed again, and Uncas appeared in the living circle. All the eyes that had been carefully examining the features of the wise man, seeking their own understanding from him, instantly shifted and now focused in quiet admiration on the upright, graceful, and perfect figure of the prisoner. However, neither the situation he found himself in nor the undivided attention he drew disturbed the composure of the young Mohican in any way. He took a careful and watchful look around him, meeting the fixed expression of hatred that darkened the faces of the chiefs with the same calm he showed toward the curious stares of the watching children. But when, finally in this proud examination, Tamenund came into his view, his gaze became locked, as if everything else had already vanished from his mind. Then, moving forward with a slow and silent step across the space, he positioned himself directly in front of the wise man's footstool. There he stood unnoticed, though sharply observant himself, until one of the chiefs informed the latter of his presence.

"What language does the prisoner use to speak to the Manitou?" demanded the patriarch, keeping his eyes closed.

"Like his fathers," Uncas replied; "with the tongue of a Delaware."

At this sudden and unexpected announcement, a low, fierce yell swept through the crowd, which could aptly be compared to a lion's growl when its anger is first stirred—a frightening sign of the fury yet to come. The impact was just as powerful on the wise man, though he showed it differently. He placed a hand over his eyes, as if to block out any sight of such a disgraceful scene, while he repeated in his low, throaty voice the words he had just heard.

"A Delaware! I have lived to see the tribes of the Lenape driven from their council fires, and scattered like broken herds of deer among the hills of the Iroquois! I have seen the hatchets of a powerful people clear entire forests from the valleys that the winds of heaven had spared! I have seen the beasts that roam the mountains and the birds that soar above the trees living in the homes of men; but never before have I encountered a Delaware so dishonorable as to slither like a venomous snake into the camps of his own people."

"The singing birds have opened their beaks," Uncas replied in the gentle tones of his own melodious voice, "and Tamenund has listened to their song."

The wise man suddenly looked up and tilted his head to one side, as though trying to hear the fading notes of a melody drifting by.

"Is Tamenund dreaming!" he cried out. "What voice reaches his ears! Have the years turned back! Will summer return once more to the children of the Lenape!"

A serious and reverent silence followed this confused outburst from the Delaware prophet. His people easily interpreted his incomprehensible words as one of those mystical conversations he was thought to have so often with a higher power, and they waited for the outcome of this divine message with deep respect. After waiting patiently for some time, however, one of the elderly men, noticing that the wise man had forgotten about the matter at hand, dared to remind him once more that the prisoner was present.

"The fake Delaware shakes with fear that he might hear what Tamenund has to say," he said. "He's like a dog that howls when the white men show him a path to follow."

"And you," Uncas replied, looking sternly around him, "are dogs that whine when the Frenchman throws you the scraps of his deer!"

Twenty knives flashed in the air, and just as many warriors jumped to their feet at this sharp and possibly deserved comeback; but a gesture from one of the chiefs held back their rising anger and brought back the appearance of calm. The task might have been more challenging if Tamenund hadn't made a movement showing he was about to speak again.

"Delaware!" the wise man continued, "you hardly deserve the name you carry. My people haven't seen bright sunshine for many winters, and a warrior who abandons his tribe when they're shrouded in darkness is twice the betrayer. The Great Spirit's law is fair. This is the way it must be; as long as rivers flow and mountains remain standing, as long as flowers bloom and fade on the trees, this is how it must be. He belongs to you now, my children; treat him with justice."

No one moved a muscle or breathed any louder or deeper than usual until the last word of Tamenund's final judgment had left his lips. Then a cry for revenge erupted all at once from the collective voices of the entire nation—a terrifying sign of their merciless plans. Amid these extended and savage screams, a chief announced in a loud voice that the prisoner was sentenced to suffer the horrible ordeal of torture by fire. The circle broke apart, and shrieks of joy mixed with the commotion and chaos of getting ready. Heyward fought frantically against those holding him; Hawkeye's worried eyes started scanning his surroundings with an especially intense look; and Cora threw herself at the old leader's feet once again, pleading for mercy.

Throughout all of these difficult moments, Uncas alone had maintained his calm composure. He watched the preparations with a steady gaze, and when his torturers came to grab him, he faced them with a firm and dignified posture. One of them, perhaps even more fierce and brutal than the others, grabbed the hunting shirt of the young warrior and tore it from his body with a single motion. Then, with a scream of wild delight, he jumped toward his unresisting victim and got ready to drag him to the stake. But at that instant, when he seemed most disconnected from any human feelings, the savage's intention was stopped as abruptly as if some supernatural force had stepped in to help Uncas. The Delaware's eyes seemed to bulge from their sockets; his mouth fell open and his entire body froze in a pose of complete shock. Lifting his hand with a slow and deliberate movement, he pointed with one finger toward the chest of the captive. His companions gathered around him in amazement and every eye was like his own, staring intently at the image of a small turtle, beautifully tattooed on the prisoner's chest in a bright blue color.

For just a moment, Uncas savored his victory, gazing calmly at the scene with a quiet smile. Then, with a grand and commanding gesture of his arm, he waved the crowd back and stepped forward before his people with the bearing of a king, speaking in a voice that rose above the murmur of admiration rippling through the gathered multitude.

"Men of the Lenni Lenape!" he declared, "my people support the earth! Your weak tribe stands upon my shell! What fire that a Delaware could kindle would burn the descendant of my ancestors," he continued, pointing with pride to the simple markings on his skin; "the blood that flows from such lineage would extinguish your flames! My people are the forefathers of all nations!"

"Who are you?" demanded Tamenund, rising at the startling tones he heard, more than at any meaning conveyed by the language of the prisoner.

"Uncas, son of Chingachgook," the captive replied humbly, turning away from the tribe and lowering his head respectfully in acknowledgment of the other man's character and age; "a son of the great Unamis."[1]

[1] Turtle.

"Tamenund's time is almost here!" the wise man declared; "the day has finally given way to night! I thank the Great Spirit that someone is here to take my place at the council fire. Uncas, the son of Uncas, has been found! Let the eyes of a dying eagle look upon the rising sun."

The young man stepped onto the platform with light but confident steps, making himself visible to the entire restless and curious crowd. Tamenund held him at arm's length for a long time, studying every detail of his handsome facial features with the unwavering gaze of someone remembering happier times.

"Is Tamenund a boy?" the confused prophet finally cried out. "Have I dreamed of so many winters—that my people were scattered like drifting sands—of white men, more numerous than the leaves on the trees! Tamenund's arrow would not frighten a young deer; his arm has withered like the branch of a dead oak; a snail would be faster in a race; yet Uncas stands before him as they once went to battle against the pale faces! Uncas, the panther of his tribe, the eldest son of the Lenape, the wisest chief of the Mohicans! Tell me, you Delawares, has Tamenund been sleeping for a hundred winters?"

The calm and profound silence that followed these words clearly revealed the deep reverence with which his people received the patriarch's message. No one dared to respond, though everyone listened with breathless anticipation of what might come next. Uncas, however, gazing at his face with the affection and respect of a beloved child, relied on his own elevated and recognized status to offer a reply.

"Four warriors from his tribe have lived and died," he said, "since Tamenund's friend led his people into battle. The bloodline of the turtle clan has flowed through many chiefs, but all have returned to the earth from which they came, except Chingachgook and his son."

"It's true—it's true," the wise man replied, a sudden flash of memory shattering all his pleasant dreams and bringing him back to the harsh reality of his people's history. "Our elders have often spoken of two warriors from the ancient bloodline who were in the hills of the white men; why have their places at the Delaware council fires remained vacant for so long?"

At these words, the young man lifted his head, which he had kept slightly bowed in respect, and raised his voice so the crowd could hear him, as if he wanted to explain his family's principles once and for all. He declared loudly:

"We once slept where we could hear the salt lake speaking in its rage. Back then, we were rulers and chiefs over the land. But when a pale face appeared on every stream, we followed the deer back to the river of our people. The Delawares had vanished. Few warriors from all their numbers remained to drink from the stream they cherished. Then my fathers declared, 'Here we shall hunt. The waters of this river flow into the salt lake. If we travel toward the setting sun, we will discover streams that flow into the great lakes of fresh water; there a Mohican would perish, like sea fish in clear springs. When the Great Spirit is prepared and commands "Come," we will follow the river to the sea and reclaim what is ours.' This, Delawares, is what the children of the Turtle believe. Our gaze is fixed on the rising sun, not toward the setting sun. We understand where he comes from, but we do not know where he travels. That is sufficient."

The Lenape men listened to his words with all the respect that superstition could inspire, finding a hidden appeal even in the symbolic language the young chief used to express his thoughts. Uncas himself observed the impact of his brief explanation with perceptive eyes, and slowly abandoned the commanding presence he had taken on as he noticed his listeners were satisfied. Then, allowing his gaze to drift across the quiet crowd gathered around Tamenund's raised seat, he first spotted Hawkeye bound with ropes. Moving quickly from where he stood, he pushed through to reach his friend's side; slicing through the bindings with a swift and fierce cut of his knife, he gestured for the crowd to step back. The Indians quietly complied, and once again they arranged themselves in their circle, just as they had before his arrival among them. Uncas grasped the scout's hand and brought him before the patriarch.

"Father," he said, "look at this pale face; a just man, and the friend of the Delawares."

"Is he a son of Minquon?"

"Not so; a warrior known to the Yankees, and feared by the Mohawks."

"What reputation has he earned through his actions?"

"We call him Hawkeye," Uncas answered, speaking in the Delaware language, "because his aim is always true. The Mingoes know him better for the deadly shots he delivers to their warriors; they call him 'The Long Rifle'."

"The Long Rifle!" Tamenund exclaimed, opening his eyes and looking at the scout with a stern expression. "My son has made a mistake in calling him friend."

"I call him that because he has proven himself to be exactly that," the young chief replied with great composure, maintaining a steady demeanor. "If Uncas is welcome among the Delawares, then Hawkeye is welcome here with his friends."

"The pale-faced man has killed my young warriors; he has earned a fearsome reputation for the devastating attacks he has launched against the Lenape."

"If a Mingo has whispered that much in the ear of the Delaware, he has only shown that he is a singing-bird," said the scout, who now believed that it was time to defend himself from such offensive accusations, and who spoke like the man he was addressing, though he modified his Indian metaphors with his own distinctive ideas. "That I have killed the Maquas I am not the man to deny, even at their own council-fires; but that, knowingly, my hand has never harmed a Delaware, goes against the nature of my gifts, which is friendly to them, and all that belongs to their nation."

A quiet murmur of approval spread among the warriors, who glanced at one another like people just beginning to realize their mistake.

"Where is the Huron?" Tamenund demanded. "Has he stopped my ears?"

Magua, whose emotions during that scene where Uncas had emerged victorious can be much better imagined than put into words, responded to the summons by stepping boldly in front of the elder.

"The fair Tamenund," he said, "will not keep what a Huron has lent."

"Tell me, my brother's son," the wise man replied, looking away from Le Subtil's dark expression and turning with relief to

Uncas's more honest face, "does this stranger have a conqueror's authority over you?"

"He has none. The panther might fall into traps set by women, but he is powerful and knows how to jump through them."

"The Long Rifle?"

"Laughs at the Mingoes. Go, Huron, ask your squaws the color of a bear."

"The stranger and the white maiden who came into my camp together?"

"Should journey on an open path."

"And what about the woman that Huron left with my warriors?"

Uncas made no reply.

"And what about the woman that the Mingo brought into my camp?" Tamenund repeated seriously.

"She belongs to me," Magua shouted, shaking his fist triumphantly at Uncas. "Mohican, you know that she is mine."

"My son remains quiet," Tamenund said, trying to understand the meaning behind the expression on the young man's face as he turned away in grief.

"That's right," came the quiet reply.

A brief and striking silence followed, during which it became very clear how reluctantly the crowd accepted the fairness of the Mingo's claim. Finally the wise man, who alone had the power to decide, spoke in a steady voice:

"Huron, leave."

"As he arrived, is it just Tamenund," the cunning Magua demanded, "or does he come with hands full of the trust of the Delawares? The lodge of Le Renard Subtil is empty. Make him powerful with his own people."

The old man thought to himself for a while; and then, leaning his head toward one of his respected companions, he asked:

"Are my ears open?"

"It is true."

"Is this Mingo a chief?"

"The first in his nation."

"Girl, what do you want? A great warrior is taking you as his wife. Go! Your bloodline will not end."

"It would be a thousand times better," cried the horrified Cora, "than to suffer such humiliation!"

"Huron, her thoughts are with her family's home. A reluctant bride creates a miserable household."

"She speaks with the tongue of her people," Magua replied, looking at his victim with bitter irony.

"She comes from a people who are merchants, and she will negotiate even for a kind glance. Let Tamenund say what needs to be said."

"Take the wampum, and our love."

"Nothing here except what Magua brought."

"Then leave with your own people. The Great Manitou forbids that a Delaware should be unjust."

Magua moved forward and grabbed his prisoner firmly by the arm; the Delawares stepped back without saying a word; and Cora, as if she knew that protesting would be pointless, got ready to accept her fate without fighting back.

"Stop, stop!" Duncan shouted, rushing forward; "Huron, show mercy! Her ransom will make you wealthier than any of your people have ever been known to be."

"Magua is a red-skin; he wants not the beads of the pale faces."

"Gold, silver, gunpowder, and lead—everything a warrior needs will be in your home; everything that befits the greatest chief."

"Le Subtil is very strong," shouted Magua, forcefully shaking the hand that gripped Cora's unresisting arm; "he has his revenge!"

"Powerful ruler of Providence!" Heyward cried out, pressing his hands together in anguish, "how can this be allowed! I beg you for mercy, just Tamenund."

"The Delaware has spoken," replied the wise man, closing his eyes and sinking back into his chair, exhausted from both the mental and physical effort. "A man does not speak twice."

"A chief shouldn't waste time taking back words he's already spoken—that's both wise and sensible," Hawkeye said, gesturing for Duncan to stay quiet. "But it's also smart for any warrior to think carefully before he buries his tomahawk in his prisoner's skull. Huron, I don't like you, and I can't say that any Mingo has ever been treated kindly by me. It's reasonable to assume that if this war doesn't end soon, many more of your warriors will face me in the forest. Think about it, then—would you rather bring a prisoner like him back to your camp, or someone like me, a man your people would be thrilled to see captured and defenseless?"

"Will 'The Long Rifle' give his life for the woman?" Magua demanded, hesitating, since he had already started moving to leave the place with his captive.

"No, no; I haven't said that much," Hawkeye replied, pulling back with appropriate caution when he noticed how eagerly Magua was listening to his suggestion. "It would be an unfair trade to exchange a warrior in his prime, at the height of his strength and value, for even the finest woman on the frontier. I might agree to go into winter quarters now—at least six weeks before the leaves change color—on the condition that you release the young woman."

Magua shook his head and made an impatient gesture for the crowd to move aside.

"Well, then," the scout continued, with the thoughtful expression of someone who hadn't completely decided; "I'll include 'Killdeer' in the deal. Take it from an experienced hunter—there's no rifle like it between the provinces."

Magua still refused to respond, continuing his attempts to scatter the crowd.

"Maybe," the scout continued, his fake composure slipping away as much as the other man showed he didn't care about making a trade, "if I agreed to teach your young warriors how to properly use this weapon, it might resolve the small disagreements we have."

Le Renard angrily commanded the Delawares, who continued to surround him in an unbreakable circle, hoping he might consider their peaceful offer, to clear his way, warning them with his fierce stare that he would make another appeal to the perfect justice of their "prophet."

"What is destined to happen will eventually come to pass," Hawkeye continued, turning to face Uncas with a sorrowful and humble expression. "That scoundrel knows he has the upper hand and he's going to use it! May God bless you, young man; you've discovered friends among your own people, and I hope they'll prove as loyal as some others you've encountered who had no Native blood. As for myself, I'll have to die sooner or later; it's fortunate, then, that there are only a few who will mourn my passing. When all is said and done, those devils probably would have succeeded in taking my scalp anyway, so a day or two won't make much difference in the eternal scheme of things. God bless you," the weathered frontiersman added, turning his head away, then immediately looking back at the young man with longing in his eyes; "I cared deeply for both you and your father, Uncas, even though our skin colors aren't the same, and our natural abilities are somewhat different. Tell the Sagamore that I never forgot about him during my darkest hours; and as for you, remember me sometimes when you're on a successful hunt, and you can count on this, young man, whether there's one heaven or two, there's a way in the afterlife for good men to reunite. You'll find the rifle where we concealed it; take it, and keep it in my memory; and listen carefully, lad, since your heritage doesn't prevent you from seeking revenge, use it somewhat freely against the Mingoes; it might help ease the sorrow of losing me, and bring peace to your heart. Huron, I accept your terms; set the woman free. I am your captive!"

A quiet but clearly audible murmur of approval rippled through the crowd at this noble offer; even the most fierce Delaware warriors showed satisfaction at the courage of the proposed sacrifice. Magua stopped, and for a tense moment, one could say he hesitated; then, looking at Cora with an expression that strangely combined brutality and respect, his decision became permanently set.

He showed his contempt for the offer by tilting his head back and said in a calm and determined voice:

"Le Renard Subtil is a great chief; he has only one mind. Come," he added, placing his hand too familiarly on the shoulder of his captive to urge her forward; "a Huron is no gossip; we will go."

The young woman pulled back with dignified feminine restraint, and her dark eyes flashed with anger, while the rich color rushed like a fleeting ray of sunlight into her temples at the insult.

"I am your prisoner, and when the time is right, I'll be ready to follow you, even to my death. But there's no need for violence," she said coldly. Then, turning immediately to Hawkeye, she added: "Noble hunter! I thank you from the bottom of my heart. Your offer won't work, and I couldn't accept it anyway, but you can still help me in a way that's even greater than your generous plan. Look at that poor, broken child! Don't abandon her until you've brought her to civilized people. I won't say," she continued, gripping the scout's rough hand tightly, "that her father will reward you—because someone like you is above earthly rewards—but he will thank you and give you his blessing. And believe me, the blessing of a good and elderly man carries weight in Heaven's eyes. How I wish I could hear just one word from his lips in this terrible moment!" Her voice caught, and for a moment she couldn't speak. Then, stepping closer to Duncan, who was holding her unconscious sister, she went on in a quieter tone, though her emotions and feminine nature were locked in a fierce battle: "I don't need to tell you to treasure what you'll have. You love her, Heyward, and that love would hide a thousand flaws, even if she had them. She is kind, gentle, sweet, and as good as any person can be. There isn't a single fault in her mind or body that would disgust even the proudest among you. She is beautiful—oh, how incredibly beautiful!" She placed her own lovely but less radiant hand tenderly on Alice's pale forehead, brushing back the golden hair that framed her face. "And yet her soul is as pure and perfect as her appearance! I could say so much more—perhaps more than calm judgment would allow—but I'll spare both you and myself—" Her voice faded away, and she bent her head over her sister's form. After giving her a long, passionate kiss, she stood up, and with a face as pale as death but without a single tear in her burning eyes, she turned away and said to the savage with all her former dignity: "Now, sir, if you're ready, I will follow."

"Yes, go," Duncan shouted, placing Alice in the arms of an Indian girl; "go, Magua, go. These Delawares have their laws, which prevent them from holding you; but I—I have no such duty. Go, evil monster—why are you waiting?"

It would be hard to describe the look on Magua's face as he heard this threat to pursue him. At first, there was a fierce and obvious show of joy, but then it was immediately replaced by an expression of cunning coldness.

"The words are open," he replied with satisfaction, "The Open Hand may enter."

"Wait," Hawkeye shouted, grabbing Duncan by the arm and forcibly holding him back; "you don't understand how cunning that devil is. He's trying to lead you into a trap where you'll be killed—"

"Huron," Uncas interrupted, having followed the strict traditions of his people by listening carefully and seriously to everything that had been said; "Huron, the Delaware people receive their sense of justice from the Great Spirit. Look at the sun. It's now shining through the upper branches of the hemlock tree. Your path ahead is short and clear. When the sun appears above the treetops, there will be men following your trail."

"I hear a crow!" Magua shouted with a mocking laugh. "Go!" he continued, waving his hand dismissively at the crowd, which had gradually parted to let him through. "Where are the women of the Delawares! Let them send their arrows and their guns to the Wyandots; they will have deer meat to eat, and corn to tend. Dogs, rabbits, thieves—I spit on you!"

His final mocking remarks were heard in complete, ominous silence, and with these sharp words still on his lips, the victorious Magua walked unhindered into the forest, followed by his submissive prisoner, and shielded by the sacred laws of Indian hospitality.

---

# Chapter XXXI.

"Fluellen.—Kill the boys and the baggage carriers! This is expressly against the laws of war; it is as complete an act of villainy, mark you now, as can be committed in the world."
—King Henry V.

As long as their enemy and his captive remained visible, the crowd stayed completely still, as if held in place by some force that favored the Huron; but the moment he vanished from view, they became restless and stirred by intense and overwhelming emotion. Uncas held his position on higher ground, watching Cora's figure until the colors of her clothing merged with the forest leaves; then he climbed down and, moving quietly through the crowd, vanished into the same lodge he had recently left. A handful of the more serious and observant warriors, who noticed the flashes of rage in the young chief's eyes as he passed by, followed him to the spot he had chosen for his contemplation. Following this, Tamenund and Alice were taken away, and the women and children were told to scatter. During the critical hour that followed, the camp looked like a disturbed beehive, with everyone simply waiting for their leader to appear and show them the way toward some distant and significant journey.

A young warrior finally emerged from Uncas's lodge and walked deliberately with a solemn, ceremonial pace toward a small pine tree that grew in the cracks of the rocky ledge. He stripped the bark from its trunk, then returned to where he had come from without saying a word. Another warrior soon followed him, removing all the branches from the young tree and leaving behind a bare, marked trunk. A third warrior painted the post with dark red stripes. The men outside received all these signs of the nation's leaders preparing for war in grim and foreboding silence. At last, the Mohican himself appeared again, wearing nothing but his belt and leggings, with half of his noble face hidden beneath a menacing coat of black paint.[1]

> [1] A tree that has been partially or completely stripped of its bark is called "blazed" in local terminology. This term comes directly from English, where a horse is described as blazed when it has a white marking.

Uncas walked with slow and dignified steps toward the post, which he immediately began circling with measured paces, resembling an ancient dance, while raising his voice in the wild and irregular chant of his war song. The sounds reached the extremes of human vocal range; sometimes melancholy and exquisitely mournful, even matching the melody of birds—and then, through sudden and startling changes, making the listeners tremble with their depth and power. The words were few and frequently repeated, moving gradually from a kind of prayer, or hymn, to the Divine, to a declaration of the warrior's purpose, and ending as they began with an acknowledgment of his own reliance on the Great Spirit. If it were possible to translate the rich and melodious language in which he spoke, the song might read something like this: "Manitou! Manitou! Manitou! You are great, you are good, you are wise: Manitou! Manitou! You are just. In the heavens, in the clouds, oh, I see many spots—many dark, many red: In the heavens, oh, I see many clouds."

"In the woods, in the air, oh, I hear the whoop, the long yell, and the cry: In the woods, oh, I hear the loud whoop!"

"Manitou! Manitou! Manitou! I am weak—you are strong; I am slow; Manitou! Manitou! Give me help."

At the end of what could be called each verse, he paused by holding a note that was louder and longer than usual, perfectly matching the feeling he had just expressed. The first ending was serious and meant to show deep respect; the second was vivid and almost frightening; and the third was the famous and terrifying war cry that exploded from the young warrior's lips like all the horrible sounds of battle combined into one. The final verse was like the first—humble and pleading. He sang this song three times, and each time he danced in a circle around the post.

At the end of the first round, a serious and highly respected Lenape chief followed his lead, singing his own words to music with a similar style. One warrior after another joined the dance, until all those with any reputation and leadership were part of its intricate movements. The scene now became wildly frightening; the fierce-looking and threatening faces of the chiefs gained even more intensity from the terrifying sounds in which they blended their deep, throaty voices. Right then Uncas drove his tomahawk deep into the post and raised his voice in a shout that could be called his personal war cry. This action announced that he had taken on the chief leadership role in the planned expedition.

It was a signal that awakened all the sleeping passions of the nation. A hundred young men, who had previously been held back by the uncertainty of their youth, rushed in a wild group toward what they believed was the symbol of their enemy, and tore it apart, piece by piece, until nothing remained of the trunk except its roots in the ground. During this moment of chaos, the most brutal acts of war were carried out on the pieces of the tree, with as much apparent savagery as if they were living victims of their cruelty. Some were scalped; some received the sharp and quivering axe; and others suffered from stabs of the deadly knife. In short, the displays of enthusiasm and fierce joy were so great and unmistakable, that the expedition was declared to be a war of the nation.

The moment Uncas delivered the blow, he stepped outside the circle and looked up at the sun, which had just reached the point when the truce with Magua was set to expire. This fact was quickly communicated through a meaningful gesture, along with a matching cry; and the entire excited crowd abandoned their mock battle, with sharp cries of delight, to prepare for the more dangerous trial of actual warfare.

The entire appearance of the camp changed in an instant. The warriors, who were already armed and painted for battle, became as motionless as if they were unable to show any extraordinary display of feeling. Meanwhile, the women rushed out of their lodges, mixing songs of celebration with cries of mourning in such a strange way that it would have been hard to tell which emotion was stronger. However, no one stood around doing nothing. Some carried their most precious belongings, others took their children, and still others helped their elderly and sick relatives into the forest, which stretched out like a lush green carpet against the mountainside. Tamenund also withdrew there with quiet dignity, after a brief and moving conversation with Uncas; the wise elder parted from him with the same reluctance a parent would feel when leaving a long-lost child who had just been found again. During this time, Duncan escorted Alice to a safe location, and then went looking for the scout, his face showing how eagerly he too was anticipating the coming battle.

But Hawkeye was too familiar with the war songs and recruitment rituals of the natives to show any interest in what was happening around him. He simply glanced occasionally at the number and quality of the warriors who, from time to time, indicated their willingness to follow Uncas into battle. In this regard, he was quickly satisfied; for, as had already been observed, the young chief's influence rapidly encompassed every fighting man in the tribe. Once this crucial matter was so satisfactorily resolved, he sent an Indian boy to retrieve "killdeer" and Uncas's rifle from the location where they had hidden their weapons when approaching the Delaware camp; this was a strategy that served two purposes, since it protected the weapons from sharing their owners' fate if they were held as prisoners, and allowed them to appear among the strangers more as victims than as men equipped with means of defense and survival. In choosing someone else to carry out the task of recovering his treasured rifle, the scout had not forgotten any of his usual caution. He understood that Magua had not arrived alone, and he also understood that Huron spies were monitoring the movements of their new enemies along the entire edge of the forest. It would have been deadly for him to attempt this mission himself; a warrior would have faced no better outcome; but a boy would not likely encounter danger until after his purpose was discovered. When Heyward joined him, the scout was calmly waiting for the outcome of this plan.

The boy, who had received thorough training and possessed considerable cunning, walked casually across the clearing toward the woods with his chest swelling with pride from such trust and all the aspirations of youthful ambition. He entered the forest at a spot some distance away from where the rifles had been hidden. The moment he disappeared behind the leafy bushes, however, his dark figure could be seen sliding like a snake toward the coveted weapons. He succeeded in his mission, and within moments he emerged racing across the narrow gap that bordered the base of the slope where the village was located, moving with the speed of an arrow and carrying a weapon in each hand. He had actually reached the rocky cliffs and was bounding up their steep sides with remarkable agility when a gunshot from the forest demonstrated just how precise the scout's assessment had been. The boy responded with a weak but scornful cry, and immediately a second bullet was fired at him from a different section of the woods. In the next instant he appeared on the plateau above, raising his rifles in victory as he moved with the bearing of a champion toward the celebrated hunter who had bestowed upon him such an honorable mission.

Despite the intense concern Hawkeye had shown for his messenger's safety, he took back "Killdeer" with such satisfaction that it temporarily pushed all other thoughts from his mind. After inspecting the rifle with a knowledgeable eye, opening and closing the firing pan ten or fifteen times, and performing various other equally crucial tests on the mechanism, he turned to the boy and asked with obvious kindness whether he had been injured. The young man looked up at him with pride, but remained silent.

"Ah! I see, boy, those villains have wounded your arm!" the scout said, examining the injured limb of the patient victim, where a deep cut in the flesh had been caused by one of the bullets. "But some crushed alder bark will work like magic. For now, I'll bandage it with a strip of wampum! You've started your career as a warrior young, my brave lad, and you'll probably carry many honorable battle scars to your grave. I know plenty of young men who have taken scalps but can't display a mark like this one. Go!" After wrapping up the arm, he declared, "You'll become a chief!"

The young man left, feeling more pride in his bleeding wound than the most conceited nobleman could feel about his fancy decorations; and he walked among his peers as someone who drew widespread admiration and jealousy.

But during a time filled with so many serious and important responsibilities, this single act of youthful courage didn't receive the widespread attention and praise it would have gotten under less dangerous circumstances. However, it had succeeded in alerting the Delawares to where their enemies were positioned and what they planned to do. As a result, a group of warriors better equipped for the job than the weak but brave boy was sent to drive out the hidden attackers. The mission was completed quickly, since most of the Hurons retreated on their own once they realized they had been spotted. The Delawares pursued them far enough from their own camp, then stopped to wait for further orders, worried about being drawn into a trap. With both groups now hiding themselves, the forest became as silent and peaceful as a calm summer morning in complete isolation could make it.

The calm yet restless Uncas gathered his chiefs and organized his forces. He introduced Hawkeye as a proven warrior who had been tested many times and had always shown himself worthy of trust. When he saw that his friend received a warm welcome, he gave him command of twenty men who, like Hawkeye himself, were quick, skilled, and determined. He explained to the Delawares what position Heyward held among the white soldiers, and then offered him a position of equal responsibility. However, Duncan refused the command, saying he was ready to serve as a volunteer alongside the scout. After making these arrangements, the young Mohican assigned various native chiefs to fill the different leadership roles, and since time was running short, he gave the order to move out. More than two hundred men obeyed him willingly but quietly.

Their entry into the forest went completely undisturbed; they didn't encounter any living creatures that could either sound an alarm or provide the information they needed, until they reached the hiding places of their own scouts. Here they stopped, and the leaders gathered to hold a quiet council meeting.

At this meeting, various plans of action were proposed, though none had the kind of bold character that would satisfy their passionate leader. If Uncas had followed his own instincts, he would have led his warriors into battle without hesitation and settled the conflict through immediate action; but such an approach would have gone against all the established practices and beliefs of his people. He was therefore forced to embrace a cautious strategy that his current state of mind found detestable, and to listen to counsel that made his fierce spirit restless, especially with the vivid memory of Cora's peril and Magua's arrogance fresh in his thoughts.

After a disappointing meeting that lasted many minutes, a lone person was spotted approaching from the enemy's position, moving with such obvious urgency that it seemed he might be a messenger bringing peaceful proposals. However, when he came within a hundred yards of the shelter where the Delaware council had gathered, the stranger paused, seemed unsure about which direction to go, and eventually stopped completely. Everyone's attention now focused on Uncas, as if looking for guidance on how to move forward.

"Hawkeye," the young chief said quietly, "he must never speak to the Hurons again."

"His time has come," said the brief scout, pushing the long barrel of his rifle through the leaves and taking his careful and deadly aim. But instead of pulling the trigger, he lowered the muzzle again and allowed himself a moment of his distinctive amusement. "I mistook the fellow for a Mingo, as sure as I'm a wretched sinner!" he said; "but when my eye traveled along his ribs looking for a spot to place the bullet—would you believe it, Uncas—I spotted the musician's instrument; and so, it turns out to be the man they call Gamut, whose death would benefit no one, and whose life, if his voice can do more than just sing, might prove useful to our purposes. If sounds still hold their power, I'll soon strike up a conversation with the good man, and in a voice he'll find more pleasant than the words of 'killdeer'."

So saying, Hawkeye set aside his rifle and crawled through the bushes until he was close enough for David to hear him, then tried to recreate the musical performance that had carried him so safely and triumphantly through the Huron camp. Gamut's refined musical ear couldn't easily be fooled (and truthfully, it would have been hard for anyone other than Hawkeye to make such a sound), so having heard these sounds once before, he immediately recognized where they were coming from. The poor man seemed relieved from his state of great confusion; following the direction of the voice—a task that was nearly as challenging for him as charging into enemy fire—he quickly found the hidden singer.

"I wonder what the Hurons will think of that!" said the scout, laughing, as he grabbed his companion by the arm and pushed him toward the back. "If those scoundrels are close enough to hear us, they'll say there are two people who can't keep quiet instead of one! But here we're safe," he added, pointing to Uncas and his friends. "Now tell us the story of the Mingo tricks in plain English, and without any dramatic changes in your voice."

David looked around at the fierce and wild-looking chiefs with silent amazement, but reassured by seeing familiar faces, he quickly recovered his composure enough to give a thoughtful response.

"The enemy forces are out there in large numbers," David said, "and I'm afraid they're up to no good. There's been a lot of shouting and wild celebrating going on, along with sounds so terrible I won't repeat them, coming from their camps over the past hour. It's been so bad that I actually had to escape to the

Delaware territory looking for some peace and quiet."

"Your ears might not have gained much from that trade if you had been faster on your feet," the scout replied with a touch of dryness. "But regardless of that; where are the Hurons?"

"They're hiding in the forest between here and their village in such large numbers that common sense would tell you to turn back immediately."

Uncas looked along the line of trees that hid his own group and spoke the name of:

"Magua?"

"Is among them. He brought in the young woman who had been staying with the Delawares; and, after leaving her in the cave, has positioned himself like an enraged wolf at the head of his warriors. I don't know what has disturbed his spirit so deeply!"

"He has left her in the cave, you say!" Heyward interrupted. "It's good that we know where it is! Can't we do something to help her right away?"

Uncas looked intently at the scout before asking:

"What does Hawkeye say?"

"Give me twenty rifles, and I'll head right along the stream, passing the beaver lodges to meet up with the Sagamore and the colonel. You'll hear our war cry from that direction—with this wind, the sound will easily carry a mile. Then, Uncas, you push forward with the main attack; when they get within shooting range, we'll hit them with a strike that—I stake my reputation as an experienced frontiersman on this—will make their battle line bend like a flexible ash bow. After that, we'll take the village and rescue the woman from the cave; then we can finish this business with the tribe either the white man's way, with a decisive blow and clear victory, or the Indian way, using stealth and cover. There might not be much sophisticated strategy in this plan, major, but with courage and patience, we can make it work."

"I really like that idea," Duncan exclaimed, realizing that the scout's main goal was to free Cora. "I think it's excellent. Let's try it right away."

After a brief discussion, the plan was finalized and made clearer to all the groups involved; the various signals were assigned, and the leaders went their separate ways, each heading to their designated position.

---

# Chapter XXXII.

"But plagues will spread, and funeral fires will multiply,
Until the great king, without paying a ransom,
Sends the dark-eyed maiden back to her own Chrysa."
—Pope.

While Uncas was positioning his warriors, the forest remained completely silent and seemed as empty as it had been on the day God first created it, except for those gathered in the war council. A person could look in any direction through the long, shadow-filled passages between the trees, but nothing could be seen that didn't belong to the tranquil and sleeping landscape.

Here and there a bird could be heard rustling among the beech tree branches, and sometimes a squirrel would drop a nut, causing the group to glance quickly toward the sound for a moment. But as soon as these brief disturbances ended, they could hear the wind whispering overhead, moving through that green and rolling canopy of forest that stretched endlessly across the vast landscape, broken only by streams or lakes. The wilderness that stretched between the Delawares and their enemies' village seemed untouched by human presence, so profound and peaceful was the silence that enveloped it. However, Hawkeye, whose responsibility placed him at the front of this mission, understood the nature of those they were about to face too well to trust this deceptive calm.

When he saw his small group gathered together, the scout cradled "Killdeer" in the crook of his arm and made a quiet gesture indicating they should follow him. He led them several yards back toward the rear, into the streambed of a small brook they had crossed while moving forward. There he stopped, and after waiting for all of his serious and alert warriors to gather around him, he spoke in the Delaware language, asking:

"Do any of my young men know where this path will take us?"

A Delaware warrior extended his hand, spreading two fingers apart while showing how they connected at the base, and he replied:

"Before the sun moves its own width across the sky, the small stream will flow into the large river." Then he added, pointing toward the location he had mentioned, "together they provide enough water for the beavers."

"I figured as much," the scout replied, looking up through the gap in the treetops, "based on the direction it's flowing and how the mountains are positioned. Men, we'll stay hidden along its banks until we pick up the scent of the Hurons."

His companions gave their usual quick sounds of agreement, but when they realized their leader was about to personally guide them forward, one or two gestured that something wasn't right. Hawkeye, who understood what their meaningful looks meant, turned around and saw that the singing-master had been following their group this entire time.

"Do you realize, my friend," the scout asked seriously, and perhaps with a touch of pride from knowing his own worth, "that this is a group of rangers selected for the most dangerous missions, and placed under the leadership of someone who, though another person might say it more modestly, won't likely let them sit around doing nothing. It might not be five minutes, and it certainly won't be more than thirty, before we step on the body of a Huron, whether alive or dead."

"Even though you haven't told me your plans in so many words," David replied, his face slightly reddened and his normally calm, expressionless eyes now burning with an unusual intensity, "your men have brought to mind the sons of Jacob marching into battle against the Shechemites, who had wickedly sought to marry a woman from a people blessed by the Lord. I have traveled a great distance and shared many experiences, both good and bad, with the young woman you're looking for. And while I'm not a warrior by nature, I'm prepared for battle and ready to fight—I would gladly strike a blow to defend her."

The scout paused, seemingly considering the likelihood of such an unusual recruitment before responding:

"You don't know how to use any weapon. You're not carrying a rifle; and trust me, whatever the Mingoes take, they'll gladly give back."

"Though I'm not a boastful and bloodthirsty Goliath," David replied, pulling a sling from beneath his multicolored and rough clothing, "I haven't forgotten the example of the Jewish boy. I practiced extensively with this ancient weapon of war in my youth, and perhaps the skill hasn't completely left me."

"Yes!" said Hawkeye, examining the deerskin strap and leather covering with a cold and discouraging look; "that thing might work against arrows, or even knives; but these Mengwe have been equipped by the French with a good rifled barrel for each man. Still, it appears to be your natural ability to remain unharmed in the midst of gunfire; and since you have been protected so far— major, you have left your rifle cocked; a single shot fired too early would mean exactly twenty scalps lost for nothing—singer, you can come along; we might have need of you when the shouting begins."

"Thank you, my friend," David replied, gathering stones from the brook like his royal namesake had done; "while I'm not one who seeks to kill, if you had sent me away, my conscience would have been deeply troubled."

"Remember," the scout added, tapping his own head meaningfully at the exact spot where Gamut was still tender, "we're here to fight, not to make music. Until the general war cry is given, nothing should make a sound except the rifle."

David nodded to show he agreed with the terms, and then Hawkeye took another careful look at his followers before giving the signal to move forward.

Their path followed the streambed for about a mile. Although the steep banks and dense bushes along the water provided protection from being easily spotted, they took every precaution known for defending against Indian attacks. A warrior crept rather than walked on each side, positioning himself to steal occasional glimpses into the forest. Every few minutes the group stopped completely and listened for enemy sounds, using hearing so sharp it would be almost impossible for civilized people to imagine. Their journey proceeded without interference, however, and they arrived at the place where the smaller stream joined the larger one without any sign that anyone had noticed their movement. At this point the scout stopped once more to read the signs of the forest.

"We're likely to have a good day for a fight," he said in English, speaking to Heyward and looking up at the clouds that were beginning to move in wide formations across the sky. "Bright sunlight and a shining gun barrel don't help with accurate shooting. Everything works in our favor—they have the wind, which will carry their noise and gunpowder smoke toward us, and that's no small advantage. For us, it means we can fire first and then get a clear view afterward. But our cover ends here. Beavers have controlled this stream for hundreds of years, and between what they've eaten and the dams they've built, you can see there are many stripped tree stumps but very few living trees left."

Hawkeye had, in fact, accurately described the scene that stretched out before them in those brief words. The stream varied dramatically in width, sometimes rushing through narrow cracks in the rock formations, while at other times spreading across vast stretches of low-lying ground, creating small bodies of water that could be called ponds. Along its banks lay the decaying remains of dead trees in every stage of decomposition, from those that creaked on their unstable trunks to others that had only recently lost their rough bark that so mysteriously holds their life force. Several long, low mounds covered in moss were scattered throughout the area, resembling monuments to a bygone era and its long-vanished inhabitants.

The scout carefully observed all these small details with a seriousness and attention they had probably never received before. He was aware that the Huron camp was located just half a mile upstream, and with the typical worry of someone who feared a concealed threat, he felt deeply disturbed by finding no sign whatsoever of his enemy's presence. Several times he considered giving the command to charge forward and attack the village by surprise, but his experience quickly warned him against such a reckless plan. He then strained to listen, filled with anxious uncertainty, for any sounds of conflict from the direction where Uncas had been positioned, but he could hear nothing except the wind's whisper as it began to sweep across the forest canopy in powerful gusts that suggested an approaching storm. Finally, giving in to his uncommon restlessness rather than relying on his expertise, he decided to force a confrontation by revealing his troops and advancing carefully but steadily up the stream.

The scout had been standing while making his observations, protected by a thicket, and his companions still lay in the bottom of the ravine where the smaller stream flowed out; but when they heard his quiet yet clear signal, the entire group crept up the bank like dark ghosts and silently positioned themselves around him. Gesturing toward the direction he wanted to go, Hawkeye moved forward, with the group splitting into single file and following so precisely in his footsteps that they left behind what appeared to be the trail of only one man, except for Heyward and David.

The group had barely emerged from cover when a barrage of gunfire from a dozen rifles erupted behind them; a Delaware warrior leaped high into the air like an injured deer before collapsing full-length to the ground, dead.

"Oh, I was afraid something wicked like this would happen!" the scout shouted in English, then quickly switched to his adopted language and added: "Take cover, men, and attack!"

The group scattered immediately at the command, and before Heyward had fully recovered from his shock, he discovered himself standing alone with David. Fortunately, the Hurons had already retreated, and he was protected from their gunfire. However, this situation was clearly going to be brief; the scout demonstrated how to continue their withdrawal by firing his rifle and moving quickly from tree to tree as his enemy gradually gave up ground.

It appeared that the attack had been launched by a very small group of Hurons, which nonetheless kept growing in size as it fell back toward its allies, until the return gunfire became nearly equal to that maintained by the advancing Delawares. Heyward plunged into the fighting, and copying the essential caution of his companions, he fired rapid shots with his own rifle. The battle now became intense and deadlocked. Few suffered wounds, since both sides kept their bodies as well protected as possible behind the trees; never actually exposing any part of themselves except when taking aim. But the odds were slowly turning against Hawkeye and his group. The sharp-eyed scout recognized his peril without understanding how to solve it. He realized it was more dangerous to withdraw than to hold his position, while he observed his enemy deploying men on his flank, which made the task of keeping themselves covered so extremely difficult for the Delawares that it nearly stopped their gunfire entirely. At this troubling moment, when they started to believe the entire hostile tribe was slowly surrounding them, they heard the war cries of fighters and the clatter of weapons echoing beneath the canopy of the forest at the location where Uncas was stationed, a valley that essentially lay below the ground where Hawkeye and his party were fighting.

The impact of this assault was immediate and brought great relief to the scout and his companions. It appeared that while his own surprise attack had been expected and therefore failed, the enemy had been misled about his intentions and the size of his force, leaving insufficient troops to withstand the fierce charge of the young Mohican. This became doubly clear from the swift way the forest battle moved upward toward the village, and from the sudden decrease in the number of attackers facing them, as these enemies rushed to help defend what had now become the main point of resistance.

Encouraging his followers with his voice and his own example, Hawkeye then gave the command to advance against their enemies. The attack, in that rough type of combat, simply involved moving from one piece of cover to another, getting closer to the enemy; and in this movement he was immediately and successfully followed. The Hurons were forced to retreat, and the location of the battle quickly shifted from the more open terrain where it had started to a place where those under attack found dense brush to take shelter behind. Here the fight dragged on, difficult and apparently uncertain in outcome; the Delawares, though none of them were killed, began to bleed heavily due to the disadvantageous position they found themselves in.

In this crisis, Hawkeye managed to position himself behind the same tree that provided cover for Heyward; most of his own fighters were within shouting distance, slightly to his right, where they kept up rapid but ineffective fire against their well-protected enemies.

"You're a young man, major," the scout said, letting the butt of "killdeer" drop to the ground and leaning against the barrel, somewhat tired from his earlier efforts. "It might be your calling to lead armies someday against these devils, the Mingoes. Here you can observe the strategy behind Indian warfare. It's based primarily on a steady hand, sharp vision, and good protection. Now, if you had a company of Royal Americans with you here, how would you deploy them in this situation?"

"The bayonet would make a road."

"Yes, there's solid reasoning in what you're saying, but a person has to consider, in this wild country, how many lives he can afford to lose. No—cavalry," the scout went on, shaking his head like someone deep in thought; "cavalry, I'm embarrassed to admit, will eventually determine the outcome of these battles. The animals are superior to men, and we must rely on horses in the end. Put an iron-shod hoof against a Native American's moccasin, and once his rifle is fired empty, he'll never pause to reload it."[1]

[1] The American forest allows horses to pass through easily, since there's little underbrush and few tangled thickets. Hawkeye's strategy is the one that has always proven most successful in battles between whites and Indians. Wayne, during his famous campaign on the Miami, took enemy fire while his troops were in formation; then he had his dragoons circle around the flanks, driving the Indians from their hiding places before they could reload. One of the most prominent chiefs who fought in the battle of Miami told the writer that the red men couldn't fight the warriors with "long knives and leather stockings"; he was referring to the dragoons with their sabers and boots.

"This is a topic we should probably discuss at another time," Heyward replied; "should we attack?"

"I don't see anything wrong with a man using his quiet moments for helpful thinking," the scout responded. "As for rushing in, I don't much like that idea, since we'd have to sacrifice a life or two in the process. But still," he continued, tilting his head to listen to the sounds of the distant fighting, "if we're going to help Uncas, we need to deal with these enemies blocking our path."

Then, turning with a quick and determined manner, he called out loudly to his Indians in their own language. His words were met with a shout, and at a given signal, each warrior made a swift movement around his particular tree. The sight of so many dark bodies flashing before their eyes at the same moment drew a hurried and therefore ineffective volley from the Hurons. Without pausing to catch their breath, the Delawares leaped in long bounds toward the woods, like panthers pouncing on their prey. Hawkeye was at the front, wielding his fearsome rifle and inspiring his followers through his example. A few of the older and more clever Hurons, who had not been fooled by the trick that had been used to draw their fire, now delivered a close and deadly discharge from their weapons and proved the scout's concerns justified by bringing down three of his leading warriors. But the impact was not enough to stop the momentum of the charge. The Delawares burst into the cover with the savagery of their nature and eliminated every trace of resistance through the violence of their attack.

The fight lasted only a moment, with both sides grappling hand to hand, before those under attack quickly retreated until they reached the far edge of the thicket, where they held onto their cover with the kind of stubborn determination often seen in hunted animals. At this crucial moment, when the outcome of the battle was once again uncertain, a rifle shot rang out behind the Hurons, and a bullet came whistling from some beaver lodges located in the clearing behind them, followed by the fierce and terrifying cry of the war-whoop.

"There speaks the Sagamore!" Hawkeye shouted, responding to the cry with his own booming voice. "We've got them surrounded now, front and back!"

The impact on the Hurons was immediate. Demoralized by an attack from a direction that gave them no chance for protection, the warriors let out a collective cry of frustration, and retreating as a group, they scattered across the clearing, thinking only of escape. Many were struck down during their attempt, falling to the bullets and strikes of the pursuing Delawares.

We won't stop to describe the meeting between the scout and Chingachgook, or the more emotional conversation that Duncan had with Munro. A few quick and rushed words were enough to explain the situation to both groups; then Hawkeye, pointing out the Sagamore to his men, handed over the main authority to the Mohican chief. Chingachgook took on the position that his birth and experience gave him such a distinguished right to, with the serious dignity that always gives strength to the commands of a native warrior. Following in the scout's footsteps, he led the group back through the dense brush, his men scalping the fallen Hurons and hiding the bodies of their own dead as they moved forward, until they reached a spot where the scout was satisfied to stop.

The warriors, who had caught their breath after the previous battle, were now positioned on a small patch of flat ground dotted with enough trees to hide them. The terrain dropped off sharply ahead of them, and below they could see a narrow, dark, tree-filled valley stretching for several miles. It was through this thick and shadowy forest that Uncas was still fighting against the main force of the Hurons.

The Mohican and his companions moved forward to the edge of the hill and listened with experienced ears to the sounds of battle. Several birds circled above the tree-covered floor of the valley, startled from their hidden nests, and scattered wisps of smoke that appeared to be dissolving into the air drifted up from the treetops, marking places where the fighting had been intense and prolonged.

"The battle is moving up the slope," Duncan said, gesturing toward the sound of fresh gunfire erupting in the distance. "We're positioned too close to the middle of their formation to make any real impact."

"They'll move toward the hollow where the cover is thicker," the scout said, "and that will put us in a good position on their flank. Go, Sagamore; you'll barely have enough time to give the war cry and lead the young warriors forward. I'll handle this fight with warriors of my own race. You know me, Mohican; not a single Huron will cross that ridge to get behind you without 'Killdeer' taking notice."

The Indian chief paused for another moment to study the signs of the battle, which was now moving quickly up the slope—clear proof that the Delawares were winning. He didn't actually leave his position until he was warned of how close both his friends and enemies had come by the bullets from his allies, which started hitting among the dry leaves on the ground like pieces of hail that fall before a storm breaks. Hawkeye and his three companions pulled back a few steps to find cover and waited for the outcome with a composure that only extensive experience could provide in such a situation.

Soon the sound of rifle fire began to fade from the woodland echoes and started to sound like weapons being fired in open space. Then warriors began appearing one by one, forced to the edges of the forest and regrouping as they entered the clearing, as if this were the location where they would make their final stand. Others quickly joined them, until a long line of dark figures could be seen clinging to whatever cover they could find with the stubbornness of desperate men. Heyward started to become restless and looked anxiously toward Chingachgook. The chief sat on a rock with only his composed face visible, watching the scene with eyes as steady as if he had been positioned there simply to observe the battle.

"The time has come for the Delaware to strike!" said Duncan.

"That's not right, that's not right," the scout replied; "when he picks up the scent of his friends, he'll let them know he's here. Look, look; those rogues are gathering in that cluster of pine trees, like bees settling down after flying. By God, even a woman could fire a bullet right into the middle of that group of dark-skinned men!"

At that moment the battle cry rang out, and a dozen Hurons were struck down by gunfire from Chingachgook and his warriors. The shout that came next was met by a lone war cry from the woods, and a yell echoed through the air that seemed as though a thousand voices had joined together in one massive roar. The Hurons wavered, abandoning the middle of their formation, and Uncas emerged from the forest through the gap they had created, leading a hundred warriors.

Waving his hands from side to side, the young chief showed his followers where the enemy was, and they scattered to chase them down. The battle now split apart, with both groups of the defeated Hurons seeking safety in the woods once more, fiercely pursued by the triumphant Lenape warriors. Perhaps a minute had gone by, but the sounds were already fading in different directions, gradually becoming less clear beneath the echoing canopy of the forest. One small group of Hurons, however, had refused to look for cover, and were retreating like cornered lions, moving slowly and defiantly up the slope that Chingachgook and his warriors had just abandoned to join more directly in the fight. Magua stood out in this group, both because of his fierce and wild appearance, and because of the proud commanding presence he still displayed.

In his eagerness to speed up the chase, Uncas had left himself almost completely alone; but the instant he spotted Le Subtil, every other thought vanished from his mind. He let out his war cry, which brought back about six or seven warriors, and ignoring how outnumbered they were, he charged at his enemy. Le Renard, who had been watching this move, stopped and waited to face him with hidden delight. But just when he believed the recklessness of his hot-headed young attacker had put him at his mercy, another battle cry rang out, and La Longue Carabine could be seen charging to help, followed by all his white companions. The Huron immediately turned around and began a swift retreat up the slope.

There was no time for greetings or congratulations; Uncas, unaware that his friends were present, kept chasing his enemies with the speed of the wind. Hawkeye shouted at him to take cover, but it was useless; the young Mohican ignored the dangerous gunfire from his enemies and quickly forced them to flee as fast as his own reckless charge. It was lucky that the chase didn't last long and that the white men had a good position to help, or the Delaware would have soon left all his companions behind and become a victim of his own recklessness. But before such a disaster could occur, both the hunters and the hunted entered the Wyandot village, close enough to strike at each other.

Energized by being near their homes and weary from the pursuit, the Hurons finally took their stand and battled around their council lodge with the desperate fury of those who had nothing left to lose. The attack and its outcome resembled the swift passage and devastation of a tornado. Uncas's tomahawk, Hawkeye's strikes, and even Munro's still-strong arm were all active during that brief moment, and the earth was soon littered with their fallen enemies. Yet Magua, despite being bold and greatly exposed to danger, managed to escape every attempt on his life, protected by the kind of legendary immunity that ancient poetry attributed to its favored heroes. Letting out a cry that conveyed volumes of rage and frustration, the cunning chief, upon seeing his warriors defeated, fled from the scene with his only two remaining companions, leaving the Delawares busy stripping the dead of the bloody spoils of their triumph.

But Uncas, who had searched for him unsuccessfully in the chaotic fight, leaped forward in pursuit; Hawkeye, Heyward and David continued pressing close behind him. The most the scout could accomplish was to keep his rifle's muzzle slightly ahead of his friend, which served him perfectly as a protective shield. At one point Magua seemed ready to make another final attempt at revenge for his losses; however, abandoning this plan as soon as he revealed it, he jumped into a cluster of bushes, where his enemies followed him, and suddenly disappeared into the cave entrance already familiar to the reader. Hawkeye, who had only held back from shooting out of concern for Uncas, let out a cry of triumph and announced loudly that they now had their prey cornered. The pursuers rushed into the long, narrow entrance just in time to catch sight of the retreating figures of the Hurons. Their movement through the natural corridors and underground chambers of the cave was accompanied by the screams and cries of hundreds of women and children. The place, viewed in its dim and flickering light, looked like the shadows of hell itself, where miserable spirits and wild demons were darting about in great numbers.

Uncas continued to focus intently on Magua, as though his entire existence revolved around this single pursuit. Heyward and the scout maintained their pursuit close behind him, driven by the same motivation, though perhaps not quite as intensely. However, their path was growing increasingly complex through these shadowy and dim corridors, and their glimpses of the retreating warriors became less clear and less frequent. For a brief moment, they thought they had lost the trail entirely, until they spotted a white robe fluttering at the far end of a passage that appeared to ascend up the mountain.

"It's Cora!" Heyward exclaimed, his voice a wild mixture of horror and delight.

"Cora! Cora!" Uncas called out, leaping forward like a deer.

"It's the maiden!' shouted the scout. 'Courage, lady; we come! we come!'"

The pursuit continued with an energy made ten times stronger by this sight of their prisoner. However, the path was rough, uneven, and in some places almost impossible to cross. Uncas threw aside his rifle and jumped forward with reckless speed. Heyward foolishly copied his actions, though both men were quickly reminded of this rash decision when they heard the roar of a gun that the Hurons had managed to fire down through the rocky passage, the bullet from which even gave the young Mohican a minor wound.

"We have to get closer!" the scout shouted, making a desperate leap past his companions. "Those villains will pick us off one by one from this distance, and look—they're using the girl as a human shield!"

Though his words went unnoticed, or more accurately unheard, his companions followed his example and through extraordinary effort managed to get close enough to the fleeing figures to see that Cora was being carried between two warriors while Magua directed their escape route and method of flight. At that instant, all four silhouettes stood out sharply against a break in the sky before they vanished from sight. Nearly driven mad by frustration, Uncas and Heyward pushed their already seemingly impossible efforts even harder, and they emerged from the cave on the mountainside just in time to observe the path taken by those they were chasing. The trail led upward along the slope and remained both dangerous and difficult to navigate.

Weighed down by his rifle, and perhaps not driven by as strong a concern for the prisoner as his companions, the scout allowed the others to move ahead of him slightly, with Uncas taking the lead ahead of Heyward. Moving in this formation, they overcame rocks, cliffs, and obstacles in an amazingly short time that, under different circumstances and at another moment, would have seemed nearly impossible to navigate. However, the eager young men were rewarded when they discovered that the Hurons, burdened by carrying Cora, were falling behind in the chase.

"Stop, dog of the Wyandots!" shouted Uncas, brandishing his gleaming tomahawk at Magua; "a Delaware girl commands you to stop!"

"I won't take another step!" Cora shouted, coming to an abrupt halt on a rocky ledge that jutted out over a steep cliff, not far from the mountain's peak. "Kill me if you want to, you despicable Huron; I refuse to go any further."

The maiden's supporters lifted their tomahawks with the wicked delight that demons are believed to feel when causing harm, but Magua stopped their raised arms. After throwing the weapons he had taken from his companions over the cliff, the Huron chief pulled out his knife and faced his prisoner with an expression where opposing emotions battled intensely.

"Woman," he said, "choose; the wigwam or the knife of Le Subtil!"

Cora paid him no attention, but fell to her knees, lifted her eyes and extended her arms toward the sky, speaking in a gentle yet trusting voice:

"I am yours; do with me as you see fit!"

"Woman," Magua repeated in a harsh voice, trying unsuccessfully to catch a glimpse from her calm and radiant eyes, "choose!"

But Cora neither heard nor paid attention to his demand. The Huron's body shook in every muscle, and he raised his arm high, but let it fall again with a confused expression, like someone who was uncertain. Once more he fought with himself and lifted the sharp weapon again; but just then a piercing scream was heard above them, and Uncas appeared, jumping wildly from a terrifying height onto the ledge. Magua stepped back; and one of his helpers, taking advantage of the opportunity, plunged his own knife into Cora's chest.

The Huron leaped like a tiger toward his offending and already retreating countryman, but Uncas's falling body came between the unnatural enemies. Distracted from his target by this interference, and driven to fury by the murder he had just witnessed, Magua plunged his weapon into the back of the fallen Delaware, letting out an inhuman cry as he performed the cowardly act. But Uncas rose from the strike, like a wounded panther turning on its enemy, and knocked Cora's killer to the ground with an effort that drained the last of his fading strength. Then, with a fierce and unwavering stare, he looked toward Le Subtil, and showed through his expression everything he would have done if his power hadn't abandoned him. Le Subtil grabbed the weakened arm of the defenseless Delaware, and drove his knife into his chest three separate times, before his victim, still keeping his eyes fixed on his enemy with a look of undying contempt, dropped dead at his feet.

"Have mercy! Please, have mercy! Huron," Heyward shouted from above, his voice nearly strangled with horror; "show mercy, and you will receive it in return!"

Raising the blood-stained knife toward the pleading young man, the triumphant Magua let out a cry so fierce, so wild, and yet so filled with joy, that it carried the sounds of savage victory to the ears of those who battled in the valley a thousand feet below. He received a response from the scout, whose tall figure could be seen moving quickly toward him along those treacherous cliffs, with steps as bold and reckless as if he had the ability to fly through the air. However, when the hunter arrived at the scene of the merciless slaughter, the rocky ledge was occupied only by the dead.

His sharp eye quickly assessed the victims below, then swept across the challenging climb ahead of him. A figure stood at the mountain's peak, right at the edge of the dizzying height, with raised arms in a terrifying threatening pose. Without pausing to identify the person, Hawkeye lifted his rifle; but a rock that struck one of the fleeing people below revealed the angry and flushed face of honest Gamut. Then Magua emerged from a crack in the rocks, and stepping with cool detachment over the body of his last companion, he jumped across a wide gap and climbed up the rocks at a spot where David's arm couldn't reach him. One leap would take him to the top of the cliff and guarantee his escape. Before making the jump, though, the Huron stopped, and shaking his fist at the scout, he yelled:

"The pale faces are dogs! The Delawares are women! Magua leaves them on the rocks for the crows!"

Laughing with a harsh, grating sound, he made a frantic leap but fell short of reaching his target, though his hands managed to grab hold of a bush growing at the edge of the cliff. Hawkeye's body had crouched down like a wild animal preparing to pounce, and his entire frame shook so intensely with anticipation that the barrel of his partially raised rifle wavered like a leaf trembling in the breeze. Rather than wearing himself out with useless struggles, the crafty Magua let his body hang down to the full length of his arms and found a rocky ledge where his feet could find support. Then, gathering all his strength, he tried again and succeeded enough to pull his knees up onto the mountain's edge. It was at this moment, when his enemy's body was most compact and vulnerable, that the scout's trembling weapon was brought up to his shoulder. The surrounding stone cliffs themselves were no more steady than his rifle became during the single moment it discharged its shot. The Huron's arms went limp, and his body sagged backward slightly, though his knees remained in place. Casting a merciless glare at his opponent, he raised a hand in fierce defiance. But his grip gave way, and his dark figure could be seen plummeting through the air headfirst for just a brief moment, before it swept past the border of bushes clinging to the mountainside during its swift plunge toward death.

---

# Chapter XXXIII.

"They fought like brave men, long and well,
They covered that ground with fallen Muslim warriors,
They conquered—but Bozzaris fell,
Bleeding from every wound.
His few surviving comrades saw
His smile when their loud cheer rang out,
And the bloody battlefield was won;
Then saw in death his eyelids close
Peacefully, as if settling into a night's rest,
Like flowers at sunset."
—Halleck.

The sun found the Lenape the next day as a nation in mourning. The sounds of battle had ended, and they had satisfied their ancient hatred and avenged their recent conflict with the Mengwe by destroying an entire community. The dark and smoky atmosphere that hung around the place where the Hurons had made camp clearly revealed the fate of that wandering tribe, while hundreds of ravens that fought above the mountain peaks or swept in noisy flocks across the vast stretches of forest provided a terrifying guide to the battlefield. In short, anyone experienced in reading the signs of frontier warfare could easily have followed all those unmistakable signs of the merciless destruction that follows Indian revenge.

Still, the sun rose on the Lenape as a nation in mourning. No cries of victory, no triumphant songs, could be heard celebrating their success. The last warrior had returned from his deadly mission, only to remove the fearsome symbols of his violent work and join his people in their grief as a devastated nation. Pride and celebration were replaced by humility, and the most intense human emotions had already given way to the deepest and clearest expressions of sorrow.

The lodges stood empty, but a wide circle of serious faces surrounded a nearby area where every living thing had gathered, and where everyone now stood together in profound and solemn silence. Although people of every social standing and age, both men and women, and from all walks of life, had come together to form this living wall of bodies, they were all moved by the same feeling. Every gaze was fixed on the center of that circle, which held the focus of such intense and shared interest.

Six Delaware girls, with their long, dark, flowing hair falling loosely across their chests, stood apart, and only showed signs of their presence as they occasionally scattered sweet-smelling herbs and forest flowers on a bed of fragrant plants that, under a covering of Indian robes, held all that now remained of the passionate, noble-spirited, and generous Cora. Her body was wrapped in many layers of the same simple fabric, and her face was hidden forever from the sight of men. At her feet sat the grief-stricken Munro. His elderly head was bent nearly to the ground, in forced acceptance of Providence's blow; but a hidden torment wrestled about his wrinkled brow, which was only partly hidden by the disheveled locks of gray hair that had fallen, unattended, on his temples. Gamut stood beside him, his humble head uncovered to the sun's rays, while his eyes, restless and troubled, seemed to be equally torn between that small book, which contained so many peculiar but sacred teachings, and the person for whose sake his soul longed to offer comfort. Heyward was also nearby, leaning against a tree, and trying to suppress those sudden waves of grief that demanded all his masculine strength to overcome.

While this group might easily be imagined as sad and melancholy, it was far less moving than another that occupied the opposite side of the same area. Sitting as he had in life, with his body and limbs positioned in solemn and dignified composure, Uncas appeared dressed in the most magnificent ornaments that the tribe's wealth could provide. Elaborate feathers swayed above his head; wampum, throat pieces, bracelets, and medals decorated his body abundantly; yet his lifeless eyes and empty features too powerfully contradicted the false story of pride they were meant to tell.

Directly in front of the corpse, Chingachgook sat without weapons, war paint, or any decorations except for the bright blue tribal markings permanently tattooed on his bare chest. Throughout the long time the tribe had gathered there, the Mohican warrior had maintained a steady, worried gaze on his son's cold and lifeless face. His stare was so fixed and intense, and his posture so unchanging, that a stranger might not have been able to distinguish the living from the dead, except for the occasional flashes of inner torment that crossed the dark features of one, and the deathly stillness that had permanently settled on the face of the other. The scout stood nearby, leaning thoughtfully on his own deadly weapon of revenge, while Tamenund, supported by the tribal elders, sat in an elevated position where he could look down upon the silent and grieving gathering of his people.

Just inside the inner edge of the circle stood a soldier, dressed in the military uniform of a foreign nation; and beyond the circle was his war horse, positioned in the center of a group of mounted servants, apparently ready to begin some long journey. The stranger's clothing revealed that he held an important position close to the commander of the Canadian forces; and who, as it now appeared, having found his peaceful mission thwarted by the savage violence of his allies, was willing to become a quiet and sorrowful observer of the results of a conflict that he had arrived too late to prevent.

The day was approaching the end of its first quarter, and the crowd had still maintained its breathless silence since dawn.

No sound louder than a muffled sob could be heard among them, and not even a limb had moved during that extended and agonizing time, except to carry out the simple and moving rituals that were performed occasionally in memory of the deceased. Only the patience and endurance of Native American strength could sustain such a display of detachment, which now seemed to have transformed each dark and still figure into stone.

At last, the wise leader of the Delaware people extended his arm and, leaning on his attendants' shoulders, stood up with such frailty that he seemed like a completely different person from the man who had addressed his people just the day before, now barely able to stand steady on his raised platform.

"Men of the Lenape!" he said, in quiet, deep tones that sounded like a voice carrying some prophetic message: "the face of the Great Spirit is hidden behind a cloud! His eye has turned away from you; His ears are closed; His voice gives no response. You cannot see him; yet His judgments stand before you. Let your hearts be open and let your spirits speak truthfully. Men of the Lenape! the face of the Great Spirit is hidden behind a cloud."

As this simple yet terrible announcement reached the ears of the crowd, a silence as deep and profound followed as if the revered spirit they worshipped had spoken the words without using human voice; and even the lifeless Uncas seemed alive compared with the humbled and submissive crowd that surrounded him. As the immediate impact, however, slowly faded away, a quiet murmur of voices began a kind of chant to honor the dead. The sounds came from women, and were hauntingly soft and mournful. The words had no regular pattern, but as one woman stopped another continued the praise, or lament, whatever it might be called, and expressed her emotions in whatever language her feelings and the moment inspired. At times the speaker was interrupted by widespread and loud outbursts of grief, during which the girls around Cora's funeral bed pulled the plants and flowers randomly from her body, as if confused by sorrow. But, in the gentler moments of their mourning, these symbols of purity and sweetness were placed back in their spots, with every sign of tenderness and regret. Though made less coherent by many widespread interruptions and outbursts, a translation of their language would have contained a structured melody, which, in essence, might have shown a series of connected thoughts.

A young woman, chosen for this responsibility based on her status and abilities, began with humble references to the qualities of the fallen warrior, decorating her words with those eastern imagery that the Native Americans likely carried with them from the far reaches of the other continent, and which create a connection linking the ancient stories of both worlds. She named him the "panther of his tribe" and portrayed him as someone whose moccasin left no mark on the morning dew, whose leap resembled that of a young deer, whose gaze shone brighter than a star in the darkness of night, and whose voice in combat rang as loud as the thunder of the Great Spirit. She spoke of the mother who gave birth to him and emphasized strongly the joy she must experience in having such a son. She asked him to tell her, when they would meet in the realm of spirits, that the Delaware women had wept over the burial place of her child and had proclaimed her fortunate.

Then, those who followed changed their tone to something gentler and even more compassionate, speaking with the delicacy and sensitivity that women possess about the foreign young woman who had departed from the world above so close to the time of his own death that the Great Spirit's intentions could not be ignored. They urged him to treat her with kindness and to show patience with her unfamiliarity with the skills so essential to a warrior's well-being. They spoke of her extraordinary beauty and her courageous spirit without any trace of jealousy, the way angels might be expected to appreciate superior virtue, explaining that these qualities would more than make up for any minor gaps in her upbringing.

After this, others took their turn speaking directly to the young woman, using the gentle, soft words of affection and love. They encouraged her to stay positive and not worry about what lay ahead. A skilled hunter would be by her side, someone who knew how to take care of her every need; and a brave warrior would protect her from any harm. They assured her that her journey would be enjoyable and her troubles few. They warned her not to waste time mourning for the friends she'd left behind or the places where her father had lived, telling her that the "blessed hunting grounds of the Lenape" had valleys just as beautiful, rivers just as clean, and flowers just as fragrant as the "heaven of the pale faces." They told her to pay attention to what her companion needed and never forget the natural differences that the Manitou had wisely created between men and women. Then, breaking into an enthusiastic chorus, they sang together about the Mohican's character. They declared him to be noble, brave, and kind—everything a warrior should be and everything a woman could love. Using distant and clever imagery, they revealed that during their brief time together, they had noticed with the sharp insight that women possess, where his heart truly lay. The Delaware girls had not caught his attention! He came from a people who had once ruled the shores of the great salt water, and his heart had drawn him back to those who lived near his ancestors' burial places. Why shouldn't such feelings be supported! Anyone could see that her bloodline was purer and more distinguished than others in her tribe; her actions had shown she could handle the dangers and challenges of wilderness life; and now, they concluded, the "wise one of the earth" had brought her to a place where she would find kindred souls and could live happily forever.

Then, shifting their tone and focus, they began speaking about the young woman who was crying in the nearby dwelling. They likened her to snowflakes—just as pure, white, and radiant, yet equally vulnerable to melting under summer's intense heat or freezing solid in winter's harsh cold. They had no doubt she was beautiful in the eyes of the young leader, whose appearance and grief seemed to mirror her own; however, while they never openly stated such a judgment, it was clear they considered her inferior to the woman they were mourning. Even so, they didn't deny her the recognition that her exceptional beauty rightfully deserved. Her curls were likened to the abundant shoots of a grapevine, her eyes to the blue expanse of the sky, and they acknowledged that even the most pristine cloud, glowing with sunlight, was less captivating than her radiant complexion.

During these and similar songs, nothing could be heard except the soft murmurs of the music, which was made even more haunting by the occasional outbursts of sorrow that served as its refrains. The Delawares themselves listened as if they were under a spell, and their expressive faces clearly showed how deeply and genuinely they felt for the singers. Even David willingly listened to these beautiful voices, and well before the chant had finished, his expression revealed that his spirit was completely captivated.

The scout, who was the only white man among them who could understand the words, allowed himself to be slightly stirred from his thoughtful position and turned his head to the side to grasp their meaning as the girls continued speaking. However, when they talked about what lay ahead for Cora and Uncas, he shook his head like someone who understood the mistake in their innocent beliefs, and returning to his leaning position, he kept it throughout the ceremony—if it could be called a ceremony—which was so deeply filled with emotion, until it was complete. Fortunately for both Heyward and Munro's ability to maintain their composure, they did not understand the meaning of the strange sounds they were hearing.

Chingachgook stood as the only exception to the fascination shown by the Native American portion of the crowd. His expression remained unchanged throughout the entire scene, and not a single muscle moved in his stern face, even during the most intense or heartbreaking moments of the mourning ritual. The lifeless body of his son was everything to him, and all his other senses seemed to have shut down so that his eyes could take one last look at the features he had cherished for so long, and which would soon be hidden from his sight forever.

In this stage of the funeral ceremony, a warrior highly celebrated for his military achievements, and particularly for his service in the recent battle, a man with a stern and serious bearing, slowly stepped forward from the crowd and positioned himself near the deceased.

"Why have you left us, pride of the Wapanachki?" he said, speaking to the lifeless ears of Uncas, as if the empty body still possessed the abilities of the living man; "your time has been like that of the sun when in the trees; your glory brighter than his light at noonday. You are gone, youthful warrior, but a hundred Wyandots are clearing the thorns from your path to the world of the spirits. Who that saw you in battle would believe that you could die? Who before you has ever shown Uttawa the way into the fight? Your feet were like the wings of eagles; your arm heavier than falling branches from the pine; and your voice like the Manitou when He speaks in the clouds. The tongue of Uttawa is weak," he added, looking about him with a sorrowful gaze, "and his heart exceeding heavy. Pride of the Wapanachki, why have you left us?"

He was followed by others, each taking their turn, until nearly all the distinguished and talented men of the nation had sung or delivered their words of honor over the spirit of the fallen leader. After each person finished, another profound and reverent silence settled over the entire gathering.

Then a quiet, deep sound could be heard, like the muffled accompaniment of distant music, rising just high enough in the air to be audible, yet so unclear that both its nature and where it came from remained matters of guesswork. It was followed by another strain, then another, each in a higher pitch, until they built upon the ear, first as long, drawn-out and frequently repeated exclamations, and finally as actual words. Chingachgook's lips had parted enough to reveal that this was the father's lament. Though no eye turned toward him and no one showed the slightest sign of impatience, it was clear from the way the crowd lifted their heads to listen that they absorbed the sounds with an intensity of attention that only Tamenund himself had ever commanded before. But they listened without success. The melodies rose just loud enough to become understandable, then grew fainter and more trembling, until they finally faded from hearing, as if carried away by a passing breeze. The Sagamore's lips closed, and he remained silent in his place, staring with his fixed gaze and motionless body, like some being that had been shaped by the Almighty's hand with human form but without a human spirit. The Delawares, who recognized from these signs that their friend's mind was not ready for such a tremendous test of strength, loosened their focus; and with natural sensitivity, they seemed to direct all their thoughts to the funeral rites of the unknown young woman.

One of the elder chiefs gave a signal to the women who had gathered in the part of the circle where Cora's body lay. Following the sign, the girls lifted the bier to shoulder height and moved forward with slow, measured steps, singing another mournful song in honor of the dead as they walked. Gamut, who had been closely watching these rituals that he considered pagan, now leaned his head over the shoulder of the grief-stricken father and whispered:

"They're carrying the remains of your child; shouldn't we follow and watch them be buried with a Christian burial?"

Munro jumped as if the final trumpet had blown in his ear, and after casting one worried and rushed look around him, he stood up and followed the modest procession, carrying himself like a soldier but bearing the complete weight of a father's grief. His friends gathered around him with a sorrow too deep to be called mere sympathy—even the young Frenchman joined the procession, with the manner of a man who was genuinely moved by the early and tragic death of someone so beautiful. But when the last and most humble woman of the tribe had taken her place in the wild yet organized formation, the men of the Lenape drew their circle tighter and formed once more around Uncas, as quiet, as solemn, and as still as they had been before.

The location selected for Cora's burial was a small hill where a group of young, vigorous pine trees had grown, creating a somber and fitting canopy over the area. When they arrived, the girls set down what they were carrying and waited for several minutes with their typical patience and natural shyness for some sign that those who were most emotionally affected approved of the preparations. Finally, the scout, who was the only one familiar with their customs, spoke to them in their own language:

"My daughters have done well; the white men thank them."

Pleased with this confirmation of their good intentions, the girls went ahead and placed the body in a coffin skillfully and attractively made from birch bark. They then lowered it into its dark and final resting place. The ritual of covering the remains and hiding the signs of freshly turned earth with leaves and other natural materials followed the same simple and quiet customs. But when these kind souls who had carried out these sorrowful yet caring duties had finished this much, they paused uncertainly, showing they weren't sure how much further they should go. It was at this point in the ceremony that the scout spoke to them again:

"My young women have done enough," he said. "The spirit of the pale face doesn't need food or clothing, since their gifts match the heaven of their race. I see," he added, looking at David, who was getting his book ready in a way that showed he intended to lead them in sacred song, "that someone who knows Christian customs better is about to speak."

The women stepped back modestly, and after being the main participants in the scene, they now became humble and focused observers of what came next. While David spent time expressing the devout feelings of his soul in this way, not a hint of surprise or a glance of impatience showed on their faces. They listened like people who understood the meaning of the unfamiliar words, and seemed as though they experienced the combined emotions of grief, hope, and acceptance that the words were meant to communicate.

Thrilled by what he had just seen, and possibly stirred by his own hidden feelings, the singer surpassed his typical performance. His deep, resonant voice held its own when compared to the gentle tones of the women, and his carefully controlled melodies carried, at least for those who were his intended audience, the extra strength that comes from understanding. He concluded the hymn just as he had begun it, surrounded by profound and reverent silence.

When the final notes had reached the listeners' ears, the secretive, nervous glances and the general yet restrained movement of the crowd revealed that something was expected from the father of the dead man. Munro appeared to understand that the moment had arrived for him to make what is perhaps the greatest effort that human nature can achieve. He removed his hat, exposing his gray hair, and looked around at the anxious and silent group that surrounded him with a steady and composed expression. Then, gesturing with his hand for the scout to pay attention, he said:

"Tell these kind and compassionate women that a heartbroken and dying man sends them his gratitude. Let them know that the God we all worship, though we call Him by different names, will remember their kindness; and that the time will come soon when we can gather around His throne without any differences based on gender, social status, or race."

The scout listened to the shaky voice with which the veteran spoke these words, and slowly shook his head when they were finished, like someone who doubted their effectiveness.

"To tell them this," he said, "would be like telling them that snow doesn't fall in winter, or that the sun burns brightest when the trees have lost all their leaves."

Then he turned to the women and shared the other person's gratitude in a way he thought would best suit his audience. Munro's head had already dropped to his chest, and he was quickly falling back into his sorrowful state when the young Frenchman mentioned earlier gently touched his elbow. Once he had caught the attention of the grieving old man, he pointed toward a group of young Indians who were approaching with a light but tightly covered stretcher, and then pointed upward toward the sun.

"I understand you, sir," Munro replied, his voice strained but steady. "I understand you completely. This is God's will, and I accept it. Cora, my dear child! If a broken-hearted father's prayers could help you now, how truly blessed you would be! Come, gentlemen," he continued, glancing around with an expression of dignified calm, though the pain that flickered across his weathered face was too intense to hide, "our work here is finished; let us go."

Heyward was relieved to follow orders that would take them away from a place where he felt he was losing control of his emotions with each passing moment. As his companions climbed onto their horses, he managed to find a moment to squeeze the scout's hand and confirm the agreement they had made to meet again at the British army's outpost. Then, eagerly mounting his horse, he rode up beside the stretcher, where only quiet, muffled crying revealed that Alice was inside. In this formation, with Munro's head once again hanging down toward his chest, and Heyward and David riding behind them in grieving silence, escorted by Montcalm's officer and his soldiers, all the white men except Hawkeye disappeared from the sight of the Delawares and vanished into the endless forests of that territory.

However, the bond that had connected these simple forest dwellers with the strangers who had briefly entered their lives through shared tragedy could not be easily severed. Many years went by before the legendary story of the white maiden and the young Mohican warrior stopped entertaining them during long nights and exhausting journeys, or ceased to inspire their young and courageous men with thoughts of revenge. The other participants in these significant events were not forgotten either. Through the scout, who continued for years to serve as a connection between them and the civilized world, they discovered in response to their questions that the "Gray Head" had soon joined his ancestors—brought down, as they mistakenly thought, by his military defeats; and that the "Open Hand" had taken his surviving daughter deep into the settlements of the white people, where her tears had finally stopped flowing and had been replaced by the cheerful smiles that better matched her happy disposition.

But these events happened later than the time our story covers. Abandoned by everyone of his own race, Hawkeye came back to the place where his heart drew him, pulled by a connection that no artificial tie could ever break. He arrived just in time to get one final glimpse of Uncas's face, as the Delawares were already wrapping him in his burial clothes of animal skins. They stopped to allow the devoted woodsman his yearning, lingering look, and when he was finished, they covered the body completely, never to be opened again. Then another procession formed like the previous one, and the entire tribe gathered around the chief's temporary grave—temporary because it was fitting that someday his bones should be laid to rest among those of his own people.

The movement, just like the emotion, had happened at the same time and affected everyone. The same solemn expression of sorrow, the same complete silence, and the same respect shown to the chief mourner were displayed around the burial site as had already been described. The body was placed in a peaceful position, facing the rising sun, with weapons and hunting tools nearby, ready for the final journey. A gap was left in the protective covering that shielded the body from the earth, allowing the spirit to connect with its physical form when needed; and everything was hidden from detection and protected from attacks by wild animals, using methods unique to the native people. The physical rituals then ended and everyone present turned their attention to the more spiritual aspects of the ceremonies.

Chingachgook became the focus of everyone's attention once again. He hadn't spoken yet, and people expected to hear something comforting and meaningful from such a famous chief during such an important moment. Understanding what the people wanted from him, the stern and disciplined warrior lifted his face, which had recently been hidden in his robe, and looked around with a steady gaze. His tightly pressed and expressive lips then parted, and for the first time throughout the lengthy ceremonies his voice could be clearly heard. "Why are my brothers mourning?" he asked, looking at the dark group of saddened warriors who surrounded him; "why are my daughters crying? A young man has traveled to the happy hunting-grounds; a chief has lived his life with honor. He was good; he was faithful; he was brave. Who could deny this? The Great Spirit needed such a warrior, and He has summoned him away. As for me, the son and the father of Uncas, I am a marked pine tree in a clearing made by the white men. My people have disappeared from the shores of the great lake and the hills of the Delawares. But who can claim that the serpent of his tribe has lost his wisdom? I am alone—"

"No, no," cried Hawkeye, who had been staring with a longing expression at his friend's stern face, maintaining something like his usual composure, but whose inner strength could bear no more; "no, Sagamore, not alone. The natural traits of our races may be different, but God has positioned us to walk the same road. I have no family, and I can also say, like you, no tribe. He was your son, and a Native American by birth; and it's possible that your blood connection was closer—but if I ever forget the young man who has so often fought beside me in battle, and rested beside me in times of peace, may He who created us all, regardless of our skin color or our natural gifts, forget me! The boy has departed from us for now; but, Sagamore, you are not alone."

Chingachgook took hold of the hand that the scout had reached across the freshly turned soil in a moment of deep emotion, and in a gesture of friendship, these two strong and fearless frontiersmen leaned their heads together as burning tears dropped to the ground, moistening Uncas's grave like raindrops falling from the sky.

In the midst of the terrible silence that greeted such an outburst of emotion from the two most famous warriors of that area, Tamenund raised his voice to dismiss the crowd.

"That's enough," he said. "Go, children of the Lenape, the Great Spirit's anger isn't finished. Why should Tamenund remain? The white men are masters of the earth, and the time of the red men hasn't come again yet. My day has lasted too long. This morning I saw the sons of Unamis happy and strong; and yet, before night has fallen, I have lived to see the last warrior of the wise race of the Mohicans."

# Thank You For Reading

**You've Just Read a Piece of the Greatest Library Ever Rebuilt**

Thank you for reading.

This book is one of thousands we're restoring, reimagining, and translating as part of the **Modern Library of Alexandria** — a global movement to preserve and share humanity's most important ideas.

What was once lost to fire and time is now rising again — not just as memory, but as living, breathing knowledge, freely accessible to all.

**What You Can Do Next:**

- **Keep Reading.**

  Discover more legendary works — in beautiful print, audiobook, or digital form — at LibraryofAlexandria.com.

- **Build Your Own Library.**

  Every title is available as a paperback, hardcover, or collectible boxset — at true printing cost. Craft a personal library worthy of display.

- **Spread the Light.**

  Share this book. Tell others about the movement. Help us translate every timeless work into every language, so no reader is ever left behind.

By finishing this book, you've already taken part in something extraordinary.

**Join us at LibraryofAlexandria.com**

Together, we're rebuilding the greatest library the world has ever known.

With appreciation,

**The Modern Library of Alexandria Team**

**Visit:**
**www.libraryofalexandria.com**
**Or scan the code below:**

www.ingramcontent.com/pod-product-compliance
Lightning Source LLC
Chambersburg PA
CBHW011959050726
47499CB00010BA/3219